FROM THE PUBLISHERS OF THE WASHINGTONIAN MAGAZINE

# WASHINGTON: The Official Bicentennial Guidebook

EDITED BY NANCY LOVE

This is the official Washington Bicentennial guidebook authorized by the Bicentennial Commission of the District of Columbia, Inc.

DC76 TM

AMERICAN REVOLUTION BICENTENNIAL 1776-1976

WASHINGTONIAN BOOKS

Photo credits:
Page 120 Paul S. Conklin; page 138 Robert R. Fonda; page 87 Robert de Gast; pages 10, 26, 88, 102, 152 Libby Joy; front cover Robert Lautman; page 118 Jerry Wachter Ltd.; pages 172, 188 Bill Weems; page 4 United Press International; page VIII courtesy of Washingtoniana Division, Martin Luther King Library; maps Sabban.

Designed by James True

Published by Washingtonian Books
1218 Connecticut Avenue NW
Washington, DC 20036



Library of Congress Catalog number 75-7415
ISBN number 0-915168-02-2 (paper)
0-915168-05-7 (cloth)

# Foreword

The city of Washington did not exist in 1776. But today it is the American city that most fully embodies the political philosophy of our founding fathers and the history of the republic they created. Here, along the tree-lined avenues named after states of the union are all the famous buildings and monuments that symbolize our federal heritage: The White House, the Capitol, the Supreme Court, the Lincoln and Jefferson Memorials, the Washington Monument.

When Washington and Jefferson were planning the nation's capital in the last decade of the 18th century, they thought of a small government town within a ten-square-mile area set aside as the District of Columbia. But that town has since grown into a city of three million people, a city which has burst across the District lines into nearby Virginia and Maryland.

Thus, Washington has become more than the nation's capital. It is a major American city in its own right with all the urban problems and opportunities found in other great cities. From the point of view of Washington residents, the federal government simply represents their principal local industry.

All of this gives Washington a somewhat split personality—a dual role as a city belonging to all Americans and as a city for its own residents. The two Washingtons sometimes seem to be miles apart.

This guidebook is intended to give the visitor an appreciation of both Washingtons, a chance to go beyond the picture-postcard facade into the more human city rich in cultural and recreational resources.

**Laughlin Phillips, Editor-in-Chief**
**Washingtonian Books**

# Contents

# Key

*An asterisk marks places and events of special Bicentennial interest.

**H**—A facility that is accessible to the handicapped.

**HP**—A facility that is accessible to the handicapped through use of a special entrance or if arranged in advance.

**AE**—American Express

**BA**—Bank Americard

**CB**—Carte Blanche

**MC**—Master Charge

**DC**—Diner's Club

**CC**—Central Charge

**Restaurants:** Cost determined by price of an evening meal for two including a round of drinks, an inexpensive bottle of wine, tax, and tip:
Very Inexpensive—under $15
Inexpensive—$15-$25
Moderate—$25-$35
Expensive—$35-$45
Very Expensive—over $45

**Telephone numbers:** Area codes are noted when it is necessary to use them when dialing from Washington, D.C.
All 800 numbers are toll-free.

**Admission charge:** All admissions are free unless indicated otherwise.

**Parking:** Convenient free and pay parking facilities are noted wherever possible.

BRADBURY PIANOS

# Chapter One

WASHINGTON

# Then and Now

J. TIMBERLAKE GIBSON

Washington began as a planned city. It did not spring up around a fort or trading post like Pittsburgh, nor on a natural harbor like New York City. In the manner of Brasilia, the fabricated capital of Brazil, it was hewn out of wilderness on a designated spot. However, there was no large government subsidy for its completion as there was for Brasilia, nor was it an "instant city" like the new town of Columbia, Maryland. Washington City grew slowly, and at times painfully, on swamp and farmland on the Potomac River near the flourishing ports of Georgetown and Alexandria, Virginia.

In 1789, when George Washington became President, one of the many pressing problems of the new government was to find a site for a capital that would be acceptable to various factions. Back in 1783, there had been an unfortunate confrontation when a group of unpaid Revolutionary War veterans menaced the Continental Congress at Philadelphia. Local authorities refused to protect Congress, which was forced to move to Princeton, New Jersey. As a result, Congress decided that a city must be *created* far from the influence of local or national politics, thereby insuring safety to the government, which presumably would be subject to the physical violence of excited pressure groups. At the time it was a sound idea. Now, however, thanks to rapid air and surface transportation, the capital city can qualify as the Pressure Group Center of the western world.

The Continental Congress favored a location near the center of the country, and when the neighborhood of Georgetown was suggested it seemed a defensible choice, based on its relative convenience to all parts of the nation as it was then constituted. Many rival areas were put forward by Northerners—an attractive spot on the Delaware River near Trenton, and another near Germantown, Pennsylvania, preferred by Vice President John Adams. Naturally, the South favored the Potomac area, and a lively regional spat ensued. Thomas Jefferson, Secretary of State, settled the matter by an adroit compromise. He invited Treasury Secretary Alexander Hamilton, who represented the New York anti-Potomac faction, to a lavish lunch with a group of Southern statesmen. As the fine food and wines mellowed the opponents, the astute Jefferson assured Hamilton that the South would yield on the knotty issue of national debt assumption (a problem of concern to Hamilton) if Hamilton would support the Potomac site for the new capital.

A "residence bill" was passed authorizing the President to pick the actual land for the capital, not to exceed 10 miles in length and width, a river tract including both Georgetown and Alexandria. Maryland ceded 69.25 square miles and Virginia 30.75; the Virginia portion was returned in 1846 because its residents were dissatisfied with the whole experience. Washington was designated a "Federal City" to be governed by committees of Congress and three commissioners selected by the President, an arrangement that lasted until 1802. As long as he lived, George Washington called it "the Federal City," embarrassed at the official name, "Washington City in the District of Columbia."

Now there was a location and a format for government, but there was neither money nor a plan. Fortunately, both were forthcoming—$120,000 from Virginia and $72,000 from Maryland for public buildings. And there was a planner in the wings. Washington had been impressed with a Frenchman, a friend of the Marquis de Lafayette, Pierre Charles L'Enfant, who had fought in the Revolution and had renovated the City Hall in New York where Washington gave his inaugural address. L'Enfant had grand ideas. Here was a chance to plan a great capital from scratch. He had the foresight to see the staggering potential of the new nation—so he thought big, so big in fact that the plan he submitted boggled the minds of 1791, especially those of the newly appointed commissioners, who loudly declared the man mad. Ordinary streets were to be 100 to 110 feet wide, avenues 160 feet wide, and a main avenue—Pennsylvania—bordered by a great Mall, would connect the legislative building with the President's palace.

Perhaps you may agree with the commissioners as you attempt to drive around one of L'Enfant's circles during rush-hour traffic. Actually, L'Enfant did not complete his work. He was removed by President Washington (at the insistence of the commissioners) because he was too slow completing the job. Surveyors Andrew Ellicott and Benjamin Banneker completed the map and survey.

After the death of Washington, President Adams had the unpleasant duty of forcing Congress to convene in the new permanent seat of government on the first Monday of December, 1800. Everyone including John Adams felt that he was leaving the center of Western civilization (Philadelphia) for the Wilderness (Washington City). Everyone was right. On June 15, 1800, the exile was begun. Government clerks—all 126—came by whatever means available. State archives and papers arrived by sea.

The execution of L'Enfant's grand design got off to a poor start. There were 109 brick houses, 263 frame houses, and a diffuse population of about 3,000. Secretary of the Treasury Oliver Wolcott echoed the general sentiment when he said: "There are few houses in any one place, and most of them small, miserable huts. The people are poor and as far as I can judge they live like fishes by eating off each other. You may look in any direction . . . without seeing a fence or any other object except brick kilns and temporary huts for more laborers." At least the kilns and laborers offered hope for more buildings. Aaron Burr called Pennsylvania Avenue, "a long cow trail . . . good for shooting partridges . . . nested among the elder bushes." A French diplomat felt he was surely being punished for past sins by being condemned to reside in such a city. Not one room in the White House was finished. Abigail Adams used the East Room for drying clothes.

In 1802 Congress provided for a mayor to be appointed by the President, and for an elected city council. By 1812, the mayor was elected by the city council; eight years later by the inhabitants. This arrangement lasted until 1874.

During the Jefferson and Madison administrations (1801-1817) Dolley Madison, who held what was surely Washington's first "salon," became the undisputed queen of society. During the War of 1812 the British burned most of the public buildings, including the Capitol and the President's House, all but putting the city permanently out of business. Dolley Madison courageously delayed her flight so that she could rescue valuable documents and Gilbert Stuart's portrait of George Washington. The Madisons moved into Col. John Tayloe's Octagon House on New York Avenue NW (now restored and occupied by the American Institute of Architects) while their house was being rebuilt, and soon afterwards they were entertaining again and bolstering the flagging spirits of the capital.

By 1820, Washington City had become a fact, though debate continued as late as 1870 whether to seek a better place for the nation's capital. The city had become so civilized by the time of John Quincy Adams's administration that in 1826 a license for a tavern keeper cost $60. In addition to the ever-increasing number of federal buildings, there were now four banks, one insurance company, three asylums, a library, five burying grounds, 14 churches, seven wharves, and three colleges (including Columbia College, which later became George Washington University). There were many taverns and boardinghouses where the transient population lived. Even elegant residences began to appear, like that of Stephen Decatur on Lafayette Square, now handsomely restored by the National Trust for Historic Preservation and used as its headquarters.

In 1842 Charles Dickens visited Washington. His derision set the tone for visiting English journalists during the next 100 years. "Washington consists of spacious avenues that begin in nothing and lead nowhere," said Mr. Dickens. He should have seen it in 1800! But the city was growing and mellowing. One could now reach New York by railroad. In 1844 F. B. Morse unveiled his telegraph. Messages could be transmitted between Paris, London, and Washington in a matter of minutes. What had God wrought? God and man together had wrought an increasingly pleasant city for its 51,000 inhabitants.

In 1847 an event occurred of utmost importance to the city and to the nation. A building was started that would do much to make Washington a center of culture in the coming years. James Smithson, the illegitimate son of the Duke of Northumberland, left the United States $515,169 "to found at Washington, under the name of the Smithsonian Institution, an establishment for the increase and diffusion of knowledge among men." In spite of the opposition of a suspicious and provincial Congress, which still didn't trust those British, John Quincy Adams managed to implement the completion of the building that is now the brownstone Gothic castle on the Mall, designed by architect James Renwick Jr. The Smithsonian has become one of the great museums of the world where everything valuable, dear, or significant to the nation could be preserved, from George Washington's surveying instruments, and the inaugural gowns of our First Ladies, to Lindbergh's *Spirit of St. Louis.* It is a laboratory, a school, and through the years has assembled one of the world's most comprehensive collections of art, science and technology, historical objects and artifacts. Today the Smithsonian Institution includes not only the museums on the Mall such as the National Museum of History and Technology, the Hirshhorn, and the National Museum of Natural History but also the National Zoo and the Renwick Gallery, as well as libraries and information services.

In 1860 when Albert Edward, Prince of Wales, visited the capital, the whole nation bubbled with excitement. The city had come a long way in the half century since his Royal Highness's countrymen had chased our President out of town, burned his house, and stolen his wine. This time the Prince just drank our wine and danced with the swooning belles of society.

Somewhat before the Prince's visit, the cornerstone of the present Washington Monument was laid with such notables in attendance as President Polk and Daniel Webster. After much initial excitement it attained a height of 150 feet before construction lagged due to congressional apathy. Public-spirited citizens decided to carry on with privately donated funds. In lieu of money, states and nations sent pre-cut stones. Among them was an ancient block from Rome, generously given by Pope Pius IX. In the middle of the night, the valuable stone was stolen by the anti-Catholic Know-Nothing Party and dumped into the Potomac, where it doubtless remains to this day. Construction faltered again and remained stymied for 40 years before the monument was finally completed in 1888.

During the Civil War the population almost doubled, a growth so explosive that it took another decade for living and service facilities to catch up with demand. Post-war visitors to the Capitol were agog at the new gaslights, flushing toilets, and showers for congressmen. Pennsylvania Avenue was jammed with commercial traffic, lined with shops such as Brady's famous photography studio, and the great City Market. Visitors gawked at the self-important government clerks who were making such lavish annual salaries as $600. Horace Greeley said the capital was a place of high rents, deep mud, bad food, and disgusting morals. He did his best to get here just the same.

The city's sizable number of blacks increased rapidly during the post-war

*1963 Civil Rights March on Washington; march director A. Philip Randolph at right, Roy Wilkins second right, the Rev. Martin Luther King seventh from right.*

expansion. Although many of the newcomers were unskilled farm workers, the city had a stable population of scholars, lawyers, and professionals, such as civil rights spokesman Frederick Douglass, who became Minister to the Republic of Haiti. His home, Cedar Hill, was designated a National Memorial in 1962 and has become a significant museum open to the public. The black community had a series of newspapers. Thanks to funds provided by the Freedmen's Bureau, and the energy and foresight of a handful of blacks, Howard University was founded in 1867 and has remained a seat of black culture in this country.

In 1874 the District's franchise to vote was revoked by Congress, partly because Alexander "Boss" Shepherd, who had been head of the Public Works Board, bankrupted the city treasury (although it must be admitted that the money was well spent to install sewers, cover the miasmic Tiber Creek, and pave the streets). Congress then established a commission form of government with three commissioners nominated by the President and confirmed by the U.S. Senate. Congress continued to keep a tight rein on the budget. This form of government was in effect until 1967.

By 1876, 100 years after the signing of the Declaration of Independence, the raw mud hole first seen by President John Adams now boasted 150,000 people, of whom 43,404 were blacks. There were excellent hotels such as the Willard ($4.50 daily) where Julia Ward Howe had written "The Battle Hymn of the Republic," the famous National at 6th Street and Pennsylvania Avenue ($4 a

night) where John Wilkes Booth plotted against the Administration, and the Wormley Hotel at 15th and H Streets, owned by James Wormley, a talented black who served what many thought was the best food in town. Lodgings were available in numerous rooming houses at $25-$100 monthly. There were reasonably priced and excellent catering services that delivered meals daily right to one's front door. The President and his cabinet periodically held "open" receptions, which were announced in the *Evening Star*, the city's largest and most important newspaper.

Horse-drawn streetcars like the Washington and Georgetown Street Railway traversed the city—fare 5¢. Carriages of various kinds could be rented for 75¢ to $2.25 hourly. The city had become an important rail terminus. Each rail line had a separate station and many grade crossings that cut across the city streets, making them dangerous and congested. By 1877 there were 119 telephones in government offices, which presumably kept 238 bureaucrats busy. The first electric light appeared in 1881, the first electric streetcar in 1888.

Churches of many denominations attracted large congregations. Several of these can still be seen, including St. John's Episcopal designed by Benjamin Latrobe (called the "Church of the Presidents") at 16th and H Streets NW and St. Patrick's at 10th and F Streets NW. Six well-established black churches served a prosperous and rapidly growing black population. Of those remaining, two of the better known are the Metropolitan African Methodist Church at 1518 M Street NW and St. Mary's Episcopal Church at 728 23rd Street NW, which still looks the way James Renwick intended.

The assassination of President Lincoln, subsequent trial of the conspirators, and the impeachment and trial of President Andrew Johnson titillated a population ever more desirous of sensation. It wasn't long before the scandals of the Grant administration kept the newspapers and public happy.

New tycoons with bulging bankrolls came to Washington. They tried it, liked it, built huge mansions, married the natives or into the diplomatic set, and provided a colorful and high-stepping society. Some, like William Collins Whitney (Secretary of the Navy) and John Wanamaker (Postmaster General) were lured here by cabinet positions.

In the 1800s two important official structures increased the city's list of showplaces: the State-War-Navy Building at 17th Street and Pennsylvania Avenue NW (now the Old Executive Office Building) and the Washington Monument, finally opened to the public by President Cleveland. It was 555½ feet high, at that time the tallest building in existence. Americans were puffed with pride, but only briefly; the French finished the Eiffel Tower a year later—985 feet (although the Monument remains the tallest *masonry* structure).

A giant step forward for the District was the elimination of the many crisscrossing railroad tracks in front of the Capitol. They were rerouted to converge at the new Union Station, completed in 1907 at a cost of $21.8 million. Patterned after the Baths of Diocletian, it remains one of the most impressive structures in the city, with its wide vistas, Columbus fountain, and allegorical statues. It is beginning a new life as a National Visitor Center in 1976.

With the conclusion of World War I, Washington continued to grow. The war prosperity of the Democrats was followed by the Republican "normalcy" of Warren G. Harding, ending in the Tea Pot Dome scandals that shook the nation. "Silent Cal" Coolidge restored propriety to the White House, but Republican prosperity ended with the Wall Street crash of October 29, 1929, followed by the crushing defeat of Herbert Hoover. The stage was set for the biggest show the city of Washington had yet seen. In 1932, Franklin Delano Roosevelt was swept into office, the New Deal was born, and Washington thrived.

"We have nothing to fear but fear itself," said FDR when he took office. Immediately the new administration cut all federal salaries by 15 percent, which caused more fear than fear itself to 28,000 homeowners who were forced to sell. But soon bureaucracy burgeoned, and jobs increased from 62,000 to 93,000. Alphabet agencies sprang up everywhere—the AAA, CCC, TVA, SEC, NRA.

Meanwhile, the National Gallery of Art, a gift of former Secretary of the Treasury, Andrew Mellon, added to the charm of the city and the pleasure of the nation. Not so successful was the Palladian style and location of the projected Jefferson Memorial on the Tidal Basin. Women objectors, led by Eleanor "Cissy" Patterson, publisher of the *Times Herald,* chained themselves to the cherry trees to protest the architecture of the monument and its obstruction of the river view.

Eleanor Roosevelt's dedication to good works inspired both hostility and admiration. The long-neglected rights of blacks were high on her priority list. When the Daughters of the American Revolution wouldn't allow contralto Marian Anderson to sing at Constitution Hall, Mrs. Roosevelt saw to it that she had a bigger, world-publicized appearance on the steps of the Lincoln Memorial.

Gradually, in the late '30s, economic stability was returning to the country, but another threat appeared—the rise of militarism in Germany and Japan. The country was strongly isolationist, however, until the Japanese attacked Pearl Harbor on December 7, 1941. Truly "the Arsenal of Democracy" would be severely tested as the stunned nation turned to Washington for leadership. The next two decades would make Washington a great world capital.

When British Prime Minister Winston Churchill visited Washington in the last months of 1941, his speech to Congress gave strength to a people staggered, yet mostly untouched by disaster. Soon the new war activity overran the already jammed city, as the population grew to 750,000. Annual events such as the Cherry Blossom Festival were called off "for the duration" to discourage people from coming to town. There were blackouts to conserve power and to foil an enemy attack. Bars were jammed as liquor consumption, always sizable, went up; suicide rates and radical fringe activities plunged.

Visitors today would scarcely recognize wartime Washington. Downtown (F and G Streets between 7th and 16th Streets) was teeming morning, noon, and night. Both sides of the Reflecting Pool from the Washington Monument to the Lincoln Memorial were bordered with "temporary" buildings. Fronting on Constitution Avenue the Navy and Munitions buildings, built during World War I as "temporaries," still stood. An additional group of "tempos" cluttered the park across from the Willard Hotel. Some of these buildings survived into the 1970s.

The New Deal and World War I had led to unprecedented growth in Washington, but even that growth was small compared to that following World War II. At the end of the war, Washington was the capital of the most powerful nation the world had ever seen. Since the United States was the only major nation that had not suffered destruction of its homeland in the war, it found itself with a global role. Washington became the nerve center for the country's expanding international activities. What had been a sleepy, suburban-like Southern town before the war became, almost overnight, the capital of the nonCommunist world.

What happened to the State Department provides the most striking example of what the country's new worldwide responsibilities meant to the city. As late as 1930, the State Department had 4,726 employees. By 1975, that number reached 12,122, and the range of diplomatic activities for which the State Department was responsible had expanded accordingly.

The creation of new countries following the breakup of European colonial empires after World War II had a direct physical impact on Washington. In 1937 there were 61 foreign diplomatic delegations in the city. Now there are 126, and the city's diplomatic community numbers more than 10,000. Most of the embassies are clustered along Embassy Row, that stretch of Massachusetts Avenue northwest of Dupont Circle. But others can be found scattered throughout the District, and a few have located in the suburbs.

The growing interdependence of the world economy, the complexities of foreign aid, and the importance of U.S. policy in the development of the Third World have pushed Washington into a dominant role in world finance. Washington already is home to the International Bank for Reconstruction and Development (World Bank), the International Monetary Fund (IMF), and the U.S. Export-Import Bank, among others.

All this overseas involvement has given Washington a unique, international flavor, a feeling of excitement and bustle that simply did not exist before the war. But that excitement, that feeling of being at the center of things, is not just the result of Washington's transformation into a world capital. Since World War II the city also has played an increasingly important role in the domestic affairs of the nation. As well as the nation's political capital, Washington has become, as historian Constance McLaughlin Green put it, "the capital of all major American interests and aspirations."

In the past 20 years, three new cabinet-level departments have been created and scores of smaller offices and agencies within older executive branch departments have sprung up. The names of national associations representing every conceivable industry, business, professional, and special interest group fill page after page in the Washington telephone directory, each here to see that federal policy makers are responsive to their opinions.

Since 1950 the population of the metropolitan area has grown from 1,507,848 to over 3.1 million, making Washington one of the fastest growing cities in the country. But statistics do not tell the whole story. The growth of the last three decades has altered the city physically almost beyond recognition; it has changed its residents' living, working, traveling, and recreational habits; it has brought many of the social ills—and the social graces—common to most large American cities. It even has changed the District of Columbia's form of government.

To begin with, the demand for office space has triggered a construction boom that shows no sign of slowing down. Following the example of the Pentagon, more and more federal agencies have located their offices outside the District of Columbia.

Entire new communities have appeared, many of them clustered around Interstate 495, the Beltway that circles the District. Other new highways radiating from the Beltway have encouraged more suburban development. Most of these communities are typical of the sprawl to be found in the suburbs of any large American city, but two of them, Reston in Virginia and Columbia in Maryland, were planned "new towns" that received worldwide attention.

By their very presence, federal installations beyond the District line influenced private industries to locate offices nearby. Dozens of aerospace, engineering, and research and development firms have moved their headquarters to the outskirts of Washington, most of them along the Interstate 270 corridor. The highly educated, highly paid employees of these firms, and their counterparts in the more technological branches of the federal government, have helped make Maryland's Montgomery County one of the richest communities in the nation. The population of Northern Virginia has a distinctly military tone since so many residents there work in the Pentagon and related agencies in Arlington and Fairfax counties.

The suburban federal office and the new suburban highway are both symptom and cause of other social changes profoundly affecting the recent history of Washington. One such change is the substantial increase in the black population and the corresponding "white flight" to the suburbs. In 1950 blacks comprised 35 percent of the District's population. Today, over 70 percent of the District's population is black. The influx of hundreds of thousands of hopeful, but in many cases unskilled, rural blacks has placed tremendous strain on the inner city. Unable to compete for better-paying jobs, many blacks have been locked into festering, ever widening slums.

But the greatest barrier to the District's ability to cope with its new challenges was the archaic way in which it was governed. Until recently, the District surely had one of the worst municipal governments in the country. It had, in fact, no government of its own at all. District affairs were run by the U.S. Congress through standing Senate and House committees with little understanding of, much less sympathy for, an urban area with a rapidly changing population. Congress provided minimal funds to the District, watched idly while the inner city deteriorated, and stymied local efforts that began in the early 1940s to regain home rule for the District. That goal was finally achieved in 1974 when Congress, whose own membership had changed significantly, passed a home rule bill and relinquished much of the control of District affairs it had held since the 1870s. The District's first elected government in 100 years, with Mayor Walter Washington at its head, took office in 1975.

President John F. Kennedy took an interest in local Washington affairs that extended to its physical appearance, and his concern sparked a reevaluation of what enormous growth was doing to the city. He squelched a 1958 plan to tear down the beautiful old houses bordering Lafayette Park across from the White House and replace them with dull federal office buildings. He also gave his blessing to a Plan for the Year 2000 that should bring the design of the city more in line with Pierre L'Enfant's original concept. Under his administration a Pennsylvania Avenue Plan was begun, which may eventually make Pennsylvania Avenue the impressive, verdant thoroughfare that it was meant to be. The Southwest Redevelopment Project, planned under President Truman, began to take shape under Kennedy. At that time the Southwest area of the city included some of the District's worst slums. Except for a few historic buildings, 550 acres were cleared and a variety of apartment and office buildings, town houses, restaurants, and theaters were built.

The Kennedy administration's preference for Georgetown living may also have helped stimulate somewhat the growing trend of young, white professional families to move back into the inner city, and to buy and restore old town houses as their homes. The restoration of Georgetown has long been complete, and homes there are now among the most expensive in the city. Intensive restoration of Capitol Hill homes also has caused property values to skyrocket in a 15-block area around the Capitol. Other centers of restoration can be found in the Adams-Morgan neighborhood of Northwest and the streets around Logan Circle.

The restoration movement, coupled with strenuous citizen efforts to preserve beautiful and historic buildings of the past amid continuing rapid growth, is just one sign of Washingtonians' new pride in their vibrant, livable city. Another is the phenomenal growth in the city's cultural opportunities and attractions. Just 20 years ago, Washington had the reputation of being a cultural backwater. Today it is unquestionably the nation's second most active city in nearly all areas of the arts. In the performing arts, the Kennedy Center, since its opening a few years ago, has established itself as a major performing arts showcase. The reputations of the National Symphony and the Washington Opera Society grow yearly. Many theaters flourish, among them the Kreeger Theater and the Arena Stage, home of one of the nation's most accomplished regional repertory companies. The Folger Theatre Group presents its innovative, electric productions in a replica of a Shakespearean theater built within a library that houses the world's foremost center of Elizabethan scholarship. Wolf Trap National Park for the Performing Arts opened in 1971 as the nation's first national park dedicated to the arts, with an enormous outdoor stage that has offered the world's best ballet, opera, and dramatic companies. Ford's Theatre, the National Theatre, the D.C. Black Repertory Company, and at least a dozen smaller theatrical companies also flourish.

In the visual arts, the collections of the National Gallery, the Hirshhorn Museum and Sculpture Garden, the Museum of African Art, the Corcoran Gallery, the Phillips Collection, the Freer Gallery, the National Portrait Gallery, the National Collection of Fine Arts, the Barnett-Aden Collection (temporarily housed in the Martin Luther King Library) are among the most outstanding in the country. Scores of thriving commercial galleries have sprung up in the past 10 years or so.

During the 1960s Washington also became the nation's protest center. It was not a new development: In 1894 Washington was the goal of "Coxey's Army," and in 1932 thousands of Bonus Marchers camped on the Capitol grounds and built shanties across the Anacostia River until forcibly dispersed by Gen. Douglas MacArthur and his aide Dwight D. Eisenhower. The first of the recent demonstrations was perhaps the most impressive. Hundreds of thousands of Americans converged on the city in 1963 to protest the continued inequities of racial injustice and to hear the Reverend Martin Luther King make his historic "I Have a Dream" speech from the steps of the Lincoln Memorial. Most of the other demonstrations of the '60s protested the Vietnam War and they escalated in violence and disruption as the war escalated. But the event with the most direct and lasting consequences for the city itself was not a demonstration but a riot—the explosion of black rage in the slums of the city that followed the murder of Dr. King in Memphis in April of 1968. Whole blocks of Washington were burned. The city is still working to erase the scars of that riot and the conditions that made it possible.

Those scars are a visible reminder that Washington as a city, not just as the seat of a government with worldwide influence, shares the problems of every large American metropolitan region. But residents of the Washington area are coming to realize that they have a common stake in their solution, that they all are Washingtonians, whether they live in the District of Columbia, or in the Northern Virginia and Maryland suburbs. The attainment of home rule for the District has given them a potent new weapon with which to attack those problems. The nation's 200th anniversary has a special significance in this city and may lead to new directions for its future. It will be a future in which the state of the city, the state of the nation, and the state of the world will be ever more closely bound together.

INFORMATION
NATIONAL PARK

Chapter Two

# Advice to Travelers

PHYLLIE THEROUX

Washington was originally criss-crossed with cowpaths; embassy personnel drew hardship pay; and more than one First Lady eschewed Washington for reasons of health; but the city has long since pulled itself together. Millions of visitors now flock to the capital every year, and during the Bicentennial years even more are expected to come for special events and to visit national shrines. Washington is a popular tourist town, but it can be confusing—even to the people who live here. The bus system is more complex, taxis function differently, and traffic regulations are different than in most cities. Rooms and information are both often difficult to find. This chapter tells you where to bed down for the night, how to get into town, the best way to get around once you're here, how to find the right tours, and other basic survival information. There are also special sections for the foreign and for the handicapped visitor.

For direction on Bicentennial sights and events, consult the agencies and operators listed in the sections on Visitor Information and Tours in this chapter.

## Arrival

### Airports

There are three major airports serving Washington: National, Dulles, and Baltimore-Washington International.

**National Airport,** located five miles outside the District Line, serves in-country flights only, including the shuttle service to New York. For sheer dramatic entry into the city, nothing can compete with following the contour of the Potomac as you sweep down onto the runway. The subsequent ride across any of the bridges into town is spectacular. This being said, National leaves almost everything to be desired.

Some airlines have built large, modern terminals, but the prevailing impression National leaves is one of confusion and eyesore. The authorities express vague hopes for establishing multilingual signs, but there is no information booth, no foreign currency exchange, and the parking facilities are hardly jet-era.

Transportation from National into the District, Maryland, and Virginia is by limousine, taxi, or bus. It takes from 20 to 40 minutes to downtown Washington, depending on traffic conditions. The airport limousine costs $2 to the Statler Hilton (16th and K Streets NW) and $2.50 to the Washington Hilton (1919 Connecticut Avenue NW). For information call 471-9801. Taxis are more expensive (approximately $3.10 to the Statler Hilton; $3.40 to the Washington Hilton). One should determine in advance exactly what the particular cab company charges. Virginia cabs are metered; District cabs charge by the zone within the city of Washington and by mileage when traveling interstate. (See section on taxis for additional information.) The #11 Metrobuses (except #11-W) run every 15 minutes to Washington, Maryland, and Virginia. The charge is 50¢-80¢ depending upon your destination. The Washington Metrobus stop is at 10th Street and Pennsylvania Avenue NW. (For additional information call Metro: 637-2437.)

The airport has a coffee shop, restaurant, and airlines club lounges for card-carrying members.

**Dulles International Airport,** designed by the late Eero Saarinen, is a peaceful, space-age facility located 30 miles out in the Virginia countryside. Although it serves many of the international flights coming into Washington, it is still largely underused as a terminal. (See section on Foreign Visitors for detailed list of services to international visitors.)

It takes 45 minutes by car to downtown Washington (longer in rush hours). Limousine service to and from the Statler Hilton (16th and K Streets NW) is $2.75. (For information call 471-9801.) Taxis cost about $18 to downtown Washington. There are also two Metrobuses that serve Dulles. They depart from Dulles at 10:02 am and 4:19 pm with stops at Herndon, Reston (10:02 bus only), Tyson's Corner, Falls Church, and Rosslyn, Virginia, and 15th and K Streets NW. Fare is $1—a bargain if you can spare the time. The Metrobuses depart from the District for Dulles at 8:39 am and 2:39 pm, stopping at 33rd and M Streets NW, Rosslyn, Falls Church, and Tyson's Corner.

Dulles has dining facilities, airlines club lounges for card-carrying members, and several gift shops, some duty-free.

**Baltimore-Washington International Airport,** 25 miles from the District line, has received high ratings on all counts. It services both national and overseas flights, has a brand new international terminal and customs clearing area, and has taken some trouble to be of assistance to the traveler. An information center in the main lobby is open from 7 am-11 pm and can either provide information or can direct one to the proper place to obtain it. In the baggage-claim area there is a bank of toll-free, hotel-reservation telephones, a Traveler's Aid office, and a back-up phone when the Traveler's Aid office is closed. (See section in this chapter on Foreign Visitors for detailed list of services to international visitors.)

A traveler may use the airport phones for only 10¢ to call either Washington or Baltimore.

Transportation from the airport is by limousine or taxi. The charge is $3.50 to 16th and K Streets NW (the Statler Hilton) by airport limousine. Limousines leave every half hour. To the Bethesda Holiday Inn, Silver Spring Sheraton Motor Inn, and College Park Quality Inn, the price is $4. From any of these locations to the airport, reservations are required three hours in advance (information and schedules: Airport Limousine Service, 347-7766). Taxi service into Washington is $20 per cab-load of four people. It takes approximately 50 minutes to the Statler Hilton.

The airport has both restaurants and cocktail lounges, game rooms, a liquor store, and special club lounges for card-carrying airline members.

## Bus

**Greyhound** (11th Street and New York Avenue NW) and **Continental Trailways** (12th Street and New York Avenue NW) are the two companies that serve Washington on a scheduled basis. Their terminals, a block apart, are on the edge of the downtown business and shopping district. Taxis are easy to catch outside, and the main Metro bus terminal is at 14th and K Streets NW.

## Car

The city anticipates a large influx of cars during the Bicentennial. At publication time, however, there were no definite fringe parking arrangements. Robert F. Kennedy Stadium (East Capitol and 22nd Streets SE), the Pentagon (across the 14th Street Bridge, in Arlington, Virginia), and the south post of Fort Myer (below Arlington Cemetery on the west side of Arlington Memorial Bridge) are proposed fringe parking sites. Transportation from these sites to the Mall is planned. The Department of Highways and Traffic plans to alert the incoming motorists to fringe parking facilities with "trailblazer" signs beginning some distance from the city, and to provide low-cost shuttle service into town.

Otherwise, the traveler should be advised that parking in the city is limited and relatively expensive. Commercial lots can cost as much as $3.50 a day, although certain lots are free with "park and shop" validation from area stores.

### Train

**Union Station** is the terminal for all trains serving Washington. Located virtually next door to the Capitol, it is within minutes of the downtown hotel area. However, while it is being converted to the National Visitor Center, an ambitious facility designed to greet, inform, and orient visitors, the station is somewhat lacking in amenities. There is a Traveler's Aid office, a cafeteria/coffee shop, some magazine racks, car rental agencies, and a lot of uncomfortable wooden benches. Free carts to push your luggage are available. Transient parking is abominable, but there is commuter valet parking. When the center is completed, trains will arrive at a terminal next door. There should be better parking facilities and a Metro station from which to catch rapid-transit cars to other parts of the city. Now buses and taxis pull up outside the front of Union Station. Taxis are shared, and sometimes there is a wait.

## Climate

Washington teeters on the edge of qualifying as a southern clime, with a short but glorious spring and a summer that is fried-egg hot. The fall is long and crisp and although the leaves aren't as vivid as those in New England, there is enough color and blue sky to clarify any heat-muddled thoughts left over from muggier months. Winter is capricious, with cold days alternating with warm. There are usually two or three good snowfalls, never expected, and the city generally folds its tents when they do come, since only half the motorists buy snow tires.

Opinions as to the best season to visit Washington vary between spring (particularly during the April Cherry Blossom Time) and fall (when the city is operating at full strength). There is absolutely nothing wrong with June, July, and August that air-conditioning can't cure, although the lines outside of major tourist attractions increase to alarming proportions. Should you come mid-winter, be sure to prepare for cold and rainy weather: warm coat, gloves, boots, and an umbrella. It can rain during any season, although Washington is not known for prolonged rainy spells.

## Where to Stay

Hotels and motels listed are either well known, have been personally sampled, or come to us with positive recommendations. The list is by no means complete, but should be helpful as a starting point. Visitors are strongly urged to make reservations before arriving in the Washington area, and may want to consider one of the alternate housing options mentioned at the end of this section.

Prices for accommodations are based on the lowest rate for a single room at the time of publication as follows: Deluxe ($34 and up), Expensive ($27-$33), Moderate ($24-$26), Inexpensive ($12-$23), and Bargain ($11 and under). "Children free" means the hotel will supply an extra bed in parents' room without charge; "children extra" means that there is either an extra charge for each child in the room or for each extra bed needed. Unless otherwise indicated, there is no charge for pets; all rooms have air conditioning, television, and a private bathroom; parking at motels and motor inns is free.

### Near Airports

#### NATIONAL AIRPORT

**Crystal City Marriott Hotel,** 1999 Jefferson Davis Highway (521-5500, 800-228-9290).

Expensive. 1½ miles south of 14th Street Bridge on Route 1. Free airport transportation. Large, luxurious hotel with heated pool, miniature golf, dining room, coffee shop, cocktail lounge. Pay valet parking. Children under 12 free. Pets allowed.

**Holiday Inn—National Airport,** 1489 Jefferson Davis Highway (521-1600, 800-238-5400).

Inexpensive. 1¼ miles north of National Airport on Route 1. Free airport transportation. Restaurant, cocktail lounge, pool. Adjacent to shopping plaza. Garage. Children under 12 free. Kennels.

**Hospitality House Motor Inn,** 2000 Jefferson Davis Highway (920-8600).

Moderate. 1½ miles south of 14th Street Bridge on Route 1. Free airport transportation. Rooftop pool, restaurant, and dancing. Children under 12 free. Pets allowed.

**Howard Johnson's Motor Lodge—National Airport,** 2650 Jefferson Davis Highway (684-7200).

Moderate. 1¾ miles south of 14th Street Bridge on Route 1. Free airport transportation. Brand new motel with rooftop pool, lake swimming, 2 restaurants, cocktail lounge. Children under 18 free. No pets.

**Quality Inn—Pentagon City,** 300 Army Navy Drive (892-4100).

Moderate. 1 mile south of 14th Street Bridge. Free airport transportation. Just opened. Year-round pool, 2 restaurants, revolving rooftop bar. Free garage parking. Children under 17 free. No pets.

**Sheraton National Motor Hotel,** Columbia Pike and Washington Boulevard (521-1900, 800-325-3535).

Expensive. ¾ mile west of National Airport. Free airport transportation. Brand new, year-round pool and sundeck, 2 restaurants (including a rooftop restaurant with entertainment), cocktail lounges. Free garage parking. Children under 17 free. Small pets allowed.

**Twin Bridges Marriott Motor Hotel,** Routes 95 and 1 (628-4200).

Moderate. ¼ mile south of 14th Street Bridge. Free airport transportation. A very complete facility, with pool, wading pool, seasonal ice skating, 3 dining rooms, coffee shop, cocktail lounge. Children under 12 free. Pets allowed.

### DULLES INTERNATIONAL AIRPORT

**Dulles Marriott Hotel,** Dulles International Airport (471-9500, 800-228-9290).

Moderate. Pool, dining room, cocktail lounge. Free overnight parking. Children under 12 free. Pets allowed.

**Holiday Inn Motor Inn,** 1000 Sully Road (471-7411, 800-238-5400).

Inexpensive. 1¼ miles east of Dulles, on Route 28. Free airport transportation. Heated pool, wading pool, dining room, cocktail lounge. Children under 12 free. Kennels.

**Sheraton Inn—Reston** (620-9000, 800-325-3535).

Moderate. 5½ miles east of Dulles, junction Route 602 and Dulles Access Road, Exit 3. Free airport transportation. New hotel with pool, sauna, tennis, dining room, cocktail lounge. Free parking. Children under 17 free. Pets allowed.

### BALTIMORE WASHINGTON INTERNATIONAL AIRPORT

**Friendship International Hotel,** Baltimore Washington International Airport (301-761-7700).

Inexpensive. Swimming pool, dining room, cocktail lounge. Free parking. Children under 12 free. No pets.

**Holiday Inn—Airport,** 6500 Elkridge Landing Road (301-796-8400, 800-238-5400).

Inexpensive. 2½ miles north of airport. Free airport transportation. Heated pool, wading pool, dining room, cocktail lounge. Children under 12 free. Kennels.

## Washington, DC

**Allen Lee,** 2224 F Street NW (331-1224).

Bargain. Small downtown hotel popular with theater performers and visitors who will sacrifice luxury to save money. Half of the rooms have private baths. No dining facilities. No parking. No family rate. No pets.

**Anthony House,** 1823 L Street NW (223-4320).

Inexpensive. Restaurant. No parking. Children free. No pets.

**Barbizon Terrace,** 2118 Wyoming Avenue NW (483-1350).

Moderate. Off Connecticut Avenue. A motor inn. No dining facilities. Limited pay parking. One child allowed free, additional children extra. No pets.

**Bellevue,** 15 E Street NW (638-0900).

Inexpensive. On Capitol Hill. One of the older resident and guest hotels. Clean, decently decorated rooms with a slightly collegiate dorm atmosphere. Cafeteria. Free parking. Children extra. Group rates. No pets.

**Burlington Hotel,** 1120 Vermont Avenue NW (785-2222).

Inexpensive. Off Thomas Circle. A modernized older hotel, with dining room. Free parking. Children under 14 free. Pets allowed.

**Channel Inn Motel,** 650 Water Street SW (554-2400).

Moderate. A modern motor inn with swimming pool, boat docking facilities, 2 restaurants, coffee shop, cocktail lounge. Children under 12 free. No pets.

**Connecticut Inn,** 4400 Connecticut Avenue NW (244-5600).

Inexpensive. Located away from downtown area, but not far from National Zoo. Restaurant adjacent. Parking in garage. Children under 12 free. Pets allowed, providing they aren't left in room unattended or unleashed in lobby.

**Christian Inn,** 1509 16th Street NW (483-6116).

Bargain. Once an elegant apartment house, but now a budget hotel with pleasant ambience. Fairly attractive rooms, some without air-conditioning. Carry-out coffee shop on premises that makes room deliveries. No parking. No family rate. No pets.

**District Guest Quarters Apartment Hotel,** 801 New Hampshire Avenue NW (785-2000).

Deluxe. Located in Foggy Bottom near State Department. All rooms equipped with kitchens, sunny and neat as a pin. Rooftop pool, bellman. No dining room, but continental breakfast available. Pay valet parking. Children extra. Pets up to 25 lbs. allowed at a charge.

**Dupont Plaza,** 1500 New Hampshire Avenue NW (483-6000).

Moderate. On Dupont Circle. Modern hotel with refrigerators and wet bars in every room. Pay parking. Children under 14 free. Pets allowed.

**Ebbit,** 1000 H Street NW (628-5034).

Inexpensive. Walking distance from the Mall. Remodeled, small hotel with European air and reputation for meticulous care and service. Restaurant, coffee shop. No parking. Children free. No pets.

**Embassy Row,** 2015 Massachusetts Avenue NW (265-1600).

Deluxe. On edge of Embassy Row, near Dupont Circle. One of the best and newest luxury hotels with rooftop pool, good restaurant, multilingual personnel. Pay valet parking. Children under 12 free. Small animals allowed at a charge.

**Envoy Motel,** 501 New York Avenue NE (543-7400).

Inexpensive. Routes 50 and Alternate 1, ½ mile south of Baltimore Washington Expressway. Pool, dining room. Children free. Pets allowed.

**Executive House,** 1515 Rhode Island Avenue NW (232-7000).

Moderate. Fairly new hotel with refrigerators in all rooms, heated rooftop pool, restaurant, bar. Free parking. Children under 12 free. Pets sometimes permitted.

**Francis Scott Key,** 600 20th Street NW (NA8-5425).

Inexpensive. Close to White House, State Department, and Kennedy Center. Small hotel, not luxurious. Vietnamese restaurant on premises. No parking. Rate reductions for stays longer than one week. Children extra. No pets.

**Georgetown Dutch Inn,** 1075 Thomas Jefferson Street NW (337-0900).

Expensive. Near C & O Canal, south of M Street NW. Has apartment units and penthouse suites, some rooms with kitchenettes. Pool, fine restaurant (La Grenouille). Free parking. Children under 15 free. Pets allowed.

**Georgetown Inn,** 1310 Wisconsin Avenue NW (333-8900).

Expensive. In the heart of Georgetown. Beautifully decorated motor inn with uniformed coachman at the front door, lots of extras, good service, 4 elegant dining rooms, cocktail lounge. Free valet parking. Children extra. No pets.

**Gramercy Inn,** 1616 Rhode Island Avenue NW (347-9550).

Expensive. Off Scott Circle. Rooms have sitting areas and bar areas with refrigerators. Swimming pool. Free parking. Children under 14 free. Special weekend rates. Pets allowed.

**Gralyn Hotel,** 1745 N Street NW (785-1515).

Inexpensive. Just off Connecticut Avenue. Once the Persian Embassy, small and charming with lovely outdoor patio and garden. Dining room serves breakfast only. Free parking in nearby lots. Children extra. No pets.

**Harrington,** 11th and E Streets NW (638-8140).

Inexpensive. In main downtown and theater district. Large, old hotel used by lots of high school groups, has seen better days but is spotlessly clean. Good cafeteria, cocktail lounge. Free overnight parking. Group rates. Pets allowed.

**Hay-Adams,** 16th and H Streets NW (638-2260).

Deluxe. One of the best locations in the city, overlooking White House and Lafayette Park. Distinguished, charming old hotel with lots of paneling, antiques, and extras galore. Dining room, cocktail lounge. Pay valet parking. Children under 14 free. No pets.

**Holiday Inn,** 1900 Connecticut Avenue NW (332-9300, 800-238-5400).

Inexpensive. North of business district near Kalorama Triangle area and embassies. Pool, dining room, cocktail lounge, standard Holiday Inn amenities. Children under 12 free. Kennel.

**Holiday Inn,** 1615 Rhode Island Avenue NW (296-2100, 800-238-5400).

Inexpensive. Convenient downtown area. Pool, restaurant, bar, standard Holiday Inn amenities. Garage. Children under 12 free. Kennels.

**Holiday Inn—Parkway,** 2700 New York Avenue NE (832-3500, 800-238-5400).

Inexpensive. On Routes 50 and Alternate 1. Pool, restaurant, cocktail lounge. Children under 12 free. Pets allowed.

**Hotel John Kilpen,** 2310 Ashmeade Place NW (462-4336).

Bargain. Just off Connecticut Avenue in Kalorama Triangle. Few amenities, bath and air-conditioning extra. Simple dining room offers a hearty, inexpensive breakfast. No parking. Children extra. Pets allowed.

**Howard Johnson's Hotel,** 2601 Virginia Avenue NW (765-2700).

Moderate. Across the street from Watergate Hotel, near Kennedy Center. Refrigerators in rooms. Pool, dining room, cocktail lounge. Free parking garage. Children free. No pets.

**Hyatt Regency,** 400 New Jersey Avenue NW (800-228-9000).

Expensive. Scheduled to open January 1976. Near Capitol. Restaurants, ballrooms, night club, cocktail lounge, coffee shop. Pay valet parking. Children under 14 free. Group rates available. Small pets allowed.

**Jefferson,** 1200 16th Street NW (347-4707).

Expensive. Not far from White House. Not an ultra-modern hotel, but has instant service, homey comfort, beautiful rooms, and extras. Attractive restaurant and bar. No parking facilities. Children under 14 free. No pets. No credit cards, but personal checks accepted.

**Loews L'Enfant Plaza,** 480 L'Enfant Plaza SW (484-1000).

Deluxe. Within walking distance of Mall and Smithsonian, but away from main nightlife of older Washington. Luxurious, brand-new hotel with every amenity: refrigerators, thick towels, lavish furnishings. 2 restaurants, 1 with entertainment and dancing. Theater and shopping at doorstep. Pay valet parking. Children under 14 free. Pets allowed.

**Madison Hotel,** 15th and M Streets NW (875-1000).

Deluxe. Elegantly decorated hotel with excellent staff and lots of extra touches (refrigerators, saunas, massages, interpreters, package wrapping). Fine restaurant (The Montpelier Room) and 2 other more informal restaurants, cocktail lounge. Pay valet parking. Children extra. Pets allowed at a charge.

**Mayflower,** 1127 Connecticut Avenue NW (347-3000).

Moderate. In center of business and shopping district, near White House. Primarily a businessmen's and convention hotel, yet a good choice for anyone who wants convenience and location without sacrificing amenities. Notary and stenographic service available. Pay valet parking. Children under 18 free. Pets allowed.

**Mid-Town Motor Inn,** 1201 K Street NW (783-3040).

Inexpensive. Close to bus terminals. Dining room (open weekdays, until noon on weekends), cocktail lounge. Children free. Pets allowed.

**National,** 1801 I Street NW (628-5566).

Inexpensive. Within walking distance of principal Washington attractions. An old, recently redone, small hotel with no frills. Coffee shop. Pay parking in adjacent garage. Children free. No pets.

**Pick-Lee House,** 15th and L Streets NW (347-4800).

Inexpensive. Good location, comfortable, dining room (closed on weekends), cocktail lounge. Pay parking facilities. Children under 12 free. Pets allowed.

**Presidential,** 900 19th Street NW (331-9020).

Bargain. A small hotel with a plain but clean and pleasant decor. No dining facilities. No parking. Children free. Group rates available. No pets.

**Quality Inn—Capitol Hill,** 415 New Jersey Avenue NW (638-1616).

Moderate. Hotel with pool, dining room, cocktail lounge. Some rooms with water beds. Free garage. Children under 12 free. Pets allowed.

**Quality Inn—Thomas Circle,** Massachusetts Avenue and Thomas Circle NW (737-1200).

Moderate. Brand new hotel with swimming pool, dining room, cocktail lounge. Free parking. Children under 16 free. No pets.

**Ramada Inn,** 10 Thomas Circle NW (783-4600, 800-228-2828).

Moderate. New, large hotel with pool that is domed for winter use. Dining room, cocktail lounge. Free valet parking. Children under 12 free. Small pets allowed.

**Regency Congress Inn,** 600 New York Avenue NE (546-9200).

Inexpensive. On Routes 50 and Alternate 1. A motel with pool, sauna, dining room. Children extra. Pets allowed.

**Roger Smith,** 18th and Pennsylvania Avenue NW (298-7200).

Inexpensive. Near White House. Breakfast only. Pay parking lot next door. Children under 13 free. Pets allowed.

**Rock Creek Hotel,** 1925 Belmont Road and 20th Street NW (462-6007).

Inexpensive. A motor inn 1 block east of Connecticut Avenue. Coffee shop (open until 1:30 pm, closed Sunday). Children extra. No pets.

**Royal Motel,** 1917 Bladensburg Road NE (526-7500).

Inexpensive. On Routes 50 and Alternate 1. Pool, dining room. Children extra. Pets allowed.

**Sheraton Carlton,** 16th and K Streets NW (638-2626, 800-325-3535).

Expensive. Near White House. Distinguished, recently remodeled hotel with 2 dining rooms, cocktail lounge. Pay valet parking. Children under 18 free. No pets.

**Sheraton Park Hotel and Motor Inn,** 2660 Woodley Road NW (265-2000, 800-325-3535).

Expensive. Washington's largest hotel, some distance from downtown but in lovely park setting. Favorite spot for conventioneers, political gatherings, and many Washingtonians who enjoy the winter ice skating and outdoor swimming pool. Entertainment and dancing in Lamp Post Lounge. 2 other restaurants, cocktail lounge. Pay garage. Children under 12 free. Many package plans available. Pets allowed.

**Shoreham Americana Hotel and Motel,** 2500 Calvert Street NW (234-0700).

Expensive. Very large hotel on edge of Rock Creek Park, newer motel just below main hotel. Several public rooms, swimming pool, sauna. Many dining facilities, including coffee shop, dinner theater in Blue Room, and Marquee Lounge where political satirist Mark Russell is a leading attraction. Pay parking lot. Children under 14 free. Pets allowed.

**Skyline Inn,** 10 I Street SW (488-7500).

Moderate. New motel not far from Arena Stage, but not in main business district. Pool, dining room, cocktail lounge. Free parking. Children under 11 free. Pets allowed.

**Statler Hilton,** 16th and K Streets NW (393-1000).

Expensive. Large, downtown hotel, commercial but good location. Many public rooms, including Trader Vic's, 2 other restaurants, and a lounge with dancing. Many shops and services. Adjacent pay valet parking. Children free. Pets allowed.

**Tabard Inn,** 1739 N Street NW (785-1277).

Inexpensive. Small hotel on semi-residential street just off Connecticut Avenue. No elevator, but very charming British ambience. Each room has fireplace (nonworking). Book-lined downstairs library, breakfast room on premises, Iron Gate Inn restaurant across the street. No parking. Children extra. Pets allowed.

**Washington,** 15th Street and Pennsylvania Avenue NW (638-5900).

Moderate. One of the city's older, large hotels. Rooftop restaurant with breathtaking view of White House and monuments. Pay parking. Children under 14 free. Pets sometimes allowed.

**Washington Hilton,** 1919 Connecticut Avenue NW (483-3000).

Expensive. New, large hotel located north of business district. Popular with conventions, vacationing families. Extra services include children's room-service menu, babysitting, interpreters, and public stenographic service. Hotel literature translated into five languages. Swimming pool, wading pool, tennis courts, dining room, coffee shop, cocktail lounges. Pay garage. Children free. Variety of package plans. Pets allowed.

**Watergate,** 2650 Virginia Avenue NW (965-2300).

Deluxe. A hotel-apartment-business complex overlooking Potomac River adjacent to Kennedy Center. 75 percent of units are suites. Good service, free indoor pool and health club, excellent restaurant, cocktail lounge. Adjacent Les Champs shopping mall has more dining possibilities. Pay valet parking. Children under 12 free without extra bed. Monthly rates. Pets allowed.

**Wellington,** 2505 Wisconsin Avenue NW (337-7400).

Deluxe. An apartment hotel on hill overlooking Georgetown. Huge rooms, residential ambience, small pool, excellent French restaurant (La Toque closed Sundays). Pay parking. Children under 12 free. No pets.

## Maryland

### BETHESDA

**Bethesdan Motor Hotel,** 7740 Wisconsin Avenue (656-2100).

Inexpensive. On Route 240, exit 19 off Route 495. Pool. No dining facilities. Children under 12 free. Pets allowed.

**Colonial Manor Motel,** 11410 Rockville Pike (881-5200).

Inexpensive. Capital Beltway (Route 495), Exit 19, beyond Bethesda business district. Pool, dining room. Children under 10 free. Pets allowed in certain rooms.

**Holiday Inn,** 8120 Wisconsin Avenue (652-2000, 800-238-5400).

Inexpensive. A hotel with heated rooftop pool and sauna. Some rooms with refrigerators. Restaurant with dancing and entertainment. Free garage parking. Children under 12 free. Small pets allowed.

**Linden Hill Hotel,** 5400 Pooks Hill Road (530-0300).

Inexpensive. Off Route 240 at junction of Routes 270 (70S) and the Capital Beltway (495). Pool, sauna, massage, indoor tennis (extra charge), restaurant. Free parking. Children extra except infants. No pets.

**Ramada Governor's House Motor Hotel,** 8400 Wisconsin Avenue (654-1000, 800-228-2828).

Inexpensive. On Route 240. Pool, dining room, cocktail lounge. Children under 18 free. Pets allowed.

**United Inn of America,** 8130 Wisconsin Avenue (656-9300).

Inexpensive. Near National Institutes of Health, Bethesda Naval Hospital. Some rooms with water beds. Free continental breakfast. Children under 12 free. Pets allowed.

### SILVER SPRING

**Georgian Motel,** 7990 Georgia Avenue (588-8520).

Inexpensive. Dining room closed Mondays. Children under 12 free. No pets.

**Holiday Inn,** 8777 Georgia Avenue (589-

0800, 800-238-5400).
Inexpensive. Pool, dining room, coffee shop. Children under 12 free. Kennels.

**Quality Inn,** 8040 13th Street (588-4400).
Inexpensive. 1 block off Route 20. Pool, restaurant. Children under 16 free. Small pets allowed.

**Sheraton Silver Spring,** 8727 Colesville Road (589-5200, 800-325-3535).
Inexpensive. On Route 29. Heated winterized pool, 2 dining rooms. Free valet parking. Children under 18 free. Small pets allowed.

**Silver Spring Motel,** 7927 Georgia Avenue (587-3200).
Inexpensive. On Route 20. No pool or dining room, but restaurant opposite premises. Children extra. Small pets allowed.

## Virginia

### ALEXANDRIA

**Brookside Motel,** 6001 Richmond Highway (765-5100).
Inexpensive. 1½ miles south of Alexandria on Route 1. Pool. No dining facilities, but near restaurants and shopping. Children extra. Pets allowed.

**Guest Quarters,** 100 S. Reynolds Street (370-9600).
Moderate. ¼ mile east of junction of Route 95 and Duke Street. A new hotel, popular with the military and families. Pool and wading pool. Large, comfortable suites with kitchen units. No restaurant, but several in area. Free parking. Rates by day or week. Small extra charge for children if accompanied by both parents; with one parent charged at the double rate. No pets.

**Holiday Inn,** 6100 Richmond Highway (765-0500, 800-238-5400).
Inexpensive. 2 miles south of Alexandria on Route 1, within 10-minute drive of Mount Vernon and Woodlawn Plantation. Pool, restaurant. Children under 12 free. Pets allowed.

**Holiday Inn—No. 2,** 2460 Eisenhower Drive (960-3400, 800-238-5400).
Inexpensive. Capital Beltway (Route 495), Exit 2. Pool, dining room, cocktail lounge. Children under 12 free. Pets allowed.

**Howard Johnson's Motor Lodge,** 5821 Richmond Highway (768-3300).
Inexpensive. On Route 1, just off Capital Beltway (Route 495), Exit 1 S. Pool. Adjacent restaurant. Extra for waterbeds. Rental cars and sightseeing tours available. Children extra. Pets allowed.

**Quality Inn Olde Colony,** First and N. Washington Streets (548-6300).
Inexpensive. 1 block east of Route 1 on George Washington Memorial Parkway. Pool. Adjacent restaurants and theater. Free continental breakfast. Bus and walking tours available. Free parking. Children under 12 free. No pets.

**Travelers Motel,** 5916 Richmond Highway (768-2510).
Inexpensive. 1½ miles south of Alexandria on Route 1. Pool. Adjacent restaurant. Children extra. No pets.

**Wagon Wheel Motel,** 7212 Richmond Highway (765-9000).
Inexpensive. Wading and Olympic-sized pools, playground, dining room, sightseeing services. Weekly rates. Children under 12 free. Small pets allowed.

### ARLINGTON

**Arva Motor Hotel,** 2201 Arlington Boulevard (525-0300).
Inexpensive. 2 miles west of Memorial Bridge on Route 50. Pool, dining room. Adjacent to shopping plaza. Children extra. No pets.

**Cherry Blossom Motor Inn,** 3030 Columbia Pike (521-5570).
Inexpensive. 1 week minimum rental, features suites and kitchenettes. Pool. Adjacent restaurant. Children under 12 free. Pets sometimes allowed.

**Holiday Inn,** 2485 S. Glebe Road (979-4100, 800-238-5400).
Inexpensive. Route 95, 3¼ miles south of 14th Street Bridge. Public bus service to Washington; sightseeing tours leaving from premises. Pool, dining room, cocktail lounge. Children under 12 free. Pets allowed.

**Holiday Inn—Key Bridge,** 1850 N. Fort Myer Drive (522-0400, 800-238-5400).
Inexpensive. 2 blocks northwest of Key Bridge in Rosslyn area. Pool, sauna, dining room. Children under 12 free. Kennels.

**Key Bridge Marriott,** 1401 Lee Highway (524-6400, 800-228-9290).
Moderate. Well-located, just across Potomac River from Georgetown. Pool, wading pool, excellent restaurant (The Chaparel), cocktail lounge. Children under 12 free. Pets allowed.

**Quality Inn Motel—Central,** Arlington Boulevard and N. Court House Road (524-4000).
Inexpensive. 1½ miles southwest of Memorial Bridge on Route 50. Pool, dining room. Children under 16 free. Pets allowed.

**Quality Inn Motel—South Gate,** 2480 S. Glebe Road (979-4400).
Moderate. 3¼ miles south of Memorial Bridge. Pool, wading pool, miniature golf, playground, restaurant. Children under 16 free. Kennels.

**Ramada Inn Rosslyn,** 1900 N. Fort Myer Drive (527-4814, 800-228-2828).

Moderate. 1 block northwest of Key Bridge. Pool, 2 restaurants, cocktail lounge. Children under 18 free. Kennels.

## Alternate Housing

**Holiday Hosts, Inc.,** P.O. Box 1108, Langley Park, MD (434-4336).

Modeled after the Bed and Breakfast plan of Europe, Holiday Hosts arrange accommodations for tourists in inspected and approved private homes. Many of them are in the suburbs within 20-30 minutes of the District, and are ideally suited for the auto traveler. There are also many in-town houses on major bus lines.

While most range from $10 for a single room to $21 for a family of four per day, there are a few less-expensive accommodations available. These rates include a continental breakfast.

For families with young children, some hosts allow the use of their kitchens for preparation of a picnic lunch or supper. Many hosts will also babysit in the evening for a reasonable fee.

The host families include engineers, government employees, lawyers, working students, artists, and doctors who have expressed an interest in sharing their homes during the Bicentennial. It is recommended that visitors write or phone as early as possible for accommodations.

Holiday Hosts will send a tourist packet, including maps, special events, and tourist attractions for $3.

**Camping** (see Chapter 7 for information).

**American Youth Hostel,** 1501 16th Street NW (387-3169).

For members only (membership $5-$10 a year), the hostel holds 65 people in dormitory-style rooms, with four to five beds in each, at $3 a night. Strictly for the knapsack-on-my-back crew. Nonresidents must clear out after 10 pm; lights are out by 11 pm. The kitchen is open for cook-it-yourself breakfast and dinner.

# Getting Around the City

## Street System

Pierre L'Enfant did not leave the city's development to chance. The Capitol was designated as the real and symbolic center of the city, sitting at the intersection of four quadrants—Northwest, Northeast, Southwest, and Southeast. North Capitol and South Capitol Streets divide the east and west quadrants; the center of the Mall divides the north and south quadrants. Numbered streets intersect with letter streets and there are four roughly identical sets of each. It is an easy system to master, once you give it a little thought.

The one-syllable letter streets are followed by two-syllable name streets in alphabetical sequence, then by three-syllable name streets, so that if your Aunt Frances lives in the 3800 block of Warren Street NW, you know that she lives in the Northwest section of Washington, in the second alphabet, between 38th and 39th Streets. One thing to remember is that there are no B or J Streets, but B is replaced by Independence and Constitution Avenues. Therefore if you want an address in the 1100 block of 20th Street, it would be in the block between L and M in the appropriate quadrant.

Visitors have been known to complain about the circles that interrupt the peaceful flow of traffic in Washington. Originally, these circles were designed so that soldiers could fire in any direction to protect the White House from foreign or domestic insurgents. Some are convinced that the circles were put there to confuse the enemy, and that it is the motorist who is now the enemy. Remember when you enter a circle that motorists within the circle have the right of way. Watch for signs that might direct you to a particular lane, and have faith that the street you entered on will pick up 180° on the other side.

Finally, there are certain broad avenues, the most famous being Pennsylvania, that cut across the city. You will find that these avenues serve as the city's major arteries to and from town. The maps in this book should help you navigate.

As for bridges, they span either the Potomac into Virginia or the Anacostia into Maryland, and are used as reference points for most driving instructions.

An eight-lane Beltway (Route 495) girdles the District, and allows one to bypass Washington entirely, or permits access to the District from several exits. Be sure to know in advance which exit you want; the signs can be confusing.

## Traffic Regulations

The speed limit is 25 miles per hour or as posted. Unless otherwise indicated, there is no right turn at a red light after stopping. Rush hours in Washington are 7:00-9:30

am and 4:00-6:30 pm with no parking allowed on major downtown streets during these hours. One should note that during rush hour on certain main arteries traffic flow is reversed: three lanes during rush hour, two lanes at all other times; certain streets become completely one-way. Rock Creek Parkway, for instance, which carries motorists north and south, becomes completely one-way going downtown during the morning rush hour and reverses during afternoon rush hour. Also, left turns are banned at some intersections during rush hour. Read all signs.

Parking fines are $5; $10 if your car is on a main street. Towing away is rare, but tickets are inevitable.

## Bus

Metrobuses criss-cross the city and cost 40¢ (exact change required, but refunds can be obtained from Metro offices); the rate increases by zones once you cross the Maryland or Virginia line. Getting to your destination may require changing buses, but transfers within the District are free. The fleet is an uneven mixture of new, carpeted vehicles and older, graffiti-engraved models, but all are heated and air-conditioned, and a tolerable way to travel if you get the hang of the complex route system. A call to 637-2437 will give you route and schedule information between 6 am and midnight. Free maps and schedules are available from Metro, 600 5th Street NW, Washington, DC 20001, or from Metro garages and ticket offices.

The Downtowner is a special mini-bus that runs from 6th and K Street SW to Connecticut and N Street NW, which takes you through the shopping and business district for only 25¢, or for nothing if you use a transfer from a regular bus going in the same direction. If you only wish to travel up and down F Street, the main downtown shopping street, you can ride for 10¢. For the Bicentennial there is promise of a shuttle bus on Constitution Avenue and stepped-up service along 17 routes to the Mall.

## Subway

The Regional Rapid Rail System (usually referred to as Metro) will revolutionize Washington transportation when it is completed. Limited downtown service over four-and-a-half miles of track is scheduled to start in 1975.

## Taxis

District taxi cabs charge on the zone system and do not have meters. Hanging behind the front seat of every licensed taxi is a zone map with the prices for crossing from one zone to another. Single and group-rate charges are also explained on the chart. Another surprise to out-of-towners is the practice of sharing cabs in Washington (everywhere but at National Airport). The driver should clue you in on what route conflict may be involved when you join or are joined by other passengers, but if he doesn't, don't be embarrassed to ask whether you are going to be taken out of your way.

Taxis are relatively inexpensive in the District: one person can ride from the White House to the Capitol for 85¢ (one zone), and from the White House to the Shoreham Hotel for $1.25 (two zones). The same rides for two people would cost $1.20 and $1.60 respectively. Additional charges for taxis are: 50¢ for ordering a cab by telephone; $1 for any bag or trunk in excess of three cubic feet; 25¢ for a wait; and after the first five minutes, 25¢ for each five minutes.

Maryland and Virginia cabs have different fare systems, and the same ride to and from National Airport can vary. Also, District cabs go onto an interstate mileage fare system when they cross the District line.

Finally, there are cabs known to the trade as "gypsy cabs," licensed by the States of Virginia or Maryland. They operate as independent carriers and should be avoided because of their high rates. They can be identified by the dome light on the cab roof and a plastic sign, magnetically clipped to the side of the car saying "Taxi." If you hail a cab without a company name and telephone number on the outside, don't get into it. You'll be considerably poorer if you do. Overcharge complaints should be sent in writing to the Washington Metropolitan Area Transit Commission, 1625 I Street NW, Washington, DC 20006.

## Car Rentals

There are plenty of car rental agencies to choose from (check Yellow Pages). Their rates vary, so it pays to shop around. For instance, at last check, **Budget Rent-A-Car** (800-228-9650) had a favorable day rate for people who plan to do a lot of driving, since it includes 100 miles before there is an added mileage charge. On the other hand, if you aren't going to drive that much, **Na-**

**tional Car Rental** (783-1000) and **Avis** (683-6700) had equally advantageous rates computed on a base plus mileage. **American International Rent-A-Car** (800-527-6346), while not competitive on day rates, had a weekend price that was hard to beat. Be sure to check economy car rates and weekend specials.

## Limousines

**Diamond Sightseeing Tours** (546-9800) provides a car and chauffeur for $12.50 an hour for business purposes, or $14.50 an hour for sightseeing. **Gray Line** (393-2227) has the same service, at a slightly higher cost, $14 and $16 respectively, and **Carey Limousines** (892-2000) charges $14 for business and $15 for sightseeing.

All of these limousine rentals have a three-hour minimum requirement.

## Bicycles

Washington is a relatively flat, rolling city, and within the past five or six years, bicyclists have successfully lobbied for better, safer, and more trails throughout the city and beyond. You might consider renting a bike for the day and tooling around some perfectly lovely parts of the city that are designed for cyclists—notably the Rock Creek Park trails and the C & O Canal towpath. (See Chapter 7.)

# Tours

**Alexandria Community Y,** 602 Cameron Street, Alexandria, VA (549-0111). This community organization offers tours conducted by enthusiastic, knowledgeable volunteers who can speak French, Spanish, Italian, or Arabic. A minimum of 10 people are required; the charge is $1 per person per hour, which includes coffee or tea, and a reservation, upon request, for lunch or dinner at one of Alexandria's better restaurants. A bus can be provided at extra charge. Tour reservations must be made at least one week in advance.

**Diamond Sightseeing Tours,** 201 F Street NE (546-9800). Diamond Tours has eight different packages, ranging from $7 to $28.50; reduced rates for children. Depending upon the size of the tour, a limousine or bus is used, with a driver-lecturer. Twenty-four-hour advance reservations are requested, but are not mandatory for individuals. Literature is available in most downtown and suburban hotels. There is free pick-up and delivery from your hotel. It should be mentioned that for the two-day tour of the Washington area (the tourist returns to his lodgings at the end of the day) Diamond's fare is almost half the Gray Line fare, with no perceptible difference in the tours.

**Doorways to Olde Virginia,** P.O. Box 7053, Alexandria, VA 22307 (548-0100). Custom-tailored tours of Alexandria and its neighboring plantations. Charge is $1 per person per hour.

**Gray Line Tours,** 1010 I Street NW (DI 7-0600). Gray Line runs the city's largest sightseeing operation with eight local and seven out-of-city tours, and more being added to the itinerary. Driver-lecturers narrate the tours. Group rates; reduced rates for children; children under five free. There is free pick-up and delivery from most major downtown hotels.

**Soul Journey,** Box 336, Washington, DC 20044 (337-5132). Soul Journey offers an innovative bus tour that shows visitors the city's important black landmarks. The Frederick Douglass home, the Museum of African Art, Howard University, and the Mary McCleod Bethune memorial are among the points of interest included. The guides are qualified historians and the driver also comments on sights of tourist interest. When in operation (check for latest schedule) tours leave on Saturday mornings at 10 am. They last approximately four hours and lunch is available at an extra charge. Group rates; reduced rates for children; children under six free. The tour starts across the street from the National Theatre at the District Building, 13½ Street NW and Pennsylvania Avenue. Phone reservations are taken until Friday evening. Soul Journey also offers a Friday evening dinner and theater tour and a Saturday evening dinner and night-on-the-town tour.

**Tourmobile,** 900 Ohio Drive SW (638-5371 for recording; 737-7880 for information, reservations). Tourmobile is a sightseeing service that takes visitors to the U.S. Capitol, Washington Mall, and Arlington Cemetery. A fleet of 88-passenger shuttle trams run at frequent intervals between marked pick-up points. One ticket is good for the entire day and allows the purchaser to board and reboard as many times as desired. Each tram has a narrator who provides a running commentary. There are three basic tours and group rates are available. Prices are subject to change, but present prices run from $1.25 to $3.00 for adults, with reductions for children, clergy, and military.

**Washington Whirl-Around,** 2262 Hall Place NW (337-1855). Washington Whirl-Around, Inc., is an organization of five knowledgeable women who decided some years ago there was a need for unusual and unique group activities that the usual bus tours around Washington didn't fill. Using their contacts, club memberships, and sophisticated knowledge of the city, they conduct half- and full-day tours of museums, galleries, embassies, historic homes, and national monuments in an individual and innovative fashion. A typical tour is the "American Art" tour, which takes in the Renwick Gallery and several others, and ends up at the Decatur House for lunch and a speaker. A "Women in Politics" seminar is very popular, and there are several programs revolving around the Bicentennial celebration. Transportation is by chartered bus; a minimum of 40 people required.

**The Wilson Boat Line,** 6th and Water Streets SW (Ex 3-8304). The Wilson Line runs up and down the Potomac from late March through Labor Day, ferrying passengers to Mount Vernon or on Potomac River cruises. There are refreshments on board, and the captain indicates the points of interest.

There are several day and evening possibilities: The daily cruise to Mount Vernon (alternating times depending upon the month), a High School River Cruise (running through June 6 every night but Sunday), and a Moonlight Cruise (June 7 to Labor Day). Depending upon the cruise, there are varying bands, types of refreshments, and fares.

# Visitor Information

## District

**The Washington Area Convention and Visitor's Bureau,** 1129 20th Street NW (659-6423 for personnel; 727-8866 for recorded message). Monday-Friday 9 am-5 pm. The Visitor's Bureau, on the second floor of the Washington Board of Trade, provides a variety of maps, hotel, motel, and tour information, some in foreign languages. Write, phone, or stop in. A call to 727-8866 is answered by a recording about the week's entertainment at local and suburban theaters, plus telephone numbers for the Smithsonian Institution, National Park Service, and the National Archives for additional recordings about their particular events.

**The Public Citizen Visitors Center,** 1200 15th Street NW (659-9053). Monday-Friday 9 am-5 pm; Saturday 9 am-1 pm. This is not your usual tourist's center. A brainchild of Ralph Nader, and run by three paid staff members and several volunteers, the center tries to alert visitors to more than just the usual monuments and public buildings in Washington. Here is the place to find out what congressional committee meetings you can attend that day and where to best see your government in action. It has been known to advise on everything from the voting record of a congressman to where to eat cheap.

Located five blocks from the White House, the center has a library and a 55-seat auditorium where documentaries are shown free. For a stamped, self-addressed envelope, it will send anyone a biweekly calendar of Washington events and, on request, will provide students with information on government and public issues for their high school studies.

**The National Park Service** (Washington area parks information 426-6700; Dial-A-Park daily activities 426-6975). The Park Service hopes that by July 1976 the National Visitor Center at Union Station will be completed. At the present time, it mans seven kiosks at the monuments, in Lafayette Park, and on the Mall that hand out maps and information of all kinds (not all are open in winter). The Dial-A-Park recordings give a rundown on facilities operated by the Park Service, which include everything from ice skating to Ford's Theatre.

**U.S. Environmental Protection Agency Visitor's Center,** first floor of the West Tower, Waterside Mall, 401 M Street NW (755-5713). Monday-Friday 9 am-4 pm. Parking at Mall. Featured are exhibits, tours (by prearrangement), and publications describing the causes and growth of pollution, how technology can combat pollution, and programs under way to control the environment. The center is very attractive, and has large, full-color exhibits, closed-circuit television, and a multivisual slide show.

## Alexandria, Virginia

***The George Washington Bicentennial Center,** 201 S. Washington Street (750-6677). Daily 9 am-5 pm. Limited, free, off-street parking. This is a state-owned facility that provides information, exhibits, and a film about Virginia in the Revolutionary era. The center will furnish you with preplanned trips to points of interest in the state, put you in contact with private tour groups in Alexandria, and make free hotel reservations for individuals or groups throughout the state. The shop here has a unique selection of Bicentennial wares (see Chapter 10).

***The Alexandria Tourist Council,** Ramsay House, 221 King Street (549-0205). Daily 10 am-4:30 pm; closed Thanksgiving, Christmas, and New Year's Day. This organization offers a variety of printed material on shopping, dining, and historic sites in Alexandria (brochures are available in 10 languages). Nonresidents of Alexandria will receive an "honorary citizen" badge, which allows them to park in a metered or limited-parking zone free for up to three days. Twice a day (at 10:30 am and 1:30 pm) a 13-minute color film of Alexandria's history is shown (additional shows can easily be arranged with advance notice).

The Alexandria City Recreation Department provides free individual walking tours following the film at Ramsay House, for those visitors who are not part of a group. The schedule is: August 31-April 1 1:45; May 3-August 30 10:45 and 1:45. The tour lasts approximately one hour.

The council will book free group tours, conducted by volunteers and tailored to the particular age and interest of the participants. At least two or three days' notice is required for this service.

# Foreign Visitors

## Information and Assistance

**International Visitors Service Council** (IVIS), 801 19th Street NW (872-8747). Monday-Friday 9 am-5 pm. IVIS is an efficient organization staffed by Washingtonians who do not charge for their services. Just call and IVIS can put you in contact with someone who speaks your native language in a matter of minutes. It has approximately 45 different possibilities in its "language bank." IVIS will also provide (48-hour notice required) a personal interpreter escort service. Other services: assistance in securing professional babysitters; advice on hotels having foreign language capabilities; arrangement for home hospitality (must be requested in person at IVIS office); a list of churches with services conducted in foreign languages; and maps and literature on the Washington area.

**Traveler's Aid,** 1015 12th Street NW (347-0101, Monday-Friday 9 am-5 pm); Union Station (Monday-Friday 9 am-4 pm, Saturday 10 am-4 pm); National Airport (daily 10 am-9 pm); Dulles International Airport (daily 10 am-9 pm). This is a volunteer organization designed to help travelers in need of emergency assistance.

**Gateway Receptionist Program,** Dulles International Airport. Daily noon-8:30 p.m. This facility is maintained by the U.S. Travel Service for the purpose of helping foreign travelers through customs, health, immigration, and agricultural inspections. A visitor information booth is planned for 1976.

**Information Center** and **Travelers Aid,** Baltimore-Washington International Airport (see Airports in this chapter). Airport employees form a pool of interpreters for these agencies to call upon when foreign travelers need assistance. After hours, airport police will find an interpreter.

## Foreign Newspapers and Publications

**Universal Newsstands,** 405 11th Street NW, 735 14th Street NW, 503 14th Street NW, and 603 15th Street NW. Some open 7 days a week and until midnight. Spanish, French, Italian, and German newspapers and magazines.

**General Newsstand,** 1796 Columbia Road NW. Monday-Friday 6 am-7:30 pm; Sunday 6 am-7 pm. Sells Latin-American, French, German, and Italian magazines, and some foreign language newspapers.

**The Library of Congress,** First Street and Independence Avenue SE. Monday-Friday 8:30 am-9:30 pm; Saturday 8:30 am-5 pm; Sunday 1 pm-5 pm. Newspapers from most foreign capitals are available free of charge for use in the main reading room.

Most embassies have reading rooms open to nationals, with newspapers available. Hours are generally 9 am-5 pm weekdays.

## Currency Exchange

Money can be exchanged at the following locations:

**Deak & Co.,** 1800 K Street NW. Monday-Friday 9 am-5:30 pm; Saturday 10 am-2 pm.

**Downtown branches of major banks,** Monday-Friday 9 am-2 pm; Friday also 4 pm-6 pm.

**Dulles International Airport,** same hours as banks, but may possibly expand hours.

The city's larger hotels also have currency exchange services.

## Local Customs

In Washington dress is usually an individual matter. Coat and tie for men are *de rigueur* in only some restaurants; women can wear pants suits or dresses.

Tipping for meals is 15-20 percent; taxis the same; and in hotels, train stations, and airports the customary tip or charge for carrying bags is 50¢ per bag. Do not leave shoes outside your door for shining, unless the hotel specifically states that it offers this service.

An entire course in diplomacy and political etiquette could be offered to help the neophyte thread his or her way through the Washington scene, but it is probably enough to mention here that a congressperson should be addressed as "Mr." or "Ms. Smith." Senators are always called "Senator Smith," and ambassadors, "Ambassador Smith." Of course, should you bump into the President, you would say, "Excuse me, Mr. President."

It is not a good idea to walk in sparsely populated areas of town at night. Washington, like other urban centers, is not immune from street crime, and unless you are in a group, you should stick to well-lighted, well-traveled streets.

## Shopping

Most stores are open from 9:30 or 10 am to 5:30 pm. Many stay open Monday and Thursday nights until 9 pm, and some are open every evening. A number of stores also operate on Sundays, at least for part of the day. Stores are usually open on legal holidays, except for Christmas, Thanksgiving, and Easter Sunday.

Personnel offices in most of the larger stores will locate foreign-speaking employees to assist shoppers.

## Interpreter Services

**International Visitors Service Council** (see Information and Assistance section in this chapter). The best bet for foreign visitors who need an interpreter is to check with IVIS about interpreter escort service.

**The Guide Service of Washington,** 15 E Street NW in the Bellevue Hotel (628-2842), provides interpreters for in-town and out-of-town trips. Four hours for $35 is standard, or $60 for eight hours. Reservations several days in advance are necessary. The guides pride themselves on knowing the area's history and giving a comprehensive in-depth explanation of the city.

**Berlitz School of Languages,** 1701 K Street NW (331-1160) offers interpreters with a wide variety of languages from Arabic to Swahili. Romance languages interpreters are $20 per hour, $140 for an eight-hour day. Other languages cost $25 per hour, or $160 per day. The interpreters are not sightseeing guides. They will translate whatever your own guide says to your language, or communicate your needs.

## Language Assistance Mall Area

*Seeing the Smithsonian* ($2) is an overall

guide to the Mall museums, which has been translated into French, Spanish, German, and Japanese. It can be purchased at bookstores in the Smithsonian museums. There are also free brochures in the same languages in all of the various Smithsonian-operated museums, and at the Museum of History and Technology a floor plan in translation is available.

Also, the Smithsonian Castle (or the Smithsonian Building) shows an orientation slide show, with subtitles in French, German, and Spanish.

At the Museum of History and Technology the first system of telephone tapes in translation has been installed. At the entrance to the museum are telephones that the visitor can pick up and receive an orientation to the museum. The National Gallery has foreign language tours.

## Handicapped Visitors

Washington sights will be much easier for handicapped visitors to see by 1976, when government buildings are all supposed to be up to acceptable standards. It is still best to call ahead to determine whether a specific tour or place is possible for a person with a particular disability.

**Tourmobile** is ready and willing to take on nonambulatory passengers. The driver will put the person on board, collapse the wheelchair, reassemble it when the bus stops at a site, take the passenger off the bus, and help him back when he wishes to resume the tour.

The **National Park Service** is installing ramps and graded walks in the Mall area, to be finished by the spring of 1976, and the park-ranger-operated kiosks will have a fleet of eight-passenger, battery-operated vehicles on call, should a physically incapacitated tourist wish to ride around the Mall. There is no charge.

The **Great Falls Park** in Virginia is completely equipped for the handicapped visitor, from the specially designed parking areas, ramps leading to the walkway, lowered drinking fountains, restroom facilities, and a covered picnic pavilion with a concrete ramp and landing.

A plan to prepare maps of the D.C. area for dual use of blind and partially sighted persons is being prepared by the U.S. Geological Survey, and will be in all public buildings by January of 1976.

The Smithsonian publishes *A Guide to the Smithsonian* in braille which can be borrowed from any of the museum information desks or from the Martin Luther King Library (901 G Street NW) or any of the 50 regional libraries under the Library of Congress Division for the Blind throughout the country.

The **National Gallery of Art** can arrange private tours for the blind. Reservations must be made in advance through the Education Department (737-4215, ext 272) of the gallery. The gallery also provides wheelchairs, at no charge, for visitors who need them.

At the **Museum of Natural History,** a map prepared in large type for the partially sighted explains the contents of the rooms. The "Discovery Room" is a particularly recommended exhibit due to its tactile nature. By the summer of 1975, a cassette tour specially prepared for the blind will be installed and ready to use.

In this book, the use of the symbol H indicates a facility that is accessible to the handicapped; HP indicates one that is partially accessible and requires advance arrangements or use of a special entrance.

## Chapter Three

# Seeing the City Walking Tours

**TONY WRENN**

These tours are planned for walking, with the exception of the Arlington Cemetery area and the Monument and Memorials tour where the distances between some attractions may make driving more practical. Washington is a beautiful city to walk in. Its flowers and street trees, open green spaces, low buildings, and the absence of overhead electrical and telephone cables, give the city a feeling of spaciousness seldom found in this country.

In selecting sites to include in the tours, we gave preference to those open to the public—in Washington these are legion, and in most cases free (exceptions are noted).

A few words of caution: Parking is difficult in most of the tour areas. Use public transportation if at all possible. During the peak seasons lines may be long. Plan enough time for waiting. Washington is the quintessence of the changing city; everything from telephone numbers to addresses shift overnight. It is best to check before going to avoid disappointment.

The intent here is to guide the visitor to the places that might interest him, knowing that most of them provide guided tours and/or free or inexpensive literature that will fill in the details when he gets there. In some cases we have noted particularly helpful publications that are available in various locations. Here are some others we recommend to make your visit more enjoyable. All can be purchased at the bookstore of the National Trust for Historic Preservation and the McGraw Hill Book Store in the Museum of History and Technology (see Chapter 10).

Wrenn, Tony, *Walking Tours: Washington, D.C.,* Parks and History Association, Washington, 1975.

American Institute of Architects, *A Guide to the Architecture of Washington, D.C.,* 2nd ed. New York, Frederick A. Praeger, 1974.

Foundation for the Preservation of Historic Georgetown, *A Walking Guide to Historic Georgetown.* Washington, 1971.

Landmarks Society of Alexandria, *Historic Homes and Landmarks of Alexandria, Virginia,* 14th ed. Alexandria, 1974.

Maddex, Diane, *Historic Buildings of Washington, D.C.* Pittsburgh, Ober Park Associates, 1973.

Goode, James M., *The Outdoor Sculpture of Washington, D.C.* Washington, Smithsonian Institution Press, 1974.

In all the tour areas there are many sights worth seeing that are not described in the text. By all means, walk with your eyes open and discover for yourself not only the richness of the city's architecture and history, but also of its parks, shops, and all of the amenities of the city that residents find a source of pleasure and pride.

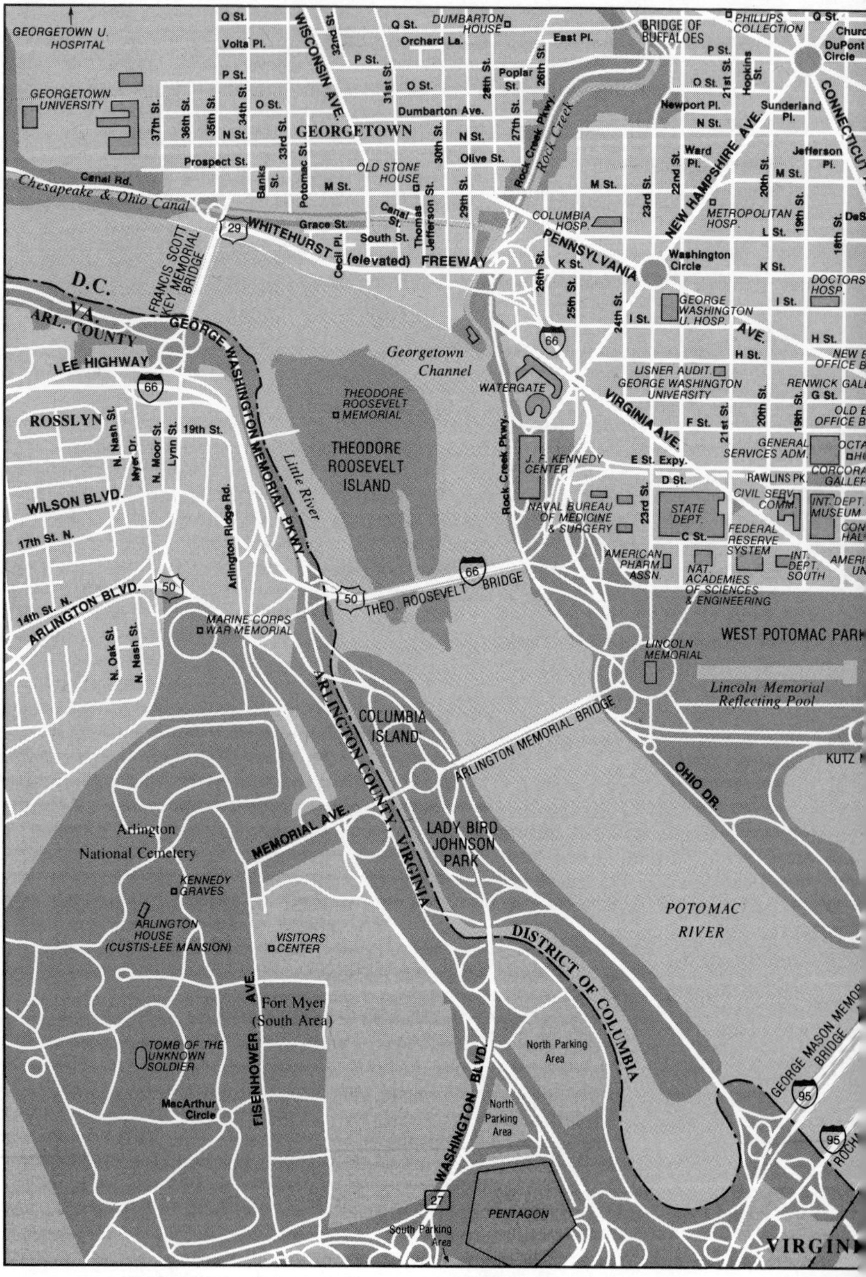
GEORGETOWN U. HOSPITAL
GEORGETOWN UNIVERSITY
Q St.
Volta Pl.
P St.
O St.
N St.
37th St.
36th St.
35th St.
34th St.
33rd St.
WISCONSIN AVE.
32nd St.
31st St.
30th St.
29th St.
28th St.
27th St.
26th St.
Q St.
DUMBARTON HOUSE
Orchard La.
P St.
O St.
Dumbarton Ave.
Poplar St.
East Pl.
GEORGETOWN
Prospect St.
Banks St.
Potomac St.
M St.
OLD STONE HOUSE
N St.
Olive St.
Canal Rd.
Chesapeake & Ohio Canal
Grace St.
Canal St.
Thomas St.
Jefferson St.
South St.
Cecil Pl.
WHITEHURST (elevated) FREEWAY
29
FRANCIS SCOTT KEY MEMORIAL BRIDGE
Rock Creek Pkwy.
Rock Creek
BRIDGE OF BUFFALOES
PHILLIPS COLLECTION
Q St.
DuPont Circle
CONNECTICUT
P St.
O St.
Newport Pl.
N St.
Ward Pl.
21st St.
Hopkins St.
Sunderland Pl.
Jefferson Pl.
NEW HAMPSHIRE AVE.
M St.
23rd St.
22nd St.
20th St.
19th St.
18th St.
COLUMBIA HOSP.
METROPOLITAN HOSP.
L St.
PENNSYLVANIA
Washington Circle
K St.
K St.
26th St.
25th St.
24th St.
DOCTORS HOSP.
GEORGE WASHINGTON U. HOSP.
I St.
I St.
AVE.
H St.
H St.
66
D.C.
VA.
ARL. COUNTY
GEORGE WASHINGTON MEMORIAL PKWY.
LEE HIGHWAY
66
Georgetown Channel
WATERGATE
LISNER AUDIT.
GEORGE WASHINGTON UNIVERSITY
RENWICK GAL
G St.
VIRGINIA AVE.
F St.
OLD E OFFICE B
ROSSLYN
N. Nash St.
Myer Dr.
N. Moor St.
Lynn St.
19th St.
THEODORE ROOSEVELT MEMORIAL
THEODORE ROOSEVELT ISLAND
Little River
Rock Creek Pkwy.
J. F. KENNEDY CENTER
E St. Expy.
D St.
GENERAL SERVICES ADM.
RAWLINS PK.
CIVIL SERV. COMM.
WILSON BLVD.
Arlington Ridge Rd.
NAVAL BUREAU OF MEDICINE & SURGERY
23rd St.
STATE DEPT.
C St.
FEDERAL RESERVE SYSTEM
INT. DEPT. MUSEUM
17th St. N.
AMERICAN PHARM. ASSN.
NAT. ACADEMIES OF SCIENCES & ENGINEERING
INT. DEPT. SOUTH
66
THEO. ROOSEVELT BRIDGE
50
50
ARLINGTON BLVD.
14th St. N.
MARINE CORPS WAR MEMORIAL
N. Oak St.
N. Nash St.
LINCOLN MEMORIAL
WEST POTOMAC PARK
Lincoln Memorial Reflecting Pool
ARLINGTON COUNTY, VIRGINIA
COLUMBIA ISLAND
ARLINGTON MEMORIAL BRIDGE
OHIO DR.
MEMORIAL AVE.
Arlington National Cemetery
LADY BIRD JOHNSON PARK
KENNEDY GRAVES
ARLINGTON HOUSE (CUSTIS-LEE MANSION)
VISITORS CENTER
POTOMAC RIVER
DISTRICT OF COLUMBIA
Fort Myer (South Area)
EISENHOWER AVE.
TOMB OF THE UNKNOWN SOLDIER
MacArthur Circle
North Parking Area
North Parking Area
WASHINGTON BLVD.
GEORGE MASON MEMORIAL BRIDGE
95
95
27
PENTAGON
South Parking Area

Downtown Washington
and Nearby Arlington
INTERSTATE
U.S.
STATE
Route Markers
State Boundaries
0
0.5
Scale of Miles
Copyright, 1974 Washingtonian Books
Washington Magazine Inc.
All rights reserved.
This work may not be copied in whole or in part.
Map by: Roberta R. Sabban
Q St.
P St.
O St.
N St.
M St.
L St.
K St.
I St.
H St.
G St.
F St.
E St.
D St.
C St.
A St.
Logan Circle
Scott Circle
Thomas Circle
John F. Kennedy Playground
RHODE ISLAND AVE.
MASSACHUSETTS AVE.
VERMONT AVE.
NEW YORK AVE.
PENNSYLVANIA AVE.
CONSTITUTION AVE.
INDEPENDENCE AVE.
MARYLAND AVE.
LOUISIANA AVE.
NEW JERSEY AVE.
DELAWARE AVE.
NORTH CAPITOL ST.
SOUTH CAPITOL ST.
SOUTHWEST FREEWAY
SOUTHEAST FREEWAY
NATIONAL GEOGRAPHIC SOCIETY
MT. VERNON SQ.
FARRAGUT
MCPHERSON SQ.
FRANKLIN SQ.
ST. JOHN'S CHURCH
DECATUR HOUSE
LAFAYETTE PARK
BLAIR HOUSE
TRAILWAYS BUS DEPOT
GREYHOUND TERM.
MARTIN LUTHER KING MEM. LIBRARY
GENERAL ACCOUNTING OFFICE
GOVT. PRINTING OFFICE
CITY POST OFFICE
UNION STATION
Union Station Plaza
TREASURY DEPT.
WHITE HOUSE
Hamilton Pl.
NATIONAL COLLECTION OF FINE ARTS
NATIONAL PORTRAIT GALLERY
JUDICIARY SQ.
NATIONAL THEATRE
FORD'S THEATRE
PERSHING SQ.
FEDERAL CITY COLLEGE
NEW FBI
DISTRICT BLDG.
THE ELLIPSE
COMMERCE DEPT.
NATIONAL AQUARIUM
OLD POST OFFICE
IRS
JUSTICE DEPT FBI
NATIONAL ARCHIVES
MUNICIPAL CENTER
EMPLOYMENT SECURITY BLDG.
US COURT HOUSE
NEW LABOR DEPT. (UNDER CONST.)
LABOR DEPT.
FED. TRADE COMMISSION
PUBLIC LIBRARY ADM. OFFICE
SENATE OFFICE BLDGS
MUSEUM OF AFRICAN ART
MUSEUM OF HISTORY & TECHNOLOGY
MUSEUM OF NATURAL HISTORY
NATIONAL GALLERY OF ART ANNEX (UNDER CONST.)
Madison Dr.
Washington Dr.
THE MALL
Adams Dr.
SUPREME COURT
FOLGER SHAKESPEARE LIBRARY
UNION SQ.
THE CAPITOL
WASHINGTON MONUMENT
SMITHSONIAN INSTITUTION
Jefferson Dr.
HIRSHHORN MUSEUM
NATIONAL AIR & SPACE MUSEUM (UNDER CONST.)
LIBRARY OF CONGRESS
LIB. OF CONG. ANNEX
SYLVAN THEATER
FREER GALLERY OF ART
ARTS & IND. BLDG
AIR & SPACE BLDG
BOTANIC GARDEN
Rumsey Ct.
AGRICULTURE DEPT.
FORRESTAL BLDG.
TRANS DEPT.
NASA
HEW
HEW & NASA
HOUSE OFFICE BLDGS
BUREAU OF ENGRAVING & PRINTING
BUREAU OF ENGR. & PRINT. ANNEX
L'Enfant Promenade
FOOD & DRUG ADM.
FBI (IDENT. DIV.)
FOLGER PARK
POST OFFICE DEPT.
L'ENFANT PLAZA
TRANSPORTATION DEPT
HOUSING & URBAN DEVEL. DEPT
School St.
Ivy St.
Frontage Rd.
Virginia Ave.
GARFIELD PARK
Tidal Basin
JEFFERSON MEMORIAL
Banneker Circle
FRANCIS CASE MEMORIAL BRIDGE
Water St.
LANSBURGH PARK
KREEGER THEATER ARENA STAGE
NATIONAL CAPITAL PARKS HDQTRS. NAT. PARK SERV. & US PARK POLICE
WILSON LINE
Canal St.
Howison Pl.
Carrollsburg Pl.
Van St.
Half St.
Cushing Pl.
N Pl.
Washington Navy Yard
EAST POTOMAC PARK
OHIO DR.
WASHINGTON CHANNEL PARK
Fort Lesley J. McNair
Potomac Ave.
Anacostia River
FREDERICK DOUGLASS BRIDGE
DISTRICT OF COLUMBIA

# Capitol Hill

**HOW TO GET THERE:** Tourmobile to Capitol. Metrobuses to Capitol: 2, 30, 32, 34, 36, 40, 52, 54, R4; to Union Station: 2, 40, 42, D2, D4.
**PARKING:** Commercial lots behind the House Office Buildings and near Union Station.
**TIME:** Approximately 3-4 hours.
**RESTAURANTS:** Supreme Court cafeteria, House and Senate Office Buildings cafeterias, Senate restaurant (see below). For nearby places to eat see Chapter 9.

The Capitol Hill area is a good starting point for touring Washington. The Capitol itself is a must; while you are in the neighborhood there are other major sights you might consider. Access is easy by public transportation, and when you get there you will find adequate information, rest rooms, and dining spots, not only within the Capitol, but also elsewhere in the tour area.

If you have only a short time, don't miss the tours of the Capitol, Supreme Court, and Library of Congress. The Botanic Garden, along with the Folger Shakespeare Library and Museum of African Art, give the visitor a welcome respite from government and the law. Both the Folger and Museum of African Art are within the Capitol Hill residential area, a 19th-century neighborhood that is again becoming one of Washington's "in" addresses. Congressional aides, young professionals, and others are renovating town houses, and the neighborhood is an interesting example of restoration in progress, worth walking an extra block or two to explore.

When the National Visitor Center opens in 1976, Union Station will become the logical starting place not only for this tour but for all Washington tours. Transportation, orientation, and information on entertainment, touring, and dining will then be available from one central point. Before then, you may want to skip the Union Station part of the tour and begin at The Supreme Court (7).

***The Government Printing Office (1),** 710 North Capitol and G Streets NW (541-2091) is the publishing arm of the various branches of the federal government. Its publications range from guidebooks to the national parks to the *Congressional Record,* the daily journal of congressional proceedings. Although the building itself is not open to the public, the bookstore is, and well worth a visit. A large number of books on display are available there; others can be ordered from the GPO catalog. Many useful publications can be purchased at bargain prices—some for less than $1. Monday-Friday 8 am-4 pm; Saturday 9 am-1 pm. No catalog orders filled on Saturday.

Near the GPO Bookstore is the **National Guard Memorial (2),** Massachusetts Avenue and North Capitol Street NW (Justement, Elam, Gallmer, and Kidd, 1965), featuring a hall of flags and an exterior sculpture court. Within the court, statuary and panels by Felix de Weldon trace the history of the Guard.

Nearer Union Station is the **City Post Office (3),** Massachusetts Avenue and North Capitol Street NW (Daniel H. Burnham, 1914). This is the only post office in the city open 24 hours a day year-round. It is particularly busy each April 15 when income tax payers try to beat the postmark deadline for mailing returns.

***Union Station (4),** Massachusetts Avenue and First Street NE, will be the home of the National Visitor Center, which is scheduled for full operation by mid-1976 (523-5200 for information). Built in an era when the train was a prime carrier of passengers, Union Station served as a gateway to Washington for many years. Probably no other building in town has been used by so many famous people.

Before Union Station was built, railroad tracks chaotically crisscrossed a Mall cluttered with stations and other structures. In 1901, when the McMillan Commission adopted a plan for restoring parklands and open space within the city and for the construction of new government buildings, it called for the consolidation of all the train stations at one terminal. Daniel Burnham designed a Roman and Beaux-Arts building set majestically at one end of a broad, landscaped plaza stretching to the Capitol. In terms of massiveness, high visibility, and style, Union Station set the pattern for most subsequent building in Washington up to World War II.

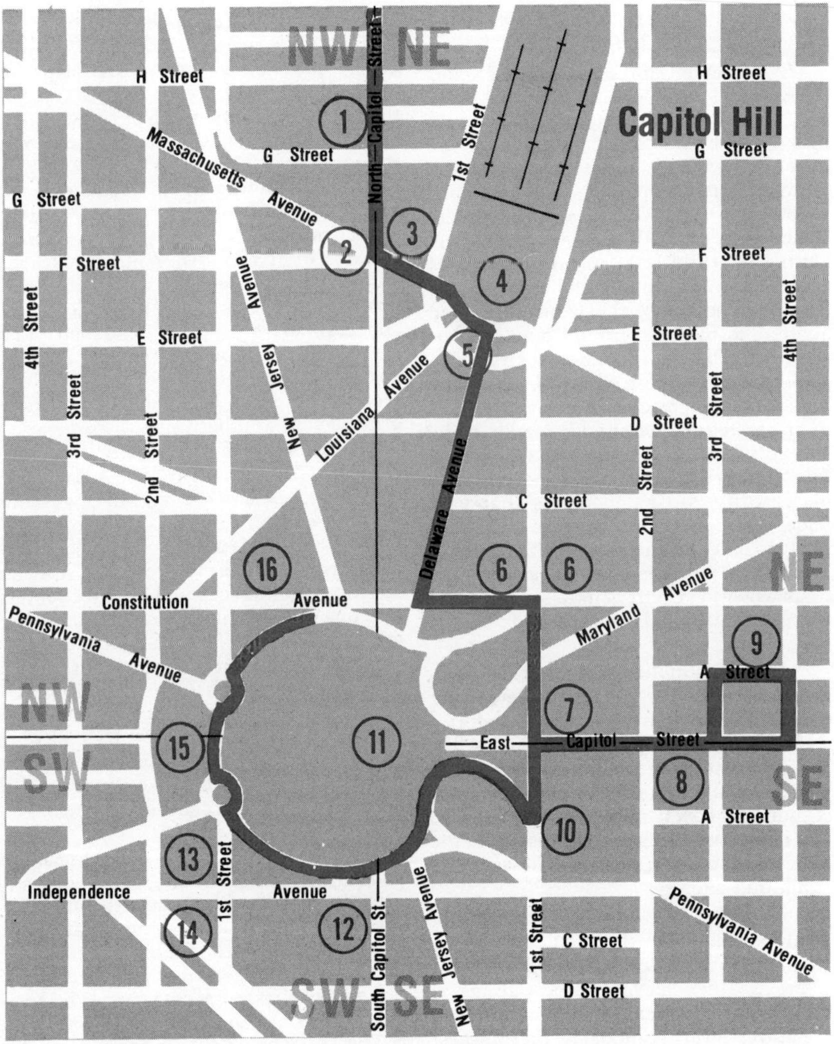


The opening of The National Visitor Center will make the building a major gateway to Washington once more. Under an agreement with the National Park Service, the terminal is being renovated and the station will become the hub of a multimedia, multipurpose, multitransportation facility. Work is under way on theaters, exhibit halls, lounges, restaurants, and an orientation-reception center capable of handling 100 people a minute. Trains will continue to use the terminal until the new station behind it is built. Parking for visitor cars is being built, and the station will be serviced by both ground-level local buses and the new Washington subway system.

The Columbus Fountain and Flagstaffs (Loredo Taft, 1912) in front of the station, and **Union Station Plaza (5),** make it pleasant and convenient to walk from the station to the Capitol. Commemorative trees line the route, and there are several landscaped areas for rest and picnicking. Toilets are near the Union Station Plaza Fountain (Bennett, Parsons, and Frost, 1933).

**The Senate Office Buildings (6)** are located on Constitution Avenue: the first is the Richard Brevard Russell Building (Carrere & Hastings, 1908), at Delaware Avenue NE; the other is the Everett McKinley

Dirksen Building (Eggers & Higgins, 1958), between First and 2nd Streets NE.

**The Supreme Court of the United States (7),** First and East Capitol Streets NE (638-0200 for recorded information) was established by the Constitution as the keystone of one of the three coequal branches of government, but had no home of its own until 1935 when the neoclassical building, designed by Cass Gilbert, was completed. During the early 1800s, a period when its decisions were shaping the form of the American republic, the Court occupied quarters in the U.S. Capitol building, but before 1805 the court often found itself dispossessed and was forced to meet in nearby homes. The Supreme Court hears its cases in an impressive room with marble walls and columns and a lofty, ornate ceiling. The Justices flank the Chief Justice in order of seniority, sitting in chairs that vary widely in appearance because each was made to order for the man who occupies it. The general public is admitted on a rotating basis when the Court is in session, but the space is limited and the wait is sometimes long.

Public tours include a short orientation, a visit to the courtroom, and a view of the elliptical spiral staircases rising six stories without interior support. The guides discuss the history of the Court, its ritual and method, and the current Justices. The tour is short and covers only the main floor, so don't miss the display on the history of the building and the Court in a lower-level exhibition hall.

One of the best popular histories of Washington institutions and buildings, *Equal Justice Under Law, The Supreme Court in American Life,* is on sale in the building. The Supreme Court cafeteria, on the lower level, is probably the plushest and one of the best in any Washington government building.

**The Folger Shakespeare Library (8),** East Capitol Street between 2nd and 3rd Streets SE (546-5370) was constructed (Paul Cret, 1932) to house not only work by Shakespeare or directly relating to him, but also other theatrical and literary work that he influenced. The exterior of the building is in the sparse neoclassical style then in vogue. Inside, the building is more reminiscent of the 16th and 17th centuries during which Shakespeare lived. The vaulted-ceiling exhibition gallery, with tile floor and oak paneling, is copied after a great Elizabethan hall. The gallery features models (including two of London's 1599-1613 Globe playhouse where Shakespeare worked), clothing, books, furniture, artifacts, manuscripts, and paintings, which either concern Shakespeare or relate to him in some way.

At the end of the exhibition gallery is the Folger's own Elizabethan theater, which, though not a replica of the Globe, is characteristic of it and other playhouses of Shakespeare's time. It is actively used throughout the year for plays, lectures, concerts, and a poetry series—many free (see Chapter 6). Monday-Friday 10 am-4:30 pm; Saturday fall only. Free tours by volunteers on Mondays at 1 and 2 pm; by prior arrangement at other times.

**The Museum of African Art** (Frederick Douglass Town House) **(9),** 316 A Street NE (547-7424), established in 1964, was the first museum in America organized to debunk traditional myths and misconceptions about African culture and to serve as an Afro-American cultural resource center. It is one of Washington's most interesting small museums. The well-lighted and uncluttered exhibit areas feature both permanent displays and changing exhibitions of carvings, furniture, fabrics, ceremonial items, paintings, and jewelry. Special exhibitions may range from one photographer's view of African culture to the paintings, fabrics, or crafts of a given area or tribal group.

A variety of publications on African art and culture, prints, jewelry, note cards, and other items are available from the museum shop, and there is also a boutique at 324 A Street adjacent to the museum, with rugs, fabrics, furniture, and a wider selection of unique jewelry and accessories. (The boutique opens at noon every day.)

The 1870s house that is the main building of the museum was the first Washington home of Frederick Douglass. He lived here for three or four years before he moved to Cedar Hill in Anacostia, which was his home until his death in 1895 (see Chapter 5). Born in slavery, Douglass escaped from his owner in 1838 and later purchased his freedom with funds donated by friends and admirers. Self-educated, he became one of the leading abolitionist spokesmen during the pre-Civil War era, using his newspaper *The North Star* to promote the cause of human freedom. The paper, begun in 1847 and named for the star that many slaves used as a guide to freedom, espoused Douglass's belief in universal rights for all citizens. Monday-Friday 11 am-5 pm; Saturday-Sunday 12 pm-5 pm. Free, though a contribution of $1 is suggested. Tours are available by prior arrangement.

A short walk around the block—3rd, A, and 4th Streets NE, East Capitol Street—will provide a good introduction to the Capitol Hill neighborhood. Houses, apartment buildings, and churches built between 1840 and 1900 show the wide diversity of styles typical of 19th-century neighborhoods.

***The Library of Congress (10),** Main Building, First Street, between East Capitol and B Streets SE (426-5458 for general information; 393-4463 for concert and ticket information). A visit to the Library of Congress may not fascinate everyone but those interested in design and decoration should not miss it. The building (Smithmeyer and Pelz; Edward Pearce Casey, 1897) was one of Washington's last great Victorian showplaces. Vaguely reminiscent of the Paris Opera, the building is full of minute and scholarly detail. A good example are the 33 keystone heads over the second-story windows, each different, which show accurate facial features of ethnic groups from the Americas, Europe, Africa, and Asia. The purpose was to inform and educate the library user even before he entered the building. Inside, the lavish use of color in mosaics, frescoes, marble, and metal is nothing short of spectacular. The approach to the visitors gallery from which the main reading room is viewed—its massive dome rising 125 feet above the floor—is one of the most exciting architectural experiences in Washington.

The guided tour takes about 45 minutes; guides discuss the collections and usually show the technical systems that keep the collections moving from the 320 miles of shelves to users who may choose from some 16 million bound volumes, only a part of the more than 72 million items in the library—possibly the world's largest. (See Chapter 5 for more information.)

In addition to regular exhibits including the Gutenberg Bible and items from presidential and other special collections, the library hosts visiting shows. At the tour and sales desk, you can buy books, catalogs, posters, note cards, and pick up free literature, including the monthly *Calendar of Events.* In addition to listing exhibits, lectures, and the like, the calendar includes the schedule of justly popular concerts (see Chapter 6). Monday-Friday 8:30 am-9 pm; Saturday until 6 pm; Sunday 11 am-6 pm. Free tours until 4 pm, weekdays only. Cafeteria and snack bar. (Note: All collections are not in the main building. Some are in the Annex, immediately to the rear of this building on 2nd Street SE; some at other locations in the Washington area. A new annex, the James Madison Building, is under construction across Pennsylvania Avenue from the main building.)

The **Fountain of Neptune** (R. Hinton Perry, 1897) is at street level in front of the library, beneath the entrance plaza and grand stairs. Surrounding the sea god are tritons, turtles, frogs, and sea nymphs on prancing mounts—half horse, half dolphin. Even in winter, without the bounce and play of water, the bronze figures, flanked by bamboo hedges, are delightful to see.

***The United States Capitol (11),** First Street between Constitution and Independence Avenues NE at East Capitol Street, visitor entrance off First Street at East Capitol Street (224-5750 for tour information; 224-3121 to reach your senator or representative). From the completion of the first section of the Capitol building in 1800 until the addition of the east front in 1961, the Capitol has undergone at least seven expansions. The variations in the cream-white colors of the facade make these easy to spot.

The list of architects responsible for the present Capitol building reads like a *Who's Who* of successful American architects including: William Thornton (1793-94), who won the original competition for the design; Benjamin H. Latrobe (1803-11, 1815-17); Charles Bulfinch (1818-29); Thomas U. Walter (1851-56); Edward Clark (1865-1902); Elliott Woods (1902-23); David Lynn (1923-54); J. George Stewart (1954-70); and, since 1971, George M. White, the present architect of the Capitol. It was Thomas U. Walter, the 1850s architect, who designed the great cast-iron dome. Visible from almost every part of Washington and its approaches, especially at night when it is brightly lighted, it has become the modern symbol of Congress.

Guided tours begin in the centrally located Crypt, where there is a sales desk with publications (*We, the People,* the official illustrated history of the Capitol is excellent), and an exhibit tracing the architectural history of the building. The 35-40 minute free tours, among the best in the city, generally cover the Crypt, the whispering gallery in the Old House of Representatives chamber, the Rotunda, and the Senate chamber and wing. Some tours may visit the House chamber and wing when there are large numbers of visitors. When the Senate and the House are in session visitors are admitted to the galleries on a rotating basis. (To visit the galleries when not on tour requires a courtesy card, available from your senator or representative.)

Like the Library of Congress, the Capitol interior decoration includes great splashes of color and symbolism. Much of the decoration is by Constantino Brumidi, who worked in the building for some 40 years before his death in 1879. On self-guided tours don't miss the Crypt, Rotunda, Brumidi corridors in the Senate wing, and House and Senate chambers.

Food in the cafeterias in the House and Senate Office Buildings is standard cafeteria fare, and it's not much better in the Senate restaurant. They are, however, among the best places in Washington to celebrity-watch.

Most congressional offices and committee rooms are located in the House and Senate Office Buildings. Committee hearings may range from the Watergate inquiry through impeachment hearings. Visitors are admitted on the basis of space available, and there are often long lines.

Starting July 4, 1976, there will be *Son et Lumière* performances at sundown at the east front of the Capitol.

**The House Office Buildings (12)** are located along Independence Avenue (which is marked B Street at this point): the Cannon Building (Carrere & Hastings, 1908), between New Jersey Avenue and First Street SE; the Longworth Building (Allied Architects, Inc., 1933), between New Jersey Avenue and South Capitol Street; and Rayburn House Office Building (Harbeson, Hough, Livingston & Larson, 1965), between South Capitol and First Streets SW.

Try to leave time for a ride on the free subway that connects the Congressional Office Buildings to the Capitol, and don't miss a chance to stroll through the Capitol grounds, one of the nation's best examples of 19th-century landscape architecture designed mainly by Frederick Law Olmsted. Capitol: Daily 9 am-4:30 pm. Free tours every 15 minutes. Last tour starts at 3:45 pm. Cafeterias in the Senate and House Office Buildings, restaurant in the Senate wing. H.

**The U.S. Botanic Garden (13),** Conservatory Building, First Street and Maryland Avenue SW (225-8333; 225-7099 for recorded information). The Conservatory Building, a combination of stone entrance and soaring aluminum and glass conservatories (Bennett, Parsons, and Frost, 1934) offers a refreshing place to pause from the weightier concerns of the capital. Within the conservatory, plant groupings range from a lush rain forest to an outstanding cactus collection, in separate temperature- and humidity-controlled environments. Fifty varieties of orchid plants put on a continuing spectacular with some 200 plants usually in blossom. Special annual shows are worth seeing. Although you cannot buy plants at the Botanic Garden, the staff does provide a referral service and will answer specific questions on plant identification and care. Daily 9 am-4 pm. Tours, for groups of 10 or more, on weekdays only, though individuals may join a tour when one is in progress. H.

To the rear of the Conservatory Building, across Constitution Avenue (First and Canal Streets SW) is the **Bartholdi Fountain (14)** and its surrounding gardens. Originally a centerpiece of the 1876 Centennial Exposition in Philadelphia, the fountain was moved to Washington at the close of the Exposition. Designed by Frédéric Auguste Bartholdi, sculptor of the Statue of Liberty, it originally symbolized fire and water, combining intermingled jets of water and gas flame. The gas has been converted to electricity and the water in the fountain is not particularly playful, but the displays of tulips and other bulbs in the spring, and annuals and perennials in the summer and fall, are spectacular.

Across the east end of the Mall you will see the Capitol Reflecting Pool (1970), and some interesting statuary **(15).** The central and largest group is the **U.S. Grant Memorial** (Henry Merwin Shrady, 1922), from which you can get one of the most impressive views of the Capitol and terraces. Grant is flanked by the **Garfield Memorial** (J.Q. Adams Ward, 1887) on one side and the **Peace Monument** (Franklin Simmons, 1877) on the other.

**The Taft Bell Tower (16),** designed by Douglas W. Orr in 1959, is to the north, across Constitution Avenue in a large, landscaped area. Though the bells are played manually only on special occasions, they chime at quarter-hour intervals from 8 am-8 pm daily, and toll each hour.

# The White House

**HOW TO GET THERE:** Tourmobile to the Ellipse. Metrobuses 30, 32, 34, 36, and all #80s to Lafayette Park.
**PARKING:** Commercial lots in areas to the north along H, I, and K Streets NW.
**TIME:** 3-4 hours.
**RESTAURANTS:** See luncheon or dinner suggestions in Chapter 9 or picnicking ideas for Lafayette Park in Chapter 7.

The White House and the Capitol represent the power centers of America. Each is also a cornerstone of the area it occupies, and each influenced the way its neighborhood grew. Both are also (having been occupied in 1800) the earliest public buildings in the federal city, and both have grown tremendously in size—paralleling the growth in power of their occupants.

The area of the White House, for all its concentrations of government, office, and other commercial buildings, remains somehow open and residential in feeling. Though there are no other residences in the immediate area, there is a human scale to the buildings surrounding Lafayette Park. Here, as in perhaps no other part of Washington, the buildings represent a historical progression of architectural styles, many the work of well-known architects. From the Georgian White House to the 1970s U.S. Court of Claims, they complement each other and their surroundings. Naturally, the White House is the main attraction, and though lines are long and visiting hours are limited, the experience is worth the wait. The Renwick and Corcoran Galleries are also musts, as are St. John's Church and Decatur House.

***The White House (1),** East Executive Avenue, visitor entrance between Pennsylvania Avenue and Alexander Hamilton Place NW (456-1414). The White House has grown from a simple Georgian house where Abigail Adams hung her wash to dry in the unfinished East Room, to a mansion with 54 rooms and 16 baths. (If office space is figured in as well, there is a total of 132 rooms.) Although the cornerstone was laid on October 13, 1792, when President and Mrs. John Adams moved into the house in November of 1800 it was far from finished. Work continued during both the Jefferson and Madison administrations. Then when the British burned Washington during the War of 1812 the building was destroyed, except for its walls. Although officially designated the President's House, the stone walls always seem to have been painted white, so it may have been called the White House from the beginning. After evidence of the fire damage was removed by white paint, however, it was thenceforth universally known as the White House.

James Hoban provided plans for the President's House, drawing from Georgian country houses in his native Ireland, and superintending both original construction and rebuilding after the fire. Benjamin Latrobe added later refinements, especially the balcony on the side facing the river and the portico at the entrance. Improvements have always kept pace with technological advances: piped water was installed in 1834, gas lighting in 1848, hot-water heating in 1853, elevators in 1881, and electrical lighting in 1891. In 1948 it was discovered that the ceilings in some rooms had dropped several inches and the house stood on foundations no longer structurally capable of supporting it. President Truman and his family moved across the street to Blair House while walls and floors were rebuilt and strengthened. The exterior walls and most of the interior detail are from the early White House.

Perhaps the White House can lay claim to being the most historic house in America. Every President since John Adams has lived there, entertaining and receiving distinguished visitors from all over the world. The President and his family share their home with the public each morning. There are usually long lines, stretching for blocks. Along the waiting route a sound system in the White House fence tells the visitor what he will see inside. Since there is no narration during the tour, it's a good idea to listen and try to remember highlights. You will need your wits about you as you are swept through a few rooms on the ground and first floors of the east wing. You are not visiting a museum but a living house of a most special kind, walking through rooms possibly used for entertaining a visiting head of state the evening before, or to be used for a luncheon for congressmen or senators just after you leave. The President's family may well be upstairs in the family quarters, and the President himself nearby. It is an experience in continuity that is unequalled elsewhere in the nation, and at few other places in the world. The wait might be long, but the tour only takes 15 to 20 minutes. *The White House, an Historical Guide,* is excellent for anyone interested in a permanent record of the history, associations, and furnishings of the White House.

Tuesday-Saturday 10 am-noon, in summer Saturday until 2 pm; closed some holidays. Visit your senator or representative to see if you can arrange to take the more leisurely tour 8 am-9 am.

***The Treasury Building (2),** East Executive Avenue between Alexander Hamilton Place and Pennsylvania Avenue NW (964-5221), is one of the most massive of the Greek Revival buildings in Washington (Robert Mills, Thomas U. Walter, 1851-69). It houses the offices of the Secretary of the Treasury, and some of the many branches he supervises. The entrance to the exhibit area in the basement of the Treasury is directly across the street from the visitor entrance to the White House. Exhibits trace the history of the Treasury and its various branches. If you are interested in architecture, the massive spaces, Greek support columns, and vaulted ceilings will make a visit worthwhile.

A sales desk in the exhibit area has commemorative presidential and other medals, presentation cases for these sets, handsome engravings, and souvenir uncirculated coin sets from the Denver and Philadelphia Mints. Other mint and uncirculated coins must be ordered by mail, but information is available here. Tuesday-Friday 9:30 am-3:30 pm; Saturday 10 am-2 pm. H.

A series of corridor exhibits on the ground floor of the Treasury Building (entrances on East Executive and Pennsylvania Avenues) will open in July. They will feature portraits, proof sets of Bicentennial coins, and a series of exhibits showing the development of coins from rough model through finished stages. Touch-and-feel exhibits for the visually handicapped and better facilities for all handicapped visitors are planned. Monday-Friday, except holidays, 10 am-4 pm.

***Lafayette Square (3),** Pennsylvania Avenue and H Street, between Madison and Jackson Places NW, with its green park, was intended as part of the President's front yard. Originally designated The President's Park, it became popularly known as Lafayette Square after the Marquis de Lafayette's visit to this country in 1824-25, when many of the events of the visit were held in houses on the square. Lafayette's statue, in the northeast corner of the park (Paul Pujol, Alexandre Falquière, and Antonin Mercie), was not erected until 1891, and though he is not the central figure in the park, the name Lafayette Park persists. Three other foreign nationals who assisted the young country in its efforts to gain freedom stand in the other corners of the park: Thaddeus Kosciuszko (Anton Popiel, 1910) is on the northeast corner; Friedrich Wilhelm Von Steuben (Albert Jaegers, 1910) is on the northwest corner; and Jean Baptiste de Rochambeau (Ferdinand Hamar, 1904) is on the southwest corner. The central figure, however, is a native-born American and authentic folk hero, who rose from humble beginnings in North Carolina to become an army hero, senator, and ultimately President. The equestrian statue of Andrew Jackson (Clark Mills, 1853) is the oldest in the park.

Over the years important persons occupied the houses on the square, and a continuity of use and human scale was established. However, the early-20th-century McMillan Plan envisioned the square as a suitable place for government expansion, and planned to surround it with neoclassical government buildings like those in the Federal Triangle. Residences began to disappear and government buildings started to take over. During the Kennedy administration that strategy was finally laid to rest. Plans developed by John Carl Warnecke and Associates preserved the historic buildings still standing, called for the demolition of the high-rise and other nonconforming buildings, and located new construction behind houses on the square. Moreover, the new government buildings are in keeping with the scale and materials of the older buildings, and are reoriented away from the square, so that their major entrances are on other streets. The character of the square was therefore reestablished and freed of much traffic it might otherwise have had to bear. It is a prime example of the way new construction can meet contemporary needs and still preserve old neighborhoods.

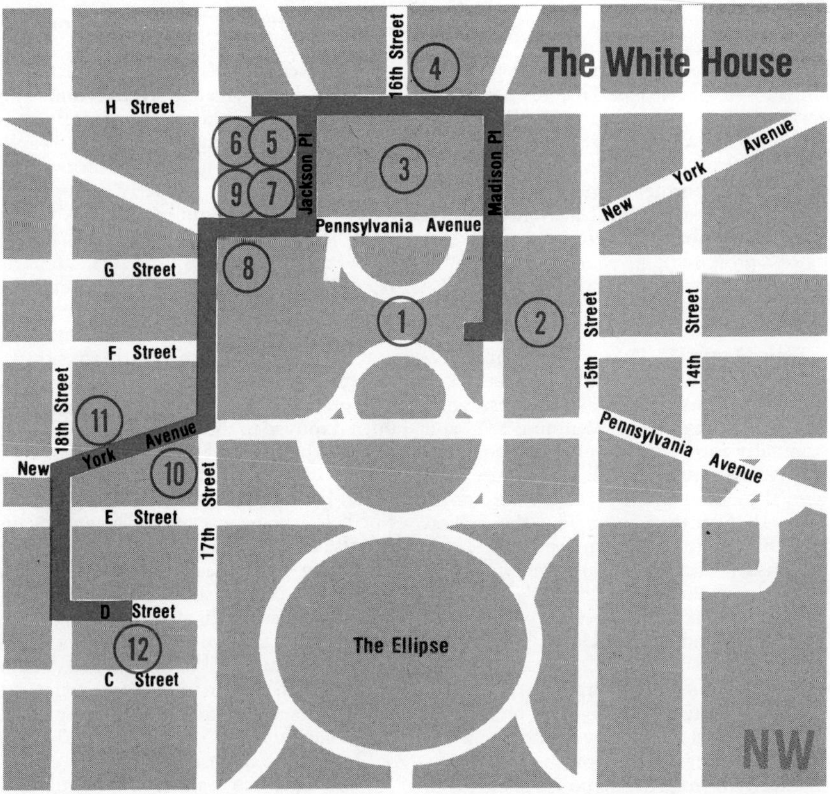


**St. John's Church (4),** 16th and H Streets NW, on the north and the White House on the south were the first two buildings on Lafayette Square. With the completion of the Cutts-Madison house to the east (H Street and Madison Place, c. 1820) and Decatur House to the west (H Street and Jackson Place, 1818) the outline of the square was formed. President and Mrs. Madison attended St. John's (Benjamin H. Latrobe, 1816) when they were at the White House, and later when they were frequent residents of the Cutts-Madison House. Mrs. Madison's association with the church continued until her death in 1849. Since Madison established the precedent of presidential attendance, every U.S. President has attended at least one service at St. John's, and pew 54 is reserved for presidential use. Still supported by an active congregation, the church has a full schedule of services, and visitors are welcome. Throughout the year there are regular Wednesday noon organ recitals, which can provide a most pleasant and welcome interlude in a day of sightseeing.

***Decatur House (5),** 748 Jackson Place NW (ME8-1204), the first private residence on the square, was constructed in 1818-19 (Benjamin H. Latrobe) for American naval hero Stephen Decatur. Shortly after he moved into the house Decatur dueled with a fellow naval officer and was killed. Subsequently the house was occupied by Vice President (later President) Martin van Buren, Vice President George Mifflin Dallas, Judah P. Benjamin, and the Russian, British, and French ministers. It was bequeathed to the National Trust for Historic Preservation in 1956, and now serves as its headquarters. Visitors can see the original house and furnishing of the era, as well as fine Victorian interiors and furnishings. There is an unexpected, well-landscaped garden to the rear of the house with massive trees.

Adjacent to Decatur House, at 740 Jackson Place, is the **Preservation Bookstore,** operated by the National Trust. The bookstore handles their publications and other books covering architecture, preservation, and legislation for preservation.

It stocks many architectural guidebooks, and you may well find one of your own home area. Decatur House, daily 10 am-4 pm; closed Christmas. Free to members, fee for others. The Bookstore, Monday-Friday 10 am-4 pm.

To the rear of Decatur House (1610 H Street) in its former carriage house is the ***Truxtun-Decatur Naval Museum (6)** (ST 3-2573). Exhibits concerning events and figures prominent in naval history, and a good collection of ship models, are on display. Daily 10:30 am-4 pm; closed holidays. H.

**Blair House (7),** 1651 Pennsylvania Avenue NW, combined with the adjacent Lee house (c. 1860), serves as the President's guest house. Constructed around 1824 and originally the home of Surgeon General of the Army Joseph Lovell, the house was owned by the Francis Preston Blair family from 1836 until acquired by the federal government in 1942. On April 18, 1861, Postmaster General Montgomery Blair, a member of President Lincoln's Cabinet, invited Robert E. Lee to visit, and offered him command of the Union Army. Lee subsequently refused in order to offer his services to his native Virginia.

Official state visitors—kings, presidents, other dignitaries—occupy the house on visits to Washington. During such visits the sidewalk in front of the house is closed to pedestrians, but though you have to stand across the street it's an excellent chance to spot VIPs as they enter and leave. Not open to the public.

**Executive Office Building** (Old State, War, and Navy Building) **(8),** southeast corner of 17th Street and Pennsylvania Avenues NW. Though it originally housed three federal departments, the building now is known as The Executive Office Building, and is used by the Vice President, his staff, and the President's staff. The most massive building of the French Second Empire style in Washington (Alfred B. Mullett, 1875-88), it has been controversial from the beginning. It follows the plan of the Treasury Building on the opposite side of the White House, and at various times there has been talk of refacing it to look like the Treasury Building. Shortly after World War II there were plans to demolish it, but fortunately that promised to be so costly that thoughts turned to restoration instead. Though not open to the public, the exterior decoration, ranging from stone walls and planters at street level to massive cast-iron chimneys, offers a visual feast from the outside.

***The Renwick Gallery (9),** northeast corner of Pennsylvania Avenue and 17th Street NW (381-5811), was originally constructed by Washington financier W. W. Corcoran to house his art collection. The building was one of the early examples of the French Second Empire style in America (1859, James Renwick), contrasting sharply with the prevailing styles in the Washington of that time. Though the building was seized by the government and used as a clothing depot during the Civil War—Corcoran was a Southern sympathizer—the gallery was later reclaimed by Corcoran and used to house his collection until it moved to the new Corcoran Gallery just south on 17th Street.

Like other structures in the area, this building came perilously close to destruction before being rescued and given new life and use during the administration of President John F. Kennedy. The new building serves as a perfect showcase for its Victorian interiors and displays featuring crafts and design. Special exhibits may show quilts, furniture, or kitchen utensils in displays that, in their manufacture and layout, are themselves excellent examples of craftsmanship and design. Daily 10 am-5:30 pm; closed Christmas.

***The Corcoran Gallery of Art (10),** 17th Street and New York Avenue NW (638-3211). It was to this building (Ernest Flagg) that the Corcoran collection moved in 1897 from what is now the Renwick Gallery. The main gallery and wing (Charles A. Platt, 1927) houses the American (based on the Corcoran Collection), William A. Clark, and Edward C. Walker collections, along with the Corcoran School of Art, one of the oldest art schools in the nation, and the only professional studio art school in Washington. Twelve full galleries are devoted to the comprehensive American collection, which includes examples from the Colonial period to the 1930s. The European collection includes a paneled 18th-century salon from the Hotel d'Orsay in Paris and a fine selection of the French Impressionists, especially Monet, Renoir, and Pissarro. Ten galleries in the museum are devoted to special exhibitions dealing with American art, with an emphasis on contemporary Washington art.

Worth a visit just for the quality, beauty, and space of its entrance atriums and grand staircase, the Corcoran is certainly one of the most important of the Washington museums, especially for anyone interested in American art. Tuesday-Sunday 11 am-5 pm; closed Mondays and holidays. Free to members. Tuesday and Wednesday free to all; other days a nominal entrance fee for nonmembers.

If you have time, two other nearby sights are worth visiting. The **Octagon House (11)** at the corner of 18th Street and New York Avenue NW, one block to the rear of the Corcoran (638-3105), is a fine Federal mansion (William Thornton, 1800). Now decorated with period furnishings and maintained by the American Institute of Architects, it is open to the public Tuesday-Saturday 10 am-4 pm; Sunday 1 pm-4 pm. One block south of the Corcoran off 17th Street at 1776 D Street NW are the ***DAR Museum and State Rooms (12)** (628-4980). In room settings you can see important examples of American decorative arts of the 18th and 19th centuries. The museum features paintings by John Copley and Thomas Sully and items associated with various figures prominent during the Revolutionary and early Federal eras. It is open Monday-Friday 9 am-4 pm.

# The Mall

**HOW TO GET THERE:** Tourmobile to points on the Mall. Metrobuses to Pennsylvania Avenue and 10th Street NW: 30, 32, 34, 36, 11, 9; or to the National Museum of History and Technology: 6, 11, 9, 17, 18.
**PARKING:** Commercial parking lots between Pennsylvania Avenue and G Street, and in the L'Enfant Plaza area at 10th Street and Independence Avenue SW.
**TIME:** Allow between 2 to 5 hours, depending on your interests.
**RESTAURANTS:** National Gallery of Art Cafeteria, National Museum of History and Technology Cafeteria, Smithsonian Associates Dining Room in The Castle (Smithsonian Associates only). For nearby restaurants see lunch section of Chapter 9.

In his plan for Washington, Pierre Charles L'Enfant envisioned the Mall as a grassy park with open space and tree-lined promenades stretching from the Capitol to a memorial to be erected to George Washington. However, the plan was largely ignored during the 19th century. A canal, later an open sewage ditch, flowed along one side of the Mall. Several public buildings, train tracks and stations, warehouses, stock pens, and other buildings were located on and adjacent to it. Early in the 20th century, work was undertaken to establish the Mall as open space, and today it is perhaps closer to L'Enfant's intent than at any other time in history.

Most of its major buildings are part of the Smithsonian Institution, one of the world's great museum and research organizations. Its riches are easily accessible to visitors; all buildings are open daily except Christmas free of charge. Many special events, both within the buildings and outside on the Mall, are also free, although there is a charge for some lectures, concerts, and other events (see Chapters 6 and 8).

The official Smithsonian guidebook *Seeing the Smithsonian* is on sale in all Smithsonian shops. It has floor plans of the buildings and short descriptions of permanent exhibits (except for the National Gallery of Art). It is possible to spend days here, so if you have only a few hours, the guide may help you budget your time.

The information services of the Smithsonian are among the best in town.
381-6264: Central information number for questions on all museums and events 9 am-5 pm.
381-5395: Special events and ticket information, live—9 am-5 pm—otherwise recorded.
737-8811 (Dial-A-Museum): Daily recorded announcements of events at various museums.
737-8855 (Dial-A-Phenomenon): Weekly recorded announcements on space satellites, planets, stars, and celestial phenomenon.

The **National Gallery of Art, East Building (1),** Madison Drive and Pennsylvania Avenue between 3rd and 4th Streets NW (I.M. Pei) is opening in stages. The first part to open will be the Connecting Link, which will include new restaurant facilities, in 1976. The East building will provide space for permanent and changing exhibits featuring many works from the National Gallery collection not previously displayed. Part of the gallery research activities will also be housed here, including the Center for Advanced Study in the Visual Arts.

***The National Gallery of Art (2),** between Constitution Avenue and Madison Drive, 4th and 7th Streets NW, entrances at 6th Street (737-4215), although established as part of the Smithsonian, is autonomously governed by its own board of trustees. Its permanent collections are made up mainly of American and European works of art, including gifts from Andrew Mellon, Joseph E. Widener, Chester Dale, Samuel H. Kress, Lessing J. Rosenwald, and some 200 other notable collectors. In addition to its own special exhibitions, the gallery hosts loan shows from around the world.

The National Gallery has a free brochure with a floor plan and all information on galleries and works of art. Leonardo da Vinci's "Ginevra de' Benci" and Raphael's "Alba Madonna" are among the finest and most popular paintings on view. The Impressionists are well represented, as are van Dyck, Rembrandt, Vermeer, Reynolds, Turner, and others. The ground floor, entered from Constitution Avenue, contains special exhibitions, but the permanent collection is on the main floor, which is entered from Constitution Avenue or the Mall. If this is your first visit to the gallery, or if your time is limited, you might want to take one of the excellent guided tours. There are three free tours: The Introductory Tour (Monday-Saturday 11 am and 3 pm; Sunday 5 pm) lasts one hour; the Painting of the Week Tour (Tuesday-Saturday noon and 2 pm; Sunday 3:30 pm and 6 pm) lasts 15 minutes; and the Tour of the Week (Tuesday-Saturday 1 pm; Sunday 2:30 pm) lasts one hour. Then there are two taped tours that allow you to go at your own pace and last about one hour: Acoustiguide is a tour with the director of the museum of his favorite paintings (also available in French, German, and Spanish); Lectour picks up recordings in various rooms and is less expensive (only in English).

Concerts, lectures, and films are frequent events at the gallery. Free concerts, often by the gallery's own symphony orchestra, are played in the delightful East Garden Court. Space is limited, so get there early if you want a seat (see Chapter 6). The cafeteria in the gallery is one of the most pleasant in the Mall area. Try to time your arrival at off-hours—it's very popular, too. Monday-Saturday 10 am-5 pm (9 pm in summer); Sunday 12 noon-9 pm; closed Christmas and New Year's Day. H.

**The National Sculpture Garden Ice Rink (3),** Constitution Avenue and Madison Drive and 7th Street NW (426-6700) is open daily for ice skating during the winter season and for miniature boat sailing during warmer months (see Chapter 7 for details). At night during the Christmas holiday season when the shrubs are draped with tiny white lights—matched by decoration of the plants on the 7th Street end of the National Gallery—and barrel fires are burning, the rink adds a festive note to the Mall.

**The National Museum of Natural History (4),** Constitution Avenue and Madison Drive at 10th Street NW (381-6264), is recognized as one of the great centers of the world for the study of man and his natural surroundings. The visitor sees less than 1 percent of the 55 million artifacts and specimens that form the basis for the work of hundreds of scientists and researchers.

The building, begun in 1911 (Hornblower and Marshall), was enlarged to its present size with additions (Mills, Petticord & Mills) in 1965. On the first floor there is literally something for everyone, ranging from a stuffed eight-ton African bush elephant—the largest ever recorded—to a life-size model of a blue whale—at 92 feet the largest animal that ever lived. The museum's most popular exhibit, however, is on the second floor. There is the famous Hope Diamond, only one of many extraordinary stones in a collection of gems, minerals, and meteorites. Daily 10 am-5:30 pm (sometimes to 10 pm in summer); closed Christmas. H.

***The National Museum of History and Technology (5),** Constitution Avenue and Madison Drive at 14th Street NW (381-6264), could certainly claim the Smithsonian's title of the "nation's attic." It includes clocks, models, a diesel railroad engine, the flag that flew over Fort McHenry while Francis Scott Key wrote *The Star Spangled Banner,* and a working post office in a 19th-century country store. Some of the other popular exhibits include a collection of First Ladies' gowns, musical instruments, and the history of printing. While the collections may be diverse, the resemblance to an attic ends there—the exhibits are well-displayed in open, well-lighted areas. A bookstore specializes in

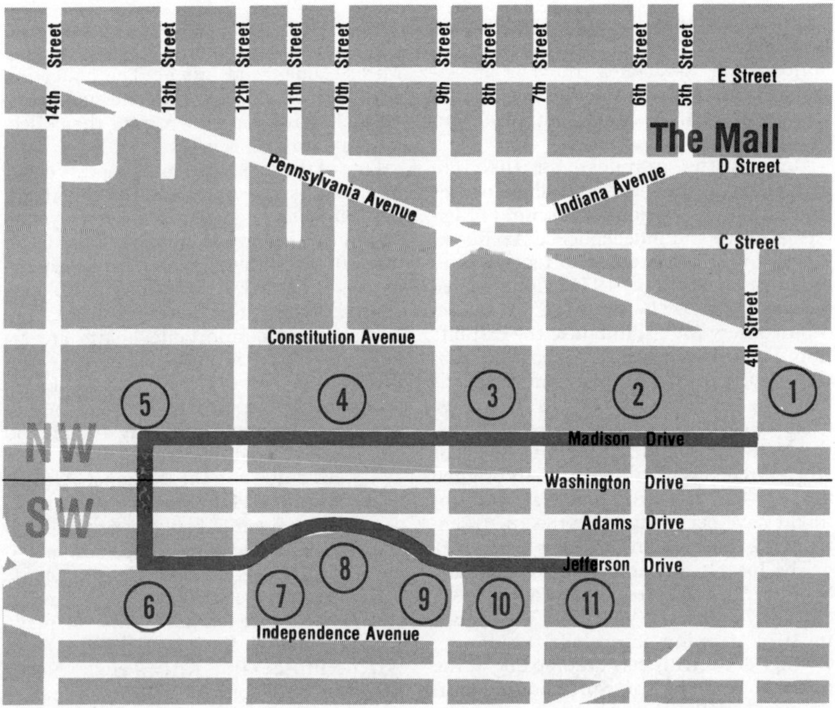


art, architecture, decorative arts, and Americana, and another shop has crafts and interesting reproductions from all over the world (see Chapter 10). There is a cafeteria in the basement.

If you are able to visit only one of the Smithsonian museums on the Mall, this is probably where you will encounter the most to interest every member of the family. Daily 10 am-5:30 pm (as late as 10 pm in summer); closed Christmas. H.

**The Department of Agriculture Administration Building (6),** entrance on Jefferson Drive near 14th Street SW, is not a must, but it does occasionally offer exhibits and free movies. Also, near the entrance is a publication sales room handling inexpensive how-to booklets on home gardening, canning, tree identification, and the like. Monday-Friday 9 am-5 pm.

Adjacent to the Department of Agriculture Building is the **Freer Gallery of Art (7)** (Charles A. Platt 1923), Jefferson Drive at 12th Street SW (381-5334), which contains one of the prime collections of Oriental and Near Eastern art in the West. The gallery also has a smaller, but important, collection of paintings by American artists, most of whom were friends or contemporaries of Charles Land Freer, who founded the collection and built the gallery.

James McNeill Whistler's Peacock Room, finished in London in 1877, is one of the fixed exhibits in the gallery, which also includes the largest single collection of Whistler's drawings, paintings, and prints. Since exhibition space is limited to a single floor, displays are continually rotated. Daily 10 am-5:30 pm; closed Christmas Day.

**The Smithsonian Building,** "The Castle on the Mall," **(8),** Jefferson Drive at 10th Street SW (628-4422), has no architectural peers in Washington—they just don't build them like that anymore. Completed in 1855 (James Renwick, Jr.), it is one of the nation's prime examples of the Gothic Revival style, and one of Washington's most important landmarks. The Smithsonian was established through a bequest from James Smithson, an Englishman who never visited this country, yet left his considerable fortune to the United States and whose tomb is in the north foyer of this building.

Originally built to house all the exhibits and activities of the Smithsonian, the building now serves limited exhibit use, but it's worth a visit to see the opulence of the Victorian furnishings in the public area. For visitors who are also members of the Smithsonian Associates, there is an Associates' reception room and cafeteria off the Great Hall. Daily 10 am-5:30 pm; closed Christmas Day.

One of the grandest Smithsonian exhibits of all is the **Arts and Industries Building—U.S. National Museum (9),** Jefferson Drive and Independence Avenue at 9th Street SW, scheduled to reopen, after restoration, in June, 1976. Constructed between 1879-81 (Cluss & Schulze, Montgomery Meigs) to house the exhibits from the 1876 Centennial Exposition that were given to the Smithsonian, it stands alone in the United States as a massive example of its style. For years it has housed the National Air and Space Museum, but when it reopens it will revert to its original purpose—to display items that were, or might have been, shown at the 1876 Centennial Exposition in Philadelphia.

The **Joseph H. Hirshhorn Museum and Sculpture Garden (10),** Independence Avenue at 7th Street SW (628-4422), opened in 1974 (Gordon Bunschaft, Skidmore, Owings & Merrill), has become one of the most popular of the Smithsonian museums. The Plaza sculptures around the circular building and the Sculpture Garden across Jefferson Drive offer the city's only outdoor collection of contemporary work.

The museum's permanent collection of some 4,000 paintings and 3,000 sculptures is a gift from Joseph H. Hirshhorn. His personal collection of modern art from the late 19th century to the present includes the work of such artists as Rodin, Picasso, Calder, Eakins, de Kooning, Matisse, Moore, Miró, Calder, and others. The collection will be increased by gifts and purchases. Special shows are drawn from the collection and outside sources.

One of the most intriguing aspects of the museum is the circular building itself. Paintings and larger works are displayed in spacious, windowless areas along the outer circle of the building. The inner gallery circle has window walls overlooking an open central court with a fountain. Plants and groupings of comfortable chairs are arranged in restful islands. The exterior wall is interrupted for one massive slice of windows, and the views of the Mall and the city beyond are spectacular. Daily 10 am-5:30 pm; closed Christmas. H.

A new home for the **National Air and Space Museum (11),** Jefferson Drive and Independence Avenue between 6th and 7th Streets SW, is scheduled to open on July 4, 1976. Designed (Gyo Obata, Helmut, Obata & Kassabaum) specifically to house aircraft and space-flight-related items, displays will range from the plane flown by the Wright Brothers at Kitty Hawk, North Carolina, on December 17, 1903, to space capsules. Rockets, experimental aircraft, and other famous planes, including the Spirit of St. Louis, will be there. Its exhibits will be the perfect foil for those in the Arts and Industries Building, where you will find the steam engines, elevators, instruments, and other materials that paved the technological way to 1903, and the 20th-century age of flight.

# Monument and Memorials

**HOW TO GET THERE:** Tourmobile to Washington Monument, Jefferson or Lincoln memorials. Metrobuses to 14th Street near Washington Monument: 52, 50, 56, 58. To Constitution Avenue near Lincoln Memorial: 80.
**PARKING:** Commercial lots north of Constitution Avenue, or the free Washington Monument parking area (off Constitution Avenue between 15th and 17th Streets), and areas at Lincoln and Jefferson memorials.
**TIME:** Approximately 2½ hours.
**RESTAURANTS:** Cafeteria in nearby Smithsonian Museum of History and Technology (and see lunch places in Chapter 9).

The area of this tour is an extension of the Mall that includes the Washington Monument grounds and West Potomac Park. Almost all of this land was reclaimed from the Potomac and its tidal marshes; it did not reach its present size and appearance until the World War II era when the Thomas Jefferson Memorial was completed. Constitution Gardens, the latest development, is not expected to be com-

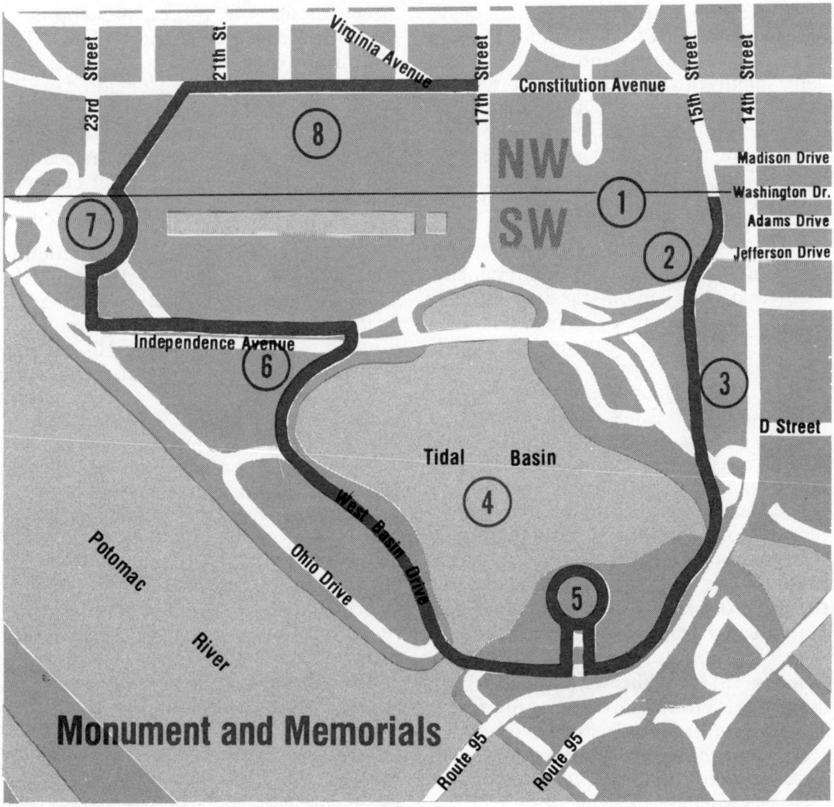


pleted until 1976.

Although the site of the Washington Monument was designated on L'Enfant's original plan for the city, it was not until the early 20th century that memorials to Jefferson and Lincoln were planned. However, the area was already being intensively used before the Lincoln and Jefferson memorials were constructed. The Tidal Basin was completed in 1897, and quickly became one of Washington's most popular beach and boating areas. When the first cherry trees were planted around the Tidal Basin in 1912, they added yet another attraction.

Although this walking tour is lengthy, it affords some of the city's best vistas of Washington, the Potomac, and Arlington, and a chance to see the wide variety of plants in the area, including the Tulip Library, and the later blooming Library of Annual Plants (at 17th Street and Independence Avenue SW), the cherry blossoms, pansies near Inlet Bridge, and azaleas and camellias near Independence Avenue and 17th Street south of the Reflecting Pool.

Open space here is extensively used for picnicking, biking, hiking, jogging, soccer, lacrosse, cricket, football, baseball, and volleyball. Spectators are generally welcome, and occasionally even asked to join in when an extra player is needed.

The entire area, including the monument and memorials, is administered and maintained by the National Park Service. For general information call Dial-a-Park (426-6975).

***The Washington Monument (1),** 15th Street between Independence and Constitution Avenues (426-6839). Young nations need heroes upon whom the populace can agree, and George Washington was perfect for the role. As general of the armies during the Revolution, his name had become a household word, and even before the site of a permanent capital was selected, the 1783 Continental Congress approved the erection of an equestrian monument to Washington. L'Enfant designated a place for it in his plan for the new city, and Washington himself, then President, approved the location. The new republic had more pressing tasks than erecting a heroic statue, however, and when Washington died in 1799 no action had yet been taken on the 1783 authorization. It was not until 1848 that work was finally started. On the eve of the Civil War when the 156-foot level had been reached, construction was halted. The monument remained at that height—the line is easily seen in the different color of the stone—until 1878 when work began again. In 1884 the capstone was set at the apex of the obelisk, and the monument finally opened to the public in 1888. It was the tallest completely masonry structure in the world (555 feet 5⅛ inches), and it has become an American symbol known around the world. An elevator ride to the top, no matter how long the waiting lines may be, is worth the wait. From there, you can see the beauty, logic, and grandeur of the city and the sweep of nearby Virginia and Maryland. March-Labor Day 8 am-midnight; rest of year 9 am-5 pm.

In the ***Sylvan Theater (2)** (c. 1917) on the Washington Monument grounds, a Shakespeare Summer Festival is presented every July and August. The theater also offers a wide variety of free concerts and other plays (see Chapter 6).

The ***Bureau of Printing and Engraving (3),** between 14th and 15th Streets, Independence and Maine Avenues SW (393-6400). All United States paper currency was printed by private firms until 1863, and it was not until 1894 that the government began to print its own postage stamps. Today the buildings of the Bureau of Printing and Engraving contain some 25 acres of floor space, where approximately 3,000 people are engaged in the design, engraving, and printing of currency, postage stamps, and more than 800 other miscellaneous products. Originally all the activities of the bureau were carried out in the red-brick-towered building at 14th Street and Independence Avenue SW (James G. Hill, 1879) which sat, at the time it was built, on the banks of the Potomac River. Work began on drainage and fill operations a few years later, and the present complex of buildings was completed in 1914 when the neoclassical revival building to the south was finished (W. B. Olmsted).

Tours enter the 1914 building from 14th Street, though the Tourmobile stop is on the 15th Street side of the building. The 30-minute tour is self-guiding. As you make your way through enclosed walks elevated above the operations floor, you are fed recorded information on what you are seeing: the printing, sorting, inspection, and binding processes for paper currency and stamps. Monday-Friday 8 am-2:30 pm; closed holidays. H.

One good way to get away from buildings for a while is to take a stroll around the **Tidal Basin (4).** Better still, rent a paddle boat at 15th Street and Maine Avenue SW (limited free parking), which will not only give you a chance for exercise and some solitude, but also good views of the cherry trees, Thomas Jefferson Memorial, and the nearby city. Rentals are reasonable.

When the Potomac River was filled in this area, silt began to accumulate in the Washington Channel. The Tidal Basin was built to restore the tidal flow through the channel in order to keep it clear. The basin also serves an additional function as a reflecting pool for the Thomas Jefferson Memorial and the cherry blossoms, which fringe it each March-April.

**The Thomas Jefferson Memorial (5),** South Basin Drive SW, at the Tidal Basin (426-6822), was designed (John Russell Pope, 1943) as an obvious tribute to the Roman taste of our only architect/President. Jefferson's design for his own home at Monticello and for the rotunda at the University of Virginia, both based on the Pantheon in Rome, gave rise in this country to the Federal style known as Roman Revival or Jeffersonian Classicism. The interior statue of Jefferson is by Rudolph Evans. Open 24 hours daily. H.

The **cherry blossoms (6)** around the Tidal Basin, East Potomac Park (Hains Point), Washington Monument grounds, and Constitution Gardens are not only Washington's harbingers of spring, but the indication that its major tourist season is about to begin. Their blooming is eagerly awaited each year, but the timing is complicated by the diverse varieties of trees and the weather. Occasionally rain spoils the show—the fragile blossoms last no more than a week under the best of conditions—and accurate predictions on blossoming time can be made no more than 10 days in advance. Of the two original varieties around the Tidal Basin, the Yoshinos have blossomed as early as March 20 and as late as April 17; the Kwanzans as early as April

14 and as late as May 1. Averaging it out, the blossoming time should be the weeks of April 5 and April 22. When they do bloom the cherry trees put on a spectacular show, especially around the Tidal Basin where the oldest trees are planted.

In a ceremony on March 27, 1912, Mrs. William Howard Taft, the First Lady, and the Viscountess Chinada, wife of the Japanese ambassador, each planted a cherry tree, the first of some 3,000 trees presented to Washington as a gift from the City of Tokyo. The original two trees survive, suitably marked, and both flower profusely each spring. In 1965, 3,800 additional trees were received from Japan, and 700 of them were planted on the Washington Monument grounds. More trees are being planted each year.

The Cherry Blossom Festival celebrates the blossoming period with parades, selection of Cherry Blossom princesses and queen, and activities throughout the area. The festival is officially opened with the lighting of a 300-year-old Japanese lantern near the original trees. Normally when the trees around the Tidal Basin are in bloom, they are lighted at night and the sight is one of the most beautiful in Washington. Since both the Jefferson and Lincoln Memorials are open 24 hours a day, it is a good time to see the blossoms and visit the memorials.

**The Lincoln Memorial (7),** Memorial Circle, between Constitution and Independence Avenues SW (426-6895). Though there were earlier attempts to erect a national memorial to Lincoln, and several designs were proposed, it was not until 1911, following the centennial of Lincoln's birth, that Congress finally authorized a commission to plan the memorial. Then the site aroused much controversy. It was little more than a swamp, with wide marshy pools said to harbor the healthiest mosquitoes in Washington, and no access by bridge or road. But ground-breaking ceremonies were finally held on February 14, 1914. Architect Henry Bacon designed a Greek temple with Daniel Chester French's statue of Lincoln as its focal point and produced a monument that is moving and rewarding to experience at any time of the day or night.

The guidebook *In This Temple,* on sale at the memorial, is excellent, especially in the details about its construction, and of more recent events there. These have ranged from Dr. Martin Luther King's "I have a dream . . ." speech, to the memorial service ending the period of national mourning for John F. Kennedy, both in 1963. Always open.

**Constitution Gardens (8),** along Constitution Avenue, between 17th and 22nd Streets NW (426-6700), is scheduled for completion in 1976 and will include a swan pond, lake, open meadows, and contoured land featuring walks, bridges, and landscaped areas reminiscent of the Boston Common. More cherry trees are being planned. There will be refreshment and other facilities in the area.

## Downtown Washington: A Civil War Tour

**HOW TO GET THERE:** Subway (when operating) from the National Visitor Center to either Judiciary Square or Gallery Square. Metrobuses to the National Collection of Fine Arts (Patent Office): 70, 72, 74, D2, D4, S2, S4, 40, 42.
**PARKING:** Commercial lots along F Street and on side streets from 7th to 10th Streets NW.
**TIME:** 3-3½ hours.
**RESTAURANTS:** Sandwich shop at National Collection of Fine Arts/National Portrait Gallery; Chinese restaurants on H Street from 6th to 8th NW; others on F and side streets (see Chapter 9).

At the beginning of the Civil War this area was the center of commercial Washington, and of much that was official Washington. The Patent Office, the District of Columbia City Hall (two of the oldest public buildings in the city), and the old Post Office were here. Cabinet members and congressmen lived in the simple houses and mansions and in boardinghouses along E, F, and G Streets. A central streetcar line ran up 7th Street—intensifying commerce along the thoroughfare and providing one of the major means of public access to the country beyond.

Though much has changed, the area remains the retail shopping center of

Washington and one of its most interesting architectural centers. It boasts a unique collection of pre-Civil War houses and public buildings, as well as many superb late-19th-century and early- 20th-century buildings. Chinatown, with its distinctive stores and restaurants, is located here too, and three of Washington's major (though perhaps among the least visited) museums: the National Portrait Gallery, the National Collection of Fine Arts (both housed in the Old Patent Office building) and the Lincoln complex (Ford's Theatre and the house where Lincoln died).

In this tour area, you can revisit the scenes of activities of the Civil War era: the scenes of Lincoln's inaugural balls, Civil War hospitals, the Surratt House (where much of the conspiracy against Lincoln was planned), Ford's Theatre, and the Petersen House (where Lincoln died). Both Lincoln and John Wilkes Booth often traveled these streets.

On the night of April 14, 1865, when President and Mrs. Abraham Lincoln arrived at **Ford's Theatre (1),** 511 10th Street NW (Museum: 426-6924), after the play *Our American Cousin* was already in progress, action on stage stopped as the orchestra began "Hail to the Chief." The capacity audience rose and began prolonged and exuberant cheering. Coming to the front of his box, the President bowed and returned to his rocking chair. At about 8:45 the theater quieted down and the play resumed. A little after 10 pm, actor John Wilkes Booth entered the theater, climbed the stairs to the second floor, and made his way to the presidential box. At about 10:15 pm he fired at point-blank range into the back of the President's head, ran to the front of the box, and jumped some 12 feet to the stage below. Already off balance, he caught his spur in one of the flags draping the box and fell heavily on his left leg—fracturing the bone just above the ankle. He was able, nevertheless, to make his way through the wings and escape. The unconscious Lincoln was carried from a presidential box never to be used again.

In 1861 John T. Ford converted the First Baptist Church of Washington to a theater. The following year he built the present theater (James J. Gifford). It soon became a well-known and popular Washington fixture, but after Booth killed Lincoln in 1865, John Ford was arrested, his theater confiscated, and he was held for 39 days before he was cleared of conspiracy. He announced that he would reopen the theater in June 1865, but the announcement aroused so much public indignation that it was again seized by the War Department. Ultimately the building was purchased by the federal government, but it was not until February 13, 1968, that Ford's was again opened to the public. Today it presents live theater once more. Though there are concessions to safety and convenience, the theater looks much as it did the night of the assassination, in the presidential box even the sofa and Washington portrait are original. However, if the President of the United States attends a play at Ford's today, he sits elsewhere. When the theater is open, costumed guides conduct 15-minute tours. A sound and light show is presented in the theater during the summer.

In the basement of the theater is the **Lincoln Museum,** devoted partly to the life of the Civil War President and partly to his assassination. Exhibits capsulize his life as lawyer, campaigner, and President. There are the clothes Lincoln was wearing the night he was shot, the boot cut from Booth's broken foot, and several of his pistols, including the actual Derringer with which he shot Lincoln. Lincoln Museum, 9 am-5 pm daily; theater, same hours (except when in use, closed after 1 pm for rehearsals).

Next door is a reconstruction of the **Star Tavern,** where Booth drank whiskey and water immediately before the assassination. Today it serves as the box office for Ford's (ticket information: 347-6260).

Directly across the street from Ford's Theatre is the Petersen House (built in 1849), also known as the **House Where Lincoln Died (2),** 516 10th Street NW (426-6830). The fatally wounded President was carried here from the theater and into the back bedroom, where he died the next morning. During the night Vice President Andrew Johnson and most of official Washington came to the house. Only a pillow on the bed where Lincoln died is original, but the entire first floor (the only part of the house open to the public) has been reconstructed and the bedroom is furnished from photographs taken that night. Some of the furnishings in the parlors do have a specific Lincoln association, since they are from the Lincoln home in Springfield, Illinois. There are no organized tours. The house is quiet and haunted by memories. You can see everything in all three rooms in

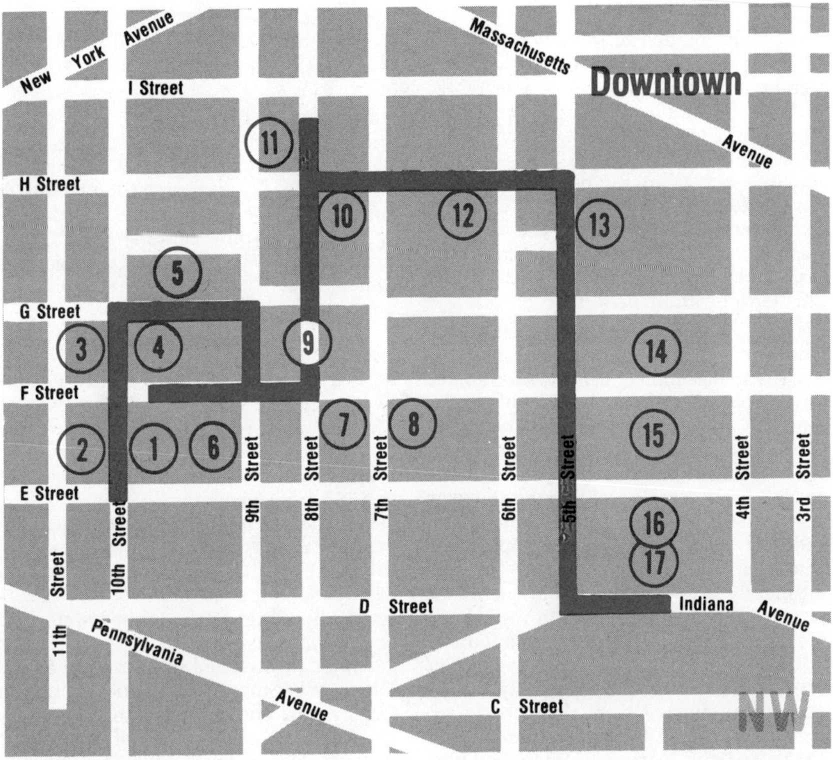


a matter of minutes.

For the most meaningful tour of the complex, begin with the sections of museum concerning Lincoln's career, visit the theater, then return to the museum to view the items in the assassin's alcove. Finally, cross the street to the House Where Lincoln Died. The hour you spend will be one of the most memorable and poignant you can experience in Washington.

**Woodward & Lothrop (3),** 10th, 11th, F, and G Streets NW, opened in 1880 as the "Boston Dry Goods House," the first major department store in Washington. Operating on the present site since 1887, the store played a significant part in developing modern retailing practices. Covering almost a full block, the present building was constructed in four stages—the oldest (and the most important architecturally), the G Street frontage (Frederick Pyle), was completed in 1902, the last on F Street in 1926. "Woodies" first floor retains much of the character and richness of the early-20th-century department store, and its Christmas windows are one of the more pleasant attractions of downtown Washington. (See Chapter 10 for shopping information.)

Facing the 10th Street side of Woodward & Lothrop is **St. Patrick's Church (4),** 619 10th Street NW (DI7-2713), the home of the oldest Catholic parish in Washington, built on land purchased in 1794. During the Civil War the second St. Patrick's Church was used as a hospital for wounded Union soldiers, as were most of the other churches in the area. This church also has a direct association with President Lincoln and the assassination, for it was attended by Mary Surratt, at whose house the conspirators met. The parish priest, convinced of Mrs. Surratt's innocence, was allowed to see her in prison only after he agreed to remain silent about the case for 25 years. After the required time had expired, he published a pamphlet that detailed his reasons for supporting Mrs. Surratt's innocence of conspiracy, a stand supported by most historians today.

It took over a decade (1872-84) to build the present church, designed in a curiously horizontal neo-Gothic style, especially beautiful in the interior. St. Patrick's is still supported by an active downtown congregation.

The main branch of the District public library system is the **Martin Luther King Memorial Library (5),** 901 G Street NW (727-1111). Completed in 1972, the library is one of the few significant contemporary buildings in the downtown area—and the only one in Washington designed by Mies van der Rohe. For anyone interested in the history of the capital city, the library's Washingtoniana collection is a particularly large and comprehensive repository (see Chapter 5 for more details).

Though F Street bears little relationship today—at least in the 900 block—to its Civil War appearance, it is of considerable interest because it figured as **Booth's escape route (6).** After he shot President Lincoln Booth made his way through the wings of Ford's Theatre, and out the back where he had left his horse. He went up the alleyway between 918 and 920 F Street, turned right, and rode eastward toward the Capitol and Southeast Washington—making his way ultimately into Maryland, and then back into Virginia. By taking a short walk down the alley, you can retrace Booth's route.

Today the 900 block of F Street contains some of Washington's best late-19th-century buildings. Among these are the Atlantic Building, 928 F Street (James G. Hill, 1887), and the National Union Building, 918 F Street (Glenn Brown, 1890). At the east end of the block are the Riggs National Bank (James G. Hill, 1901 and Arthur Heaton, 1926) and the Old Masonic Hall, more recently Julius Lansburgh Furniture Company (Adolph Cluss, 1870).

**The Old Post Office (7),** now the Tariff Commission building, F Street between 7th and 8th Streets NW, is the third oldest of the great public buildings remaining in the area. The southern section along F Street was completed in 1844 (Robert Mills). The northern section along F Street (Thomas U. Walter) was begun in 1855, but construction was slowed by the Civil War, and it was not completed until 1866. Standing almost alone in the center of the city at the beginning of the Civil War, the Patent Office and Post Office buildings served multiple uses—barracks, hospitals, supply depots—at the same time the regular government departments attempted to carry on their usual functions. When the city celebrated the end of the Civil War on April, 13, 1865 this building was one of the focal points of the city-wide illumination. Over 3,500 candles lighted its windows, and hung before its facade was a grand transparency showing a mail carrier and the words, "Behold, I bring you good tidings of great joy."

**The Hecht Company (8),** 7th and F Streets NW (J. West Wagner, c. 1885), like Woodies, is today one of Washington's best-known department stores. Though both firms have extensive new outlets in suburban shopping centers, their downtown stores continue to serve urban customers. (See Chapter 10 for shopping information.)

*The National Collection of Fine Arts and the National Portrait Gallery are housed in the **Old Patent Office (9),** between 7th and 9th, F and G Streets NW. The first major public building constructed in Washington after the Capitol and the White House, the Patent Office was started in 1836 from plans by William P. Elliot. (The other architects who worked on it over the years were: Robert Mill, 1840; Thomas U. Walter, 1852, 1862; and Edward Clark, 1867.) It's one of the largest Greek-revival buildings in the United States and one of the finest.

Although intended to house the Patent Office, it became the home of the Interior Department and the repository for many governmental collections of documents and art objects. These included paintings by Gilbert Stuart and John Singleton Copley, the Declaration of Independence, Benjamin Franklin's printing press, furniture and clothing belonging to George Washington, and material collected on various scientific expeditions. The collections increased until just before the Civil War when more than a thousand boxes and barrels were stored along corridors, and the science, history, and art collections were transferred to the then new Smithsonian building (on the Mall).

With the outbreak of the Civil War, the building assumed great importance as a major site for defense purposes, and then as one of the major Washington hospitals, visited frequently by Lincoln, Walt Whitman, and Clara Barton, who was employed as a clerk in the Patent Office from 1854 to 1857, when she was fired for her abolitionist sentiments. Whitman worked there too, for Interior's Bureau of Indian Affairs. His superiors were scandalized by his *Leaves of Grass,* and he was also fired. Lincoln's second inaugural ball was held here, and the grand illumination in this building in celebration of Lee's surrender at

Appomattox required some 6,000 candles.

After the war, the Patent Office reverted once more to performing its main functions, and the more-than-80,000 exhibited models made it one of the major tourist attractions of the city until a fire in the north and west wings of the building in 1877 destroyed most of the models. After the Department of the Interior vacated the building in 1917, and the Patent Office in 1932, the Civil Service Commission became the main occupant and remained until 1956. For a while it seemed that the great building would be replaced by a parking lot until Congress decided to transfer it to the Smithsonian Institution, to serve as a permanent home for the National Portrait Gallery and the National Collection of Fine Arts.

**The National Portrait Gallery** is, as the name implies, for portraits of persons who have affected the history and development of the United States: politicians, military personnel, explorers, actors, painters, writers, and scientists. On the second floor is the collection of portraits of U.S. Presidents, including a full-length portrait of George Washington by Gilbert Stuart. With the Lincoln portraits are life masks of his hands and his face—the young, almost boyish, unwrinkled face of the 1860 man (already 51 years old) becoming, through the cares of the wartime presidency, an old, wrinkled man by 1865. Special exhibitions are presented periodically—accompanied often by films and recordings and always by full catalogs.

**The National Collection of Fine Arts** is an outgrowth of the collection of American art originally housed in the Patent Office, and contains some 15,000 prints, drawings, sculptures, and paintings—ranging from 18th-century portraits to contemporary canvases. "Explore" and "Discover" galleries challenge children and adults to experience art (see Chapter 8). Special galleries are devoted to Winslow Homer, Washington painters, 19th-century landscapes, John Rogers groups, American Impressionists, and 20th-century painting and sculpture—among others. If time is limited, perhaps the third-floor Lincoln gallery, where President Lincoln received during his second inaugural ball, is the best place to start; the works here offer a tantalizing sampling of the collection.

The Sandwich Shop (located in the 7th Street wing of the building) offers one of the best bargain lunches in Washington. Individually crafted sandwiches and salads are ample and reasonably priced. Though the interior space is small, in good weather you can also sit in the courtyard, which is an unusually pleasant dining spot. National Collection of Fine Arts (381-5180), enter from G at 8th Street; National Portrait Gallery (381-5380), enter from F at 8th Street, entrance for the handicapped through parking ramp on G Street for both buildings. Daily 10 am-5:30 pm, except Christmas. Tours of the collection are arranged by appointment for weekdays at 10 am, 11 am, or 1 pm (381-6541); guide service in the gallery is available daily 10 am-3 pm (381-6347).

**Calvary Baptist Church (10),** 755 8th Street NW (347-8355), was organized during the Civil War by a small number of pro-Union and antislavery Baptists; the congregation acquired plans and began constructing the present sanctuary in September, 1864 (Adolph Cluss). In 1894, James G. Hill was retained to add a Sunday-school building, Woodward Hall (named for S. W. Woodward of Woodward & Lothrop, a prominent member of the congregation), and to remodel the interiors. Another addition, the Green Memorial Building (1925-29) was the work of Arthur Heaton. Inside the sanctuary the great Mohler organ, installed in 1927 (when, with more than 5,000 pipes, it was the largest in Washington), continues in use. Warren G. Harding and Chief Justice Charles Evans Hughes were both members of Calvary. During the 1921 Washington Conference on Arms Limitation, both President Harding and then Secretary of State Hughes attended Thanksgiving services at this church—together with the ministers, presidents, and heads of state attending the conference. It was probably the greatest gathering of international notables in one church within the District until 1963 when the funeral of President Kennedy was held at St. Matthew's Cathedral. Another early member of the church, Dr. E. M. Gallaudet (after whom Gallaudet College for the deaf was named), founded Washington's first mission for deaf-mutes at the church in 1885. The mission continues today with a fully staffed church for the deaf. The church is open daily (entrance through Woodward Hall) and provides a regular series of concerts on the first Sunday afternoon of each month.

**Greater New Hope Baptist Church (11),** 816 8th Street NW (EX3-9730), was built as a synagogue by the Washington Hebrew Congregation, chartered in 1852, and the oldest Jewish congregation in Washington. The building they originally used had been a Methodist church. The present building (Stutz and Pease, 1897) shows a strong Byzantine influence, especially evident in the minaret-like towers topped with octagonal open belfries and, until recently, with onion domes. Though these domes have been removed, the towers, the great Star-of-David window, and other decoration remain. In 1955 the building was sold to the Greater New Hope Baptist Church. Though it is a Washington landmark, its future is uncertain since it is in the area of the proposed site for the Eisenhower Convention Center.

None of the buildings on the west side of the 700 block of 7th Street NW are pre-Civil War, but 12 buildings survive from the 1880s. Originally constructed to serve small family businesses, with living quarters above, all are still in active commercial use. Though most of the facades are now divorced from the street by more modern street-level treatment, the floors above the street level offer a casebook example of downtown commercial Washington in the last quarter of the 19th century; with some renovation and sympathetic new construction across the street, the block would become a showcase for the best of the last half of the 19th century and of the 20th century.

**The Surratt House (12),** 604 H Street NW, is not open to the public. Mary Surratt rented the building from 1864 to 1865 and used it as a boardinghouse. It was here that John Wilkes Booth discussed his hatred of Abraham Lincoln with Lewis Paine (one of Mrs. Surratt's boarders), Mrs. Surratt's son, and other conspirators. Originally, the group planned to kidnap President Lincoln, Vice President Johnson, General Grant, and members of the Cabinet. At the last minute, when Booth saw the Confederacy collapsing, the plan changed to assassination. Only Booth was successful in carrying out his part of the plot, though Paine did attempt to kill Secretary of State William H. Seward.

After the assassination, Mrs. Surratt was arrested at home. Ironically, Paine was also arrested there when, after having hidden for three days, he returned to the Surratt house on April 17 while federal troops were searching it. Both boarder and landlady were tried by a military court and hanged.

Today the Surratt House is located in the midst of Washington's Chinatown. Chinese restaurants, grocery stores, and other businesses abound in the area, and the Chinese presence prevails even in pagoda-shaped telephone booths along the street. Every winter the celebration of the Chinese New Year brings floats, bands, dragons, firecrackers, and other festivities to the neighborhood.

**St. Mary's Church (13),** 727 5th Street NW (ME8-3250) was built by German Catholics who organized their own parish partly because of a desire to separate from the traditional Irish Catholic churches, and partly because they wanted a church where they could hear German spoken. The first church on the site was erected in 1846; it served the congregation until 1891, when the present structure was completed (E. F. Baldwin). True to the congregation for which it was being built, German Gothic architectural models were followed. The Saint Mary Mother of God Catholic Church still serves an active, though no longer German-speaking, congregation.

**The Pension Building (14),** between F and G Streets and 4th and 5th Streets NW, was built in response to the needs generated by the Civil War, which added hundreds of thousands of veterans and their wives to the pension rolls. During the years between 1885 and 1926 when the Pension Bureau occupied the building, it paid benefits to 2.7 million veterans and their dependents—some 500,000 of them from the Civil War. Intended as a memorial to veterans of the Civil War, the building (Montgomery C. Meigs, 1882-85) is essentially a modified Italian palazzo, with offices around a roofed-in center court. The Civil War motif appears in the massive terra-cotta frieze of cavalry, infantry, artillery, quartermaster corps, and medical units marching around the building, interrupted at one point by navy units. Because of the vast interior spaces, the Pension building was an instant success as the site for the inaugurals of Presidents Cleveland, Harrison, McKinley, Theodore Roosevelt, and Taft. Since the Pension Office moved out in 1926, the building has been used by a series of government agencies. Occupied at present by the District of Columbia Superior Court, it is slated for eventual use by the Smithsonian as a museum devoted to American architects and architecture. There is perhaps no building in the city better suited to the purpose.

L'Enfant intended **Judiciary Square (15),**

between 4th and 5th Streets, G Street and Indiana Avenue NW, as the site for the federal judiciary, and the three-block square has been a significant part of the cityscape since the construction of the City Hall in 1820. It was used for inaugurations beginning with Zachary Taylor's in 1849. Lincoln's second inaugural elsewhere interrupted the tradition in 1865, but it was resumed with the construction of the Pension Building to the north of the square (1885) and continued until 1909. Four court buildings have been added to the square in this century, but open space remains, dotted with trees, statuary, and pleasant walks. With the completion of the Judiciary Square subway station and the return of the old City Hall to municipal use, the square will resume its past role as one of the more beautiful and important open spaces within the city.

The first building constructed in Judiciary Square, **District of Columbia City Hall (16),** 451 Indiana Avenue NW (George Hadfield), was begun in 1820 and completed in 1849. There have been additions and renovations since, but Hadfield's design survives (especially along the Indiana Avenue facade)—making it one of the oldest and architecturally most significant public buildings in the city. Its current tenant is the federal government, but under present plans for restoration, the building will once more be returned to the city. In front of City Hall, on Indiana Avenue, stands Lott Flannery's 1868 **Lincoln Statue (17),** which was erected with funds subscribed by citizens of the District and was the first memorial in Washington to the slain President.

# Federal Triangle

**HOW TO GET THERE:** Tourmobile to either Museum of Natural History or History and Technology, walk north; almost any Metrobus to terminals at 12th Street and Pennsylvania Avenue NW.
**PARKING:** Commercial lots north of Pennsylvania Avenue.
**TIME:** 2-3 hours.
**RESTAURANTS:** Snack bars or cafeterias in most buildings.

In 1901 the McMillan Commission planned the Federal Triangle as one of several homogeneous complexes of buildings to house some of the federal agencies and departments. The Commerce, Justice, and Labor Departments, along with several independent agencies and the District of Columbia Government, eventually did move into the enclave. The Post Office Department already had a major structure in the area, the massive Richardsonian Romanesque Old Post Office (W. J. Edbrooke, 1899), which breaks up the monotony of the neoclassical facades that stretch some 10 blocks along Constitution and Pennsylvania Avenues.

Though sometimes overlooked as a tourist attraction, the triangle offers a great

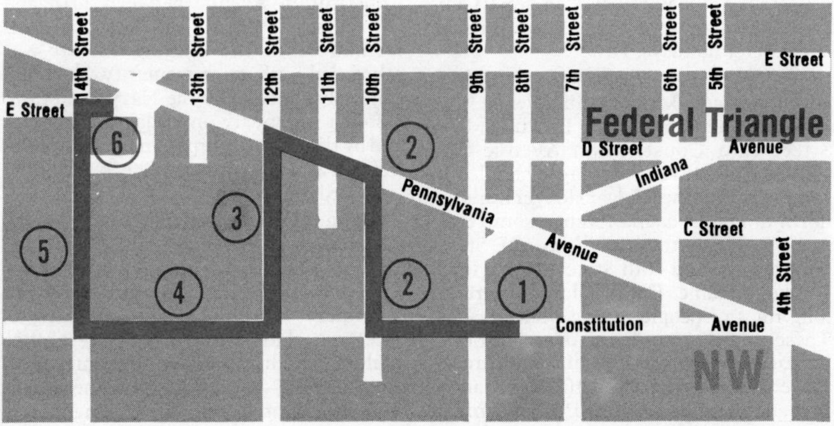

diversity of things to do and see—the National Archives, the Philatelic Exhibition Room of the Postal Service, the Federal Bureau of Investigation, and the National Aquarium.

*The **National Archives (1),** Constitution and Pennsylvania Avenues, between 7th and 9th Streets NW (963-6411 for information on records and research; 962-2000 for information on exhibits and public activities). The Constitution, the Declaration of Independence (without which we would not be celebrating a Bicentennial Year), and the Bill of Rights—all are on public view beneath the 75-foot-high Constitution Avenue Rotunda of the Archives building. They make up only a small part of the well-known records in the archives, many of which are displayed on a rotating basis. The 1937 building (John Russell Pope) has more than 20 floors containing records. They include all major American treaties: the Louisiana Purchase, the Japanese surrender document ending World War II, the Emancipation Proclamation, and such less-public documents as the Warren Commission hearings on the assassination of President John F. Kennedy. The Archives holdings include billions of pages of written material, more than five million still pictures, 82,000 reels of motion pictures, 70,000 sound recordings, and some four million maps and aerial photographs.

If you are interested in research, enter from Pennsylvania Avenue; if interested in seeing the exhibits or shopping at the sales desk, use the Constitution Avenue entrance. Exhibits: April-September weekdays and holidays 9 am-10 pm; Sundays 1 pm-10 pm. October-March weekdays and holidays 9 am-6 pm; Sundays 1 pm-6 pm. Research: Monday-Friday 8:45 am-10 pm; Saturdays 8:45 am-5 pm; closed Sundays and federal holidays. H.

**FBI Tours (2),** J. Edgar Hoover Building, 10th Street and Pennsylvania Avenue NW, or Department of Justice Building, 10th Street near Constitution Avenue NW (324-3447). The FBI tours are scheduled to be relocated to the J. Edgar Hoover Building north of Pennsylvania Avenue some time in 1975. The entrance will be on E Street between 9th and 10th Streets NW. Hours will be the same. The popular tours attract long lines of people during peak seasons. These guided tours give an overview of the history and operation of the bureau. Fingerprinting, the FBI's 10-most-wanted list, and exhibits and lectures on some of the best-known cases are a part of what the visitor sees and hears. The grand finale includes a visit to the FBI indoor firing range where weapons and target shooting are demonstrated. Used targets and expended bullets are sometimes distributed to visitors as souvenirs. Monday-Friday 9:15 am-4 pm (last tour leaves at 3 pm). H.

***Philatelic Exhibition Room (3),** United States Postal Service, Room 1315, 12th Street between Constitution and Pennsylvania Avenues NW (961-7540). In another of those paroxysms of change that afflict Washington, the Philatelic Division was scheduled to move to new quarters in L'Enfant Plaza, directly across the Mall, in early 1975. At publication time it has not yet moved, and may well be in its old quarters until early 1976. In the meantime, only a few displays such as the die proof exhibit are around, but stamps and postal stationery, special publications, and stamp-collecting kits are still being sold. The Postal Service seems to have finally realized that providing stamps for collectors is a legitimate activity of the Postal Service, so the publications and material available from the Philatelic Division are worth a look for anyone interested in collecting.

After the Philatelic Division vacates this space, it is proposed for use by the Treasury Department's Bureau of Alcohol, Tobacco, and Firearms. The exhibit will feature a brass whiskey still once owned by George Washington, other stills, and part of the bureau's collection of hundreds of guns. It will be a combination museum and public information facility. Monday-Saturday 9 am-5 pm. H.

*The **Departmental Auditorium (4),** Constitution Avenue between 12th and 14th Streets NW (967-4277). Though performances in the auditorium are not scheduled with great regularity, there are generally concerts by the Navy Band from October to January on Fridays at 7:30 pm and by the Marine Corps Band from April to May on Sundays at 2 pm. Check the bulletin board in the auditorium.

**National Aquarium (5),** lower lobby, Commerce Department Building, 14th Street between Constitution Avenue and E Street NW (967-2825). The Department of Commerce Building (York and Sawyer, 1932) is said to have been the largest office building in the world at the time of its construction—certainly it was the largest in Washington before the Pentagon was built. The department, responsible for the federal census, maintains the Census Clock in the 14th Street entrance lobby. It clicks off constant tabulations of projected changes in the population.

In the lower lobby is the National Aquarium operated by the Division of Fish Hatcheries of the Fish and Wildlife Service, Department of the Interior. Successor to the oldest aquarium in the country—in operation in various locations since 1888—it displays over 2,000 specimens of aquatic life, covering some 350 species in 67 different tanks. Fish are normally fed in the morning, a good time to visit. You'll see both fresh- and salt-water specimens. Sharks, octopuses, sightless cave fish, and many other colorful and intriguing fish are of special interest to young children. A large tank showing the results of water pollution makes a strong point. Daily 9 am-5 pm; closed Christmas Day. H.

The **District Building (6)**, 14th Street and Pennsylvania Avenue NW (Cope and Stewardson, 1908) was the first of the great neoclassical buildings constructed in the Federal Triangle. It houses the offices of the District government.

# Arlington National Cemetery

**HOW TO GET THERE:** Tourmobile from any site on the Mall.
**PARKING:** Free Arlington National Cemetery Visitor Center, Columbia Island, Iwo Jima Memorial.
**TIME:** 3-4 hours.
**RESTAURANT:** Marina at Columbia Island (see below).

Arlington House was originally part of the estate of George Washington Parke Custis (Martha Washington's grandson), who grew up at Mount Vernon with General and Mrs. Washington. Both the house and Arlington Cemetery are in Arlington County, which, during most of the lifetime of Custis, was part of the District of Columbia. The city planned by Pierre Charles L'Enfant in 1790-91 lay within the Maryland part of the District, ensuring that the government buildings would be north of the river. Virginians, finding themselves with the problems of the federal city and none of the spoils began agitating for retrocession to Virginia in the 1820s. In 1846 they won their case, and the Virginia portion of the District—all of Arlington County and most of the present city of Alexandria—was returned to Virginia.

Ironically, L'Enfant, who planned the capital, is buried in Arlington National Cemetery, which is no longer a part of the Washington that he played such a prominent part in shaping. Appropriately, however, his grave is in front of Arlington House, a site that has perhaps the best views of the city. Though the Tourmobile offers easy access to Arlington National Cemetery, the only way to get to Columbia Island or the Iwo Jima Memorial is on foot or by car. Both have free parking.

**Columbia Island (1),** just north of the 14th Street Bridge on the George Washington Memorial Parkway, was originally an island in the Potomac and a part of the Arlington estate. Today it is much enlarged by fill and the original shoreline is difficult to locate. An area along the parkway is designated as Lady Bird Johnson Park, in honor of the First Lady who did much to make Washington the beautiful city it is. Millions of daffodils were planted between the 14th Street Bridge and Memorial Bridge as a result of her efforts.

In the center of the park is the Lyndon B. Johnson Memorial Grove. A large granite boulder from an area near the Johnson Ranch in Texas provides the simple monument to the former President. His major legacy, however, will be the walks, views, and vistas, in a leafy landscaped grove under development between the marina and the Potomac.

Just north of the 14th Street Bridge, between the parkway and the Potomac, is the Navy Marine Memorial (Ernesto Begni del Piatta, 1934) one of the most beautiful of the Washington area monuments. Views across the river as you walk or drive northward from the memorial are impressive.

The snack bar at the Marina offers rather good crab cakes (the sandwiches are only passable), or you can bring your own picnic and eat at outside tables or on the lawns where you can see the boats and marine activities. Snack bar 9 am-5 pm daily (DI 7-0173).

**Arlington Memorial Bridge (2),** between the Lincoln Memorial and the Main Gate of Arlington Cemetery and Arlington House. The Memorial Bridge connecting the memorial to Civil War President Abraham Lincoln and the home of Robert E. Lee, commander of the Confederate forces, symbolizes the union between North and South. Though suggested in the 19th century, and included in the 1901 McMillan plan for Washington, the bridge was not actually begun until 1926 and not completed until 1932 (McKim, Meade, and White).

**Arlington National Cemetery Visitor Center (3),** south of Memorial Drive and the main gate to the cemetery (LI 5-6700). Although the cemetery is technically closed to private vehicles, temporary passes may be obtained at the visitor center to visit the graves of friends or relatives; permanent passes are available for the next of kin of persons buried there. For others, the best bet is either to walk or take the Tourmobile. No photographing of funerals is permitted.

The Visitor Center is a temporary structure that dispenses information and tickets for the Tourmobile. It also has exhibits on Arlington Cemetery and Arlington House with taped commentaries in five languages. The cemetery is maintained by the Department of the Army; Arlington House by the National Park Service.

Burials actually took place in the national cemetery in 1864, when the house and grounds were occupied by U.S. forces. Most of those buried in the cemetery were a part of the military forces. However, dependents, public figures, and former slaves (who flocked to Union lines during the Civil War and established Freedman's Village near the mansion) are also buried here.

A brochure on the cemetery, available at the Visitor Center, contains a map of the grounds and of the location of major graves and memorials of most interest to the visitor. The cemetery staff at the center will assist visitors in locating the graves of friends and relatives. November-March 8 am-5 pm; April-October 8 am-7 pm. Wheelchairs provided for the handicapped upon request.

The **Kennedy Gravesite (4),** Sheridan Drive, just below Arlington House. John F. Kennedy's grave is on a slope in front of Arlington House, a site he admired. There, an eternal flame marks the grave where the slain President was buried in November, 1963. Then just a grassy slope, the site is today part of a simple but large area of stone and marble, which follows the general contours of the hill (John Charles Warnecke Associates, 1967). On walls below the grave are selections from Kennedy writings.

Nearby, in an extension of the same gravesite, Senator Robert F. Kennedy, slain by an assassin's bullet in 1970, is buried beneath a simple white cross. The eternal flame on the Kennedy grave is visible at night from the Lincoln Memorial and from Memorial Bridge as one approaches the cemetery. It is just below the lighted facade of Arlington House, its flicker noticeably different from the electric light nearby. November-March 8 am-5 pm; April-October 8 am-7 pm.

George Washington Parke Custis began to build **Arlington House (5),** between Lee and Sherman Drives (557-3153), about 1804 on land inherited from his father, and completed it around 1820 (George Hadfield). Custis chose his site wisely. At the time of its completion the house stood alone on the Virginia shore, overlooking the wide river marshes. It still remains the dominant feature of the Virginia skyline.

Custis, an agricultural reformer, painter, public speaker, and writer, inherited many of the Washington mementos from Mount Vernon and spent most of his life perpetuating George Washington's memory. His only daughter married Robert E. Lee, then a lieutenant in the United States Army. After the death of Custis in 1857, the estate passed to Mrs. Lee and was to have become the Lee home. In 1861 Lee resigned from the Army and became the commander of troops of his native Virginia, and never returned to Arlington. Union forces occupied the estate shortly after Virginia voters ratified an ordinance of secession.

Throughout the Civil War the house served various military uses, and in 1864 the grounds began to be used as a military cemetery. Arlington House is now maintained as a memorial to Robert E. Lee. The slave quarters and kitchen area also contain exhibits, and there is a museum in which the story of the house and of Lee's agonizing decision to leave the U.S. Army is told through artifacts and sound. The visit to the house and museum is quiet and leisurely, and views from the mansion site

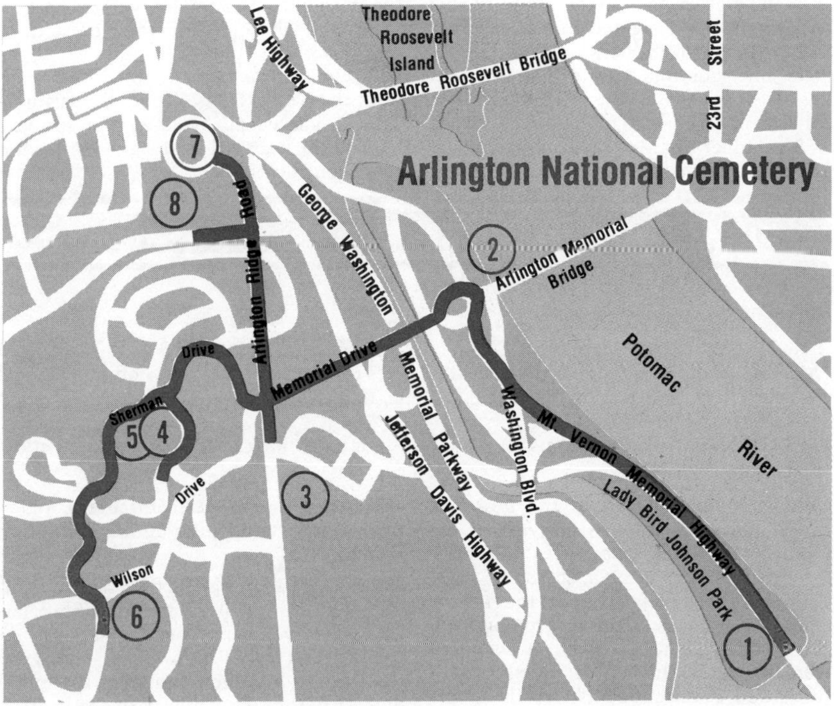


make it well worth the effort to reach it. November-March 9:30 am-4:30 pm; April-October 9:30 am-6 pm.

The *Tomb of the Unknown Soldier (6), between Wilson, Roosevelt, and Memorial Drives, is where the first of the unknown soldiers was laid to rest on Memorial Day in 1921. The present marker, a rectangular marble block, was not erected until 1931 (Lorimer Rich, architect; Thomas Hudson Jones, sculptor). On Memorial Day 1958 unknown soldiers from World War II and the Korean War joined the unknown from World War I. The Tomb Guard, provided by the Army, is composed of special troops from the Old Guard Unit stationed at Fort Myer. The ceremonial guard is posted hourly in all weather when the cemetery is open to the public; the night guard is not ceremonial. The tomb guard activities are based on the number 21, the highest honor that can be paid, as in a 21-gun salute. Movements are based on 21 steps, and stops or salutes on counts of 21 seconds.

Flags within the cemetery fly at half-staff during the day when burials are taking place in the cemetery, and at full-staff at other times. The sound of a gun salute and of a bugler mournfully playing taps can often be heard. Daily November-March 8 am-5 pm; April-October 8 am-7 pm.

The **Marine Corps War Memorial (7)**, north of Arlington National Cemetery near the intersection of Route 50 and Arlington Boulevard, commemorates the February 23, 1945 flag raising on Mount Suribachi on Iwo Jima by five Marines and a Navy hospital corpsman. Associated Press photographer Joe Rosenthal photographed the flag raising, earning himself a Pulitzer Prize, and producing what is probably the best-known photograph taken during World War II.

The sculptor, Felix W. de Weldon, used the three men who survived the war as models, and worked from photographs of the others. Lighted and available for viewing at all hours of the day and night, the monument has become a popular tourist attraction. Special units from the Marine Corps Honor Guard and Band present sunset reviews at the memorial during the summer season each Tuesday at 7:30 pm.

The **Netherlands Carillon (8)**, north of Arlington National Cemetery, between Route 50 and Arlington Boulevard, is a gift from the Netherlands to the people of this country. It was dedicated on May 5, 1960, and is the work of architect Joost W. C. Boks and sculptors E. van den Grinten-Lucker and Paul Konig—all Dutch. The bells are played Saturdays or Sundays April to September and on some holidays (call 557-8991). There is plenty of room to sit on the grass, and refreshments are not frowned upon, though litter afterward most definitely is.

A Tulip Library, maintained with gifts from the Netherlands, is near the carillon. This is succeeded by flowering annuals later in the year. All plants are marked for easy identification.

# Georgetown #1

**HOW TO GET THERE:** Metrobus—D 2 along Q Street to 27th Street NW.
**PARKING:** Some on-street parking, but it requires patience to find. Most commercial lots are near either M Street or Wisconsin Avenue, then walk to tour area.
**TIME:** Approximately 2-3 hours.
**RESTAURANTS:** For suggestions see Chapter 9. For picnicking head for Montrose Park or Dumbarton Oaks Park.

Located near the falls of the Potomac River—Little Falls is just upriver and the Great Falls some five miles beyond—Georgetown was recognized in the early 18th century as a site for a port to serve the commercial needs of the developing Piedmont of Maryland. In an era when roads were little more than Indian trails, and railroads and canals nonexistent, the rivers were the lifelines for commerce. The shops and homes of craftsmen and merchants spread up the hill away from the docks. By the time the federal city of Washington was established in 1789 Georgetown already boasted a custom house and was an official port of entry for foreign trade.

Although the port suffered some ups and downs, its growth was steady and Georgetown came to rely almost exclusively on river and canal-borne commerce. The Chesapeake and Ohio Canal, begun in Georgetown in 1828, finally reached Cumberland, Maryland in 1850. The canal brought increased traffic to Georgetown, but ultimately could not compete with the railroad that had been built between Cumberland and Baltimore. Changes in river channels and siltation due to overuse of the land along the river banks also played a part in the decline of the port.

Georgetown did not die however. Although it joined with Washington County in the District of Columbia in 1871, the appeal of the original port town remained, and has been enhanced in recent years. Homes and shops spanning many decades and architectural styles have been rehabilitated. Today Georgetown is historically significant, a prime residential area, and a lively center of shopping, dining, and entertainment.

Essentially the area of the first Georgetown tour is residential. It is on top of the hill, far above the river. Large country estates from the 18th and early 19th century, some with their grounds intact, mingle with more modest houses dating up to the early 20th century. Great public spaces, so important to Victorian America, have survived here, not only public parks, but also cemeteries—the social, artistic, and cultural epitome of that era. If you must make a choice about what stops to make along the tour route, visit Oak Hill Cemetery and Dumbarton Oaks.

You can, wander in almost any direction and find much more to see. Wisconsin Avenue and M Street are the main shopping and entertainment streets of Georgetown. The major residential area is bounded by R Street on the north, the canal on the south, Rock Creek on the east, and Georgetown University on the west.

**Mt. Zion Cemetery (1),** 27th and Q Streets NW, is one of the oldest black cemeteries in Washington. The Female Union Band Society, a group of freedmen, established a cemetery here in 1843, adjacent to the old Methodist burial ground. That cemetery, where both slaves and freedmen had been interred, came into exclusive black ownership in 1879, when its owners deeded it to black members of the Methodist congregation. Both cemeteries came to be called Mt. Zion and served the

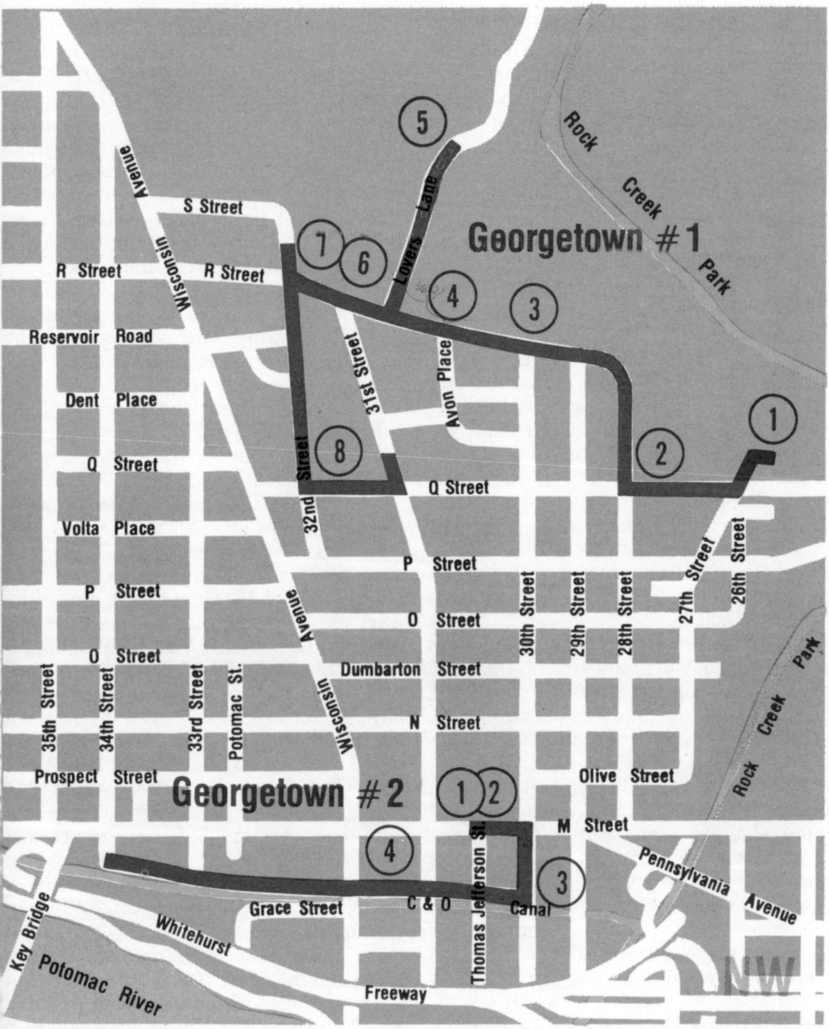


Georgetown area in the late 19th century when Georgetown residents were 35-40 percent black. The last burial was in 1952. Prime open space eagerly sought by developers, the area is proposed as a memorial park devoted to black contributions to the history of Washington. In the meantime, the cemetery is being restored.

**Dumbarton House (2),** 2715 Q Street NW (337-2288), was one of the fine early 1800s houses that marked the transition from Georgian to Federal style. It was originally at the end of Q Street and was moved to its present site in 1915 because the street was being opened to through traffic when the Q Street (Buffalo) Bridge was completed. In 1928 Dumbarton House was purchased by the National Society of the Colonial Dames of America who use it as their headquarters. The house has been restored, furnished with period pieces, and opened to the public. Daily 9 am-noon; closed Sunday and July-August. Admission fee.

**Oak Hill Cemetery (3),** R and 30th Streets NW. If the Victorian tradition of weekend visits to the cemetery ever makes a comeback, it will be cemeteries like Oak Hill that are the cause. Established in 1849, the cemetery is a landscaped park, adapting to its hillside site through a series of curving drives and terraces. Its tall cast-iron fence along R Street is a marvel of the ironmaster's art, matched by the quality of iron benches, planters, and urns within the cemetery. James Renwick's Gothic Revival Chapel (1850), and George Hadfield's Van Ness Mausoleum (c. 1820 and moved here from elsewhere) are excellent examples of the architecture of the day.

Renwick and Hadfield are only the icing on the cake: many lesser-known architects and sculptors are represented by works they proudly signed and dated. The individually designed and carved markers, tombs, and monuments often serve as obituaries, telling much more than just names and dates. Achievements, honors, dreams and poetry—both borrowed and original—adorn the stones. Symbolism is everywhere—the truncated column, inverted torch, and draped urn symbolizing death, with the angel, flower, and cross, symbolizing life after death. Many well-known people are buried here, among them John Howard Payne, who wrote "Home, Sweet Home." His monument is just inside the gate, centered in its own grassy plot. Open daylight hours.

From its period light fixtures to its views of Rock Creek and Dumbarton Oaks Park, **Montrose Park (4),** R Street at Avon Place NW, is a delightful place. Take a stroll, rest, or pursue more active recreation like tennis (see Chapter 7). Always open.

**Dumbarton Oaks Park (5),** R and 31st Streets NW (approach by Lover's Lane), is a relatively natural area behind Dumbarton Oaks House and Gardens and Montrose Park. It adjoins Rock Creek Park at the base of the hill that slopes away from the street. Chipmunks scamper about and you are likely to see opossums and raccoons, as well as many wildflowers. Daily 9 am-5 pm.

**Dumbarton Oaks House and Gardens (6),** entrance to gardens at 3101 R Street NW (232-3201). Construction of the house began about 1801. Its most recent private owners, Mr. and Mrs. Robert Woods Bliss, made the last alterations after 1920. In 1940 they gave the house and gardens to Harvard University, which now uses it as a study center. By the mid-19th century the gardens were already well developed and the grounds of Dumbarton Oaks were one of the showplaces of Washington. Today the many gardens (see Chapter 7) represent perhaps one of the last great examples of American private garden design. They have been planned to provide grand vistas and intimate corners, formal settings, and informal interludes. Every detail of texture of walks, design of gazebo, or placement of benches has been geared to make these features as much a part of the total picture as the plants themselves. Try to see as much as possible but don't miss the pebble garden where a giant mosaic of a sheaf of wheat made from cobblestones is covered with a thin sheet of water and serves as a huge birdbath. You may watch from the terrace above without disturbing the birds.

*Dumbarton Oaks, A Guide to the Gardens,* is an inexpensive booklet helpful not only for finding your way around the grounds, but also for understanding why and how they came about.

Daily 2 pm-5 pm; closed holidays and July-Labor Day, and sometimes during winter when snow or ice make the pathways hazardous.

The **Dumbarton Oaks Research Library and Collections (7),** 1703 32nd Street NW (232-3201). Most visitors come to see the art collections housed in various wings of Dumbarton Oaks House, but along the way, stop at the Music Room, which was added to the house by Mr. and Mrs. Robert Woods Bliss in 1929. They used it for private musicales, and it now serves for invitational concerts, often by world-renowned artists. In April 1947 Igor Stravinsky first performed his "Dumbarton Oaks Concerto" here. It was also in this room in 1944 that the Dumbarton Oaks Conference was held that led to the drafting of the United Nations Charter.

The collections of Greek and Roman statuary and mosaic floors, and of Byzantine art and artifacts are in the Garden Library Wing (Frederic Rhinelander King, 1963) and in earlier 20th-century wings of the house. In another wing, the Museum of Pre-Columbian Art (Philip Johnson, 1963) houses early South and Central American jewelry, pottery, and artifacts. The museum, a series of circular glass display areas arranged around an interior court is one of the most innovative and interesting contemporary structures in Washington.

A sales desk has exhaustive literature on the house, gardens, research facility, and collections. *An Introduction to Dumbarton Oaks* is an inexpensive, brief way to become acquainted with all of it.

Tuesday-Sunday 2 pm-5 pm; closed holidays and July-Labor Day.

Although they are not open to the public, many houses along the tour route and nearby streets provide excellent examples of the developing architecture and taste of some two centuries of Georgetown. One of the more interesting houses is ***Tudor Place (8)**, 1644 31st Street NW, which was built between 1794-1816, after designs by William Thornton. It is not only an important Federal mansion, but one that still has its grounds intact, and is still owned and occupied by descendants of Thomas Peter for whom it was built. Peter married Martha Parke Custis, granddaughter of Martha Washington, through whom the family inherited a significant collection of papers, furniture, and relics relating to Washington. The most impressive view of its facade is from Q Street.

From this point, you may continue west on Q Street to Wisconsin Avenue, or down 31st Street to M Street. Either direction will bring you to the commercial areas of Georgetown and to the starting point of the other Georgetown tour.

# Georgetown #2

**HOW TO GET THERE:** Any 30 Metrobus to 30th and M Streets NW.
**PARKING:** Commercial lots between M Street and the river.
**TIME:** 2 hours.
**RESTAURANTS:** Along M Street and Wisconsin Avenue and between M Street and the C & O Canal are many excellent restaurants where you can get a delicious sherbet (at Le Sorbet) or a full-course dinner (see Chapter 9 for lunch and dinner suggestions).

In this part of Georgetown there is a great concentration of specialty shops, restaurants, and night clubs fanning out along M Street and Wisconsin Avenue. It is one of the few places in Washington where businesses stay open until the early morning hours and the streets are crowded and busy almost around the clock. There are not as many museums or public buildings open to the public here—the major one is the Old Stone House—but it is an interesting urban area. When you've had enough of browsing in the shops and galleries, walk along the C & O Canal towpath. Blocks of houses and businesses that grew up along the towpath face the canal, which is still filled with water and has operating locks. The towpath continues along the canal for some 184 miles inland, providing hiking, jogging, bicycling, and other recreational opportunities (see Chapter 7). Though severely damaged during the floods that followed hurricane Agnes in 1972, the canal is now being repaired, and summer barge trips will begin in 1976.

***The Old Stone House (1)**, 3051 M Street NW (426-6851), starkly different from its later brick and frame neighbors, is believed to be the only pre-Revolutionary War house in the present District of Columbia. Built around 1764 by Christopher Layman, it was occupied by a succession of families, both as a residence and place of business. Layman probably came to Georgetown from Pennsylvania—the house has more similarities to those constructed by the German settlers in eastern Pennsylvania than it does to the more traditional English buildings of this area.

The simple Old Stone House provides good architectural contrast for the later, more pretentious residences of the rich and famous that are open to the public elsewhere in Washington and Alexandria. Its furnishings also illustrate the different way of life of a middle-class family. Layman was a cabinetmaker, and he designed the house so that the ground floor could serve his business. The kitchen is located there, too. Both are furnished as they would have been during the late 18th century. On the floor above, the dining and other rooms offer clues to the life of the tradesman after his shop was closed for the day. Wednesday-Sunday 9:30 am-5 pm (at times open daily; check by phone).

***Thomas Simm Lee Corner (2)**, M and 30th Streets NW (northwest corner). Typical of the houses constructed by the more affluent merchants and residents of Georgetown in the late 18th and early 19th centuries, the Thomas Simm Lee Corner was saved only through the concerted effort of a group of Georgetown residents, who purchased the building, undertook its restoration, and rent out the space. The restoration of this property helped to ensure the preservation of the additional buildings in the row.

Thomas Lee, friend of Washington and other leaders in the Revolutionary era, was a Maryland delegate to the Continental Congress, a staunch supporter of Revolutionary activities, and twice governor of Maryland.

The **Chesapeake and Ohio Canal (3)** was constructed to make trading by water possible from the Chesapeake Bay to the Ohio River. The goal was never attained, not because it wasn't realistic, but because the canal was being built concurrently with the railroads, which provided faster, more flexible, and cheaper transportation. The canal did exert great influence on Georgetown, however, from the time its Georgetown section was completed in the early 1830s to the time it reached its terminus in Cumberland, Maryland, in 1850. Trade from the Piedmont and mountain areas to the west supplemented the already busy coastal and ocean trade, and businesses in Georgetown boomed, especially milling. Though the canal ceased to be a competitive transportation link in the 19th century, it carried some traffic until the 1920s. Authorized for acquisition by the National Park Service in 1971, the linear C & O Canal National Historical Park now covers some 184½ miles along the canal right-of-way from Georgetown to Cumberland.

When mule-drawn barge trips on the canal resume in the summer of 1976, they will originate from the landing at 30th Street. That is also a good place to begin your walking tour of the canal. The four blocks between here and 34th Street are particularly enjoyable. Along the towpath, businesses, warehouses, and 19th-century houses still front on the canal. The rush of water through the locks and the shade of the towpath trees along the canal make it a pleasant spot for pedestrians, bicyclists, and hikers (see Chapter 7 for hiking and bicycling information).

Midway through this tour you can take a detour for a look at **Canal Square (4)**, 1054 31st Street NW (enter from the towpath, 31st Street, or M Street). For this recent commercial development architect Arthur Cotton Moore incorporated the existing walls of a C & O Canal warehouse, and other buildings along 31st Street into office and shopping space. The square contains shops and a restaurant at ground levels, and offices above. Though modernized with new roof lines and windows, the brick walls and lines of the earlier buildings remain, making it one of Washington's prime examples of contemporary use of historic structures.

From here you can resume the towpath walk or branch out into the other shopping and dining areas of Georgetown.

# Old Town Alexandria #1

**HOW TO GET THERE:** # 9 or 11 buses from Pennsylvania Avenue and 12th Street NW in the District to Oronoco and N. Washington Streets or the Bicentennial Center at Prince and S. Washington Streets.

**PARKING:** A small parking area is adjacent to the Bicentennial Center at Prince and S. Washington Streets. On-street parking is available and free permits for visitors may be secured from the Ramsay House Visitor Center at King and Fairfax Streets. Commercial parking lots are located east of Washington Street near the center of town.

**TIME:** 2-2½ hours.

**RESTAURANTS:** Light food—Hector's, 701 King Street, is good for Greek sandwiches, submarines, pizza, and Greek pastries; L'Estaminet, 127 Washington Street, a French luncheonette and carry-out for quiche, soup, and sandwiches. More ambitious dining—The Old Club, 555 S. Washington Street, features southern American dishes in a large dining room with a fireplace; Taverna Cretekou, 818 King Street, offers super, traditional Greek dishes in an attractive Mediterranean setting.

Alexandria began with a tobacco warehouse built about 1732 and the small village that developed around it. It is two years older than Georgetown, and the oldest settlement still surviving in the Washington area. Alexandria's streets evoke its early days: King, Queen, Duke, Prince, Princess, Royal, Pitt. It was from Alexandria that General Edward Braddock began his famous march into western Maryland and Pennsylvania in 1755 during the French and Indian Wars. That same year a confer-

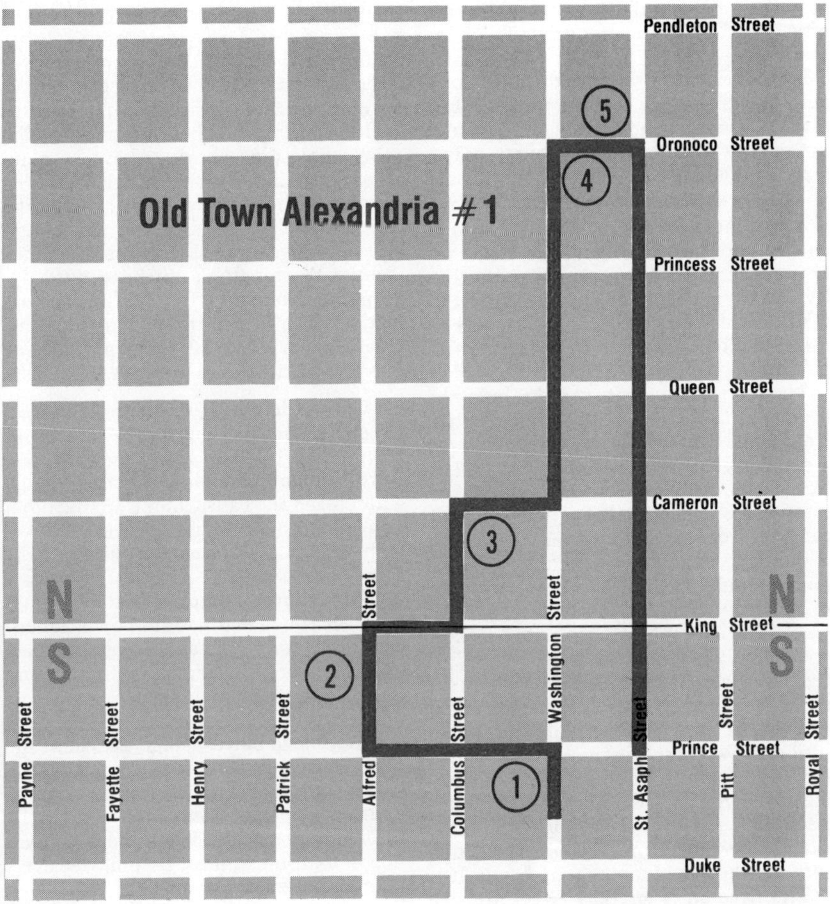


ence of five Royal Governors met in Alexandria to discuss the western territory. Among their recommendations was a tax on the colonists, one of the measures that ultimately led to the American Revolution. During that era George Washington, George Mason, and Light-Horse Harry Lee were frequent visitors to or residents of the town. The cornerstone for the 1790 survey of the District of Columbia still remains in Alexandria under the Jones Point Lighthouse, and elsewhere in town other stones marking the southern boundary are still in place. Alexandria remained a part of the District until 1846 when it was receded to Virginia.

The town served as a shipping point for tobacco and as a port of entry for the Piedmont area of Virginia as did Georgetown for the Maryland Piedmont. Farther downriver than Georgetown, it remained a port longer, both because of clearer channels and because of the availability of railroads to and from the city. The Chesapeake & Ohio Canal eventually crossed the Potomac and continued south to Alexandria. Today the town still serves as a port, especially for freighters carrying newsprint and speciality items for Georgetown, Washington, and Alexandria shops.

The movement of Federal troops across river from Washington on May 24, 1861—the day after Virginians voted in favor of an ordinance of secession—led to the first civilian and military casualties of the Civil War. Later the city became a shipping and rail center for Union supplies and an important lifeline for Union forces.

Georgetown and Alexandria, developed largely in the same manner and with much the same types of citizenry, both still have an amazing number of buildings from the past that are maintained through active private and governmental preservation efforts.

Both Alexandria tours begin in historic buildings that today serve as tourist information centers where trained personnel can provide information, brochures, maps, reservations, and advice on walks and tours within Alexandria or nearby areas.

Tour # 1 presents a before-and-after look at the effects of restoration and the reemergence of an urban area as a place to live, work, and shop. It includes both residential and commercial areas, as well as mixes of the two in various stages of rehabilitation.

There is wide diversity of sights here: the Bicentennial Center, Friendship Fire House, and Christ Church—are well worth a visit. If you have time the walk to Lee Corner and back takes in houses that are interesting and varied. Printed material available from the Bicentennial Center will make the tour more enjoyable.

***Bicentennial Center** (Lyceum) **(1),** corner of S. Washington and Prince Streets (750-6677). The Alexandria Bicentennial Center opened in 1974 with well-designed, uncluttered displays that cover the development of the area and its Revolutionary history, and regular showings of a film about Revolutionary War activities in Alexandria. In a newer addition to the rear there is a complete Virginia Tourist Information Center (see Chapter 2) and a sales shop with exceptionally tasteful items relating to local history and the Bicentennial (see Chapter 10).

The Lyceum is an 1839 Greek Revival structure of a type and sophistication rare in northern Virginia. Benjamin Hollowell, a Quaker schoolmaster, operated his Lyceum here, and the building also served as the Alexandria Library. The center will operate until the end of the Bicentennial era in 1989 when the building will revert to the city for other uses. Bicentennial Center, daily 9 am-5 pm. Museum Shop, Monday-Saturday 10 am-4:30 pm; Sunday 1 pm-4:30 pm. Adjacent free parking. H, except for film showing on second floor.

***The Friendship Fire Company (2),** 107 South Alfred Street, is maintained by the Friendship Veterans Fire Engine Company as a museum dedicated to preserving artifacts and historic memorabilia connected with fire fighting in Alexandria. The company was organized in 1774; among the treasures here are a 1775 fire engine, made in France and purchased by George Washington for the company, and other items belonging to George Washington or associated with him. The 1850s fire station in which the collection is housed is one of several excellent stations that survive within the city. The building and its adjacent cobblestone alleyway have been restored to their early appearance. Young visitors enjoy the place, and they can ring the fire bell and the bells on the various engines. Each year the association celebrates George Washington's birthday with appropriate ceremony. The celebrations are held in the street in front of the building. Tuesday-Saturday 10 am-4 pm; closed Sunday, Monday, and holidays.

***Christ Church (3),** Cameron Street, between N. Washington and N. Columbus Streets (549-1450), is one of the three pre-Revolutionary church buildings (Pohick Church and the Falls Church are the other two) in Northern Virginia designed by local architect James Wren and all built from the same basic design. Throughout its history Christ Church, completed in 1773, has been identified with well-known Americans. Two communicants whose pews are marked were George Washington and Robert E. Lee. Many other famous people have worshipped here, including Woodrow Wilson, David Lloyd George, President and Mrs. Franklin D. Roosevelt, Winston Churchill, President and Mrs. Harry S Truman, President and Mrs. Dwight D. Eisenhower, and President and Mrs. Lyndon B. Johnson. Sunday 2-5 pm; weekdays 9 am-5 pm (guides available).

***The Fendall-Lee House (4),** 429 N. Washington Street (548-0931), is one of the four houses at the corner of Oronoco and N. Washington Streets associated with the Lee family, and one of two open to the public. Because of this concentration of Lee houses the intersection is called Lee Corner. The Edmund Jennings Lee House is at 428 N. Washington Street, Robert E. Lee's Boyhood Home at 607 Oronoco Street, and Benjamin Hollowell's School next door at 609 Oronoco Street. The Fendall-Lee House, built around 1785, was occupied by various members of the Lee family until 1903. Later it was the home of John L. Lewis of the United Mine Workers until it was acquired from his estate by the Virginia Trust for Historic Preservation. Furnished with period pieces, many of which have a direct association with the Lee family, the house also maintains a collection of doll houses.

The two collections may be viewed together, or visited separately. Daily 9 am-5 pm. Admission free.

**Robert E. Lee's Boyhood Home (5),** 607 Oronoco Street (548-8454), and its twin next door are late-18th-century houses associated with Robert E. Lee. He lived in the house at 607 during his childhood, and he prepared for entrance to West Point at a school at 609 operated by Benjamin Hollowell. Here Lee studied with other sons and daughters of the Northern Virginia intelligentsia. Lee was 11 years old when his family moved to this house, and it was here and in the Hollowell School next door that he developed associations with the Lewis family of Woodlawn and the Custis family of Arlington House. Nelly Custis Lewis of Woodlawn is credited with interceding on his behalf with President Andrew Jackson to gain him quick admission to West Point, and he later married her niece Mary Custis of Arlington. The building is furnished with period pieces, many of them related directly to Lee or his family. The house is still surrounded by extensive walled gardens. Daily 10 am-4 pm. Admission fee.

The best route back to the center of Alexandria is by N. St. Asaph Street. The early brick sidewalks (with a wide variety of designs and patterns), curbing, and drains still survive for several blocks, and you will pass buildings ranging from 18th-century row houses to 20th-century developments along the route. As elsewhere in the tour area, the walk offers glimpses into alleyways and private gardens, and there are enough trees to shade the way in summer.

# Old Town Alexandria #2

**HOW TO GET THERE:** #9 or 10 buses from 10th Street and Pennsylvania Avenue NW in the District to King and Washington Streets, then walk to Tavern Square where the tour begins.
**PARKING:** Apply at Ramsay House Visitor Center, corner of King and N. Fairfax Streets for nonresident parking permits that allow free parking on metered streets. Commercial lots are located near Tavern Square.
**TIME:** 2-3 hours.
**RESTAURANTS:** Light food—The Snack Bar, 107 King Street, homemade soups and fat sandwiches to eat here or carry out; Popajohn's, 112 N. Pitt Street, a cafeteria and sandwich shop with home-style cooking; Maison des Crêpes, 111 King Street, dinner and dessert crêpes. More ambitious dining—The Warehouse, 214 King Street, American food and live entertainment; Il Porto, 121 King Street, Italian food and excellent homemade ice cream (also sold from a window on Lee Street); The Wharf, 119 King Street, good seafood and live entertainment; King's Landing, 121 South Union Street, quiche and traditional French dishes; China Gate, 310 N. Fairfax Street, fine Mandarin and Szechuan dishes.

The waterfront of Alexandria offers not only a wide variety of historic possibilities, but some of the most interesting shopping and dining in the Washington area. Specialty shops, antique shops, art galleries, and restaurants are located near King and N. Fairfax Streets and there are heavy concentrations around Tavern Square (City Hall Square) and down King Street from Fairfax Street to the Potomac River (see Chapters 9 and 10).

Architecturally this is one of the best of the tours. Buildings here range from the mid-18th century to the present, with superb examples of almost every style built in America up to the beginning of the 20th century. (The 20th-century architecture, though it successfully blends with its surroundings, cannot be said to be innovative.)

Visit the Stabler-Leadbeater Apothecary Shop, a different kind of museum; and the Torpedo Factory Art Center, where artists and craftsmen do their thing. But leave enough time to walk, window shop, sit in Tavern Square watching the fountain, or to enjoy a drink or coffee in a café or restaurant.

***Ramsay House** (Alexandria Tourist Council) **(1),** 221 King Street at N. Fairfax Street (549-0205), is a good starting point for this tour of Alexandria's Old Town. The Ramsay House, built in the mid-18th century, when it had an unobstructed view of

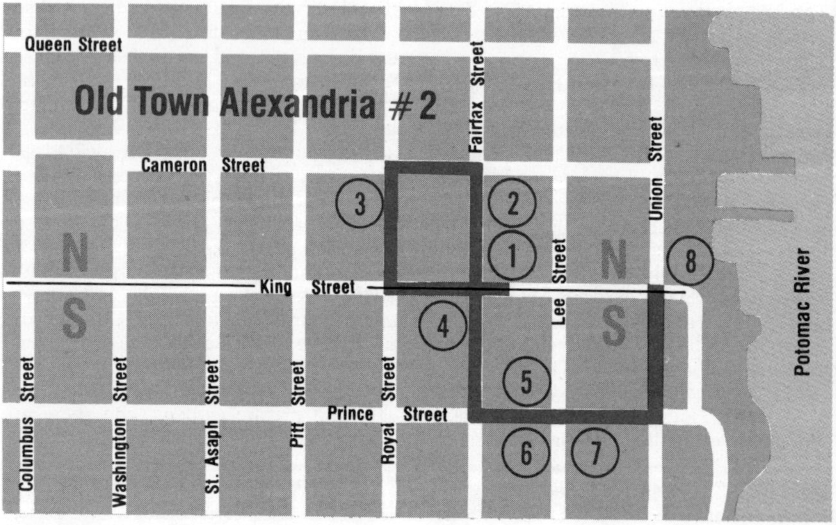


the Potomac, is oriented toward the water. Extensively restored, it now serves as the headquarters of the Alexandria Tourist Council. The council offers an information service, tour guides (arrange in advance), and valuable brochures on local activities and attractions. At the center, there is also a 13-minute color film, and displays of artifacts from local archaeological digs. Daily 10 am-4:30 pm.

When it was constructed *Carlyle House (2), 121 N. Fairfax Street (278-8880), like the Ramsay House, had an unobstructed view of the river, though its orientation and placement are totally different. While Ramsay House is a simple cottage built on a corner lot, Carlyle House is an elegant Georgian mansion, built in the center of its lot and originally surrounded by formal gardens and support buildings. John Carlyle, who built the house in 1752, was an Alexandria merchant from Scotland. It became a social and political center of great importance during pre-Revolutionary days and the beginning of the republic. General Edward Braddock made it his headquarters in 1755 while preparing to march westward to Pittsburgh (and his death) during the French and Indian Wars. In April, 1755, the Royal Governors of Virginia, New York, Pennsylvania, Maryland, and Massachusetts, summoned by Braddock, met here to discuss how the colonists could pay for campaigns against the French and Indians. An outgrowth of the meeting was the Stamp Act, certainly one of the major provocations of the Revolution.

Early in the 19th century, the Bank of Alexandria, said to have been the first native bank in Virginia, was built on a corner of the Carlyle lot. Its building and Carlyle House have both survived, and are slated to be part of a historical complex operated by the Northern Virginia Regional Park Authority. Restoration of the bank building has not yet begun, but the Carlyle House is scheduled to open on New Year's Eve, 1975, and will play a role in the Bicentennial year commensurate with its status as one of the sites where the Revolution started.

***Gadsby's Tavern (3),** 128 N. Royal Street (corner of Royal and Cameron Streets), was frequented by George Washington and other notables of the day. The first of the two taverns, known today as Gadsby's, was built about 1752. In 1794 John Gadsby, an Englishman, slave trader, and hotelier, purchased both buildings and operated them as Gadsby's Tavern. In recent times it was an American Legion Post and a popular place for Alexandria celebrations. It is now being restored, and by 1976 is scheduled once again to become an operating tavern.

**The Stabler-Leadbeater Apothecary Shop (4),** 107 S. Fairfax Street (836-9402), started in 1792 by Edward Stabler, operated continuously for nearly 150 years, serving generations of Washingtons, Lees, Custises, and other prominent local families. The interior and contents of the drugstore were acquired intact by the Landmarks Society of Alexandria, and shelves and drawers still filled with medicines, mortars, pestles, and other staples of the trade look much as they always did. Included in the collection are orders from Martha Washington (for castor oil), Nelly Custis Lewis, Robert E. Lee, and others. Lee was in the shop in 1859 when then Lt. J. E. B. Stuart brought him word from Washington that he was to go to Harper's Ferry to quell the uprising led by John Brown. A taped commentary relates the history of the shop. The Landmarks Society operates a consignment antiques shop in the adjacent building. Monday-Saturday 10 am-5 pm.

**The Atheneum** (Northern Virginia Fine Arts Association) **(5),** 201 Prince Street at S. Lee Street (548-0035). Built in the mid-19th century as a bank, this is one of the few pure Greek Revival buildings in town. The NorthernVirginia Fine Arts Association, a chapter of the Virginia Museum, uses the Atheneum as a gallery with regular exhibits, a museum shop, and occasional lectures and workshops open to the membership and general public. It also maintains a small sculpture garden. Tuesday-Saturday 10 am-4 pm; Sunday 1 pm-4 pm.

Though the Atheneum may be said to be the cornerstone of the two blocks of houses known today as Gentry Row and Sea Captain's Row, many of the houses in the two rows predate it by as much as 75 years. **Gentry Row (6),** on Prince Street between S. Fairfax and S. Lee Streets, is fairly typical of the houses built by affluent merchants and planters in the late 18th and early 19th centuries. **Sea Captain's Row (7),** on Prince Street between S. Lee and S. Union Streets, dates from the same period, but most of the houses are the smaller and simpler ones built by sea captains and tradesmen. Prince Street affords a fine architectural walking tour past 18th-century, 19th-century, and early-20th-century houses, often intermingled, stretching inland some 12 blocks.

**The Torpedo Factory Art Center (8),** 101 N. Union Street at King Street (836-8564). What do you do with a World War I torpedo factory that covers part of three downtown blocks on a city's waterfront, and is the most massive structural complex in town? You turn it into studio and sales space for local artists and craftspeople. At least, that's what the city of Alexandria did with a section of one of the buildings that spans a city block. Its exterior paint changed from battleship gray to beige, its interior turned into work space for sculptors, ceramicists, painters, lapidarists, and others—it now welcomes collectors, students, and other craftspeople who want to learn, browse, or buy. Daily 10 am-5 pm.

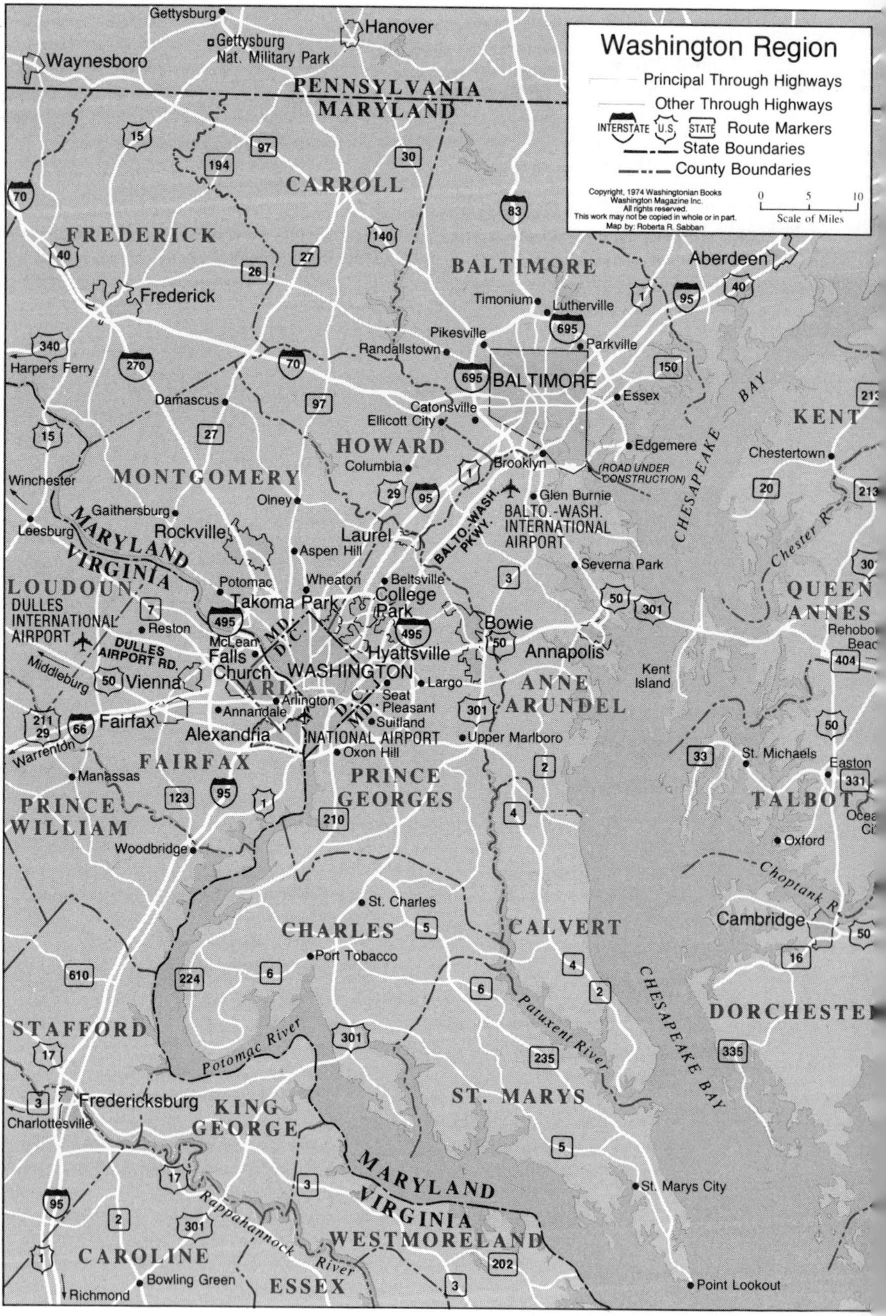

Washington Region
Principal Through Highways
Other Through Highways
INTERSTATE U.S. STATE Route Markers
State Boundaries
County Boundaries
Copyright, 1974 Washingtonian Books
Washington Magazine Inc.
All rights reserved.
This work may not be copied in whole or in part.
Map by: Roberta R. Sabban
0 5 10
Scale of Miles
Gettysburg
Hanover
Gettysburg
Nat. Military Park
Waynesboro
PENNSYLVANIA
MARYLAND
CARROLL
FREDERICK
BALTIMORE
Frederick
Aberdeen
Timonium
Lutherville
Pikesville
Parkville
Randallstown
Harpers Ferry
BALTIMORE
Essex
Damascus
Catonsville
Ellicott City
KENT
HOWARD
Edgemere
Columbia
Brooklyn
Chestertown
(ROAD UNDER CONSTRUCTION)
Winchester
MONTGOMERY
Olney
Glen Burnie
BALTO.-WASH. INTERNATIONAL AIRPORT
CHESAPEAKE BAY
Gaithersburg
Leesburg
Rockville
Laurel
BALTO.-WASH. PKWY.
Chester R.
MARYLAND
VIRGINIA
Aspen Hill
Severna Park
LOUDOUN
Potomac
Wheaton
Beltsville
QUEEN ANNES
DULLES INTERNATIONAL AIRPORT
Takoma Park
College Park
Reston
Bowie
McLean
Falls Church
MD.
D.C.
Hyattsville
Annapolis
Rehoboth Beach
DULLES AIRPORT RD.
Kent Island
Middleburg
Vienna
WASHINGTON
Largo
ANNE ARUNDEL
ARL
Arlington
Seat Pleasant
Annandale
Suitland
Fairfax
Alexandria
NATIONAL AIRPORT
Upper Marlboro
Warrenton
Oxon Hill
St. Michaels
Easton
FAIRFAX
Manassas
PRINCE GEORGES
TALBOT
PRINCE WILLIAM
Ocean City
Woodbridge
Oxford
Choptank R.
St. Charles
Cambridge
CHARLES
CALVERT
Port Tobacco
Patuxent River
DORCHESTER
STAFFORD
Potomac River
CHESAPEAKE BAY
Fredericksburg
KING GEORGE
ST. MARYS
Charlottesville
MARYLAND
VIRGINIA
St. Marys City
Rappahannock River
WESTMORELAND
CAROLINE
Bowling Green
ESSEX
Point Lookout
Richmond

# Chapter Four

# Seeing the Region

ROBERT SHOSTECK

## Annapolis, Md

Maryland's Colonial capital is only a half hour's drive from Washington via the John Hanson Highway (Route 50). The Greyhound Bus Lines offer frequent service to Annapolis. The major tourist attractions are the Colonial section of the city, the Naval Academy, and the waterfront.

If you plan to go on the walking tour of old Annapolis, we suggest that you leave your car at the all-day municipal parking lot near the Historic Annapolis office in the Old Treasury Building behind the State House. On the 1½-hour tour, well-informed guides lead you along the narrow, cobblestone streets, making frequent stops for short talks or visits. These tours start from the Old Treasury Building. Monday-Friday 10 am-1:30 pm; summer daily. You can arrange a tour by prior appointment at other times (minimum group charge is $5). If you are not up to the walking tour, get a few dimes for parking meters and drive to each of the historic sites. Begin at the ***State House,** the first peacetime U.S. Capitol. This stately building houses the legislative chambers, a flag museum, and the old chambers, including the one in which Washington resigned his military commission in 1783. Daily 10 am-5 pm. Guides take groups through the building at frequent intervals at no charge. Nearby is the ***Old Treasury Building.** Summer daily 10 am-4 pm; rest of year Monday-Friday. Opposite is historic **St. Anne's Church.** During the summer hostesses are on hand to explain the history of the church.

Drive on to College Avenue to the **St. John's College** campus. This is the third-oldest college in the United States. You can visit MacDowell Hall and pause for a few moments at the 600-year-old "Liberty Tree" where a treaty of peace was signed with the Indians in 1652. Proceed to King George Street, turning right to reach three notable Colonial homes: **Hammond-Harwood House, Chase House,** and **Ogle House.** The only one open is Hammond-Harwood House: March-October weekdays 10 am-5 pm, Sunday 2 pm-5 pm; November-February weekdays 10 am-4 pm; Sunday 1 pm-4 pm. Admission fee.

You can drive your car through the main entrance of the **Naval Academy.** Make your first stop the ***Naval Museum.** Thousands of mementos of American naval history are on display here. Daily 10 am-4:30 pm; closed Monday. To get the flavor of the Academy, and how the midshipmen live and learn, take a look at Bancroft and Memorial Halls. Guided tours of the Academy grounds (modest fee) start from the nearby Field House.

Leaving the Academy, proceed left on King George Street and right on Randall Street to the **City Dock** and **Market.** Here you can buy all kinds of seafood and unique local dishes like crab cakes and fried chicken. There is a food carry-out service

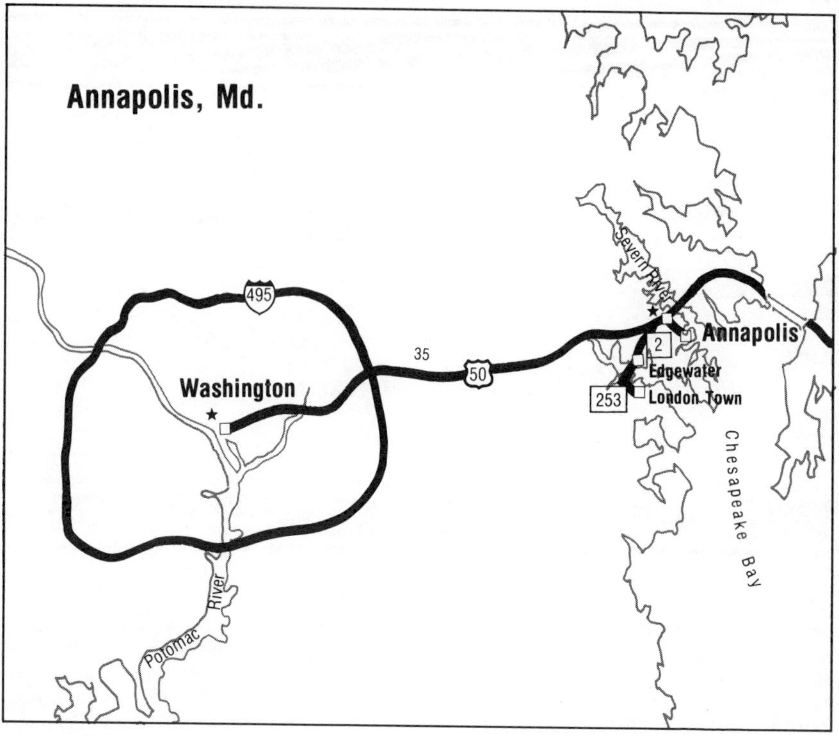


and a good raw bar. The market is closed on Tuesdays. You will also probably want to take some time to stroll past the pleasure and fishing boats tied up at the dock.

You can take a scenic cruise on the Harbor Queen, which operates daily April-October from the City Dock. The cruise includes the Naval Academy, Severn River, Chesapeake Bay, and Eastport. A boat schedule is available at the Information Center on City Dock.

Nearby is the ***Naval Historical Wax Museum,** May-October daily 9 am-9 pm; November-April 9 am-6 pm. Admission charge. Several other historic sites are worth visiting if time permits. The gardens of the ***William Paca House:** daily 10 am-4 pm. Admission charge. Enter via 1 Martin Street. Nearby **Eastport** is also of interest. This community is devoted to fishing and boating. Hundreds of boats, large and small, both sailing and power, are moored along its docks. It is across the Compromise Street Bridge.

**London Town,** overlooking the South River, once was a busy Colonial port of entry; today it is undergoing restoration. Visitors can go into the 1745 Publick House, the log barn, and other outbuildings, and stroll through the eight acres of restored gardens—probably the showiest in the Annapolis area—which include a spring walk, azalea glade, wildflower walk, and winter garden. Daily 10 am-5 pm. Admission fee. To reach London Town, go south on Route 2 to Edgewater, left at the traffic light on Route 253, then one mile to London Town Road.

**Restaurants:** Annapolis has a number of excellent eating places with the expected emphasis on seafood. Middletown Tavern on Market Space has a Colonial atmosphere and a sidewalk café. Harbour House, at dockside, specializes in seafood dishes. The 18th-century Maryland Inn, at Church Circle, offers French and continental cuisine in the Treaty of Paris Room; jazz groups play in the King of France Tavern. The Penthouse in the Hilton, facing the harbor, affords a fine view of the waterfront with your dining. Busch's Chesapeake Inn, on Route 50 near the Bay Bridge, is very popular and specializes in seafood; during the summer months, you may have to wait in line to get in. Whitehall Inn, also on Route 50, offers family-style meals.

# Baltimore, Md

Baltimore, founded in 1729, soon will celebrate its 250th anniversary. Its diverse historic monuments, outstanding art museums, and interesting shops offer a variety of choices for the visitor. The city is accessible by I-95; take the Caton Avenue Exit, go left on Wilkens Avenue, and then east into downtown Baltimore.

At some point during your tour, stop at the **Visitors Center,** 102 St. Paul Street, between Lexington and Fayette Streets, for maps and information. It is probably more convenient to first make some other stops on the center's suggested tour along the "Star Spangled Banner Trail." This tour includes about 15 attractions that could take from a few minutes to an hour each to visit.

As you enter the city at Wilkens Avenue, you come to the first of these attractions. A short distance to the right, on Monroe Street, is **Mt. Clare** in Carroll Park. Built during 1754-60, it is the oldest house in Baltimore, and was the home of Charles Carroll, a Revolutionary War patriot. It is a beautifully furnished and important example of Georgian architecture. Tuesday-Saturday 11 am-4:30 pm; Sunday 2 pm-4:30 pm. Admission fee.

Go back up Monroe Street, then right on Pratt Street to Poppleton Street, location of the Mt. Clare Station (America's first railroad station, 1830) and the **Baltimore and Ohio Transportation Museum.** This museum houses the world's largest collection of railroad cars, locomotives, models, and replicas, dating back to 1829. Wednesday-Sunday 10 am-4 pm.

Proceed east on Pratt Street, right on Light Street, and left on Key Highway, to **Fort McHenry.** En route you pass Federal Hill, a fine vantage point for a view of downtown Baltimore and the Inner Harbor. Fort McHenry, Baltimore's best-known shrine, is the birthplace of the U.S. national anthem. The fort, built in 1776, withstood a British bombardment in 1814 during which Francis Scott Key watched the bombs falling and saw the flag still flying "by the dawn's early light." Today, Ft. McHenry is operated by the National Park Service. Visitors can stroll around the star-shaped fortifications, visit the powder magazine, officers' quarters, and barracks. A 15-minute film in the visitors center depicts the history of the fort and the story of the "Star Spangled Banner." Daily 9 am-5 pm. Admission fee. Ample free parking.

Return to Key Highway, which becomes Calvert Street. Find a convenient parking space between Fayette and Lexington Streets, and walk one block to the **Visitors Center** at 102 St. Paul Street, where you will find maps and information. While in the area, stop at the **Battle Monument** at Calvert and Fayette Streets. This was erected about 1820 as a memorial to those who fell defending Baltimore during the War of 1812. On the Court House steps is a statue of Cecilius Calvert, founder of Maryland.

Nearby, at Holliday and Lexington Streets, is the **Peale Museum,** erected by artist Rembrandt Peale in 1814, now the oldest museum in the nation. On display is a large collection of prints, paintings, photographs, and memorabilia connected with Baltimore's history; there are also many fine paintings by members of the Peale family. Tuesday-Saturday 10:30 am-4:30 pm; Sunday 1:30 pm-5:30 pm.

Continue east on Fayette Street, past the Shot Tower, then right on Front and Albemarle Streets to Lombard Street. Park your car to visit three historic sites nearby. The **Shot Tower** was built in 1829 for production of gun shot. Molten lead was poured through a sieve at the top of the tower and hardened into round pellets when it fell into the tank of water below. **Carroll Mansion,** at Front and Lombard Streets, was built in 1815 by Charles Carroll, one of the signers of the Declaration of Independence. It has been restored as a public museum. Tuesday-Friday 10:30 am-4:30 pm; Sunday 1-5 pm.The **Flag House,** a block south at Pratt and Albemarle Streets, was the home of Mary Pickersgill who made the huge flag that flew over Fort McHenry and inspired Key to write the national anthem. The house has many original furnishings and relics of the War of 1812. An adjacent museum contains memorabilia of that war. Both buildings open Tuesday-Saturday 10 am-4:30 pm; Sunday 2 pm-5 pm. Admission fee includes both sites.

Turn right on Pratt Street and drive several blocks to the **USF Constellation,** at Constellation Pier. Built in 1797, this was the first ship of the U.S. Navy. It saw duty through World War II, when it served briefly as a flagship for Admiral E. J. King at Newport, Rhode Island. Daily 10 am-4 pm; Sunday noon-5 pm. Admission fee.

One of the city's two outstanding art museums, the **Walters Art Gallery** at Charles and Centre Streets, is north of the downtown area. Drive west on Pratt Street to Charles Street, then north to Monument Street. Try to park in the vicinity of the Washington Monument. The Walters is a splendid private collection that includes not only outstanding paintings but also the art and artifacts of many civilizations. Tuesday-Saturday 11 am-5 pm; Monday 1:30 pm-5 pm; Sunday and holidays 2 pm-5 pm. Tio Pepe (the Baltimore branch of the popular Spanish restaurant in Georgetown), around the corner at 10 E. Franklin Street, is a good place for lunch. For something less expensive, try the cafeteria across the street in the Peabody Institute.

**The Washington Monument,** designed by Robert Mills, was completed in 1842. The Historical Information Center at the base is open all year Friday-Tuesday 10:30 am-4 pm. Two blocks west, at 201 W. Monument Street, is the headquarters of the **Maryland Historical Society** where a large collection of manuscripts, paintings, silver, china, costumes, and artifacts on Maryland history is displayed. There are also several period rooms. The original manuscript of "The Star-Spangled Banner" can be seen here. Monday-Friday 9 am-5 pm; Saturday 9 am-1 pm.

If you have an interest in art, you will also want to visit the **Baltimore Museum of Art,** north on Charles Street, at 33rd Street. Its large collection ranges from old masters to contemporary art, and it is especially known for the Cone Collection of distinguished French Impressionist and post-Impressionist paintings. It has a Maryland Wing of reconstructed period rooms. Tuesday-Friday 11 am-5 pm; Saturday 10:30 am-5 pm; Sunday 1 pm-5 pm.

Another interesting place to visit is the **Lexington Market.** Go west on Monument Street and left on Eutaw Street, five blocks to the market on the right. This huge market, covering two city blocks, offers a variety of produce, prepared food, cheese, meat, seafood, and baked goods, including an in-

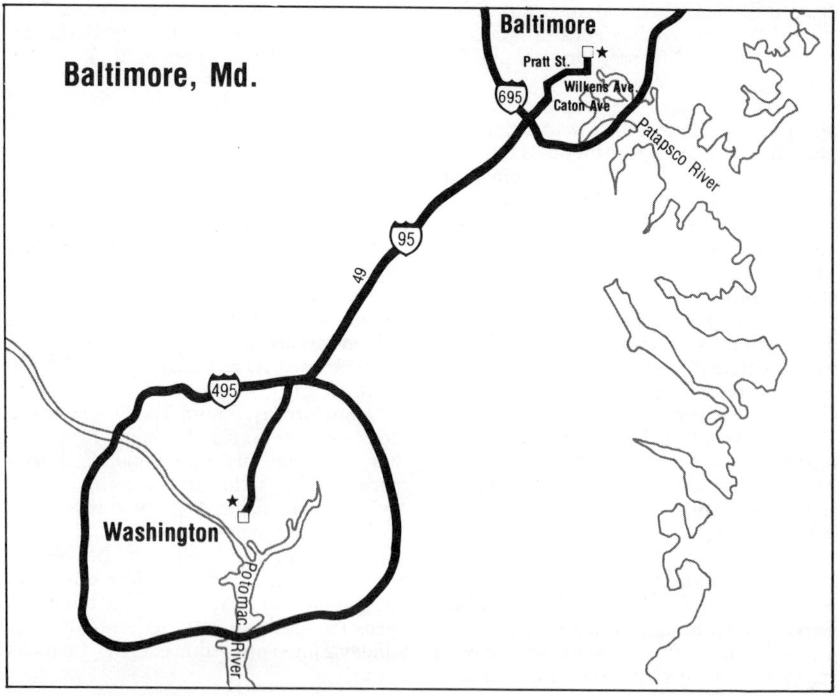

teresting variety of ethnic foods. If you are there at lunchtime, the market offers a good selection of carry-out sandwiches and fresh oysters shucked while you wait. It is one of the oldest and largest markets in the nation. Open weekdays. Public parking garage under the market.

Antique collectors may wish to visit the city's largest concentration of antique shops along Charles Street, above Saratoga, in the 200 and 300 blocks. These shops are open weekdays, usually 9 am-5 pm.

**Restaurants:** Baltimore is known for its steamed hard-shell crabs seasoned with pepper. Gordon's of Orleans Street, Orleans Street and Patterson Park Avenue, and O'Brycki's Crab House, 1729 E. Pratt Street, are two places where you can eat crabs the way the locals do—piled high on paper-covered tables, and accompanied by pitchers of beer. Thompson's Sea Girt House, 5919 York Road at Belvedere Avenue, is the place to go for good crab cakes. For a fine, but more expensive, seafood dinner try The Chesapeake, 1701 N. Charles Street. If you like Italian food, head for Baltimore's Little Italy on the waterfront where you'll find many authentic trattorias including Velleggia's, 204 S. High Street; Chiapparelli's, 237 S. High Street; and Sabatino's, 901 Fawn Street. Baltimore is also reported to have the best Jewish delicatessens south of New York. At Jack's or Attman's, 1150 and 1019 E. Lombard Street respectively, you can get carry-out sandwiches or eat on the premises. If you're interested in European cuisine, try Haussner's, 3244 Eastern Avenue, where you can admire the impressive art collection in the dining room.

## Eastern Shore, Md

The lure of Maryland's famed Eastern Shore lies in its historic towns and villages, wildlife refuges, sport fishing, and the meandering tidal rivers, salt marshes, and ponds. Although it embraces over 600 miles of shoreline, you can easily sample the Eastern Shore in a one-day trip. Take Route 50 east, and in about an hour you are on the far side of the Chesapeake Bay Bridge.

First, stop at the tiny village of ***Wye,** on Route 662. Here you can see the 450-year-old **Wye Oak,** Maryland's State Tree, and the restored 1672 ***Wye Mill,** where you can buy water-ground meal and flour. The mill operates during the summer months. The old **Wye Church,** built in 1721, is one of America's oldest Episcopal Churches. Of special interest are the high box pews, the hanging pulpit, and the silver communion service. It is open Thursday and Friday 3 pm-5 pm; Saturday 11 am-5 pm; Sunday 2 pm-5 pm. Services are held on Sunday at 11 am. Farther along Route 662 is the **Talbot County Wildlife Refuge** where you can see thousands of wildfowl. In the same area is a 19th-century "little red schoolhouse," now a museum open to the public. There is no admission fee for any of the sites in and near Wye.

Next head for **Easton,** off Route 50. A convenient stopping place is near the ***Historical Society House** at 30 S. Washington Street. This impressive Federal building contains exhibits on local history. It is open Tuesday and Friday 10 am-4 pm; summer also Saturday 10 am-4 pm and Sunday 1-4 pm. Admission fee. Two blocks away, at South and Harrison Streets, is the **Academy of Arts,** housed in a 19th-century schoolhouse. In addition to the permanent collection, works of local artists are displayed. Monday-Friday 1 pm-4 pm; summer Monday and Thursday only. There are special shows on many weekends.

At Harrison and Dover Streets is one of Easton's most elegant and oldest homes, the **Bullitt House,** built in 1790. It is not open to the public. We suggest lunch or dinner at the nearby Tidewater Inn.

Leaving Easton, proceed south on Washington Street to the **Third Haven Meeting House,** built in 1682. William Penn preached here. In Colonial days, people came to services by boat, up the Tred Avon River. Contact custodian on the grounds for admission. A donation is suggested after the tour.

Turn around, go north into the center of town and west on Route 33, nine miles to **St. Michaels,** a village almost surrounded by water. The harbor is filled with boats belonging to oystermen, crabbers, fishermen, clammers, and yachtsmen. The main attraction (in addition to the magnificent scenery) is the **Chesapeake Bay Maritime**

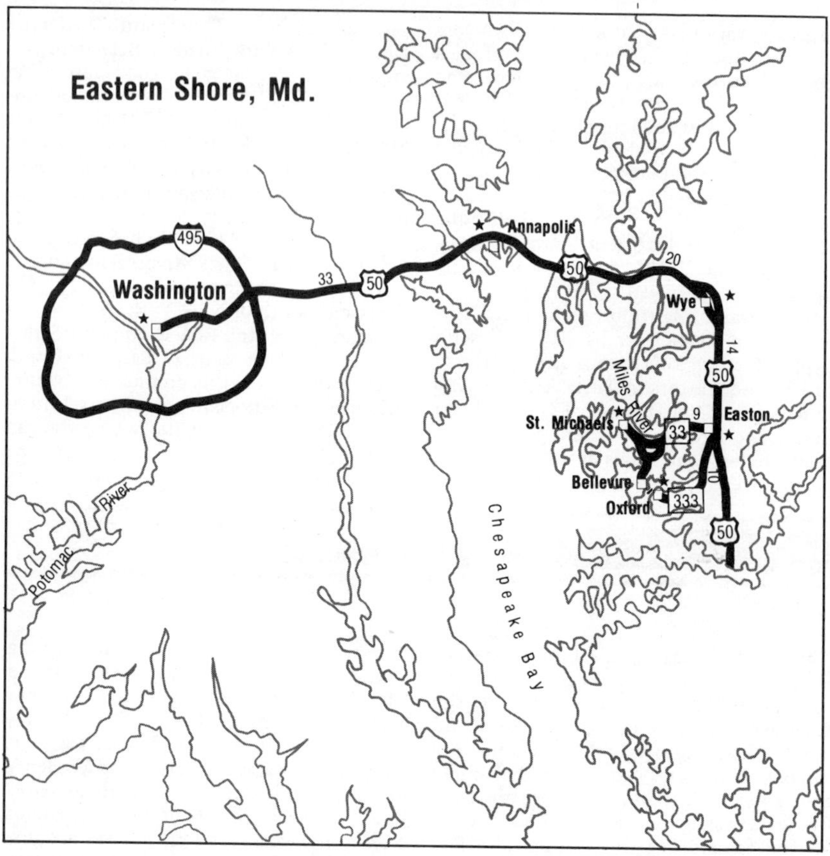


**Museum,** which has exhibits of bay memorabilia of today and yesterday, a lighthouse, lightship, and historic vessels of all sorts moored at the dock. Tuesday-Sunday 11 am-4 pm; summer 10 am-5 pm.

If time permits, take a 1½-hour historic and scenic cruise of the bay aboard "The Patriot." The boat leaves from the museum pier at 11 am, 1 pm, and 3 pm daily. For a seafood lunch, we suggest the Crab Claw Restaurant near the museum.

Take a short walk around St. Mary's Square and the Green after your museum tour. Many of the homes date from the 17th and 18th centuries. The **St. Mary's Square Museum** offers local historical exhibits. It is open April-September, Friday, Saturday, and Sunday 9 am-4 pm; other times by appointment. Small admission fee.

If time permits, try to include **Oxford** in your itinerary. An interesting and direct route is south to Bellevue and the Tred Avon Ferry (believed to be the oldest ferry in the nation) right into Oxford. Oxford was a major port of entry in Colonial times, and today is the home base for watermen who harvest the bay's seafood bounty.

The **Oxford Museum,** next to Town Hall, is open Friday, Saturday, and Sunday 2 pm-5 pm; other times by appointment. The ***Robert Morris Inn** was once the home of the financier of the American Revolution. **Applegarth's Marine Yard,** on Morris Street, still builds bay skipjacks, the traditional oystering boat. Oxford has a monument to ***Tench Tilghman,** the Revolutionary War general and aide-de-camp to General Washington, who carried the message of Cornwallis's surrender to the Continental Congress in Philadelphia. **Grapevine House,** near the center of town, is named for the huge grapevine planted there in 1810 by Captain William Willis and still flourishing.

The route home is east on Route 333, then north on Route 50.

# Southern Md

The tri-county Southern Maryland area is bounded by the Potomac River and Chesapeake Bay, and bisected by the Patuxent River. It has a rich heritage beginning with the founding of the colony in 1634. Because of its rural character, it is attractive to those interested in outdoor recreation, especially fishing, swimming, boating, hunting, and camping. There are state parks, tobacco auctions, an Amish market, and sites associated with conflicts from the Revolutionary War to the Civil War. The best way to see this region is to divide it into one-day trips to each county.

## Trip one—Calvert County

Lying between the Patuxent River and the bay, Calvert County is accessible from Route 4, which extends for almost 60 miles from the Beltway (Route 495) to Solomons Island. **Chesapeake** and **North Beaches,** together with a half-dozen smaller, privately operated, nearby beaches on the bay are the closest ones to the District. These are all popular places for fishing, swimming, and seafood; they can be approached from Routes 2 and 260.

You may want to make a brief stop at Sunderland, where Routes 4 and 2 join, to visit ***All Saints Episcopal Church.** Built in 1774, its unique Flemish bond brick walls, paneling, and Colonial footstools and pews are still intact. Always open.

**Calvert Cliffs,** 22 miles south, is at the end of a side road that begins three miles past St. Leonards. The cliffs along the bay in this area contain fossils of the Miocene Age that are somewhere around 10 to 25 million years old. A Baltimore Gas and Electric

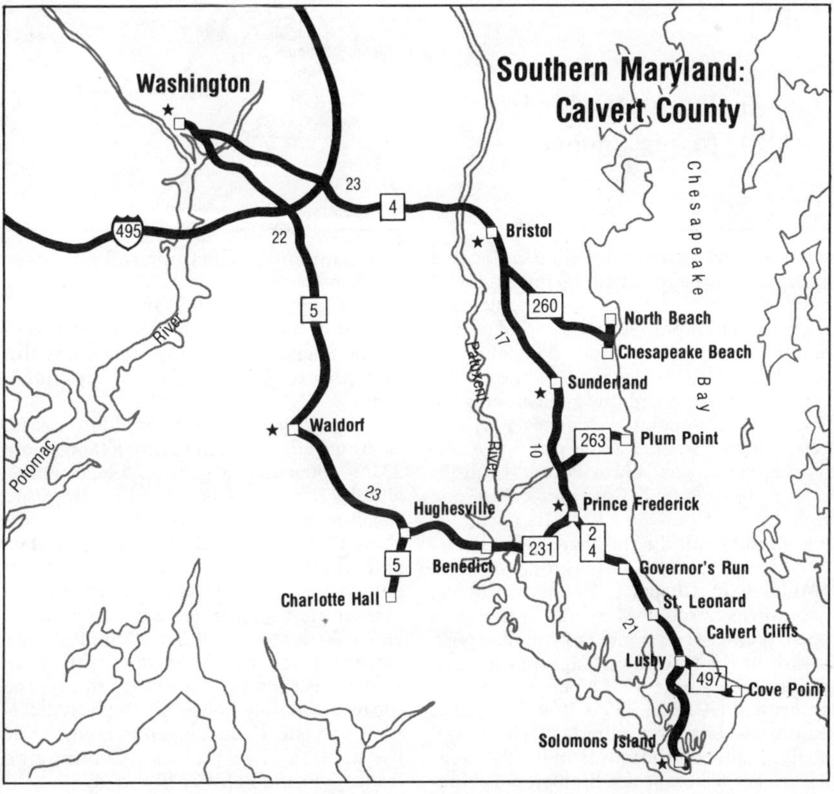

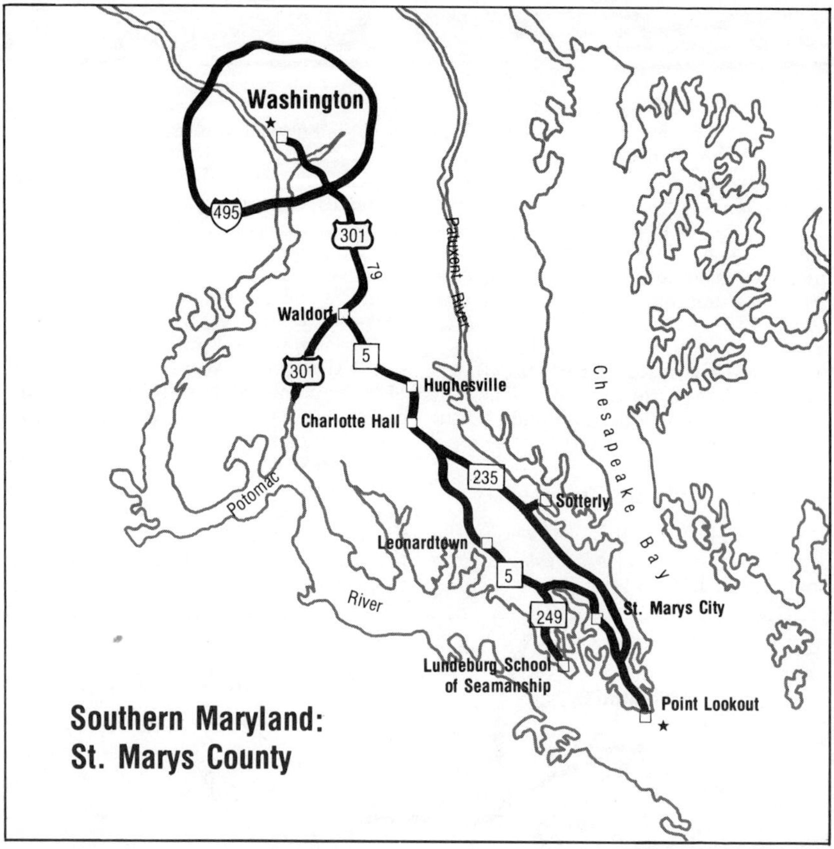


nuclear power-generating plant is located at the end of the road, and its museum and overlook are open to the public Tuesday-Friday 10 am-3 pm; Saturday, Sunday, and holidays 10 am-6 pm. Since the state park at Calvert Cliffs is not open to the public yet, fossil hunters can find good pickings at two privately-operated beaches north of here, which also offer a first-rate opportunity for swimming: **Plum Point,** six miles east of Route 4, and **Governor's Run,** one mile east on Route 509. Both are open during summer months and charge admission.

Return to Route 4 and continue to Lusby. ***Middleham Chapel** (1748) is the oldest cruciform church in Maryland. It is always open. If you are a camera fan you may wish to stop at the **Cove Point Lighthouse** three miles down Route 497. Open only by appointment (301-326-3257). Route 4 ends at Solomons Island, a popular fishing and boating center at the mouth of the Patuxent River. The **Chesapeake Biological Laboratory** maintains an aquarium and exhibits of plant and animal life of the Chesapeake Bay area. Monday-Friday 9 am-5 pm; June-August also on Saturday. The **Calvert Historical Society's Maritime Museum** is also located here. Saturday and Sunday 1 pm-5 pm.

For the return trip, stay on Route 4 as far as Prince Frederick, then turn left on Route 231 to **Benedict,** a fishing village with a well-known crab house, The Pier. If you are traveling on a Wednesday or Saturday you should visit the **Charlotte Hall Farm Market,** which offers produce and foods from Amish farms, antique stalls, and a flea market that's great for bargain hunters. Open Wednesday and Saturday mornings. To get there turn left on Route 5 to Hughesville, and go four miles south. The **tobacco auction** house at Hughesville is worth a visit if you happen to go by while the auction is in progress. Continue on Route 5 to the Beltway (Route 495).

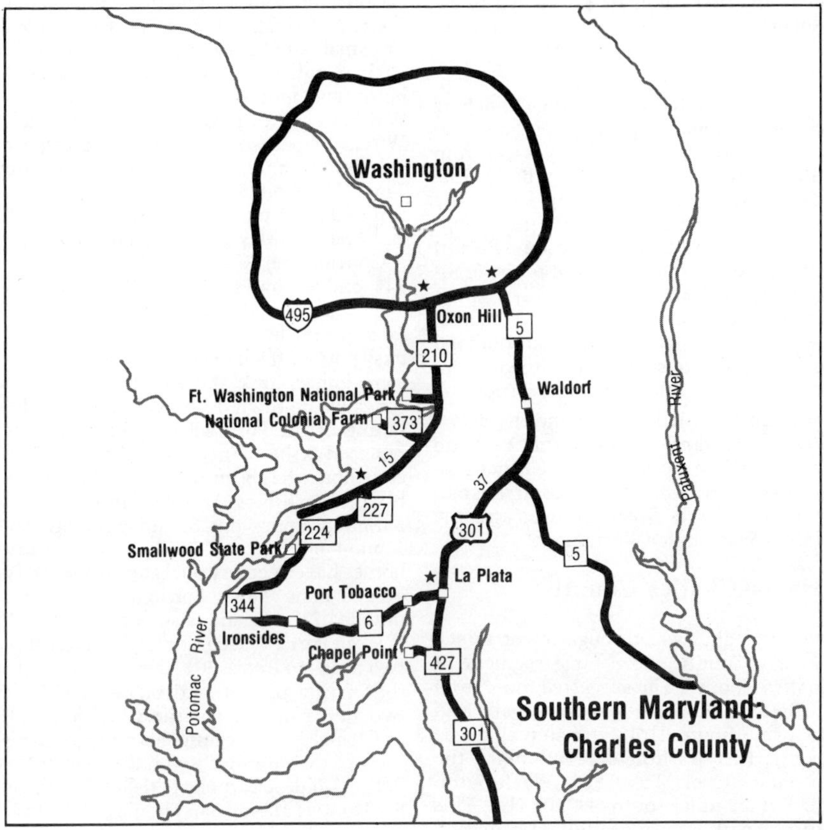


## Trip 2—St. Marys County

This county, in the heart of Southern Maryland, is accessible by Route 5. The round trip is about 165 miles. First stop can be Hughesville, if **tobacco auctions** are underway, or the **Charlotte Hall Farmers Market,** if it's market day. Both are described in the Calvert County trip above.

Healing properties were attributed to the waters of "Ye Coole Springs of Saint Maries" at **Charlotte Hall,** which was the site of the first sanitorium in the colonies. Turn right at the sign into the Charlotte Hall School grounds, then left to the white pillars. You can sample the water and get a free brochure from the school custodian describing the springs.

Bear left onto Route 235, then left on Route 245 for a visit to ***Sotterly,** a working Colonial plantation, built around 1725. The mansion, of exceptional architectural interest, is decorated with Colonial period furnishings. There is a farm museum and a gift shop on the grounds. June-October 11 am-5 pm. Admission fee.

Continue on Route 235 to **Point Lookout** where the Potomac River meets the bay. This state park is open year round, but is particularly popular during the summer when swimming, fishing, boating, picnicking, and hiking are in full swing. The Confederate Monument commemorates over 3,300 prisoners of war who died here during the Civil War.

Turn back toward Washington on Route 5. You can see the **Tulip Disaster Monument and Cemetery** from the highway. The USS Tulip, a federal gunboat, blew up near here in 1864; its crew is buried in the cemetery. ***St. Marys City,** founded in 1634, served as the Colonial capital of Maryland until 1695. Visit the replica of the original State House. Daily 9 am-5 pm; closed Monday. The Calvert Monument in nearby Trinity Churchyard marks the spot where the first colonists assembled to establish a government. Note also the Freedom of Conscience Monument.

If you are traveling on Sunday, a seven-mile detour on Route 249 to the **Lundeberg School of Seamanship** will give you an opportunity to see all sorts of vessels from sailboats to a 257-foot yacht, the *Dauntless.* Closed to the public the rest of the week. **Tudor Hall,** on Route 5 near Leonardtown, overlooks picturesque Breton Bay. The estate once belonged to the Francis Scott Key family. Tours daily 9 am-5 pm; closed Monday. Admission charge. Keep your eyes open for the quaint old jail near the courthouse in Leonardtown. Continue on Route 5 back to the District.

**Restaurants:** We recommend the Belvedere Restaurant at Lexington Park on Route 5. Closer to home, three other possibilites in Waldorf are: Waldorf Restaurant, Ben Davis Steak House, and the Martha Washington Restaurant.

## Trip 3—Charles County

This trip takes you through lower Prince Georges County and a large segment of Charles County. The suggested route from the Beltway (Route 495) is out Indian Head Highway (Route 210). First stop could be historic **Fort Washington** overlooking the Potomac River. Take Fort Washington Road, three miles south of Oxon Hill. This military park is open year round. Summer, free tours daily; otherwise weekends only. (See Chapter 5.)

***National Colonial Farm,** an 18th-century freeholders farm, is at the end of Route 373 (Bryans Point Road). May 31-Labor Day 10 am-5 pm. Admission charge. (See Chapter 8.)

Continue south on Route 210, left on Route 227, right on Route 224, seven miles to ***Smallwood State Park** (see Chapter 7). Visit **Smallwood Retreat,** the restored home and grounds of the Revolutionary War hero and early governor of Maryland, William Smallwood. You can also inspect the garden and stroll down the Nature Trail. Mansion tours May 30-Labor Day daily 10 am-6 pm; Labor Day-December 1 and March 1-May 30 weekends only.

Continue on Route 224, left into Route 344, and left on Route 6 to ***Port Tobacco.** This was originally an Indian village ruled by a queen. In Colonial days it became a busy port with wharves, warehouses, a customs house, inns, and a hotel. As the fortunes of the town declined because of the silting of the Port Tobacco River, it was replaced as the county seat by La Plata. The courthouse has been restored and contains historic exhibits. Wednesday-Friday 10 am-noon, 1 pm-4 pm; Saturday and Sunday 1 pm-4 pm. Several nearby 18th-century homes have been restored and are privately owned. The **Town Springhouse,** in the middle of the square, also is restored.

From Port Tobacco, continue on Route 6, two miles to Route 301, then Route 5 into the District, or turn south on Route 427, for two more stops. **St. Ignatius Church** (1798), at Chapel Point, commands a magnificent view of the Potomac River. It is one of the nation's oldest Catholic parishes. Nearby is **St. Thomas Manor,** early home of Jesuits in America.

**Restaurants:** If you are interested in a Maryland seafood dinner, turn south seven miles to Pope's Creek. Take Route 427 to Route 301, right to Faulkner, then right three miles to the end of the road. You will find good eating at either Captain Drink's or Robinson's crab houses.

# Frederick, Md and Gettysburg, Pa

Frederick is best known as the home of Francis Scott Key, author of our national anthem, and Barbara Fritchie, legendary heroine of John Greenleaf Whittier's patriotic poem, but its historic associations date back to the American Revolution. The town is only 30 minutes from the Beltway (Route 495), via Route 270 (70S). You can also get to Frederick by Greyhound bus. Make your first stop the **Visitors Information Center,** which you reach by going north on Route 15 to the Rosemont Avenue Exit. They suggest a walking tour of the historic downtown section and a motor tour of outlying points of interest, and have maps and literature about the area. The people at the center also will give you directions to the Municipal Parking Lot on S. Court Street.

The walking tour is about two miles, but

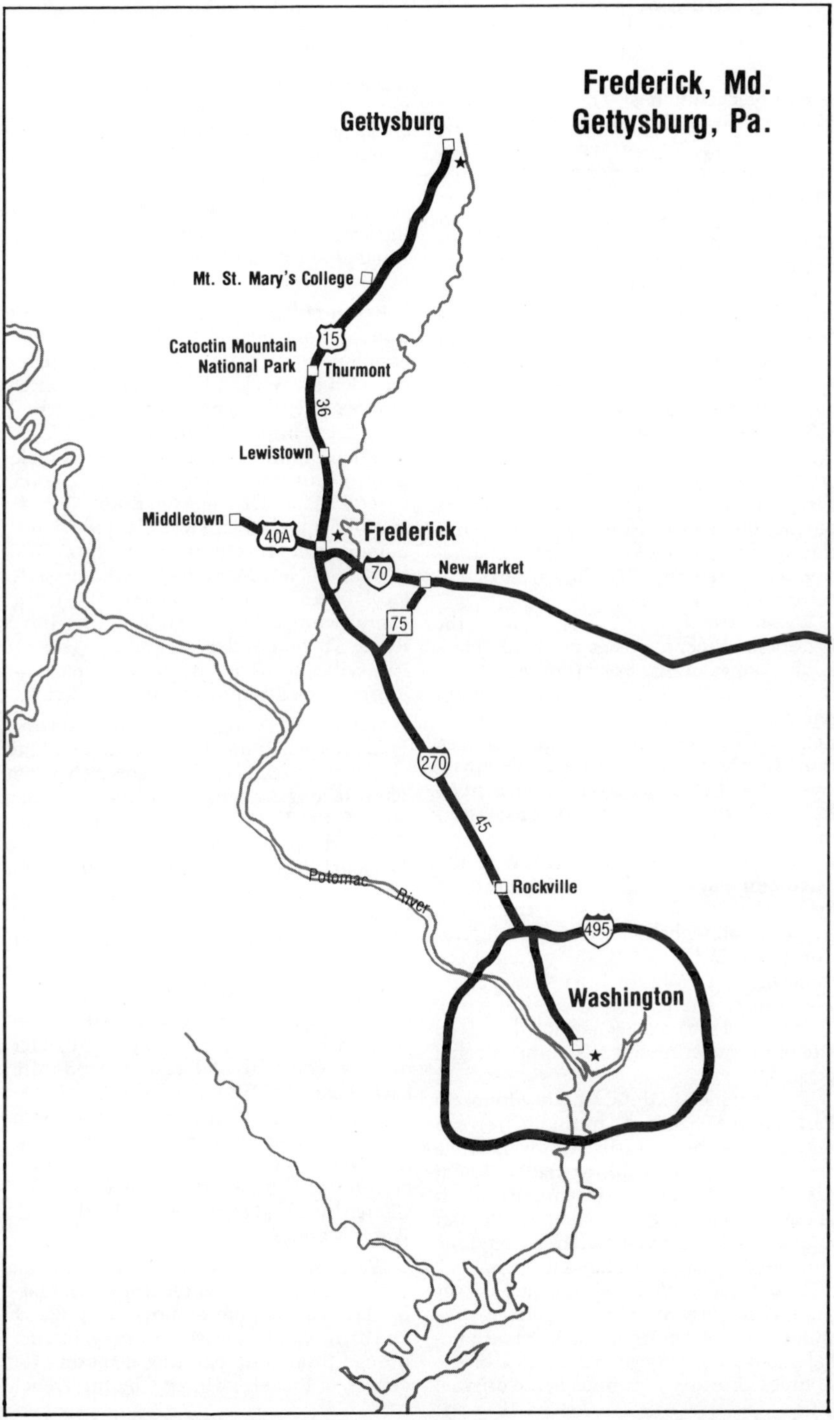
Frederick, Md.
Gettysburg, Pa.
Gettysburg
Mt. St. Mary's College
15
Catoctin Mountain
National Park
Thurmont
36
Lewistown
Middletown
40A
Frederick
70
New Market
75
270
45
Potomac River
Rockville
495
Washington

can be shortened by going west on 2nd Street instead of on 3rd Street. **Court House Square** is a must. As you approach W. Church Street, you can see the spires of three noted churches. These are usually open to visitors during the day, unless a service is in progress. You can only admire the architecture of most of the other buildings on the walking tour since they are largely occupied by offices or businesses. The **Roger Taney House and Francis Scott Key Museum** is at 123 S. Bentz Street, near the end of the tour. May-September weekends only. Admission fee. The **Barbara Fritchie House,** at 154 W. Patrick Street, combines a restored home, museum, and gift shop. March-December daily 9 am-5 pm. Admission fee.

You will have to drive to see the ***Hessian Barracks.** Go out S. Market Street, left one block on Madison Street to reach the barracks that housed Hessian prisoners during the Revolution. You can stroll through the grounds and watch the restoration in progress. In 1976 the barracks will be opened to the public.

We suggest that you visit some of the historic and scenic places in nearby Frederick County during your tour, especially those north on Route 15. If you're interested in covered bridges, there are three right in this area. One is a short distance from Lewistown on Old Frederick Road; another is three miles east of Thurmont on Route 77; the third is a mile past Thurmont, east of Route 15.

During the Revolutionary War the ***Catoctin Furnace,** three miles north of Lewistown, off Route 15 on Utica Road, supplied cannonballs used in the siege of Yorktown. In the 1860s, the plates of the ironclad ship "Monitor" were cast here. The furnace site is open at all times. The casting shed is being reconstructed, and the site of the superintendent's home is being cleared.

The entrance to the **Catoctin Mountain Park** is at the far side of Thurmont. You can take a scenic mountain drive or walk along any of the nature or hiking trails. Stop at the Visitors Center and Museum to find out about weekend programs, such as folk-craft demonstrations, that are offered from June through August. (See Chapter 7.)

Two noted Catholic shrines are on the grounds of **Mt. St. Marys College,** five miles north of Thurmont. On a mountainside above the college is a replica of the Lourdes Grotto. On campus is the original 1750 stone house of Elizabeth Ann Seton, who founded the Sisters of Charity. Both are accessible at all times.

If antique shops interest you, **New Market** is the place to visit. Thirty-one shops are located in this village near the intersection of Routes 75 and 70 (see Chapter 10).

Five miles beyond Frederick on Route 40-A is picturesque **Middletown,** noted for its neat Victorian homes and the many small produce stands and markets operated by local farmers.

**Restaurants:** Dandee Restaurant, a few miles out of Frederick on Route 40, is very popular, moderately priced, and usually crowded on weekends. It offers a limited number of entrees, but servings are generous. Cozy Inn in Thurmont offers good Maryland home cooking. The Shamrock, also in Thurmont, specializes in seafood. Peter Pan, at Urbana, on Route 355, is another popular, moderately priced restaurant with a limited menu. Mealey's Restaurant, in New Market, serves home-style local dishes. Gabriel's, in Ijamsville, offers a multicourse French style dinner (take Route 70 four miles east, then right on Ijamsville Road). Masser's Restaurant, on Route 40, is 2½ miles west of Frederick.

**Gettysburg** is only 36 miles north of Frederick on Route 15. You can combine the two in a one-day trip., especially when days are long. You may only have time for a tour of the **Gettysburg National Military Park,** which is under jurisdiction of the National Park Service. Don't worry if you have to resist the temptation to visit a dozen or more commercial "attractions" that beckon the visitor; the park is the best part.

Using the services of a licensed battlefield guide, who will go with you in your car, is a good idea, or you might prefer to park your car and take the 35-mile Battlefield Bus Tour. Of course, you can tour the battlefield at your own pace with the help of a map and brochure available at the Visitor Center. There is also a free, guided one-hour walking tour to General George Meade's Headquarters and the High Water Mark.

We suggest that you first spend some time at the Visitor Center. Take advantage of the free accurate audiovisual program and battle exhibits. Also see the cyclorama, a huge panoramic painting depicting the climax of Pickett's Charge, by the French artist Paul Philippoteaux.

Gettysburg is a very popular tourist attraction, especially in summer and on weekends and holidays. You may experience delays in getting into various places, especially restaurants, and you may encounter traffic problems. There are a great many restaurants in town that cater to tourists. These are listed in a free brochure, "This is Gettysburg," available from the Gettysburg Travel Council, Carlisle Street, Gettysburg, PA 17325.

# Charlottesville, Va

The principal attractions in this area are the homes of two noted Presidents (Thomas Jefferson's Monticello and James Monroe's Ash Lawn) and the University of Virginia, designed by Jefferson. The round-trip distance is about 240 miles, approximately five hours driving time on good roads. The best route is south on Route 66 to Route 29. Continental Trailways offers frequent bus service to Charlottesville from its terminal at 12th Street and New York Avenue NW. Plan on using a taxicab to get around if you go by bus.

Jefferson not only designed the **University of Virginia,** he also planned the curriculum and hired the faculty. Your first stop can be the Rotunda, a white-domed building visible to the right off Main Street. Jefferson adapted the design from the Pantheon and the building was first used as

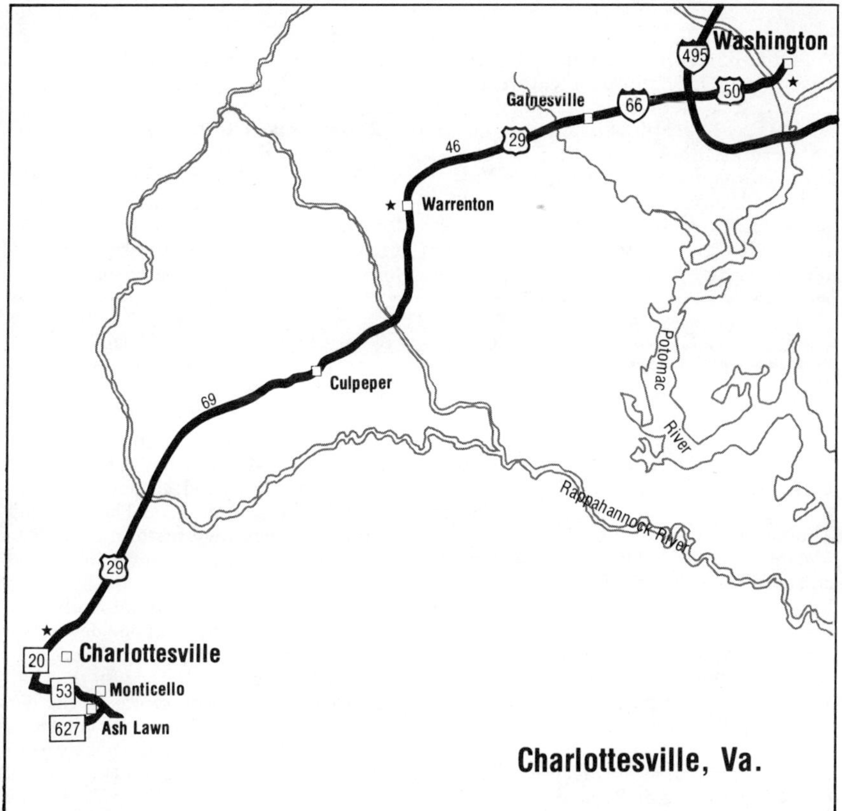

a banquet hall to honor Lafayette during his visit in 1824. From the Rotunda there is an impressive view of the lawn, a long mall lined on either side by white-columned professors' houses and some student quarters. Gracefully undulating red brick walls, the "Serpentine Walls," separate the faculty homes from other student residences. These walls are only one brick thick, but the winding design provides the necessary strength. Student-led tours from the Rotunda, through the school year daily 9:30 am-1 pm, 2 pm-5 pm; summer months weekdays only.

The **Albemarle County Court House,** built in 1803, is on Court Square. Daily 9 am-5 pm; closed Sundays and holidays. Jefferson's will can be seen in the **County Office Building** nearby.

***Monticello** was built on a leveled mountain top, 857 feet above sea level. Construction continued for over 35 years because of Jefferson's many alterations in his original design. A classic example of early American architecture, Monticello contains 35 rooms, including 12 in the basement. The dominant feature is the dome, which is over an octagonal room. Visitors see a wealth of inventions and architectural innovations that developed from Jefferson's fertile imagination—all explained during the conducted tour. The outbuildings are all located below long terraces adjacent to the main building—a unique feature. The flowers, vegetable gardens, trees, and shrubbery are very much as they were when Jefferson retired from public life to enjoy his estate. He died at Monticello in 1826 and is buried in the family graveyard. It is in a secluded spot on the mountainside, a short distance from the end of the lawn. On your grounds tour you can visit the icehouse, carriage house, stables, servants' quarters, dairy, smokehouse, kitchen, weaver's cottage, and gift shop. March 1-October 31 daily 8 am-5 pm; November 1-February 28 daily 9 am-4:30 pm. Admission fee.

***Ash Lawn,** James Monroe's home, is two miles beyond Monticello. Designed by Jefferson, this charming plantation has a magnificent boxwood garden, but it is much smaller and less pretentious than Monticello. Daily 8 am-5 pm. Admission fee.

You pass **Michie Tavern and Museum** on the road back to Charlottesville. This tavern was a favorite stopping place for travelers, and visitors today can admire the beamed, paneled rooms and the Colonial furniture and china, which look much as they did in the 18th century. Daily 9 am-5 pm. Admission fee.

**Restaurants:** The Tavern, in a 200-year-old converted log slave house, serves Southern-style luncheons 11:30 am-3 pm. In town, the Boar's Head Inn specializes in Southern-style meals. You will find more varied menus at Holiday Inn, Howard Johnson's, and Thomas Jefferson Inn.

# Fredericksburg, Va

Fredericksburg is rich in shrines of the Colonial and Revolutionary periods, and was the scene of major Civil War battles. Important figures in the town's history include Thomas Jefferson, James Madison, John Marshall, Patrick Henry, James Monroe, and John Paul Jones. The Washington family had many close associations with the town. The noted naval scientist, Matthew Fontaine Maury also lived here. Fredericksburg is barely an hour's drive from Washington along the new I-95, and Continental Trailways supplies bus service to the town.

Begin your tour at the **Fredericksburg Information Center** at Bypass Route 1 and Princess Anne Street (take the first exit to the town as you approach on I-95). Here you can get tickets for free parking, $500 in Confederate bills, and free literature on tourist attractions and accommodations, including a free tour map. Plan to walk around the downtown historic area, or to follow the green arrows and historic tour signs as you drive. There are 22 suggested stops on the route. You cannot really visit all of these historic sites in one day, so we suggest that you sample the highlights, being sure to leave some time for the Civil War battlefields and museums in the National Military Park. The travel counselor at the center can help you allocate your time. If you are planning to visit many of the attractions you should consider buying a block ticket to eight principal historic shrines for $6.26, a saving of several dollars

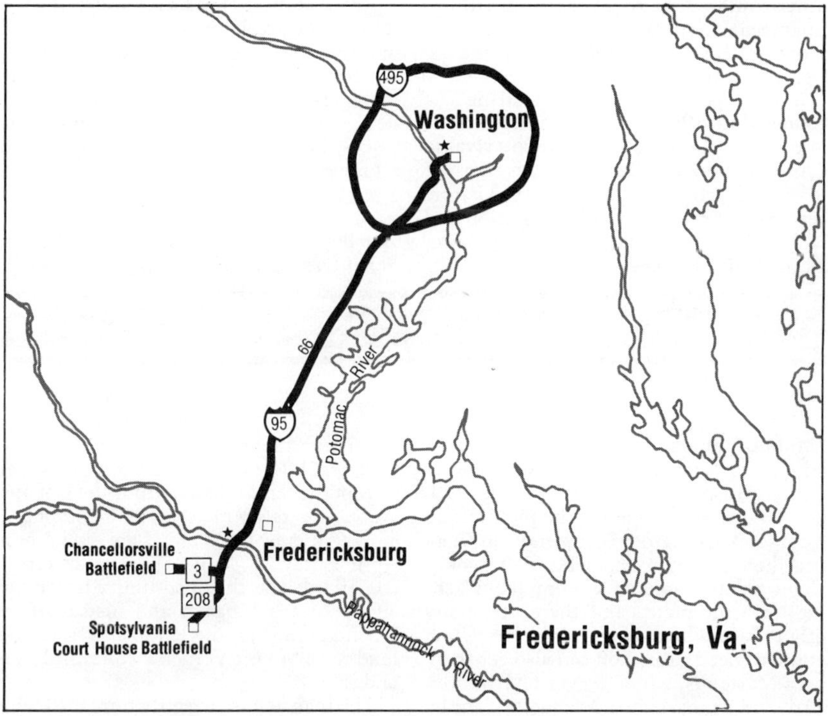


over separate admissions (children under 14 free). All of the shrines included in the tour have uniform hours; November 15-March 1 9 am-4:30 pm; March 2-November 14 until 5 pm.

We recommend that you visit the shrines and museums described below, and others if time permits, depending upon your special interests. First stop is the *__Mary Washington House__ where George Washington's mother lived from 1772 until her death in 1789. It is beautifully maintained with original furnishings and a boxwood garden in the rear. Admission charge.

The *__James Monroe Museum and Library__ contains President Monroe's furnishings, portraits, china, jewelry, and extensive library; also the desk on which he drafted the Monroe Doctrine. Admission charge.

The *__Hugh Mercer Apothecary Shop__ was founded in 1763 by Dr. Mercer, who dispensed drugs and practiced medicine. A Revolutionary War general, he died at the Battle of Princeton. Admission charge.

*__Stoner's Store and Museum__ displays over 13,000 items of merchandise typical of a large general store of the early 1800s and over 125 items of the Revolutionary War era. The gift shop sells old-fashioned candies and other nostalgic souvenirs. Admission charge.

*__Kenmore__ is a beautiful Georgian manor house, home of Colonel Fielding Lewis and his wife Betty, only sister of George Washington. Hostesses in Colonial costume take visitors on a guided tour of the house and gardens, and serve tea and gingerbread. Admission charge.

A new attraction, **Historic Fredericksburg Museum,** 619 Caroline Street, features Colonial clothing, Indian artifacts, Civil War relics, and a 19th-century children's room containing toys, furniture, and clothing. Admission charge.

The *__Fredericksburg Bicentennial Center,__ 706 Caroline Street, offers a slide presentation and picture exhibit on the town's history and the famous personalities associated with the area. Monday-Friday 8:30 am-5 pm; Saturday and Sunday 9 am-5 pm.

The **Visitors Center and Museum** of the **Fredericksburg and Spotsylvania National Military Park** is at the south end of town, on Route 1. Here you will see dioramas and other exhibits and relics that bring to life important Civil War battles. Begin your motor tour of the battlefield here, using the free guide map.

If time permits, plan on visiting the **Chancellorsville Battlefield,** 10 miles west of town on Route 3; also the **Spotsylvania Court House Battlefield,** 12 miles south of town off Route 208. Stop first at the visitors centers and museums, for orientation and maps. The military parks daily 9 am-5 pm; summer until 6 pm.

**Restaurants:** Fredericksburg has a number of excellent restaurants. In town are Princess Anne Inn (moderate prices, American food, Colonial decor), the General Washington Inn (offers a buffet each day), Kenmore Coffee Shop (moderate prices, home cooking), Palms Restaurant (Hungarian and seafood specialties), Cellar Door (an intimate place for lunch), Courtyard Mall (kosher-style food, mainly luncheons), China Garden (Chinese foods), Scheherazade Restaurant (Lebanese food).

## Mount Vernon, Va

*__Mount Vernon,__ one of America's most famous historic shrines, was the home of George Washington from 1754 until 1799. It is readily accessible via the picturesque George Washington Memorial Parkway and there is ample free parking. It is only about a half-hour's ride from the Washington Monument, and there are many other worthwhile sights nearby for which you will need a car. You can also get there by a Metrobus, which leaves hourly from 12th and Pennsylvania Avenue NW, or by the more expensive sightseeing buses (see Chapter 2). The Wilson Line excursion boat to Mount Vernon leaves from the 6th and Water Streets SW pier May 24-September 2 daily 9:30 am, 10:30 am, 2 pm, and 3 pm; April 1-May 24 2 pm only. This leisurely trip affords you the opportunity to see the sights of Washington and historic Fort Washington from the Potomac before you land near Mount Vernon's columned verandas.

The mansion is elegantly furnished with

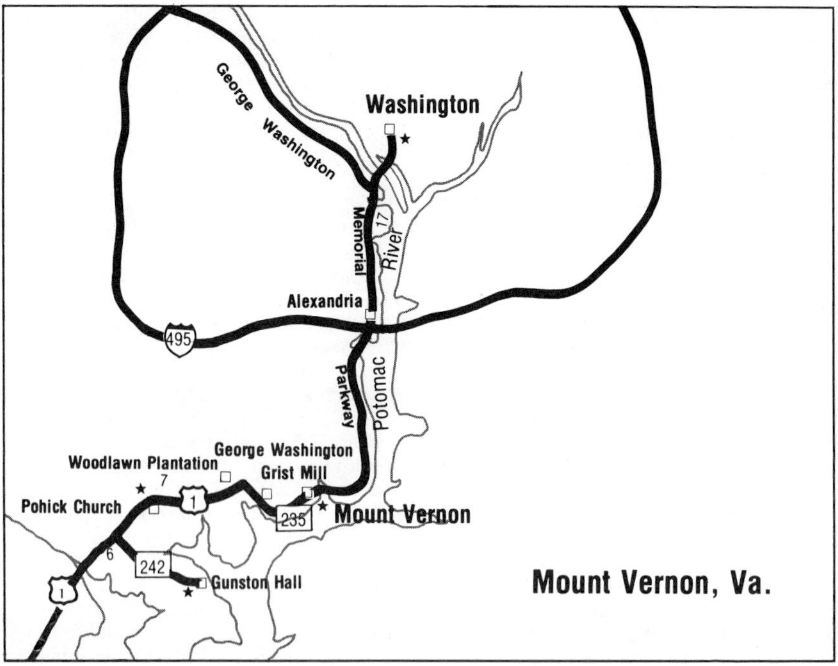

original and period pieces, and an adjacent museum contains many interesting archeological artifacts. Also close at hand are more than a dozen "dependencies"—kitchen, barn, carriage house, smokehouse, and servants' quarters. The gardens are much the same as when the Washington family strolled along the boxwood-lined paths. The Washington Tomb is nearby. March 1-October 1 daily 9 am-5 pm; October 1-March 1 only until 4 pm. Admission fee. Don't overlook the gift shop, snack bar, and Mount Vernon Inn just outside the main gate. The Mount Vernon Inn, open only for breakfast and dinner, is a good choice for a simple, well-served meal (see Chapter 9).

The **George Washington Grist Mill,** three miles west of Mount Vernon on Route 235, is open Memorial Day-Labor Day daily 10 am-6 pm. A ranger is on duty to explain the mill's history and operation. The pond, millrace, and grounds are open year-round.

Continue south on Route 1 about a half mile to **Woodlawn Plantation** on the right. This plantation was presented by George Washington as a wedding gift to his ward, Eleanor Custis, and his nephew, Major Lawrence Lewis. Woodlawn is elegantly furnished and has unusually beautiful formal gardens. There is a Touch and Try room that is delightful for children (see Chapter 8). Daily 9:30 am-4:30 pm. Admission fee.

The **Pope-Leighey House,** on the Woodlawn grounds, was designed by Frank Lloyd Wright, and moved here from Falls Church, Virginia, in 1965. This one-story home, constructed mainly of cypress, brick, and glass, is perhaps best known for its revolutionary open design that uses no walls to divide the space into separate rooms. March-October Saturday and Sunday 9:30 am-4:30 pm.

***Pohick Church,** known as "The Parish Church of Mount Vernon," was completed in 1774. George Washington and George Mason were vestrymen here. It is on Route 1, about halfway between Woodlawn and Gunston Hall, so you can stop either on your way to Gunston Hall or on your way back to Washington. Daily 9 am-5 pm.

Another worthwhile stop nearby, ***Gunston Hall,** is six miles south on Route 1, then left five-and-a-half-miles on Route 242, Gunston Hall Road. This mansion, built in 1775, was the home of George Mason, author of Virginia's Bill of Rights. It is noted for its exquisite woodwork and authentic furnishings. Be sure also to see the long boxwood allée flanked on both sides by formal gardens. For a bit of relaxation and change of scenery, we recommend that you then take a leisurely stroll along the **Barn Wharf Trail,** which starts to the right of the mansion and leads down to the wharf overlooking the Potomac River. Get a copy of the free booklet that explains the 25 marked stopping places along the trail. It's an easy 15-minute walk. Daily 9:30 am-5 pm. Admission fee.

**Restaurants:** There are several excellent restaurants in the Mount Vernon area. Cedar Knolls, overlooking the Potomac, is less than a mile north of Mount Vernon. Collingwood, also on the Parkway, is two miles north of Mount Vernon, and is open April 30-Labor Day. The Lazy Susan is in Woodbridge five miles south of Pohick Church.

## Skyline Drive, Va

Shenandoah National Park, one of the major parks east of the Mississippi River, is best known for the Skyline Drive, which winds its way along the crest of the Blue Ridge Mountains for 105 miles. Starting from Washington, a comfortable one-day trip of 194 miles provides a sampling of the park's scenic and recreational attractions from Skyline Drive's northern terminus at Front Royal to Panorama, 32 miles to the south. The suggested route is west on Routes 66 and 55 to Front Royal and Skyline Drive. Return from Panorama via Route 211. Allow about five hours' driving time, since your trip on the drive itself should be a leisurely one including stops at many of the overlooks.

**Shenandoah National Park** is open throughout the year; however, the visitor centers and many facilities are open only from early spring to late autumn. (There are plans to keep one visitor center open during the winter.) Your first stop in the park should be Dickey Ridge Visitor Center, near milepost 5 on the Skyline Drive, which offers brief orientation programs,

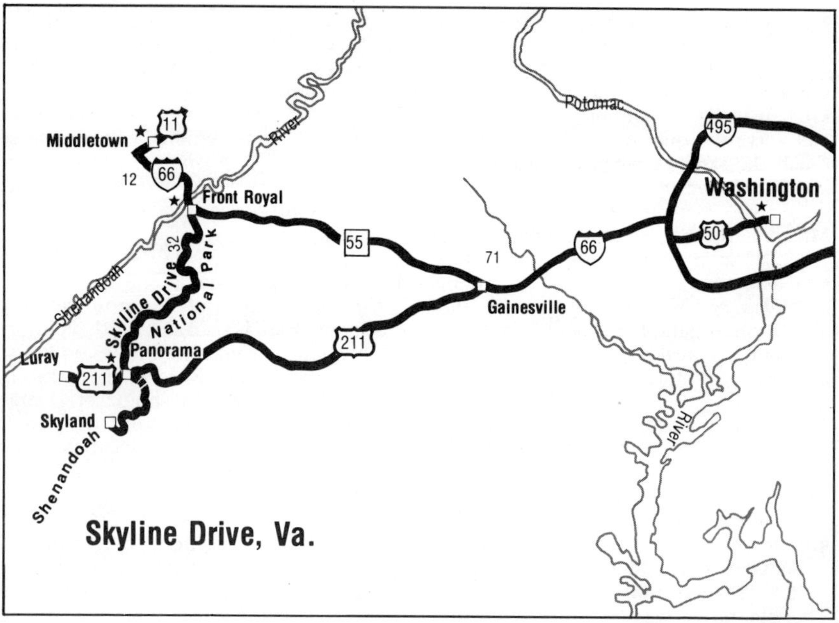


exhibits, maps, and pamphlets on the park's programs and services. Bulletin boards throughout the park list events for the week, including nature walks, field trips, and campfire programs.

There are many overlooks between Front Royal and Panorama, which provide views from heights of over 3,000 feet. Most spectacular is Hogback Overlook, where on a clear day, you can see the Shenandoah River snaking in and out through fertile farms and villages. There are picnicking facilities with fireplaces throughout the park—check for specific locations. Camera fans should bring along a filter for panoramic views, and telephoto lenses for pictures of wildlife. (See Chapter 7 for camping information.)

You may wish to extend your trip at either the Front Royal or Panorama ends of Skyline Drive. From Front Royal there are several interesting possibilities. For instance, you could spend an hour at **Skyline Caverns,** just a mile south of Front Royal. The caverns are open the entire year. Daily 9 am-sunset. Admission fee. In Front Royal you can visit the **Confederate Museum** to see pictures, documents, and memorabilia of the Civil War. Summer hours 9 am-8 pm; Sunday until 6 pm; April-May and September-October 9 am-6 pm. Admission fee.

Two miles south of town, on Route 522, is the **Front Royal Beef Cattle Research Center** of the U.S. Department of Agriculture. Visitors are welcome. A new and unusual attraction in the Front Royal area is the **Thunderbird Museum and Archeological Park,** located on the Shenandoah River six miles south of town, off Route 340. During the summer months visitors can see archeologists at work excavating artifacts that trace the history of man in this area back almost 12,000 years. Artifacts and fossil remains of animal life, unearthed in the past five years, are on display in the museum. Visitors also can stroll along a marked nature trail with outdoor exhibits and signs that tell the geological history of the area and call attention to the unusual features of plant life along the route. The park also offers canoe rentals for trips on the Shenandoah River with or without a guide, horseback riding, and hiking along a three-mile nature trail. Arts and crafts by local artisans are on display in the Arts and Handicraft Shop. Thunderbird Museum daily 10 am-6 pm. Admission fee.

Theater fans will be interested in the excellent summer stock company that stages plays at the **Wayside Theatre,** in Middletown (701-869-1776), 12 miles northwest of Front Royal, on Route 11. Adjacent is historic Wayside Inn, which serves first-rate Southern style dinners in an authentic Colonial atmosphere.

You can extend your trip from Panorama 10 miles south to **Skyland**, or to **Luray,** nine miles west on Route 211. If you continue south on the drive, consider a stop at **Little Stony Man.** The one-and-a-half-mile round-trip walk on Stony Man Trail affords a sweeping view of the Shenandoah Valley and a close-up of the wildflowers and wildlife of the area. There is also an underground river you can hear beneath the rocks and an abandoned copper mine to explore.

**Skyline Lodge** is less than three miles past Stony Man Overlook. There you will find a restaurant, local crafts and gift shop, horseback riding, and conducted nature walks. April-November. Return to Panorama, then east on Route 211 to Washington.

An alternate trip west on Route 211 takes you to the famous **Luray Caverns.** Guided tours are available at frequent intervals. Nearby is the **Car and Carriage Museum,** featuring 75 antique vehicles. Caves and museum daily year-round 9 am-sunset. Admission fee. An added feature is the **Luray Singing Tower,** with a 47-bell carillon. Recitals are given mid-March-mid-November Tuesday, Thursday, Saturday, and Sunday.

**Restaurants:** In Luray, the Caverns and Coach Restaurant is known for its Virginia dishes and home-baked breads and pastries. In Front Royal, Bell Boyd and Hi-Way Restaurants offer diverse menus, including many Southern dishes. The Panorama Restaurant at Skyline Drive and Route 211 makes the most of its mountain setting. Skyland Lodge in the park at Skyland accommodates 450 persons very efficiently (April-November 1).

## Harpers Ferry, W.Va

Harpers Ferry, intimately associated with the opening of the West and with John Brown's Raid and the Civil War, lies nestled on a mountainside in an area of unparalleled scenic beauty where the Shenandoah and Potomac Rivers have carved a passage through the Appalachian Mountains. Harpers Ferry is 65 miles from Washington, via Route 270 and Route 340. The Chessie System has train service to Harpers Ferry Saturday, Sunday, and holidays, leaving Washington at 11 am and returning from Harpers Ferry at 6:27 pm. Travel time is one hour, five minutes. You should be forewarned that the park is very crowded during summer months, especially on weekends, and you may have to wait in line for meals.

In 1747, Robert Harper established a ferry line here and later built a mill. A federal armory and arsenal began operating in 1796. The growth of Harpers Ferry was further stimulated by the coming of the Chesapeake and Ohio Canal and the Baltimore and Ohio Railroad. The town, now a National Historical Park, is in the process of being restored to look the way it did from the time of John Brown's daring raid on the arsenal here in October, 1859, that hastened the outbreak of the Civil War, until 1865.

Leave your car in the large parking lot opposite the Visitors Center in **Stagecoach Inn.** Here you can watch a short audiovisual program, see historical exhibits, and obtain a free trail guide to the park. It suggests two short walking tours. The first is a historic tour that includes the Master Armorer's House; the Arsenal Foundation; dry goods store, law office, and confectionery store on Shenandoah Street; the tavern on Potomac Street; the Virginius Island Trail to the ruins of the rifle works; John Brown's Fort on Arsenal Square; the Stone Steps to Harper House; and Jefferson Rock (so-called because Thomas Jefferson described the view from this point as, "one of the most stupendous scenes in nature"). En route are St. Peter's Catholic Church, built in the 1830s, and the ruins of St. John's Episcopal Church, built in 1852. Next to the Harper House is the row of restored Marmion Houses built between 1832 and 1850.

Another short walk you could take is up High Street, a four-block-long business street that includes antique, craft, and gift shops, and the John Brown Wax Museum. March-December daily 9 am-5 pm; January and February Saturday and Sunday 9 am-5 pm. Admission fee.

A third trip—recommended for the able-bodied and sturdily shod—is the blue-blazed trail to Maryland Heights, where the Union forces fortified the high point overlooking Harpers Ferry. Get a trail

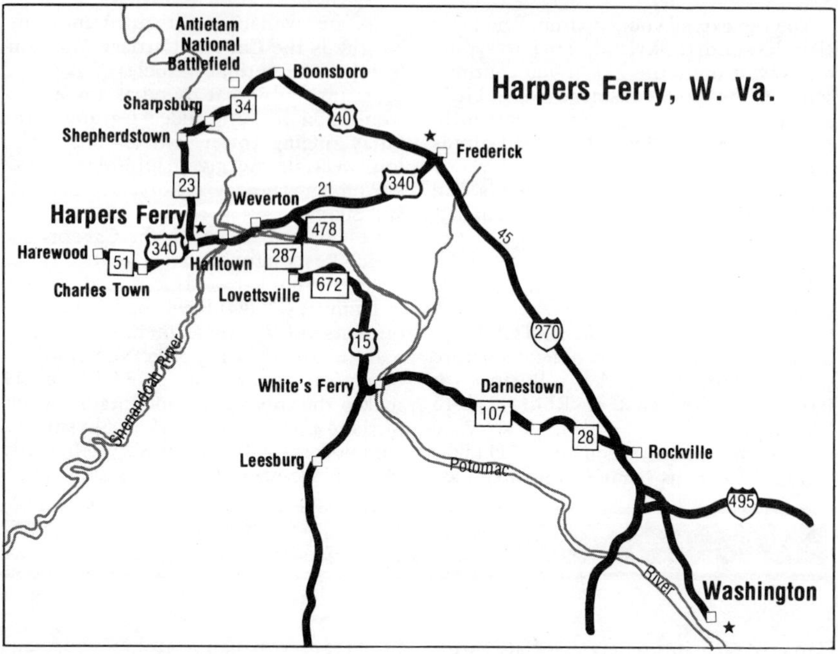


map at the Visitors Center. Overlook Cliff, less than an hour's round-trip walk, is 850 feet above sea level, and 300 feet directly above the Potomac. From this point there is an unobstructed view for many miles up the Potomac and Shenandoah Rivers. Count on spending two to three hours if you want to inspect all of the fortifications farther up Maryland Heights at an elevation of 1,400 feet. National historical park: daily 8 am-dark.

**Harpers Ferry Caverns** is two miles distant off Route 340; open daily. Admission fee. A few miles beyond is **Charles Town.** The old courthouse here was the scene of John Brown's trial. The library and museum, one block east, features a Civil War exhibit, including the wagon in which John Brown was borne to the scene of his execution. Daily 9 am-5 pm.

*__Harewood,__ on Route 51 three miles west, was the home of George Washington's brother, Colonel Samuel Washington; you can visit his office and the family graveyard.

**Restaurants:** The New Central Restaurant in Charles Town is popular. In Harpers Ferry, you can eat at the famous Hilltop House, with its commanding view from atop High Street; Cliffside Restaurant, about a mile out of town on Route 340; or at the Iron Horse, a moderately-priced restaurant conveniently located across from the railroad station.

An interesting side trip for the history buff is a visit to the **Antietam National Battlefield Site,** 13 miles north of Harpers Ferry in Maryland. Take Route 340 west to Halltown, right on Route 23, and then Route 17 into Shepherdstown, right on Route 34 into Sharpsburg, and left to the battlefield. Plan on taking the eight-mile battlefield motor tour. Stop first at the visitors center for a map. The bloody battle of Antietam changed the course of the Civil War. General Robert E. Lee failed in his first attempt to invade the North when he was stopped here by General George McClellan's superior forces. Five days after this Union victory, Lincoln issued the Emancipation Proclamation. Visitor Center daily 8:30 am-5 pm; longer hours in summer. Roads open until dark.

For the return trip, go six miles to Boonsboro, east on Route 40 to I-70, then right, and into Route 270 (70S). An alternate route from Harpers Ferry is via White's Ferry, the only ferry crossing on the Potomac River. Take Route 340 to Weverton, east on Route 478, south on Route 287 into Virginia, east on Route 672 and south on Route 15, nine miles to the toll ferry. In Maryland take Routes 107 and 28 to Route 270 and Washington.

*A good way to see Annapolis is on a harbor cruise.*

*Ghanaian weaving—a typical demonstration at the Anacostia Neighborhood Museum.*



# Chapter Five

# Other Sights

WHITNEY WATRISS

Away from the more heavily trafficked tourist routes are many more sights, curiosities, and places of interest to visit. We have selected a sampling—libraries, churches, urban development areas, embassies, museums, and so on. Be sure to see Chapter 3, 4, for museums, art collections, historic sites, nature and science centers not mentioned here.

## The Arts

**Phillips Collection,** 1600-1612 21st Street NW (387-2151). Tuesday-Saturday 10 am-5 pm; Sunday 2 pm-7 pm; closed Christmas. Tour. The Phillips has a superb art collection assembled by the late Duncan Phillips and hung in his former home, an elegant 19th-century town house. The rooms with their rich wood paneling, fine molding, and comfortable furniture are a perfect environment for viewing fine art. The permanent collection, which is hung in rotation, consists mainly of 19th- and 20th-century paintings and sculpture, along with some paintings by El Greco, Goya, and other old masters. There are also special loan shows. Tours lasting about 90 minutes are given Saturday at 3 pm or by appointment. Don't miss the free Sunday concerts in the handsome Renaissance Revival hall (see Chapter 6).

***State Department Americana Rooms,** 2201 C Street NW (632-3241). Tours by appointment Monday-Friday at 9:30 am, 10:30 am, and 3:30 pm; also 10 am and 3 pm during the summer; closed federal holidays. Tours are subject to sudden cancellation, so check before going. Commercial parking lot at 23rd Street and Virginia Avenue NW. H. In 1961 the State Department began redecorating its diplomatic reception rooms, which had been done in "motel modern," in the styles typical of the homes of wealthy Americans in the period 1740-1825. The result is an outstanding collection of period furnishings that includes fine paintings, superior Chinese Export porcelain, valuable antique rugs, and major pieces of American furniture. Many pieces have additional historical value, such as silver crafted by Paul Revere and an architectural table-desk designed by Thomas Jefferson. The rooms themselves, redone in the interior architectural styles of the period, provide an excellent backdrop. A useful booklet on the rooms is provided free. Allow about one hour.

*Note: Special arrangements will be made for the Bicentennial, beginning in 1976 and extending for several years.*

**Textile Museum,** 2320 S Street NW (667-0441). Tuesday-Saturday 10 am-5 pm; closed federal holidays. The spotlight here is on textiles of all types, with exhibits that change about every three months. Recent displays featured Egyptian tapestries, South Persian tribal carpets, African cloth, and examples of 13th- to 18th-century Turkish weaving. The permanent collection has some of the finest Oriental rugs to be found anywhere.

The museum sponsors various programs, such as illustrated lectures on rugs and the care of fabrics and, from time to time, concerts and poetry readings. A very fine shop offers anything and everything related to stitchery (see Chapter 10). The unusual reference library is particularly strong on Oriental rugs and ancient textiles.

# Embassies

Most embassies do not sponsor regular programs for the public, though from time to time they may have an open house, exhibit, or film. If you are interested in a particular country, check to see if its embassy is planning anything special.

Those embassies regularly open to the public are:

**Australian Embassy,** 1601 Massachusetts Avenue NW (797-3173). Monday-Friday 9:30 am-5:30 pm; closed federal holidays. Group tours. H, two steps. The embassy conducts group tours for up to 150 people by advance appointment; individuals may join a group by calling ahead. There are exhibits on Australian timbers, textiles, arts and crafts, and sculpture, and many native materials have been incorporated in the design and decoration of the building. During the summer, films are shown at lunch hour.

**Japanese Embassy,** 2520 Massachusetts Avenue NW (234-2266). Tours by appointment Wednesday 2:30 pm-4:30 pm May-July, September, and October; closed federal and Japanese holidays. Behind the embassy is an authentic Japanese tea house, designed by the architect Nahiko Emori, surrounded by a typical Japanese garden. The tour of the house and garden lasts about 30 minutes; only children 11 or older are admitted.

# Historic Sites

***Anderson House** (Society of the Cincinnati), 2118 Massachusetts Avenue NW (785-2040). Tuesday-Sunday 2 pm-4 pm; closed federal holidays except George Washington's birthday. Commercial parking lot on P Street between 21st and 22nd Streets NW. Anderson House epitomizes Dupont Circle at the turn of the century. The house, at that time one of the costliest ever built, was designed by Little & Browne for Larz Anderson, wealthy diplomat and prominent Washingtonian. It was completed in 1905 at a cost of $800,000. Almost nothing in the home is simple or unadorned. In 1939, Anderson's widow donated the house to the Society of the Cincinnati, an early patriotic organization in which Anderson was an active member. To the wealth of art objects already there, the society added its own considerable collection of Revolutionary War and other historic material, such as paintings by Gilbert Stuart and George Washington's correspondence. Staff is on hand to answer questions, or you may choose to buy an informative booklet on the society, the house, and the Andersons.

***Arlington Historical Society Museum,** 1805 Arlington Ridge Road, Arlington, VA (532-1453). Route 95 to Arlington Ridge Road, turn left. Sunday 2 pm-4 pm. Parking available. This small museum contains a mélange of memorabilia and historical odds and ends: Victorian clothing, Colonial furniture, old farming equipment, Jefferson Davis' desk, an old jail door, and Indian artifacts—to mention a few.

**Columbia Historical Society** (Christian Heurich Memorial Mansion), 1307 New Hampshire Avenue NW (785-2068). Monday, Wednesday, and Saturday 2 pm-4 pm; closed federal holidays. Commercial parking lots on 19th Street NW. Tours. This massive, brooding building was once the home of Christian Heurich, a German immigrant who built a fortune on beer and became a noted Washington philanthropist. Like many wealthy residents during the city's Victorian heyday, Heurich built himself a grand mansion, designed by John Granville Meyers, and ornamented with gargoyles, turrets, a carved ivory frieze, frescoes, and lavish paneling. The eclectic mixture of furnishings includes rare Japanese temple vases, a suit of Italian armor, and 16th-century tapestries. Be sure to ask for a tour since nothing is marked and there is no literature. The house is now headquarters for the Columbia Historical Society, a nonprofit organization founded in 1894 and dedicated to the preservation and dissemination of information about the District of Columbia. It has a valuable library of Washingtoniana (for details see Libraries, this chapter).

**Clara Barton House,** 5801 Oxford Road, Glen Echo, MD (229-3440). MacArthur Boulevard to Oxford Road, then follow the signs. Tuesday-Sunday 1 pm-5 pm; closed federal holidays. Parking. Built in 1892, this unusual mid-Victorian house was originally intended for storage of Red Cross supplies. In 1897 Clara Barton, founder of the American Red Cross, moved into the second floor and made the house headquarters for the organization. Most furnishings are original and belonged either to Mrs. Barton or the Red Cross. The interior of the house resembles a Mississippi riverboat, with the rooms built around a large central shaft reaching up two floors. The National Park Service has acquired the house so the hours may change.

**Colvin Run Mill** and **Miller's House,** 10017 Colvin Run Road, Great Falls, VA (759-2771). Route 123 south or Capital Beltway (Route 495) to Route 7, 5 miles west of Tyson's Corner. Saturday-Sunday 10 am-4:30 pm. Admission: adults $1, children 50¢. Parking. Tour. HP, see below. This mill is an excellent example of an early-19th-century "merchant" mill, which bought and sold grain wholesale and produced flour for retail trade as well. The design follows the then-revolutionary concept of division of labor, which was a forerunner of the modern production line. Thus, although the mill is large, it only takes one person to run the complex machinery. The Fairfax Park Authority acquired the property in 1965. Although restoration is not yet completed, corn is ground every weekend. A 45-minute tour is conducted at 11 am and 2 pm following a slide show on the mill and its reconstruction. The handicapped should make advance arrangements to drive up to the mill. Only the first floor, where the millstones are located, is easily accessible.

**Fort Ward,** 4301 West Braddock Road, Alexandria, VA (750-6425). Route 95 south to Seminary Road exit, turn left and go about a mile to Howard Street, turn left to East Braddock Road, turn right; entrance is a short distance on the left. Museum open Monday-Saturday 9 am-5 pm; Sunday 12 pm-5 pm; closed Thanksgiving and Christmas Day; park grounds and restored fort bastion open daily 9 am-sunset. Parking adjacent to the museum. H, museum only. The Confederate victory at the first Battle of Bull Run early in the Civil War prompted a massive effort to fortify Washington. Fort Ward was the fifth largest of the defenses constructed. Recently, the city of Alexandria purchased the fort's remains, restored one bastion, and opened a museum. The museum, housed in a typical Civil War fort headquarters, contains uniforms, weapons, an excellent map of the fort's system, and other relics. Don't miss the copy of an interview with Lincoln obtained four days before he delivered the Gettysburg Address. Next door to the museum is a furnished officer's hut. Though only the northwest bastion of the fort has been restored, it gives you a good idea of what Civil War fort defenses were like.

**Fort Washington,** 5210 Indian Head Highway, Fort Washington, MD (292-2112). Capital Beltway (Route 495) to Route 210 (Indian Head Highway) south to Fort Washington Road, turn right and proceed to the end of the road. Daily winter hours 9 am-5 pm; summer 9 am-dark; closed Christmas and New Year's Day. Parking available. Picnic facilities. HP. Until the Civil War, Fort Washington, an excellent example of early-19th-century coastal fortifications, was the city's only defense. It is a massive masonry structure, 833 feet in perimeter with some walls as much as seven feet thick, surrounded by a dry moat. By the 1860s the fort had become obsolete and was used mainly for administrative work. It was refortified in the 1890s with concrete gun batteries and was the major Washington defense post during World War I. In 1946 the National Park Service acquired it and began restoration, most of which is now complete. A history of the settlement of the city and the fort, illustrated in part by some splendid photographs, is displayed in a small museum at the entrance. Recordings at key points around the fort explain its fortifications and describe a soldier's life in the 19th century. Park Service rangers give tours on request, and there is an excellent free brochure with additional information. From time to time, special programs are held. The torchlight tour is particularly popular (reservation required).

**Frederick Douglass Home** (Cedar Hill), 1411 W Street SE (889-1736). Southeast Freeway to the 11th Street Bridge to Good Hope Road to 14th Street, turn right and continue to W Street. Monday-Friday 9 am-4 pm; Saturday and Sunday 10 am-5 pm; closed Christmas. Parking available. Tour. Picnic facilities. Frederick Douglass, the noted abolitionist, moved to Cedar Hill in 1877 from his home on A Street NE, now part of the Museum of African Art (see Capitol Hill walking tour, Chapter 3). He lived here until his death in 1895. After protracted litigation with some of Douglass' children, his second wife, Helen Pitts, succeeded in donating the home to the public. Most of the original furnishings are here, and the excellent restoration by the National Park Service has closely duplicated the original interior, even to the use of oil lamps and candles for light. The furnishings, library, and art in the house say much about the character of the man, the people he admired, and the breadth of his self-acquired knowledge. The regular tours, which last about 45 minutes, are very informative. There is also free literature on Douglass and the house. Check in advance for special events.

***George Washington Masonic National Memorial,** King Street and Callahan Drive, Alexandria, VA (683-2007). Route 1 south to King Street in Alexandria, turn right. Daily 9 am-5 pm; closed Thanksgiving, Christmas, and New Year's Day. Parking available. Tour. This imposing monument, built by Freemasons in honor of President George Washington, Master Mason and First Worshipful Master of the Alexandria-Washington Lodge No. 22, serves as a repository for the numerous Washington possessions and memorabilia owned by the lodge. These fascinating items are displayed in the two museums here and range from the eloquent—Washington's family Bible—to the grotesque—photographs of his dentures. The museums also contain mementos of Washington's contemporaries, as well as other curiosities, such as John Brown's handcuffs and a piece of Plymouth Rock. The memorial's tower affords one of the finest views of the metropolitan area (though Washington would not recognize the landscape he once knew so well). The rest of the building, including five floors of the tower, are devoted mainly to Freemasonry. Regular guided tours of the tower rooms begin at 9:15 am. Allow about an hour-and-a-half to browse.

**Great Falls Tavern** (C & O Canal National Historical Park), 11710 MacArthur Boulevard, Potomac, MD (299-3613). Daily 9 am-5 pm; closed Christmas. Parking. Snack bar nearby late spring-early fall. H, one step at entrance. Great Falls Tavern, originally known as Crommelin House, the only hotel built by the Canal Company, was very popular with travelers in its day. Its fortunes rose and fell, and by the turn of the century it had become little more than a refreshment stand. Today it houses a museum, hospitality center, and information room. The museum deals specifically with the canal and has a working model of a lock. A 10-minute silent film on the canal, made in 1917, is shown every hour on the half-hour at peak seasons and upon request during slack periods. A number of special programs are held; check in advance, as some require reservations.

**Lincoln Park,** East Capitol Street between 11th and 13th Streets NE. This large park is well known for its sculpture. The Emancipation Group shows President Abraham Lincoln with the Emancipation Proclamation in his right hand, his left hand extended over a slave whose shackles are broken. Erected in 1876, it was funded entirely from donations by freedmen. Recently, blacks protested the depiction of a former slave kneeling at Lincoln's feet. Some say, however, that the sculptor, Thomas Ball, intended for the slave to be rising. Judge for yourself. Opposite is a recently dedicated statue of Mary McLeod Bethune, noted black educator. It was donated by the National Association of Colored Women.

**Pierce Mill,** Beach and Tilden Streets NW (426-6908). Wednesday-Sunday 9 am-5 pm; closed Christmas and New Year's Day; check on other holidays. Parking. H. Grain was stone ground at Pierce Mill from 1820 to 1897, when the introduction of more modern methods made this mill's operations uneconomical. In its heyday, more than 70 bushels a day were ground, an amount made possible by the efficient design of the structure and machinery. Today, thanks to the National Park Service, the millstones once again produce wheat flour and cornmeal, which can be bought by visitors. Watch for special events such as demonstrations of 19th-century cooking using a wood stove and 100-year-old utensils.

While visiting the mill you might also want to stop at the **Art Barn** next door (Tuesday-Friday 1 pm-5 pm; Saturday and Sunday 11 am-5 pm; closed Christmas and New Year's Day; check on other holidays). Its two galleries, located in a barn that predates the mill, are devoted entirely to the works of Washington artists. Exhibits change every six weeks. (Not accessible to the handicapped.)

***Scottish Rite Temple,** 1733 16th Street NW (232-3579). Monday-Friday 9 am-4 pm; Saturday 9 am-noon; closed federal holidays. Commercial parking lots nearby. Tour. H, one step at entrance off the alley. Sitting on 16th Street is a good copy of one of the seven wonders of the world. John Russell Pope modeled the Scottish Rite Temple headquarters for the Southern Jurisdiction of the Scottish Rite of Freemasonry, after the tomb of Mausolus at Halicarnassus. It is an elaborate structure, full of Masonic symbolism and philosophy. Some of the rooms contain displays on eminent Masons, past and present, from George Washington to Col. Edwin E. Aldrin; the idiosyncratic collections of Masonic Grand Commanders; and loads of Masonic regalia and artifacts. The regular tours, describing the building and explaining the order, take about one hour. There is also an excellent library, reputed to be the oldest public library in the city, with one of the most complete collections on Freemasonry anywhere.

**Woodrow Wilson House,** 2340 S Street NW (387-4062). Daily 10 am-4 pm; closed Thanksgiving and Christmas. Admission: $1.25 for adults, 60¢ for students, senior citizens, military, and children (there is a combined $1.50 ticket with Decatur House). Tours. Although President Woodrow Wilson had wanted to build his own home when he left the White House, he could not afford to. Instead he bought this handsome Georgian Revival house designed by architect Waddy B. Wood (1915). After he died in 1924, his wife kept it exactly as it was and left it to the National Trust for Historic Preservation. The house is very personal and offers many insights into Wilson and his life. He was deeply involved with its decoration; it is crowded with mementos of every sort, from kewpie dolls given to him by sailors to Czechoslovakian crystal chandeliers from an unknown admirer. The library, his favorite room, houses his collection of books and reflects his enormous range of interests. On the second floor you will hear a record of his daughter singing. There is a guide on each floor to show you around. Allow about an hour to visit the three floors. The National Trust also provides a free and informative brochure on Wilson and the home.

# Libraries

Washington abounds in libraries of every size, covering every topic; it is the bibliomaniac's mecca, the information hunter's utopia. The purpose of this section is not to give you a complete list (which can be found in the *Library and Reference Facilities in the Area of the District of Columbia,* 9th edition, the American Society of Information Science, Washington, DC). Rather, it is to tell you where to look for libraries, the general rules governing their use, and to acquaint you with a few of the best or most unusual.

Most federal agencies have libraries open to the public; their collections generally cover the agency's sphere of interest, though some are broader. A few, where an agency deals in sensitive areas, are not open. City and county public libraries are a good source for local history: check the District of Columbia; Arlington and Fairfax counties and the cities of Alexandria and Falls Church in Virginia; Montgomery and Prince Georges counties in Maryland.

There are hundreds of Associations in Washington, most of which have comprehensive holdings in their respective fields. The same is true for public and private museums and galleries. Many other organizations that serve the public or are public oriented—i.e., churches, women's organizations—usually welcome nonaffiliates. Major exceptions to this general rule are those libraries, such as the National Archives and the National Library of Medicine, where staff are hard pressed to meet the needs of regular users, and therefore can only accommodate researchers with specific projects.

In general, most libraries are open for reference only, although you can arrange to borrow books through the interlibrary loan system. Almost all are free. Their hours generally parallel daily business hours, and they are closed on holidays; the exceptions are public libraries and college and university libraries. Most public libraries have equipment or facilities for the handicapped; generally others do not, with the noteworthy exception of the Library of Congress.

The libraries described here were selected because they are big, unusual, or Washington oriented, and the sample is by no means complete. All are open to the public.

**Columbia Historical Society Library,** 1307 New Hampshire Avenue NW (785-2068). Monday, Wednesday, and Thursday 10 am-4 pm. Commercial parking nearby. The society's collection is among the best on Washington, DC; much of the material dates back to the city's beginnings: letters of Dolley Madison, a broadside from the DC slave market, and city directories from 1821 on. The picture collection has 10,000 unusual prints and negatives. The material is largely uncatalogued because of a lack of funds; nevertheless, the librarians somehow know what is where.

***Martin Luther King Memorial Library,** main branch District of Columbia Public Libraries, 901 G Street NW (727-1111). Monday-Thursday 9 am-9 pm (night owl service to 11 pm for the Black Studies and Popular Section); Friday and Saturday 9 am-5:30 pm; closed federal holidays. Tours (727-1221). Free parking in underground garage; meters and commercial lots. Canteen. H. This new central branch has much to recommend it, from the collections to the building itself. The special collections on Washingtoniana (which will be highlighted during the Bicentennial) and Black Studies are excellent. An AP news ticker in the lobby is a unique feature. The **Barnett-Aden Collection,** the only major collection of black American artists in the United States, will be exhibited here through 1976. Check for special programs. The building itself, the only one in the city designed by the late architect Mies van der Rohe, has received much critical acclaim.

***Library of Congress,** First Street and Independence Avenue SE (426-5000). Main Reading Room Monday-Friday 8:30 am-9:30 pm; Saturday 8:30 am-5 pm; Sunday 1 pm-5 pm; closed most federal holidays. Snack bar. H. The Library of Congress may well be the largest library in the world, with over 72 million items on 320 miles of shelves. One of the strongest areas is Americana, but it has collections on practically anything you can think of including Federal Research, Geography and Maps, Manuscripts, Music, Orientalia, Prints and Photographs. There is also a Division for the Blind and Physically Handicapped. In addition to the Main Reading Room there are a number of others; check for hours. To use the facilities you must be over high school age. (For more information on tours, concerts, and the building see Capitol Hill walking tour, Chapter 3, and Entertainment, Chapter 6.)

**Smithsonian Institution Libraries,** Natural History and General Reference and Circulation Division, Natural History Building, 10th Street and Constitution Avenue NW (381-5382). Monday-Friday 8:45 am-5:15 pm (same hours for all Smithsonian libraries). H, use Constitution Avenue entrance. The Natural History and General Reference and Circulation Division is the main branch of the Institution's libraries. It contains a card catalogue covering all other branches, a general collection covering the areas with which the Institution deals, and a comprehensive collection on natural history, going back at least 100 years. The total holdings of the Institution are too large and varied to describe here, but they are among the most complete anywhere in their respective fields.

**Volta Bureau Library** (Alexander Graham Bell Association for the Deaf, Inc.), 1537 35th Street NW (337-5220). Monday-Friday 9 am-4:30 pm; closed holidays. This library was founded in 1887 by Alexander Graham Bell. The holdings include over 10,000 items, one of the most comprehensive collections on deafness. The archives contain unpublished primary source material as well as photographs and other memorabilia, which are displayed from time to time.

## Museums

**Anacostia Neighborhood Museum,** 2405 Martin Luther King Avenue SE (381-6691). Southeast Freeway to the 11th Street Bridge to Martin Luther King Avenue, turn right. Daily 10 am-6 pm; Saturday and Sunday 1 pm-6 pm; closed federal holidays. On-street parking (until 4 pm). H. This unusual, free-wheeling, and ever-changing museum is a result of the Smithsonian Institution's efforts to make museums more accessible to people and related to their interests. The emphasis is on black history, urban and community problems, and arts and crafts. Afro-American heritage is the basis for many activities, such as the Kwanza demonstrations (an Afro-American adaptation of the African harvest festival), exhibits such as "Blacks in the Westward Movement," displays of African artifacts, and works by local artists. Weekday programs are geared to school children, weekends to adults, and all stress participation. Whatever is going on—batik preparation, painting, pottery making—you can join in. Check in advance to see what's happening or write for the free calendar.

**B'nai B'rith Museum,** 1640 Rhode Island Avenue NW (393-5284). Monday-Friday 1 pm-5 pm; Sunday 10 am-5 pm; closed Jewish holy days and some federal holidays. Commercial parking lots nearby. H. The collection covers a wide area of Jewish history, activities, and culture, including Jews in the Revolution, American political and public life. There is an exceptional array of old and rare religious articles. Fine craftsmanship abounds, for example, in the intricate herb boxes and in the Kanof Collection of modern renderings of historic religious articles. Informative literature is available at no charge; particularly useful for non-Jews is the pamphlet on the Kanof Collection, which explains the origin and use of religious articles. A good library adjoins the museum.

***National Rifle Association Firearms Museum,** 1600 Rhode Island Avenue NW (783-6505). Daily 10 am-4 pm; closed Christmas, New Year's Day, and Easter. Commercial parking lots nearby. H, only first floor. Firearms, firearms, and more firearms—at least 1,500 of them—are on display, along with many kinds of ammunition. One exhibit, for example, shows the development of firearms through seven centuries, from the primitive hand cannon to the modern breech-loading metallic cartridge arm. Teddy Roosevelt's favorite rifle, one of King James' fowling pieces, an Asiatic repeating flintlock gun, Austro-Hungarian carbines, rare dueling pistols, and $CO_2$ gas guns are just a few of the weapons displayed. If you need more information, there is a good reference room.

## Nature and Science

**Audubon Naturalist Society of the Central Atlantic States,** 8940 Jones Mill Road, Chevy Chase, MD (652-9188). Rock Creek Parkway to Beach Drive to Jones Mill Road. Grounds open daily sunrise-sunset; information office Monday-Friday 9 am-5 pm, Sunday around 2 pm-4 pm; generally closed Saturday and federal holidays. Parking. H, house only. The Audubon Naturalist Society of the Central Atlantic States (it is independent of the National Audubon Society) has its headquarters on a beautiful 40-acre estate, Woodend. Visitors are welcome to walk around the Georgian-style house, designed by John Russell Pope and built in 1928-9, and to use the reference library. The grounds have been converted into a wildlife sanctuary and outdoor classroom, with 28 resident species of birds and various mammals. The society provides a small guidebook for the half-mile nature trail. There is also a well-marked demonstration tree farm. On Sundays at 2 pm you can join the "Discovery Walk." Pets are prohibited and picnicking is discouraged. Guided tours should be arranged well in advance.

**Lightship Chesapeake,** 1200 Ohio Drive SW (426-6897). East Potomac Park opposite the miniature golf course. Saturday and Sunday 1 pm-4 pm (hours may be extended during the summer); closed most holidays. Parking. Tours. Acquired in 1972 by the National Park Service, this decommissioned lightship has been converted into an environmental workshop with laboratory and exhibits. It is now a traveling classroom for students who want to learn about the river environment. Sea Explorers (part of the Boy Scouts) do much of the teaching and provide most of the crew. One of them will give you a tour and describe the vessel's history and present function. Below are several aquariums (containing some of the river's inhabitants) and the lab. The tour lasts about 20 minutes.

**NASA Goddard Space Flight Center,** Greenbelt, MD (982-4101). Capital Beltway (Route 495) to Exit 29 north. To open early 1976; hours will be Monday-Friday 10 am-3 pm; closed federal holidays. Parking. Tour. Restaurant. HP. The center is planning to open a permanent exhibit facility and to provide tours beginning early 1976.

**National Wildlife Federation,** 8925 Leesburg Pike, Vienna, VA (790-4000). Capital Beltway (Route 495) to Route 7 west about 2 miles beyond Tyson's Corner. Grounds open year-round; office and exhibit center Monday-Friday 8 am-4:30 pm; closed federal holidays. Parking. Nature trail. H, exhibit center only. Walk along either of the well-marked, half-mile nature trails and learn what a riprap is, how chiggers make you itch, the advantages of bats, and the effect of lichens. At the end of the trail there is a demonstration area where you can learn how to attract animals to your yard. A wide range of flora and fauna can be seen. An exhibition center is scheduled to open soon. No pets.

**United States Naval Observatory,** Massachusetts Avenue at 34th Street NW (254-4534 or 254-4569 for recorded information). Day tour Monday-Friday 2 pm; night tours see below; closed federal holidays. Parking. Established in 1844, this observatory is the oldest scientific institution of the Navy. Its primary purpose is to provide navigational information; it is the only facility in the country where fundamental positions of the principal celestial bodies are observed and determined on a continuing basis. It is also here that precise time is calculated.

Tours last about an hour during the day and a little longer at night, when visitors may view the moon through the 26-inch refractor telescope. Night tours, four per evening, are held on the average of two or three times a month. Reservations are required for night tours and must be made well in advance; only children 12 years or older are admitted. During the day children of all ages are welcome, but must be accompanied by an adult. The buildings are not heated, so dress accordingly. Tours begin at the Goldsborough Museum in Building 1 (the museum has a few displays on the observatory and its mission) and consist of an introductory lecture by a staff astronomer, followed by a movie and visits to the time service building and the 26-inch telescope.

## Religious Sites

**Christ Church,** 620 G Street SE (547-9301). Monday-Friday 9 am-3 pm; weekends call in advance; closed some federal holidays. Christ Church (the "mother" church of the Washington Episcopal parish) is attributed to Benjamin Latrobe, although subsequent additions and alterations have all but obscured his simple rectangular design. The interior was restored in 1953-4, however, and now resembles the original. A nice recent addition is the vibrant stained-glass window by Rowan and Irene LeCompte. Many distinguished Washingtonians attended services here, among them Presidents James Madison, Thomas Jefferson, and John Quincy Adams. John Philip Sousa was baptized, confirmed, married, and buried from the church.

**Congressional Cemetery,** located some distance away at 1801 E Street SE (daily 7 am-3:30 pm), is under the management of Christ Church. At one point it was the official burying ground for congressmen. It is full of artistic memorials to the famous and not-so-famous: John Philip Sousa; Pushmataha, Choctaw chief, scout, and friend of President Andrew Jackson; and many congressmen. Check at the office for locations of graves.

**Franciscan Monastery,** 1400 Quincy Street NE (526-6800). Daily 8 am-5 pm; closed

Christmas and New Year's Day. Parking. Tour. H, upper church and gardens. The buildings and grounds of the monastery reproduce many famous shrines of the Holy Land and Italy. The Byzantine church is shaped like the five-fold cross of the Holy Land and contains many chapels modeled after those in the Near East. Under the church are the catacombs, with a Martyr's Crypt, similar to those in Rome. The lovely gardens are the site of an accurate reconstruction of the grotto of the shrine at Lourdes, France, and of the Chapel of the Ascension, a replica of the 12th-century chapel built by Crusaders at Mount Olivet. These shrines, and many others, are included on the tours, which are conducted every 45 minutes and last about 25 minutes (Monday-Saturday 8:30 am-4 pm; Sunday 1 pm-4:30 pm). Visitors should wear suitable clothing.

**Islamic Mosque,** 2551 Massachusetts Avenue NW (332-3451). Monday-Thursday, Saturday, and Sunday 10 am-4 pm; Friday 10 am-11:30 am and 2 pm-4 pm; check for different summer hours. This mosque, typical of those of the Middle East, is the only one in the United States built in this style. The architecture was designed in Egypt, and most of the decorations were fashioned by Middle Eastern craftsmen. A minaret rises above the mosque, and from it Moslems are called to prayer five times a day.

The information office has a lot of literature, most of it free, describing the Islamic faith and the mosque. Staff is available to answer questions. The reference library, devoted to Islam and the Middle East, contains a few display cases with religious artifacts, such as unusual copies of the Koran.

Suitable clothing must be worn—bare midriffs and the like are not permitted—and shoes must be left at the door (the interior is carpeted).

**Metropolitan African Methodist Episcopal Church,** 1518 M Street NW (331-1426). Monday-Friday 9:30 am-4 pm; Sunday 8:30 am-3 pm. Commercial parking lots nearby. This unusual church has played a significant role in black history in Washington. Its congregation is one of the oldest, largest, and most active in the city, and many prominent blacks have been associated with it. Frederick Douglass's funeral service was held here. In recent times the activist tradition has continued, and the church has hosted various national protest groups.

The architecture, by Samuel G. T. Morsell, is fundamentally Victorian with Gothic motifs. An unusual feature is the location of the main sanctuary on the second floor. The stained-glass windows are original and bear the names of the conferences that donated them; the handsome chancel furniture is also original. In the chancel are the silver candelabra donated by Douglass. There is usually someone at the church to answer questions.

**National Shrine of the Immaculate Conception,** 4th Street and Michigan Avenue NE (526-8300). Daily 7 am-8 pm. Parking. Tours. Cafeteria. This church is the seventh largest in the world, a gargantuan structure sitting atop one of the highest points in the city. Its form follows the Latin cross and combines Byzantine, Romanesque, and contemporary styles. Made entirely of stone, brick, and tile, it is very ornate, with sculpture, carvings, and other works of art throughout. There are 56 chapels, each different. Guided tours are given on the hour Monday-Saturday 9 am-5 pm; Sunday 2 pm-4 pm and 5:15 pm September through May; every half-hour June through August. The tour lasts about 35 minutes. The Shrine also sponsors free organ recitals every fourth Friday of the month at 8 pm except during December; during the summer the recitals are given on Sunday at 7 pm. Carillon recitals are held Sunday at 3:30 pm and before concerts.

**St. Mary's Episcopal Church,** 728 23rd Street NW (333-3985). Monday-Friday 10 am-2 pm; call in advance at other times. Parking at commercial lots nearby; a few meters. H, use entrance at back of church via the alley. This beautiful red brick church was designed by James Renwick in the parish Gothic style and completed in 1887, one of the first two Episcopal churches in the city built specifically for blacks. The interior is exceptionally pleasant: a patterned tile and red marble floor; wood-decked ceiling with exposed rafters; and unusual polychromatic stenciled walls accentuating the chancel. One of the outstanding stained-glass windows is an original Tiffany; the other three, featuring saints important to blacks and the early history and growth of the church, are by the French firm Lorin of Chartres. Unlike many of Washington's churches, this one still looks the same as it did in 1887, and the congregation intends to keep it that way.

***St. Paul's Episcopal Church** and **Rock Creek Cemetery,** Rock Creek Church Road and Webster Street NW (church 726-2080; cemetery 829-0585). Daily during daylight hours. Parking. This church, possibly the oldest in the city, began as a chapel-of-ease in 1712. The present building, touted as the only Colonial church in Washington, was constructed in 1921. The claim of antiquity comes from the walls, which date back to 1771, the only part of the original building to survive a fire in 1921. Recently, the interior was restored in the Colonial style. Check for special Bicentennial events.

In its early days St. Paul's was recipient of a glebe of about 100 acres. Today, most of the acreage is part of **Rock Creek Cemetery,** founded about 1871. It is best known for the Adams Memorial with its statue of a hooded woman by Augustus St. Gaudens. The memorial was erected by Henry Adams, diplomat and author, in memory of his wife. The statue is commonly called "Grief," but neither Adams nor St. Gaudens ever named it nor did they accept "grief" as its meaning.

Many distinguished people are buried in the cemetery. A list and map are available at the entrance, where you should also apply to see the church if it is closed.

**Washington Cathedral** (The Cathedral Church of Saint Peter and Saint Paul), Wisconsin and Massachusetts Avenues NW (966-3500). Daily 9 am-5 pm; check for longer hours during the summer. Parking. HP. This exceptional 14th-century Gothic-style cathedral, begun in 1907 and funded entirely from contributions, is now 75 percent complete. When finished—around 1984—it will be one of the largest churches in the world. Built the way churches used to be, it uses no structural steel and employs workmanship of high quality: exquisite stained-glass windows, fine carving, beautifully embroidered kneeling cushions, and rare tapestries. A small museum exhibits many religious objects, such as Russian icons and Easter eggs.

In the **Rare Book Library** (Tuesday-Friday 1 pm-5 pm; Saturday 10 am-5 pm; Sunday noon-5 pm) you can see a first edition of the King James Bible, printed in 1611 and hand illuminated, and a first edition of the Book of Common Prayer, published in 1549. A gift shop (daily 9 am-5 pm) features a good selection of religious articles and literature and gift items.

The possibilities here do not end with the church itself. There is the **Bishop's Garden,** a lovely example of a walled medieval garden; two shops—the **Herb Cottage** (Monday-Friday 9:30 am-4 pm; Saturday 9 am-5 pm; closed holidays), which specializes in herbs and objects decorated with herbs, and the **Greenhouse** (Monday-Saturday 9 am-5 pm), which sells plants and fresh herbs; the wooden bridge of Japanese design near the St. Alban's School tennis courts; **St. Alban's School** itself, and the **National Cathedral School**—both run by the Cathedral.

Capable guides conduct tours of the cathedral lasting about 40 minutes (Monday-Saturday 10 am-3:15 pm; Sunday at 12:15 pm, 1:30 pm, and 2:30 pm), and they can direct you to the other sites. The cathedral is well known for its concerts: organ recitals at Sunday evensong; carillon recitals at 12:15 pm on Sunday, except during Lent, and from 5 pm-6 pm in the summer; and performances of the excellent Cathedral Choral Society (see Chapter 6).

# Urban Living

## Two Old Sections

**Dupont Circle.** Its somewhat arbitrary boundary runs along N Street NW from 15th Street to Florida Avenue, north on Florida to R Street, east on R Street to 15th Street, and south on 15th Street to N Street. In 1870, Dupont Circle and environs were an ill-defined square and unplanned tract on L'Enfant's plan. Only one house west of 17th Street on Massachusetts Avenue intruded on the woods and fields. Development began in 1871 when a syndicate of westerners invested $600,000 in real estate. The first houses set the tone—lavish mansions and diplomatic residences. Before long, Massachusetts Avenue was dubbed "millionaire's row," and the area became one of the city's most fashionable. At the same time, many modest but substantial row houses were built to accommodate the growing middle class.

Dupont Circle remained a prosperous and popular center of the city well into the

20th century. But, as so often happens, this fashionable area began to decline. Today this decline seems to have been arrested. "Millionaire's row" is pretty much intact because, although only a few are in private hands, many mansions have become embassies. Dupont Circle has been attracting artists and young professionals, and many row houses are being restored. Art galleries, coffee shops, and specialty shops flourish here. Despite deterioration and some unimaginative new building, this is still an architecturally rich area to walk around, a living museum of diverse 19th- and early-20th-century architecture and lifestyles. A few buildings are listed here either because you can see the interiors or because of some unusual feature. There are plenty more to discover for yourself.

**1785 Massachusetts Avenue** was one of the first luxury apartment buildings—one unit per floor. The architect was the well-known Henri deSibour. **1319 18th Street** (Horace Trumbauer, 1901) recently became headquarters of the American Forestry Association, which has done a good job of preserving the interior and does not mind your looking at the first and second floors. If you take advantage of this rare opportunity, you can get an idea how Washington's wealthy lived (Monday-Friday 9 am-4:45 pm). Nearby at **1801 P Street** is the Iraqi Chancery, designed by Hornblower & Marshall in 1893, one of the finest and one of a very few surviving houses influenced by H. H. Richardson. Call in advance (483-7500) if you want to see the well-preserved interiors. **The Washington Club** (private) is the very ornate building at 15 Dupont Circle. It was owned by Eleanor (Cissy) Patterson, publisher of the *Times-Herald.* President and Mrs. Calvin Coolidge lived here in 1929 when the White House was being refurbished.

**The Dupont Circle fountain** by Daniel Chester French, with three figures representing the sea, wind, and stars, is a fitting memorial to Admiral Samuel Francis duPont. At **2020 Massachusetts Avenue** is one of the most sumptuous mansions, built in 1901-2 at a cost of at least $835,000. The owner, Thomas F. Walsh, spent many years in poverty prospecting in Colorado. When he struck it rich he built a house that embodied everything he and his wife had dreamed of. The **Cosmos Club** (also private) at 2121 Massachusetts Avenue was designed by Carrere & Hastings after the Petit Trianon of Versailles.

In contrast to these mansions are the attached houses along the **2000 block of R Street**—typical of middle-class dwellings of the period. **Schwartz's Pharmacy** at the corner of R and Connecticut Avenue is where Upton Sinclair used to take the Duchess of Windsor for egg salad sandwiches. The building, unusual for Washington, has French-style apartments with large rooms, high ceilings, and French doors opening onto narrow balconies. Upton Sinclair himself lived at **1712 19th Street,** in one of the few remaining pre-Civil War wood houses in the area. At **1825 R Street** is the Tudor-style International Student Center. Walk in to see the great hall, courtyard, and refectory, and take tea from 4 pm-5 pm on Sunday. **1618 New Hampshire Avenue** is the old Perry Belmont House. He was a wealthy diplomat who spent $1 million on his mansion, and it still holds its own against the modern high-rises. Old Castle Row—three attached houses—sits at **1612-16 S Street;** it was patterned after Henderson's Castle, which once stood not far away. The Associated Press began operations in the apartment of Theodore and Frank Noyes (of the *Washington Star* dynasty) at **1616 S Street.** The tallest privately owned building in the District (156 feet) at 1614 Q Street, the **Cairo Apartments,** is now being restored. When it was built, the city was outraged by its size and passed a restriction, still in effect, limiting the height of all future buildings in the District.

**Washington Navy Yard Historic District,** 8th and M Streets SE (433-2651). Monday-Friday 9 am-4 pm; Saturday, Sunday, and holidays 10 am-5 pm; closed Thanksgiving, Christmas, and New Year's Day. Parking is limited on weekdays, available weekends. Cafeteria, closed Sunday. Tours by arrangement. H. The Washington Navy Yard is unique, the only example remaining in the city of a really fine 19th-early-20th-century industrial complex. Established in 1799, it is also the oldest naval installation in America. Its roles were many and diverse. It functioned first as the primary naval shipyard of the new nation, then became the main facility for manufacturing naval equipment. Later the yard was turned into the Navy's major munitions center. Throughout its history, the yard has been hospitable to innovation. Although Robert Fulton's early work with torpedoes was unsuccessful, Commodore John Rodgers built the first marine railway for hauling ships here, and in 1898 the first model ship basin was completed.

The yard was also critical to the growth of Washington. It was the major source of jobs in the early 1800s and remained one of the city's most important manufacturing centers throughout the 19th century.

Since the 1960s the yard has been used primarily for administrative purposes—other functions having been transferred to more modern facilities. It is fun to meander around and see the handsome old factories and officers' quarters. Three exceptionally fine buildings—**Tingey House,** the Commandant's home; **Quarters B,** for the second in command; and the **Commandant's Office**—that survived the fire of 1814 set by the Navy to prevent the yard from falling to the British are particularly worth noticing. The other quarters, constructed between 1801 and 1900, are good examples of period architecture. The industrial buildings were built for the most part between 1850 and 1900.

During the week, drop by the public relations office in Building 200 and pick up a history of the yard, along with a map and other information. A number of cafeterias are open daily except Sunday. Picnicking is allowed in the parks. The excellent library contains anything you want to know about the Navy and naval matters in general.

While in this area you might want to stop by another military establishment noted for good architecture, the **US Marine Corps Barracks** and **Commandant's House** at I and 9th Streets SE. (Call 433-4173 to arrange for an escort.) Thomas Jefferson chose the site because it was close to the Navy Yard and within easy marching distance of the Capitol. The Commandant's House, an early Federal-style building that dates back to 1801, also survived the fire of 1814. To the rear of the house are the barracks designed by Hornblower & Marshall and built between 1902 and 1906. In the quadrangle in front of the barracks the Marine Corps Band plays for the public on Friday evenings (see Chapter 8).

## Two New Neighborhoods

While some expected new towns to solve the urban housing crisis of the 1950s, others turned their attention to revamping the existing city. Washington has seen many and varying building developments; two recent ones are particularly notable: the Southwest Urban Renewal Area and the Watergate.

**Southwest Urban Renewal Area.** The boundary runs approximately along Independence Avenue from 12th Street to 3rd Street, south on 3rd to C Street, east on C to South Capitol Street, south on South Capitol Street to the waterfront, west and north along the waterfront to 12th Street.

This area was one of the earliest and most massive urban renewal efforts sponsored by the government. Begun in 1953, it covers 560 acres, most of which have been entirely rebuilt. Some believe it has been successful; critics feel that the wholesale bulldozing and subsequent construction of modern buildings has given the area a sterile quality, and point out that a middle-class enclave has been created at the expense of the lower-income residents who lived there previously.

Generally, the area can be divided into two sections. North of the freeway the space is occupied mostly by federal office buildings, with the exception of **L'Enfant Plaza,** which is a complex with a hotel, office buildings, shops, theater, and restaurants. At its southern end is **Banneker Circle,** a pleasant park, named for black mathematician Benjamin Banneker, who, along with L'Enfant, is credited with planning the city of Washington. Many well-known architects are associated with the Southwest area: The Plaza, built in 1965, was designed by I. M. Pei & Partners and Araldo Cussutta (the hotel and west office building were designed by Vlastimil Koubek); the **Forrestal Building,** headquarters of the US Army Corps of Engineers, was designed by Curtis & Davis, Fordyce and Hamby Associates, and Frank Grad & Sons; the **Department of Housing and Urban Development** was designed by Marcel Breuer and Associates and Nolen, Swinburne & Associates in 1968; and the **Nassif Building,** headquarters of the Department of Transportation, by Edward Durell Stone.

South of the freeway the redevelopment mainly took the form of residential buildings, although there are some offices, a shopping center, the waterfront with various commercial establishments, and a very fine theater. Good examples of the new residential complexes are **Tiber Island** at 429 N Street, stretching to M Street and from 6th Street to 2nd Street, designed by Keyes, Lethbridge and Condon and completed in 1965; and **Carrollsburg Square,** 1100 3rd Street and 1100 6th Street, designed by I. M. Pei, 1961-2, and Chloethiel Woodward Smith, 1972. Also note the handsome

**Arena Stage/Kreeger Theater** complex.

In case you wonder what the area used to be like, a few historic buildings somehow escaped being razed. Most are the product of the city's first real estate syndicate, formed about 1793, which at one point owned one-third of the land on sale in the city. The group was not successful; in four years it went bankrupt, but it left behind a small legacy. The **Thomas Law** (or Honeymoon) **House,** at 1252 6th Street, is one of the first houses designed by William Lovering in 1794. It was restored in 1965 and is open from time to time, though on no regular schedule. Around the corner is **Duncanson-Cranch House** at 468-70 N Street, a double house built by the syndicate, also attributed to Lovering, 1794. Nearby is the **Edward Simon Lewis House** at 456 N Street, built in 1817, well after the syndicate folded. At 1315-21 4th Street is **Wheat Row** (Lovering 1794), another syndicate product, modest in style and cost.

**The Watergate,** 2500, 2600, and 2700 Virginia Avenue NW and 600 and 700 New Hampshire Avenue NW (337-0020). Parking at commercial lot underneath the building. The Watergate was designed by Luigi Moretti and built by an Italian firm as a planned downtown community that has almost everything—shops, restaurants, recreation, open space, offices, a health club, hotel, and the Kennedy Center next door. The catch for most people is the cost, since the residential units are among the most expensive in Washington. Though the complex is mammoth, its shape—meandering and convoluted—hides its overall size, which might otherwise be overwhelming, and allows for partially enclosed green spaces with fountains and a sense of different "neighborhoods." There are places to dine inside and out, malls with unique shops, and many scenic vistas. The architecture is controversial, but the concept, while not within everyone's reach economically, is nonetheless one interesting answer to urban living.

## Two New Towns

The deterioration of urban areas spurred attempts in the '50s and '60s to develop alternatives to city living. Two new towns emerged near Washington: first Reston, Virginia, then Columbia, Maryland. Both are total communities—that is, they provide a full range of facilities, jobs, dwellings, shops, recreation, open space, and the like. Their economic fortunes have fluctuated along with the rest of the economy.

**Columbia, MD** (301-730-7700, ask for the Vistor Center). About 30 minutes. Capital Beltway (Route 495) to Columbia Pike north to Little Patuxent Parkway north to Columbia Mall and Visitor Center at Wincopin Circle. Monday-Friday 8:30 am-5 pm; Saturday, Sunday, and holidays 10:30 am-5 pm. Parking. Car necessary for touring. Started in 1963, this new town is unusual because of its wide range of facilities. Today the town has 37,000 residents of a projected 97,000. Whether or not it will ultimately succeed, and by whose definition, is still being argued. Most residents seem pleased, but critics assail the town's failure to attract a diverse population; the costly housing; and the lag in building a college and inexpensive apartments.

Make your first stop the **Visitor Center,** where there is an exhibition, a 12-minute slide show, and lots of free literature, including a map (an important adjunct). Staff is on hand to answer questions. You may take advantage of the excellent recreational facilities—many are free, others charge a reasonable rate (Columbia Park and Recreation Association—301-730-6100).

**Reston, VA** (471-4810, ask for the Information Center). About 30 minutes. Capital Beltway (Route 495) to Route 7 west to Route 606 to the Information Center at 11401 North Shore Drive. Winter Monday-Friday 10 am-5 pm; Saturday and Sunday 10 am-6 pm; summer Monday-Friday 10 am-6 pm; Saturday and Sunday 10 am-7 pm; weekend hours prevail on holidays. Parking. H. Reston was one of the first of the recent new towns, and its early history was touch-and-go, largely because businesses were not anxious to locate that far from Washington. Without industry there were too few jobs to attract residents. That has changed to some extent. In 1974 there were 23,500 inhabitants of a projected 75,000, with 4,585 employed.

Start at the Information Center, where a brochure outlines the town's history and organization and provides maps for two self-guided tours, one walking, one driving. A few examples of what to see: The Stone House, scaled for children; award-winning Washington Plaza; the imaginative Van Gogh pedestrian suspension bridge; housing clusters; and the unusual semi-star-shaped building of the U.S. Geological Survey. A two-hour tour costing $20 can be arranged by calling Miss Floyd, 471-4810.

Chapter Six

# Entertainment and Sports

THIERRY BRIGHT-SAGNIER

If you're visiting Washington for the first time and you think the city's entertainment is provided solely by the Smithsonian Institution and the United States Congress, you're in for a pleasant surprise. In recent years, the local entertainment industry has boomed; complaints that there's nothing to do after 10 pm have declined. Truth is, there's a lot to do here, regardless of your tastes.

Washingtonians no longer have to travel to New York for theater and to Baltimore for burlesque. We've got professionals in both fields, as well as a bona fide opera company and a fine symphony orchestra. More and more Broadway-bound shows try out here each season, and the many area indoor and outdoor theaters are favored stops for touring dance, opera, music, and repertory drama companies. There are the usual first-run movie houses, of course, and also a number of theaters and museums that screen classics and art films, some of which are free.

The nightclubs seem to be holding on, even in the face of a depressed economy. Many talented local performers have chosen Washington as their home base, and virtually any night of the week you can listen to Charlie Byrd's guitar, Richie Cole's alto sax, or Marshall Hawkins' bass. You can also find places to do a quick fox-trot or a slow waltz, watch some of the nation's best bluegrass performers pick and sing Appalachian blues, or perhaps meet someone interesting in a singles club.

Washington might not be a sports capital, but it fields acceptable football, basketball, and hockey teams; keeps racetracks busy a good part of the year; and offers aficionados auto racing, soccer, polo, and even rowing.

Getting around at night can be a problem. Most parking lots charge between 50¢ and 90¢ an hour, but in entertainment areas—particularly Georgetown—lots are scarce and street parking even scarcer. You might consider taking a bus, but you should probably take a cab. Metrobus after-dark service is rather spotty, and exact-change system can be a hindrance if all you have is a $20 bill.

Many hotels and motels are on main cab routes, and several companies operate all night. You might have to let the phone ring a while, but eventually you'll get an answer. That doesn't mean the promised cab will ever come, though, if you're out of the city's high-traffic areas. Try 546-2400 (Capitol Cab); 387-6200 (Diamond Cab); LI 4-1212 (Yellow Cab), or refer to the Yellow Pages. Taxis charge an extra 50¢ for responding to a call. Once you're in a major entertainment district, you won't have any trouble picking up a cab on the street. At out-of-the-way places, ask the management to call a taxi for you in advance.

The dress of Washington audiences and pub crawlers ranges from very elegant to very relaxed. Some appear at theater openings and first-night operas in black tie, and many women wear long dresses to any performance at the Kennedy

Center. But most of the places you'll want to go will demand less sartorial splendor. As a rule, the clubs and bars located in the bigger hotels prefer that men wear ties. Georgetown and Capitol Hill nightspots are by and large dress-as-you-will, but a few establishments require coat and tie after dark. Call before you go or carry a clip-on tie in your pocket. And for even more important insurance, get advance tickets or make reservations before starting out on a night on the town, especially on weekends.

# Night Life

## Nightclubs

My definition of a nightclub is a place where there is entertainment, alcohol, and in some cases, dancing. Those listed here are only a sample of what's available; they run the gamut from cheap to expensive, pushy to subdued. There's something for everyone—young or old, single or couples, gay or straight.

The recession-depression-inflation has hit the entertainment clubs rather hard. Many have been forced to cut back their live entertainment; a few have ceased to produce anything more complicated than a bottle of beer. By the time you read this, it's entirely possible that some clubs listed will be closed or vastly different. Call before you go.

Local liquor laws control the closing hours of bars and clubs. In the District most are open until the legal cut-off hour of 2 am Sunday through Thursday and 3 am Friday and Saturday. The law forbids the sale of liquor after those hours, but customers generally remain until they finish their drinks. Maryland and Virginia laws are slightly different. Most Maryland and Virginia clubs stop serving drinks at midnight and allow a half hour for customers to finish them. Unless otherwise noted, closings in the clubs listed here conform to legal closing hours.

The cover charges are usually higher on weekends than during the week and can vary depending on the stature of the performers.

### BLUEGRASS AND FOLK

Washington has been called the nation's bluegrass capital (the world bluegrass capital, incidentally, is Tokyo). Bluegrass has reached an all-time popularity in recent years, and Washington can boast of having the country's best groups on a year-round basis. The Country Gentlemen started here. The Seldom Scene, Hickory Wind, Grass Menagerie, None of the Above, Informed Sources—all are bands to watch for. The area also offers excellent folk musicians, such as Bill and Taffy of "Country Roads" fame. Many clubs feature an "open microphone" or "hootenanny" night when amateur performers take over the stage.

**The Cellar Door,** 34th and M Streets NW (337-3390). Two shows nightly, three on Saturday. Cover charge. The Cellar Door offers performers ranging from Doc Watson to Country Joe, largely folk and bluegrass with an occasional smattering of jazz. The cover charge is relatively expensive but the caliber of entertainment is high.

**Chancery,** 704 New Jersey Avenue NW (638-2500). Closed Sunday. Cover charge on weekends. The Chancery caters primarily to college students from neighboring Georgetown Law School as well as to night workers from the Government Printing Office, which makes for an interesting crowd. The music is excellent, particularly when Clayton Hambrick or Hickory Wind play there. There's dancing on Tuesdays.

**Childe Harold,** 1610 20th Street NW (483-6700). Cover charge. Childe Harold occasionally books national talents like Josh Graves, but more often relies on local people of some stature. The entertainment is in a small, friendly upstairs room with good drinks and fair sound.

**The Corsican,** 1716 I Street NW (298-8488). Open until midnight Sunday; closed Monday and Tuesday. Cover charge. The Corsican occasionally features bluegrass, but the drink prices are rather steep. It's a good talking club, though, with a pleasant atmosphere.

**The Dubliner**, 4 F Street NW (737-3773). The Dubliner is a long, narrow bar owned and managed by Hugh Kelly, a portly gentleman who has tried to duplicate the atmosphere of a true Irish pub. The place seats less than 100, and gets crowded when everyone stands to do a jig. Music is provided by the three-piece Irish Tradition composed of a fiddle, an accordion, and a guitar. The Tradition does mostly old-timey music, but occasionally cut loose with an Irish revolutionary anthem. On Thursdays, the Alexandria pipers play for an hour or two.

**Matt Kane's Bit O' Ireland,** 1118 13th Street NW (ME 8-8058). Weekend minimum. Matt Kane's is a drinking man's Irish bar. There are Irish pipe players and wandering minstrels who sing the glory of the old country. It's a favorite hangout of reporters and editors after the paper has been put to bed.

**Red Fox Inn,** 4940 Fairmont Avenue, Bethesda, MD (652-4429). Cover charge Tuesday-Saturday, and Sunday when there is live entertainment. The Red Fox is one of the nation's bluegrass meccas. Owner Walter Broderick gets reservations from all over the country and fan letters from all over the world. His stage has seen the most talented banjo, guitar, and mandolin pickers on the East Coast, and he regularly books the Seldom Scene. Celebrities drop in; congressmen and truck drivers, musicians and writers have made it a second home. Seating capacity is less than 150, so call and reserve.

**William's Restaurant,** 3014 Colvin Street, Alexandria, VA (751-1722). Cover charge on entertainment nights—Wednesday, Friday, Saturday, and Sunday. William's is another well-known bluegrass club with live bands four nights a week. It has excellent acoustics, but the usually moderate cover charge can go as high as $5 when it books national name bands.

## JAZZ

Washington is a good jazz town, though it has had its hard times, periods when jazz musicians could find few, if any, clubs to hire them. In recent years, however, there's been something of a jazz revival that has seen both traditional and mainstream artists develop their music. There are a number of nationally known jazz musicians who live and play here, and, after all, Washington has a reputation to maintain, being the birthplace of Duke Ellington.

You might look for particular bands like the New Sunshine Jazz Band or the Original Washington Monument Jazz Band. A great deal of information about who's appearing where can be obtained from the **Potomac River Jazz Club** (630-7752). The club holds weekly sessions in the Windjammer Room of the Marriott Twin Bridges Motor Hotel in Arlington, Virginia, Sundays 7:30-11:30 pm, featuring visiting groups and soloists. No cover charge.

**Blues Alley,** 1307 Wisconsin Avenue NW (337-4141). Closed Sunday. Cover charge. Blues Alley is perhaps Washington's best-known and best-loved strictly jazz club. It also has a deserved reputation for good Creole food. The club has become a stop for touring artists as well as for local musicians. Audiences are generally attentive here, and extraneous sounds, a distraction in most jazz clubs, are minimal.

**Ed Murphy's Supper Club,** 2308 Georgia Avenue NW (234-3617). Cover charge. This is a favorite with a predominantly black audience that comes to eat as well as to catch the name groups who play here.

**Embers,** 1200 19th Street NW (296-6555), is also a restaurant with above-average jazz for its diners. Call to make reservations for Friday and Saturday nights. Closed Sunday.

**Harold's Rogue and Jar,** 1814 N Street NW (296-3192). Cover Tuesday-Saturday; two drink minimum Monday; no cover Sunday. Harold's is a favorite haunt of local musicians who jam there and form free-floating bands. The place is rather small, but it helps the music. The cover pays the performers. The crowd is young and immersed in the music.

**King of France Tavern,** 20 Maryland Circle, Annapolis, MD (261-2206). Open until 1 am, closed Monday. Cover. If you're in the mood for a drive, some excellent music, and good food, you might consider a trip to this basement tavern in an 18th-century inn. The King of France, home base for Charlie Byrd, books some of the best talent around. If you're too tired to drive back, you can spend the night upstairs in the Maryland Inn. Reservations recommended.

**Mr. Henry's Upstairs,** 601 Pennsylvania Avenue SE (546-8412). Cover on weekends. Mr. Henry's is where Roberta Flack got her start, and it's hard to tell who did more for whom. We all know where Roberta Flack went, and her rise has made the Upstairs the coveted spot for performers hoping to make it big. It's dressier than most places. Reservations should be made, depending on the performer's popularity.

**Top O' the Foolery,** 2131 Pennsylvania Avenue NW (333-7784). Cover. The predominantly black crowd here is slightly older and more chic than in many other clubs. Top O' the Foolery presents the best local talents, both professional and amateur, and tends to be jammed.

**Zambezi Club,** 4021 South Capitol Street (563-4161). Closed Monday. Cover on weekends. The Zambezi features primarily black performers playing for a black audience, but everyone is made to feel welcome. Make reservations on weekends.

### ROCK AND ROLL

Washington cannot truthfully be called a rock-and-roll town, though it does have some excellent bands. Some bars feature house bands, but most club owners prefer to choose their performers from a constantly changing list of talent. Perhaps the main trouble with most rock clubs is the high decibel level, which makes conversation impossible. Most, however, are good places to dance, and the drinks are relatively cheap.

**The Bayou/Bitter End,** 3350 K Street NW (333-2897). Closed Monday. Cover. The Bayou, located in Georgetown's warehouse district beneath the Whitehurst Freeway, has tried every form of entertainment. A long time ago, it was a strip joint featuring the best of the tassel twirlers; then it featured local rock bands. In December of last year, it assumed its present name, Bitter End, and went into the big time. Some excellent performers have appeared there: James Cotton, Rory Gallagher, Jerry Jeff Walker. It's a listening and dancing club with medium-priced drinks, frequented by a relatively young and relaxed group.

**Black Greco,** 2000 L Street NW (293-2060). No cover. During the day it's a cafeteria, but at night a band plays hard rock to an audience in its middle-twenties. The house band is called The Eye, and it's a seven-piecer, unusual in size—if nothing else. Thursday and Sunday are "oldies but goodies" nights.

**Bogie's,** 1214 Connecticut Avenue NW (628-0852). Cover. Bogie's hires some big-name bands such as Dr. Hook and the Medicine Show, Canned Heat, and Stories. The house band, Foxie, is one of the District's best, so the music is good even when national names aren't there. No reservations accepted.

**Butterfly Nightclub,** 823 14th Street NW (628-0852). No cover. The Butterfly offers a change of pace from the more middle-class local clubs. It's a racially integrated place along the "adult strip," one of the many clubs, including the Silver Slipper and Benny's Rebel Room, that offer hard rock and no cover or minimum. Beware of the drink hustle. You might think the liquor you're buying is wooing the young woman who approached you, but chances are you'll be hugging only your wallet at the end of the night.

**Crazy Horse,** 3259 M Street NW (333-0400). Weekend cover. Crazy Horse was named after the celebrated Parisian nightspot, but bears no resemblance to that venerated institution. Located in the heart of Georgetown, it offers straight-ahead rock at blasting level as well as a variety of films shown simultaneously on movie screens. Some of the area's better bands gig there. Good dancing in an atmosphere of smoke and beer.

**The Keg,** 2205 Wisconsin Avenue NW (333-9594). Closed Monday. Cover. The Keg is way up front in the decibel contest with hard rock by groups like Cherry People. It has dancing and a young crowd in anything from jeans to jodhpurs. Go there on your motorcycle.

**Larry Brown's,** Connecticut Avenue and R Street NW (332-7440). Closed Sunday. Cover. In an old mansion a plush integrated club for dinner, drinking, and dancing to rock bands. Football star Larry Brown's new spot attracts a dressy late-late night crowd that begins pouring in after midnight.

**The M Club,** 3124 M Street NW (333-5955). Cover. The M Club is in the same style as the Keg, but slightly smaller. Perhaps its main advantage is its location in the heart of Georgetown.

**Reading Gaol,** P Street NW in the alley between 21st and 22nd Streets NW (833-3882). Cover Wednesday, Friday, and Saturday. Reading Gaol, near Dupont Circle, offers good drinks and good music to a sophisticated audience. It's a wood-paneled, homey place with an excellent sound system. Reading Gaol, however, features rock only on certain nights. Call before you go.

**The Showboat Lounge,** 2477 18th Street NW (265-0830). Cover. The Showboat is where guitarist Charlie Byrd began his career, but now it's a soul/rock club where some of the area's better black bands play regularly. The club is mostly patronized by ultra-chic black customers. The Columbia Road and 18th Street area has some other good entertainment worth checking out.

**COMEDY**

**The Marquee Lounge,** Shoreham Americana Hotel, Calvert Street and Connecticut Avenue NW (234-0700). Two shows nightly. Minimum Friday and Saturday; no cover. The attraction here is political satirist Mark Russell, who every night for the past decade, has verbally sliced to ribbons the administration, Congress, and foreign policy. The customers here include conventioneers, the well-heeled from Georgetown, and representatives of all political persuasions—and everyone has a good time, even when they're the butt of the humor. Dancing between shows to a middle-of-the-road house band.

## Singles Bars

Washington has a large population of unattached men and women who frequent bars designed to facilitate meetings and casual relationships. Many of these do not feature live music or any form of entertainment; the crowd is left to amuse itself. The idea is to buy a drink and walk around. There are no cover charges.

**The Aeroplane,** 1207 19th Street NW (223-3617). Closed Sunday. The Aeroplane draws young, relatively urbane, well-informed professionals who gather here after work. The bar area is small and tends to be packed after 5 pm, but the wood paneling and conviviality make it an attractive spot.

**Charing Cross,** 3027 M Street NW (338-2141). This is not by design a singles place, but it does attract a number of unattached people. The motif is an American version of an English pub. The atmosphere is extremely relaxed, and the ales and Italian food are good, especially the pasta dishes.

**Clyde's,** 3236 M Street NW (333-9180). Clyde's is the parent of virtually every "exposed-brick-and-wood-paneling" saloon in Georgetown, and by far the most successful. It's not exclusively a singles club, but singles go there; it's not high class, but bejeweled ladies and Cardin-suited men enjoy its atrium. In its three rooms you'll find good hamburgers, omelettes, and a great jukebox.

**The Exchange,** 1831 M Street NW (833-1495). This very popular singles bar is designed to look like a miniature stock exchange, complete with a "big board." You might have to search for it, since it's located in the basement of Mrs. French's plant store. Bankers, ad men, and, yes, stockbrokers go to the Exchange. There is entertainment in the back room Tuesday-Friday and in the front room Saturday.

**Fran O' Brien's,** 1823 L Street NW (296-3918). Frannie's is a favorite of sports-minded singles. There are pictures of Redskins and Bullets players and a huge television set to follow the games. There's also a rock band at night, which plays new and old music.

**The Guards,** 29th and M Streets NW (695-2350). The Guards is a coat-and-tie place after dark, the quintessential singles club for people in their late twenties and early thirties. The setting is posh; the drinks rather expensive. The technique here is to roam around meeting people until one strikes up a conversation worth pursuing.

**Mr. Henry's Georgetown,** corner of M Street and Wisconsin Avenue NW (337-4333). Mr. Henry's, though not exclusively gay, has for a long time provided homosexuals as well as straights with a quiet place to meet. Located as it is on Georgetown's main intersection, it also is a stopping place for what's left of the Georgetown street people, who particularly like the spaghetti dinner (all you can eat for $2).

**Jenkin's Hill,** 223 Pennsylvania Avenue SE (544-6600). Jenkin's, on Capitol Hill, boasts that it has Washington's longest bar, which might or might not be true. Hill lawyers and students mix here, and it's not unusual to see one of our public servants quaffing a few after a hot Senate debate. The drinks are steep, but good.

**Pall Mall Restaurant,** 3235 M Street NW

(965-5353). Paul Mall is a favorite of Redskin football players and their ladies, as well as with people who like a convivial and sporty atmosphere. There's dancing nightly to a good rock band.

**Ventuno 21 Supper Club,** 1119 21st Street NW (466-2616). Ventuno's has several attractions—including a large dance floor, a top band, and no cover or minimum—that seem to appeal to affluent singles in their late twenties and early thirties.

## Dancing

### BALLROOM

If you prefer to dance to the beat of a different (and slower) drum, Washington has rooms, often in large hotels or motels, where bands play more traditional dance music. Some of these spots also have floor shows.

The **Marriotts** and **Holiday Inns,** for instance, often feature entertainment and dancing. The entertainment differs from hotel to hotel, but there is no cover or minimum. Reservations are recommended, especially on Saturday nights.

**Alexander's Three Penthouse Restaurant,** 1500 Wilson Boulevard, Rosslyn, VA (527-0100). Closed Sundays. Located on the top floor of the Rosslyn Hotel, Alexander's offers a choice view of Washington to enjoy while you fox-trot to your heart's content.

**Apple of Eve,** Loews L'Enfant Plaza Hotel, 480 L'Enfant Plaza East SW (484-1000). Closed Sundays. The Apple, a dimly lit restaurant in one of Washington's classier hotels, offers dancing and entertainment after 9 pm.

**Four Oaks Restaurant,** Washington Hilton Hotel, Connecticut Avenue and Columbia Road NW (483-3000). The Hilton is a favorite of conventioneers and others who are used to traveling around the world Hilton-style. The lavish Four Oaks provides danceable music for a coat-and-tie crowd on Friday and Saturday evenings after 8 pm.

**Port O' Georgetown,** 1054 31st Street NW (338-6600). No dancing Sundays. The Port is a large restaurant with exposed brick walls and a nautical theme in Canal Square, Georgetown's quaint old/new shopping mall. Its attractions include dining, dancing, and a floor show.

**Ramada Inn,** 901 N. Fairfax Street, Alexandria, VA (683-6000). Closed Monday. A show, dancing to a combo, a vocalist singing Broadway show tunes—and on Sunday afternoons a buffet instead of the regular dinner.

### DISCOTHÈQUES

Discothèques are staging a comeback in Washington. However, they come and go quickly. Here are a few current favorites.

**Boccaccio,** 3204 M Street NW (333-6767). No cover. Boccaccio is located above the Rive Gauche Restaurant at the corner of Wisconsin Avenue and M Street. A long time ago this was Whisky À-go-go, the District's first discothèque. Now it is done in more-or-less European decor and frequented by a relatively sauve crowd. The dancing is good and so are the drinks.

**East India Sporting Club,** 2915 M Street NW (965-2350). No cover. The India Club is known as one of Georgetown's elite singles places where the Beautiful People like to go. It is very posh and drinks are on the expensive side.

**Le Club Zanzibar,** 2015 L Street NW (833-9565). No cover. Le Club Zanzibar is for stylish people who all seem to have money. The crowd is not all gay, but one does get the feeling that straights are in the minority. The Zanzibar is housed in what was once a carwash, and is decorated in New York disco fashion. It offers excellent recorded music and the latest word on fashion.

## Coffeehouses

If alcohol and late hours are not your thing, you might try Washington's coffeehouses. No hamburger and donut places these, but real coffeehouses in the old European tradition of wandering guitarists and itinerant poets. Most coffeehouses are affiliated with a religious organization, but no one does any proselytizing.

**The Iguana,** Vermont Avenue and N Street NW (667-1377). Friday and Saturday 8:30 pm-midnight. The Iguana is Washington's oldest coffeehouse. It serves a legendary 5¢ cup of coffee and hosts amateur lutenists, banjo pickers, and guitar strummers who play and wander off into the night.

**New Friend's Coffeehouse,** Quaker House, Decatur Street at Connecticut and Florida Avenues NW (483-3310). Tuesday-Saturday 6 pm-11:30 pm; Friday until midnight. There is entertainment Friday nights, lectures and poetry readings on

Wednesdays, and chess on Tuesdays.

**Potter's House,** 1658 Columbia Road NW (265-6816). Open nightly except Tuesday 8 pm-11:30 pm. Located in the racially mixed Adams-Morgan area, the Potter's House is posh as coffeehouses go. It has open forums with well-known Washingtonians and some entertainment. Expect to spend at least $2.

# Music and Dance

Music, particularly during the summer months, is everywhere in Washington; but year-round, you can hear classical music performed by solo artists or symphony orchestras, attend jazz and rock concerts, watch opera or ballet. Although it has only a few resident companies, such as the National Symphony, the Washington Opera Society, and the Capitol Ballet Company, Washington regularly hosts the Philadelphia Orchestra, the Metropolitan Opera, and many other distinguished ensembles.

Although some performances are costly to attend, there are many musical events offered without charge, often featuring such first-class performers as the Juilliard String Quartet and the Washington National Symphony.

## Admission Charge

**Capital Centre,** Landover, MD (350-3900). Off Capital Beltway (Route 495) Exits 32E and 33E. The Capital Centre, although relatively new, has already become a cultural center of sorts. It hosts numerous sports events (see Sports in this chapter), but it also serves as the largest auditorium around for rock and soul concerts. The biggest acts have played there: The Who, James Brown, Johnny Cash, B. B. King, Linda Ronstadt. In spite of its size, it's designed so that no seat is farther than 200 feet from the stage, and a color television screen is suspended from the ceiling for added viewing. Show times and prices vary. Tickets available at downtown ticket office, 18th Street NW between K and L Streets, and at ticket agencies.

**Carter Barron Amphitheatre,** 16th Street and Colorado Avenue NW (723-2435). The outdoor Carter Barron Amphitheatre was once one of the city's best and most famous theaters. After several years of primarily black rock music, it is going back to hosting a wider variety of performing artists, including the National Symphony Orchestra, Alvin Ailey Dance Company, and a Shakespearean repertory company, as well as popular musicians such as the O'Jays, the Blue Oyster Cult, and Kris Kristofferson. The program runs for 12 weeks during the summer months.

**Constitution Hall,** 18th and D Streets NW (638-2661). Constitution Hall has been the scene of excellent concerts, both classical and popular, although it stays away from hard-rock shows, preferring jazz, bluegrass or folk. The hall is small, comfortable, and homey. Tickets for most performances are reasonably priced. The box office is open Monday-Saturday 10 am-10 pm; Sunday noon-6 pm.

**Hayfield High School,** 7630 Telegraph Road, Alexandria, VA (971-8920). Hayfield has become the area's best bluegrass-country concert hall. The performances, held either in the auditorium or in the gym, are friendly and relaxed. Call Ticketron for show times and prices.

**John F. Kennedy Center for Performing Arts,** 2700 F Street NW (872-0466). The Kennedy Center is a lavish cultural showcase overlooking the Potomac River and Virginia skyline. It houses four separate theaters: the Concert Hall, Opera House, Eisenhower Theater, and the American Film Institute Theater. The Kennedy Center is worth a visit, even if you don't plan to attend a performance there. Many of the furnishings are gifts from foreign countries, and no expense was spared on details that are sometimes lost in the vastness of the interior. There are free guided tours every day from 10:15 am-1:15 pm, leaving every 15 minutes from parking level A. The tours take between 35 and 45 minutes. The National Park Service presents free Rooftop Talks about the capital, weekends from 11 am-4 pm, on the Roof Terrace.

If you're too early for a performance, you might consider having a drink in the lobby, or dinner before or after a show in one of the rooftop restaurants—the Promenade cafeteria, the intimate Gallery Café, or the elegant Grande Scène.

Parking is easy, since the complex has a huge underground garage that charges as you enter ($2). The arrangement makes for a usually quick getaway after a performance, but it can slow down your arrival, so allow some extra time before the curtain. Metrobus lines 80 and 81 go to the Center.

Musical performances are presented in either the Concert Hall (ticket information 254-3776) or the Opera House (254-3770). The box office hours for both are Monday-Saturday 10 am-9 pm; Sunday noon-9 pm. The Concert Hall has evening performances at 8:30 pm and matinees at 3 pm; the Opera House has evening performances at 8 pm and matinees at 2 pm on Wednesdays and Saturdays. It is difficult to hear dialogue past the middle of the Opera House, and the acoustics in the front rows of the Concert Hall leave something to be desired. You should also be aware that many of the seats in the upper tiers of the Concert Hall have obstructed sight lines. These are sold at bargain prices and, since the sound is just as good as any place else in the house, are very much in demand (and if you can get one on a front row you can see the stage by leaning forward).

In addition to hosting local and international dance, opera, vocal, and orchestral groups and soloists, Kennedy Center also books notable rock and rollers and jazz greats. Among the local companies that perform at the center are the Capitol Ballet Company, the National Symphony Orchestra, and the Washington Opera Society.

*Capitol Ballet Company,* 1200 Delafield Place NW (TU2-4039). This Washington-based professional ballet troupe is an outgrowth of the Jones-Haywood School of Ballet. Its future is uncertain, but it plans to perform at the Kennedy Center Opera House.

*National Symphony Orchestra,* John F. Kennedy Center (785-8100). The National Symphony performs year-round in the Concert Hall. Led by Antal Dorati or a guest conductor, and featuring distinguished soloists, the orchestra often plays three times a week during its subscription season (October-May). In the summer, in addition to concerts at Kennedy Center, it also plays at Wolf Trap Park Farm (see below) and participates in the National Capital Park's annual Summer in the Parks Program. Watch for performances of the recently formed National Symphony Quartet and National Symphony Chamber Orchestra.

*Opera Society of Washington,* 2000 P Street NW (296-8660). The local opera company performs three operas at the sumptuous Kennedy Center Opera House from February-April. The leading roles are filled by international professional stars. In May the company presents chamber opera in Lisner Auditorium. The Opera House is also the scene of performances by the New York City Opera, Bolshoi Opera, and other national and international opera troupes.

**Lisner Auditorium,** George Washington University, 21st and H Streets NW (676-6800). Lisner is one of the Washington Folklore Society's favorite places. It has brought Pete Seeger there several times, as well as other famous musicians. Once in a while, there will be a rock concert, but these are rare. The Washington Ballet Company performs the Nutcracker Suite during the Christmas season.

**Merriweather Post Pavilion,** Columbia, MD (953-2424). Mid-June to mid-August daily 7 or 8 pm. About 40 minutes from Washington. Capital Beltway (Route 495) to Columbia Pike north to Patuxent Parkway. The Pavilion, an outdoor theater with a partial roof, stages a variety of rock, pop, and classical concerts. It is the summer home of the Baltimore Symphony Orchestra from June-August. (For information about the Baltimore Symphony summer or winter schedule, write to 120 W. Mt. Royal Avenue, Baltimore, MD 21201.)

**Shady Grove Music Fair,** Shady Grove Road, Rockville, MD (301-948-3400). About 35 minutes. Take Route 270 (70S) to Shady Grove Exit. Tuesday-Sunday 8 pm; matinees Saturday and Sunday 3 pm; some Saturdays 7 pm and 10:30 pm. Tickets also at Ticketron. At one time only a summer theater, Shady Grove is now open year-round. It books all kinds of well-known pop groups—jazz, country, soul, and rock.

**Smithsonian Institution,** Box Office: Arts and Industries Building, 900 Jefferson Drive SW (381-5395). In addition to films and lectures (some free) that it sponsors, the Smithsonian Division of Performing Arts schedules musical events ranging from traditional to modern and from jazz to folk in the Museum of Natural History, the

Museum of History and Technology, and the Hirshhorn Museum. They are usually held in the evening, and some are preceded by free afternoon workshops. Reduced prices for members.

**Washington Performing Arts Socitey,** 1300 G Street NW (393-4433). The society acts as the impresario for several series of symphony, vocal, small ensemble, and solo performances in the Concert Hall of the Kennedy Center from October to May, Friday and Saturday at 8:30 pm; Sunday at 3 pm. These are sold by subscription, but single-performance seats are available at the Washington Performing Arts Society office or at the Concert Hall ticket office. The society also brings performing artists to Kennedy Center, Lisner Auditorium, and other places. Tickets also available at Ticketron and Records & Tapes Ltd.

**Wolf Trap Farm Park,** Vienna, VA (938-3800). About ½ hour from Washington. Take the Capital Beltway (Route 495) to Wolf Trap Exit. Performances Tuesday-Sunday 8:30 pm; Sunday matinee 3:30 pm. Park open noon-9 pm daily. Refreshment tent. Picnicking on grounds. The Farm's covered Filene Center is a Kennedy Center without walls, presenting a summer cornucopia of opera, ballet, jazz, theater, rock—you name it. The combined indoor-outdoor facility seats close to 3,500 people, and if you want to sit on the lawn, you can buy a ticket for as little as $2. Although dinner is available at the refreshment tent, it is recommended that you bring your own picnic. The '75 season includes appearances by the Metropolitan Opera, the New York City Ballet, Stan Kenton, and many others. Wolf Trap's own student company stages a few operas and musicals each season featuring visiting professional artists.

## Free

**The Anacostia Neighborhood Museum,** 2405 Martin Luther King Avenue SE (381-6691). The museum presents a Sunday Performing Arts Program once a month. Local talents play blues, jazz, and gospel. There are also amateur dance troupes, poetry readings, and drama.

**The United States Capitol** (224-3121). Pop concerts by the Armed Forces Bands can be heard at 8 pm Monday, Tuesday, Wednesday, and Friday during the summer months on the steps of the Capitol.

**The D.C. Department of Recreation Concerts.** The Department of Recreation sponsors free concerts ranging from rock music to opera.

The *Ambassador's Orchestra and Showmobile Revue* (829-7050) presents rock and soul concerts to a teenage audience. The concerts are given at various locations and times, so it's best to call for details.

The *Baroque Arts Chamber Orchestra* (629-7226) plays one Tuesday a month at Alice Deal Junior High School (Fort Drive and Nebraska Avenue NW) and gives Thursday night chamber concerts at various other locations.

*The Civic Opera* (629-7347) presents four operas a year, including two at the Kennedy Center and one at the Lisner Auditorium.

**Adventure Theater,** Glen Echo Park, MacArthur Boulevard and Goldsboro Road, Glen Echo, MD (229-3009 or 229-3031). The National Park Service sponsors folk and bluegrass concerts here at irregular intervals during the winter, for which there is an admission charge. From July to October the Park Service holds free Sunday evening bluegrass performances by such notables as Grass Menagerie and autoharp virtuoso Brian Bowers.

**The Library of Congress,** First Street and Independence Avenue SE (393-4463). Usually Thursday and/or Friday at 8:30 pm. The Library's concerts are one of the biggest bargains in town. For a service charge of 25¢ you get a seat in the intimate 500-seat Library auditorium where you will hear the Juilliard String Quartet and other artists whose repertoire ranges from medieval to modern. Tickets are available the Monday before the performance at 8:30 am at the Campbell Music Company, 1300 G Street NW (two to a customer). If you call Campbell's (347-8464), they will hold tickets for you until 1 pm Tuesday. The only problem is getting through on the telephone.

**Jefferson Memorial** band concerts. Wednesday 8 pm June-August, the U.S. Army Fife and Drum Corps, accompanied by the U.S. Army Band and Choir, plays a *Torchlight Tattoo.* It's one of the city's more impressive shows. Take a pillow, a blanket, and go early.

*The Watergate Concerts,* pop concerts by the Armed Forces Bands, are held at the

Jefferson Memorial on Sunday, Tuesday, Thursday, and Friday 8:30 pm June-August. Call National Capital Parks (426-6700) for more information.

There is more military music on Fridays at 8:15 pm May-September at the *Marine Corps Barracks.* These are free, but make reservations at least a week in advance. The band concert is followed by a drill and marching show.

**National Gallery of Art,** 6th Street and Constitution Avenue NW (737-4215). Sunday 7 pm September-June. The National Gallery presents concerts played by its own orchestra, as well as by chamber groups of the highest caliber. The concerts are given in the East Garden Court, amidst an abundance of flowers, leaves, and steam that do very little for acoustical quality. However, it is a charming setting.

**National Shrine of the Immaculate Conception,** 4th Street and Michigan Avenue NE (LA 6-8300). A carillon concert every fourth Friday of the month at 7:30 pm followed by an organ concert.

**Organization of American States** (OAS), 17th Street and Constitution Avenue NW (381-8353). Irregularly on Wednesday nights, from November to April, the OAS presents classical music by performers of North, Central, and South America. You need an invitation that can be picked up at 1735 I Street NW or ordered by mail.

**Phillips Collection,** 1612 21st Street NW (387-2151). Sunday 5 pm September-May. The artists are soloists who play in a handsome room hung with Rouaults and Monticellis. Glenn Gould is a Phillips graduate, and many young musicians got their start here.

**Festival of American Folklife.** On the Mall. June 25-29, July 2-6 in 1975; throughout the summer in 1976. The Smithsonian and the National Park Service bring in the best rural artists from many parts of the country. They play everything from black blues to white gospel. If you can bear the summer heat and humidity, plan to spend a few hours there. If you're a musician yourself, check out the workshops taught by people who really know what they're talking about. The festival also includes demonstrations of arts and crafts, folk dancing, local foods, and occupational skills.

**St. John's Church,** 1525 H Street NW (DI 7-8766). Wednesday 12:10 pm. Guest organists play a wide selection of works at this regular lunch hour concert.

**Summer in the Parks Programs,** sponsored by the National Capital Parks (NCP), 1100 Ohio Drive SW (426-6975). As part of this program the National Symphony gives 20 free evening concerts at various locations. Small concerts by mostly local performers are scheduled around town during the lunch hour.

**Sylvan Theater,** Washington Monument grounds (426-6975). Performances at varying times during spring and summer. Natives consider it a treat. It's outdoors, right in the center of town, and free, if you don't mind sitting on the grass. Otherwise, it's a dollar. The Sylvan offers everything in the performing arts, including music, ballet, and theater. The Jefferson Airplane has played here, and a professional Shakespearean company is in residence every summer.

**Washington Cathedral** (The Cathedral Church of St. Peter and St. Paul), Wisconsin and Massachusetts Avenues NW (WO 6-3500). The cathedral has carillon recitals at 12:15 pm Sunday (except during Lent) and 5 pm-6 pm in summer. The well-known organ recitals at Sunday evensong have been discontinued until February 1976. The Cathedral Choral Society performs three concerts at the cathedral in the spring, for which there is an admission charge. The Choral Society also performs with the National Symphony and at other locations.

**Washington Ethical Society,** 7750 16th Street NW (882-6650). There's a free concert by the Contemporary Music Forum the third Monday of every month. The Ethical Society also has a bluegrass sing-out the third Friday of each month and a folk music open sing on the first Friday of each month. These both cost $1.

**Y.W.C.A.,** Barker Hall, 17th and K Streets NW (638-2100 Ext. 58). The Young Women's Christian Association holds a Music Hour where young Washington soloists or groups, chosen by audition, perform on Sundays at 3 pm. The Friday Morning Music Club gives concerts on Fridays at 11 am (649-5291 for information).

# Theater

Some people have unkindly suggested that the best shows in town are acted out several months a year on the House and Senate floors. Well, there's been a lot of competition lately. The Kennedy Center, National, and Ford's theaters have been booking Broadway-bound shows and touring companies in great numbers. And the old Howard Theatre has opened and plans to bring in theatrical and musical greats as it used to. There are many interesting professional and semiprofessional local companies, numerous university and amateur companies of varying skills and talents, and about a dozen dinner and summer theaters (generally located in nearby Virginia and Maryland).

To find out what's playing where and when, check the newspapers, *The Washingtonian* magazine's "Where and When" section, and *Forecast FM,* which specializes in area entertainment. As a rule, it's wise to buy tickets in advance, but it's not always necessary to make a trip to the theater to get them. The Kennedy Center and the National will accept phone orders and you can charge tickets on any major credit card (Kennedy Center offers special theater weekend packages, too). The Talbert Ticket Agency, 15th Street and Pennsylvania Avenue NW (628-5575 or ME 8-5900); Ticketron, 1101 17th Street NW and other locations (659-2601); and other agencies provide tickets to most area shows for a minimal service charge.

Some theaters have special rates for students, senior citizens, military, and/or children. Groups rates are worth looking into if you're traveling with more than four people. Be wary of scalpers trying to sell you tickets. There has been a rash of counterfeit tickets sold by unauthorized vendors. Theaters are not responsible and will not honor them.

## Theater Houses

**Ford's Theatre,** 511 10th Street NW (347-6260). Tuesday-Friday 7:30 pm; Saturday 6 and 9:30 pm; matinees Thursday and Sunday 3 pm. Box office Monday-Friday 10 am-8 pm; Saturday 10 am-10 pm; Sunday noon-4 pm. The theater where Abraham Lincoln was assassinated has been restored by loving hands that spared no detail. The only concessions made to modern theatergoers are slightly softer (but not too soft) seats and a better lighting system. The best seats available are in the center section; avoid the seats located on either side of Row E since the sight lines are not good. Ford's Theatre is relatively small and a good house for one-man shows and intimate reviews. Because of its historical associations, a touch of the past seems to rub off on both spectators and performers.

Before or after the show, you might want to visit the house across the street where Lincoln was taken after John Wilkes Booth shot him (see Civil War walking tour, Chapter 3). Commercial parking lots are plentiful in this neighborhood.

**Howard Theatre,** 620 T Street NW (462-6400). Ticket prices and showtimes vary. The Howard Theatre is one of Washington's historic landmarks. Opened in 1910, it was the scene of 60 years' worth of great performances before it closed in 1970, a victim of the Washington riots. In its time, it featured performers such as Danny Kaye, Duke Ellington, and Sarah Vaughn. Now totally rebuilt and refinished, it is going modern. The 1300-seat theater will present Redd Foxx, the Spinners, Moms Mabley, and other current headliners. The Howard hopes to become a Washington center for multiple attractions ranging from black blues shows to pre-Broadway openings. Season tickets and group rates available; tickets can be purchased through Ticketron.

**John F. Kennedy Center for the Performing Arts,** 2700 F Street NW. Eisenhower Theater (254-3600; instant charge 254-3080); Tuesday-Saturday 7:30 pm; Saturday and Sunday matinees 2 pm. Opera House (254-3770; instant charge 254-3050;); daily 8 pm; Saturday and Sunday matinees 2 pm. (See Kennedy Center entry under Music and Dance in this chapter for information on restaurants, parking, and other facilities.) The Eisenhower Theater is an elegant hall that seats 1100 people. It offers a variety of productions ranging from classic to contemporary by Broadway-bound or touring companies. While the Eisenhower Theater specializes in straight theatricals, the larger Opera House, in addition to opera and a spectacular ballet schedule, presents musicals and plays aimed at a larger audience. But one must pay for the Kennedy Center opulence. Ticket prices can be steep, and scalpers occasionally get two or even three times the face value of the tickets when they peddle them at the door.

**National Theatre,** 1321 E Street NW (628-3393; instant charge 254-3952). Monday-Saturday 8 pm; Wednesday and Saturday matinees 2 pm. Box office Monday-Saturday 10 am-9 pm. The National Theatre is now run by the management of the Kennedy Center and offers the same kind of fare as the Eisenhower Theater (you can purchase National tickets at the Eisenhower box office). The acoustics are good, the sight lines are excellent, and one can't help but be impressed by this theater's musty grandeur. There's plenty of parking nearby in a commercial lot or across the street in the District Building's parking lots.

**Shady Grove Music Fair,** Shady Grove Road, Gaithersburg, MD; Rockville post office (948-3400). Shady Grove is a huge theater-in-the-round that hosts traveling Broadway musical comedy companies, headed up by at least one big star. Also big-name jazz, country, soul, and rock groups. The drive is scenic and the setting beautiful.

## Companies

**American Society of Theatre Arts,** 612 12th Street NW (628-8368). Wednesday-Sunday 8 pm; dark during the summer. This young company is experimenting with original and other contemporary drama, as well as performing classics from time to time. Their present tiny theater is threatened with demolition, so check location before going.

**Arena Stage and Kreeger Theater,** 6th and M Streets SW (638-6700). Performances Tuesday-Saturday 8 pm; Sundays 7:30 pm; weekend matinees 2:30 pm. Arena Stage has been called Washington's most innovative theater group. Its modern theater is located in the Southwest where urban renewal has transformed a large area near the river (see Urban Living, Chapter 5). The location has one big advantage, easy parking. There's a free lot next to the theater (come early to find a space), or you can generally find street parking close by.

Arena, as its name indicates, is a theater-in-the-round. It has the latest equipment, the seats are comfortable, the sound is excellent. Theater-in-the-round, according to directors and performers, is demanding and calls for strong acting; the Arena Company is equal to the challenge and deserves its international reputation as one of the country's finest regional troupes. The repertoire has included such classics as *The Cherry Orchard* and Shakespearean plays, as well as contemporary plays such as *Indians, Raisin,* and *The Great White Hope.* The season runs from September until July unless a play is held over into the summer by popular demand. The best seats are rows C and D on all four sides; the best boxes F, I, and C.

**The Kreeger,** in the same complex, is one of the city's smaller and more intimate theaters. Hours and prices are the same as those of Arena Stage and so is the quality.

**Back Alley Theater,** 1365 Kennedy Street NW (723-2040). Performance times vary. Back Alley is Washington's oldest community theater and has staged some good plays in its small theater. That doesn't guarantee security, of course, and because of that, the scheduling of plays is somewhat erratic.

**D.C. Black Repertory Company,** Last Colony Theater, 4935 Georgia Avenue NW (291-2877). Performances Wednesday-Saturday 8 pm; Sunday 7 pm. This group is used to successful seasons, but like other struggling companies in the city, it is in need of funds. The Last Colony is small, but the sound and sight lines are excellent. What the company lacks in money it makes up in imagination and style. It operates year-round, generally presenting five black-oriented plays and one or two high-quality performances by the D.C. Black Repertory Dance Company that are a delight to both white and black audiences.

**Folger Theatre Group,** Folger Shakespeare Library, 201 East Capitol Street SE (546-4000). Performances Tuesday-Sunday 8 pm; Sunday matinee 3 pm. Everything about this enterprise is small: the stage, the company, and the theater itself (a replica of one from Shakespeare's day), which seats less than 200 people. But the company does a fine job with both classics and new plays. The few plays it puts on during the season are well attended, so get there early because seats are not reserved.

**Washington Area Feminist Theater,** Mount Vernon College, 2100 Foxhall Road NW (986-1783). This ambitious group presents plays written, directed, and performed by women. Their idea is not to prosyletize for the women's movement, but rather to give women an opportunity to do jobs in the theater usually performed by men. There are generally two shows a week. Schedules and prices vary.

## Amateur

**Catholic University,** Hartke Theater, Harewood Road NE (529-3333). October-May Monday-Saturday 8 pm; Sunday matinee 2:30 pm. Box office Monday-Sunday 10 am-6:00 pm. Performances here are of professional quality. Catholic University has for several years put on top-notch shows, performed by students mixed with a few visiting professional actors. Six plays are presented each season. Helen Hayes, Cyril Ritchard and Geraldine Fitzgerald have appeared there. Parking is easy, but if you're coming in from the Northwest section of town, consult a map. Half-price tickets are available during the "student rush" a few minutes before curtain time, but don't count on it: the theater is quite small and the performances popular enough to ensure a good house.

**Little Theatre of Alexandria,** 600 Wolfe Street, Alexandria, VA (683-0496). Performances Tuesday-Friday 8:30 pm; Sunday matinee 3 pm. Box office Monday-Saturday 1 pm-4 pm, 7 pm-9 pm; Sunday 1:30 pm-3:30 pm. The company of the Little Theatre presents a number of plays both indoors and outdoors. During the summer, its shows are held in the courtyard of Gadsby's, a 172-year-old tavern at 400 Cameron Street, which was one of General Washington's headquarters during the French and Indian War.

**The Theater Lobby,** 17th Street and St. Matthew's Court behind St. Matthew's Cathedral. This local amateur group has endured more than 25 years and endeared itself to Washingtonians. There are only 75 seats available for any performance, and all are generally filled. The Theater Lobby has put on such plays as *Waiting for Godot* and *The White House Murder Case.* It has fathered one famous actor, George C. Scott. Times and prices vary.

## Summer Theater

Summer tourists will have a few more interesting choices, the "summer theaters," which operate only from May to October. Some are a distance from Washington, but often worth the drive. You might plan an all-day excursion and take a picnic lunch or feast in one of the nearby inns.

**The Olney Theatre,** 2001 Olney-Sandy Spring Road, Olney, MD (924-3400). About 45 minutes. Georgia Avenue north to Route 97, 10 miles to intersection with Route 108, right on 108, 1½ miles on the left. Performances Tuesday-Saturday 8:30 pm; Sunday 2 pm and 7:30 pm. Box office daily 10 am-9 pm. Olney Theatre is an offshoot of Father Gilbert Hartke's Catholic University theater. It offers good, solid performances at varying prices. You might consider dining at the Olney Inn before the performance.

**Sylvan Theater,** Washington Monument grounds (426-6975). Performances Tuesday-Sunday 7:30 pm. Reserved seats $1, grass free. The Shakespeare Summer Festival at this outdoor theater is as close to heaven as you can get in Washington if you're a Shakespeare fan. One play is staged from mid-July to mid-August each year by a professional Shakespeare company. (See Music for other performance information.)

**Wayside Theater,** Middletown, VA (703-869-1776). About 1½ hours. Take Beltway (Route 495) to Route 66 to Route 81 north to Middletown exit. Wayside is known for the quality of its productions, and makes a good excursion, especially when you include dinner at the nearby inn. Call for prices and hours of performance.

## Dinner Theaters

Many people scoff at dinner theater, but even more people regularly attend and enjoy it. The advantages are obvious: you can get a good meal and a fairly good performance without having to change location, and when one considers the price of food and entertainment, dinner theaters are a bargain.

There are a dozen dinner theaters in the area, and with the exception of the Shoreham Americana, most are located some distance from the District. As a rule, they offer musical comedies and other light fare with professional and semiprofessional actors in the cast. The dinner theaters listed vary in price and performance time. Give them a call before going, and get directions.

**Arlingtonian Dinner Theater,** 4019 Wilson Boulevard, Arlington, VA (524-3935).

**Burn Brae Dinner Theatre,** Route 29 at Blackburne Road, Burtonsville, MD (384-5800).

**Cedar Knoll Dinner Theatre,** George Washington Parkway, 7 miles south of Alexandria, VA (360-7880).

**Garland Dinner Theatre,** Columbia, MD (301-730-8311).

**Harlequin Dinner Theatre,** 1330 Gude Drive, Rockville, MD (340-8515).

**Hayloft Dinner Theatre,** Manassas, VA (591-8040).

**Lazy Suzan Dinner Theater,** Route 1, Woodbridge, VA (550-7384).

**Mosby Dinner Theatre,** Route 7 at Goose Creek Inn, Fairfax, VA (471-4481).

**Shoreham Americana Blue Room Dinner Theater,** 2500 Calvert Street NW (234-0700).

**Villa Rosa Dinner Theater,** 813 Ellsworth Drive, Silver Spring, MD (588-6226).

# Film

## Repertory

**American Film Institute,** Kennedy Center for the Performing Arts (785-4600). Daily 6 or 6:30 pm and 9 pm; weekend matinees 2 pm. The Institute has a growing archive of American films ranging from kid's movies to pornos. It also shows representative foreign films in its cozy theater. During the same week you can see seven Mickey Rooney features or 20 Walt Disney cartoons, depending on the focus of the current series. The theater, incidentally, only seats 240 people, which coupled with AFI's low ticket prices, can make it difficult to get in. The AFI will send out program announcements on request.

**Biograph,** 2819 M Street NW (333-2696). Continuous showings. Specializes in old or unusual movies. Prices vary but are always low. The Biograph also features special midnight shows for night owls who might be interested in seeing Richard Nixon's *Checkers Speech* or *Pink Flamingos.* A favorite is *Reefer Madness,* a 1930 number warning against the dangers of marijuana. The Biograph is also a favorite of music fans who can catch up on films of the Bangladesh concert, *Monterey Pop,* or *Woodstock.*

**Circle and Inner Circle,** 2105 Pennsylvania Avenue NW (331-7480). Continuous showings. This two-theater house is probably the favorite of Washington-based college students. It offers double features for rock-bottom prices, as well as several film festivals every year. An entire week might be devoted to Humphrey Bogart, another to Jean Paul Belmondo, and another to the works of Luis Buñuel. There's a foreign film festival and, at the end of every year, a week's showing of the year's best movies. And the Circle probably sells the best and most generous box of popcorn in Washington.

**Key,** 1222 Wisconsin Avenue NW (333-5100). Continuous showings. Another of the houses that shows oldies but goodies, classics, foreign favorites, and off-beat current products. Like the Biograph, it also has special midnight shows, and special midnight crowds.

## Free Films

Several museums and institutions show free movies regularly.

**The Corcoran Gallery of Art,** 17th Street and New York Avenue NW (638-3211). Lunchtime movies every Tuesday noon-1 pm about classic and modern art.

**The National Gallery of Art,** 6th Street and Constitution Avenue NW (737-4215). Films on art.

**National Geographic Society,** 17th and M Streets NW (296-7500). Full-length movies are shown during the summer in the auditorium.

**The National Archives,** 8th Street and Pennsylvania Avenue NW (962-2000). Thursday 7:30 pm, Friday noon and 2 pm. Films on a variety of subjects.

**The Renwick Gallery,** 17th Street and Pennsylvania Avenue NW (628-4422). Second and fourth Thursday of each month 11 am, 12:15 pm, and 1:30 pm. The "Creative Screen" series concentrates on crafts and design.

**The Smithsonian Institution,** 10th Street and Constitution Avenue NW (737-8811) presents various free films ranging from Felix the Cat cartoons to documentaries, which are shown at the Hirshhorn Gallery, the Museum of Natural History, and the Museum of History and Technology

## Radio and Television

**Radio stations:** Classical music, WGMS (AM 570; FM 103.5); classical music and enlightenment, the local Public Broadcast Radio station WETA (FM 90.9); all news, WAVA (AM 780; FM 105.1) and WTOP (AM 1500); progressive and rock WHFS (FM 102.3); middle-of-the-road music, WASH (FM 97.1); jazz and rhythm and blues, WHUR (FM 96.3).

**The Voice of America** (330 Independence Avenue SW, 755-4744), the radio broadcasting arm of the U.S. Information Agency, gives tours Monday-Friday at 9, 10, and 11 am and 1, 2, 3, and 4 pm (closed federal holidays). The tour lasts about 45 minutes and includes visits to the master control room, studio rooms, USIA exhibit, and discussions on the program.

**Television Channels:** Network affiliates—Channel 4 (WRC) NBC; Channel 7 (WMAL) ABC; Channel 9 (WTOP) CBS. Channel 5 (WTTG) is unaffiliated and shows more movies and reruns than the other channels. The UHF channels—Channel 20 (WDCA), shows more movies than the rest; Channel 26 (WETA) and Channel 53 (WNVT) are both PBS affiliates and show a lot of educational programs, often identical ones.

Some of the locally produced television shows welcome studio audiences. Call to inquire.

## Sports

### Auto Racing

**Beltsville Speedway,** Powder Mill and Springfield Roads, Beltsville, MD (490-2300). Friday 8 pm-11 pm. Children under 12 free. The racing is mostly stock car and, occasionally, demolition derby.

### Basketball

**The Capital Bullets** are the hottest professional basketball team in the country. They play at the Capital Centre, Capital Beltway and Central Avenue, Landover, MD (350-3900) from October to early April. Weekday games at 8:05 pm, Sunday game time varies. You can see big-time **collegiate basketball** at the University of Maryland's Cole Field House, College Park, MD (454-2121).

### Boating

**Rowing:** If you get up early enough (about 8 am), you may want to wander to one of the bridges crossing the Potomac (Key Bridge and Memorial bridge are both good) to see one of the rowing crews working out. The team from Georgetown University is among the best in the nation and often challenges other teams on the river. Check in the newspapers for dates.

**Powerboat Regattas:** The President's Cup Regatta, held in early June on the Potomac, is a spectacular event. There are many powerboat regattas held in the Annapolis area May-September. Contact the Division of Tourism, 2525 Riva Road, Annapolis, MD (301-267-5517) for details.

**Sailing:** Annapolis is the largest sailing

center in this area and hosts a number of racing events as well as the largest outdoor sailboat show, held every year in October. The Division of Tourism, 2525 Riva Road, Annapolis, MD (301-267-5517) has information on specific events. Contact the individual sailing associations to find out their schedules.

## Cricket

**The British Commonwealth Cricket Club** (265-5050) holds its tournaments on the grounds of West Potomac Park from April-October. They are usually held at 2 pm on Saturdays and Sundays, but it's best to call first.

## Football

**The Washington Redskins,** led by mercurial George Allen and quarterbacked by Billy Kilmer and Sonny Jurgensen, make their home at RFK Stadium from

*The Washington Bullets are a prime attraction at the Capital Centre.*

September-December. There are rarely tickets available for their regular season games, but you can see the Redskins play their pre-season games at the stadium in August and early September. Call 466-2222 for ticket information.

## Ice Hockey

The Washington area now has a professional ice hockey team, **The Capitals,** who play at the Capital Centre, Capital Beltway and Central Avenue, Landover, MD (350-3900) from October to early April. The Capitals are generally acknowledged as the worst team in the league—they hold the National Hockey League record for most consecutive defeats—but many people enjoy going to their games to give moral support.

## Horse Racing

### HARNESS RACING

**Laurel Raceway,** Route 1, Laurel, MD (725-1800). Monday-Saturday 7:30 pm July-September.

**Rosecroft Raceway,** 6336 Rosecroft Drive, Oxon Hill, MD (248-8400). Monday-Saturday 8:00 pm April-July. Closed Preakness day.

### STEEPLECHASE

The annual **Fairfax Steeplechase Races** are held in September at Glenwood Park Race Course, Middleburg, VA (759-2025). Local county hunt clubs sponsor races in the spring and fall on weekends. Check the newspapers for specific events.

### THOROUGHBRED

**Bowie Race Course,** Bowie, MD (262-8111). Bowie, open from January-March and May-July, has one of the fastest tracks around, but doesn't attract the top horses who usually race in Florida during the winter months.

**Laurel Race Course,** Laurel, MD (725-0400). October-December 1 pm; 12:20 pm after Thanksgiving. The Washington DC International, one of racing's most important events, is held at Laurel in November. This 1½-mile invitational race features the best stake horses in the world.

**Pimlico Race Track,** Belvedere and Park Heights Avenue, Baltimore, MD (301-542-9400). March-May 1 pm. Pimlico is the home of the Preakness, the second event in the Triple Crown. The Preakness is held every year in May, near the end of Pimlico's season.

**Shenandoah Downs; Charles Town Race Course,** Charles Town, W. VA (737-2323). Late January-early December Monday-Friday, 7:15 pm, Saturday 6:15 pm. There is night racing at Shenandoah Downs and neighboring Charles Town Race Course.

## Lacrosse

Pro lacrosse, now in its second season in the Washington area, is a big success. **The Maryland Arrows** play box lacrosse at the Capital Centre (350-3900) April-September weekdays 8 pm, Sundays 7 pm. The games are exciting, fast-moving, and rough. There are also many college lacrosse teams in the area. Call the individual schools for schedules.

## Polo

**The Potomac Polo Club** has matches every Friday at 8:30 pm and Sunday at 4 pm from June-October at Travilah and Glen Roads, Potomac, MD (223-4069). There are also irregularly scheduled polo matches held in West Potomac Park.

## Rugby

**The Potomac Rugby Union** has games all around the area with most of the area's universities participating. The games are held from March-June at varying times. For more information write Matt Godek, 5055 Seminary Road, Apartment 904, Alexandria, VA 22311.

## Soccer

Washington's pro soccer team, the **Diplomats** (587-0252), plays at RFK Stadium April-August, Wednesday and Friday 7:30 pm, Sunday 2:30 or 5:00 pm. The Diplomats Pro Soccer Club is one of 20 teams in the North American Soccer League, the third largest professional league in North America.

## Tennis

Washington tennis fans get several chances to see the world's top players. The **Virginia Slims Tennis Tournament,** held annually in late January, is part of the women's professional tennis circuit. The **Xerox Tennis Classic,** held annually in March, attracts many of the finest male players. Check newspaper listings for dates and location.

Chapter Seven

# Outdoors

KATHERINE JANKA

There is a limit to touring museums and monuments. You know when you've reached it: your neck is sore from gazing upwards to read inscriptions; all the famous paintings are starting to look alike; you left your umbrella at any one of the last five buildings you visited; and you still haven't found anyone who can give or sell you an aspirin.

In Washington, there is ample opportunity to give yourself a break from the usual tourist haunts. Washington is blessed with a wide variety of outdoor recreation possibilities and with enough mild weather to enjoy them. Take to the fresh air in many easily accessible parks or gardens, on hiking or cycling trails, on golf courses or tennis courts, and in campgrounds or forests. You can stay right downtown and picnic in a grassy "pocket" park, or you can drive into nearby Maryland or Virginia and camp overnight in a national park.

The National Park Service is especially concerned with encouraging outdoor recreation for visitors to Washington during the Bicentennial. National Capital Parks (NCP), its arm in the Washington area, provides literature about park activities that can be obtained at the kiosks located at monuments and other sightseeing stops. In addition, NCP is providing senators and representatives with literature to pass on to their constituents; so a call or letter to them should yield advance information on park activities in the area or call directly.

### DISTRICT OF COLUMBIA

**National Park Service,** C Street between 18th and 19th Streets NW 20240 (343-4747).

**National Capital Parks,** 1100 Ohio Drive SW 20242 (426-6700).

**Dial-a-Park:** a recording about current activities of Washington area National Parks (426-6975).

**District of Columbia Department of Recreation,** 3419 16th Street NW 20010 (629-7226).

### MARYLAND AND VIRGINIA

**Maryland National Capital Park and Planning Commission** (Montgomery County), 8787 Georgia Avenue, Silver Spring, MD 21907 (589-1480).

**Maryland National Capital Park and Planning Commission** (Prince Georges County), 6600 Kenilworth Avenue, Riverdale, MD (277-2200).

**Maryland Department of Parks and Forests,** State Office Building, Annapolis, MD 21404 (District Forester's Office, Laurel, MD: 776-5411).

**Virginia Department of Conservation and Economic Development,** Division of Parks, 501 Southern State Building, Richmond, VA 23219 (804-770-2132).

**Virginia State Travel Bureau,** 906 17th Street NW, Washington, DC 20006 (293-5350).

**Northern Virginia Regional Park Authority,** 11001 Popes Head Road, Fairfax, VA 22030 (278-8880).

# City Parks

**Anacostia Park,** along the Anacostia River between South Capitol Street and Benning Road SE (National Capital Parks: 426-6917). Open daily. Parking. Rest rooms. This huge park sprawls along the southeastern bank of the Anacostia River across from the Washington Naval Yard, several marinas, and some nonscenic industry. There are ball fields, picnic areas, playgrounds, tennis courts, and a swimming pool—making this one of the most complete parks in the area as far as facilities are concerned. The setting, however, is somewhat stark, with few trees or hills for landscape relief. A number of "park nodes" are under construction at Anacostia, scheduled for completion in 1975. These small, paved pavilions will be enclosed with latticework and roofed, and should make Anacostia a good place to picnic when weather is dubious. There will be a skating rink, picnic tables and grills; and the equipment for shuffleboard, pitching horseshoes, and other games.

**Battery-Kemble Park,** Chain Bridge Road, just below Loughboro Road NW. Open daily during daylight hours. Parking. Latrines. A small gem of a park, Battery-Kemble is noted as an ideal area for sledding and tobogganing on those rare occasions when it snows in Washington. It is also a good place to picnic. Tables and grills are scattered about the slopes and woods, and there is a lot of thick grass for those who like their outdoor meals closer to the ground. Except for some frisbee throwing, games are almost impossible because of the hilly terrain.

**East Potomac Park,** southwest of the Tidal Basin, Ohio Drive SW (426-6700). Open daily. Parking. Rest rooms. Snack bar. This 327-acre peninsula between the Washington Channel and Potomac River is a good place if you are itching to stroll at water's edge but don't want to leave the city. A path following along the water is bordered by cherry trees and benches and offers a good opportunity to watch sailboats and cruisers. The park is flat and open, with a small picnic area, playground, and miniature golf course. A swimming pool, a rather flat golf course, tennis courts, and bicycle rentals attract sporting types and are discussed later in this chapter. At the tip of the peninsula, called Hains Point, the National Capital Park Service has a large headquarters with a visitors center.

**Glover-Archbold Park,** running north-south from MacArthur Boulevard and Canal Road NW to Van Ness Street and Wisconsin Avenue NW. Take bus number D-4 to MacArthur Boulevard and Foxhall Road. Open daily. Street parking near entrances. Bordering on Foxhall Road and Georgetown University, the southern end of this heavily wooded park cuts through one of the loveliest—and wealthiest—sections of Northwest Washington. To enjoy this part of the park, start from the nature trail (designated by markers) at 44th Street and Reservoir Road NW. From there you can walk south to the Chesapeake and Ohio Canal or north along Foundry Branch Stream. The park is particularly popular with bird watchers. At its northern end, the trail starts at Van Ness Street NW, a half-block west of Wisconsin Avenue, and takes you through a large open field on your way into the woods. Some picnic tables are available along the way.

**Meridian Hill Park,** 16th Street between W and Euclid Streets NW. Open daily. Street parking. An urban mesa that affords a treetop view of the city, Meridian Hill resembles an Italian Renaissance garden complete with immense cascading fountains, numerous statues, and trees and shrubs planted in formal rows. Sadly, it has aged beyond its former elegance, as evidenced by cracked walkways, patched walls, and broken statuary. Picnic tables and benches are provided. This is not a safe place to explore after dark.

**Montrose Park,** R Street at Avon Place NW. Take a number 30 or 32 bus up Wisconsin Avenue to R Street and walk east about three blocks to the park. Open daily. Street parking. Rest rooms. A favorite Sunday strolling spot for Georgetown residents, Montrose Park is designed to be used, not just viewed. It has some large trees and shaded pathways, but it is mostly open, grassy, and ideal for games or picnicking. A playground, tennis courts, and picnic tables are provided. Separating Montrose Park from Dumbarton Oaks just to the west is a cobblestone path called Lover's Lane, a main route between Georgetown and Baltimore during the 18th century and a peaceful walk where many a romance bloomed during the 19th and 20th centuries. Oak Hill Cemetery borders on Montrose Park as it slopes down to Rock Creek Park. The beautiful, wooded cemetery was founded in 1849 and is the burial site of many prominent local figures, including Edwin M. Stanton, Lincoln's Secretary of War, and John Howard Payne, composer of "Home Sweet Home."

**Rock Creek Park,** along Rock Creek, cutting through Northwest Washington from the intersection of Virginia Avenue and the Potomac River north into Maryland (426-6834). Open all year. Parking lots at various picnic areas. Rest rooms. Algonquin Indians once lived along Rock Creek, fishing in its waters long before it became polluted and hunting along its shores before roads were built and people moved in. Later, settlers built gristmills and a sawmill along the creek, which then became a center for small local industry. Today, the 1,754-acre area, four miles long and a mile wide, is a wooded park alive with cars, bicycles, and picnickers, but large enough to still have plenty of quiet paths.

From the many parking turnouts along Rock Creek Parkway, you can picnic in cleared areas, explore the paths through the woods, or along the creek's edge. Plant life is abundant, with colorful wildflowers and hundreds of daffodils blooming in spring, and trees turning breathtaking colors in fall. There are about 15 miles of trail in the park, with footbridges across the creek. Conducted nature walks are offered periodically. For a map of the park and schedule of walks, phone the number above or stop at the park headquarters and visitors center on Beach Drive, south of Military Road.

Among the numerous sports offered in the park are horseback riding, tennis, bicycling, and golf, discussed under those headings later in this chapter. Swimming, wading, and fishing are not permitted in the creek because it is polluted. The **Rock Creek Nature Center** (see Chapter 8), **Pierce Mill,** and **Art Barn** (see Chapter 5) are interesting places to visit in the park.

The major roadways through the park, Beach Drive and Rock Creek Parkway, are heavily traveled by local commuters and are extremely crowded during rush hours, so try to plan your visit between 10 am and 4 pm.

**Theodore Roosevelt Island.** Take Theodore Roosevelt Bridge to George Washington Memorial Parkway on the Virginia side of the Potomac River; follow signs to parking area for Roosevelt Island (426-6922). Open daily, 9 am-dark. Rest rooms. A man who delighted in nature and supported conservation before it became a popular cause, the nation's twenty-sixth President would have found this peaceful setting a particularly fitting memorial. Its 88 acres of swampland, marshland, and woodland, traversed by two-and-a-half miles of walking trails, are alive with plants and animals that thrive in their natural habitat. On the high ground in the center is the formal memorial, dedicated in 1967—a large oval terrace with an impressive, 17-foot-high, bronze statue of Roosevelt.

## Picnicking in the City

Thousands of Washington office workers wouldn't think of lunching anywhere but outside in good weather. There always seems to be a park within walking distance, no matter where you are in downtown Washington, and that means benches to sit on, grass to recline on, and trees to shade you. If you are in the right park on the right day, there will even be music to entertain you, compliments of the city's "Summer in the Parks" program (phone Dial-a-Park, 426-6975, for details). Of course, there are also pigeons, and an occasional panhandler, but these inconveniences are hardly noticeable in the face of a sunny day.

Many of the parks and gardens included in this chapter are good places to picnic, and most have tables and grills. More convenient, however, are the smaller parks right downtown:

**Dupont Circle** (intersection of Connecticut, New Hampshire, and Massachusetts Avenue NW). There is almost always something going on here: crowds clustered around a bongo-drum player, guitar players strumming by the fountain, or people simply picnicking and sunning. There are a number of carry-outs nearby on Connecticut Avenue and on 18th Street where you can buy your picnic supplies.

**Farragut Square** (between I and K Streets just east of Connecticut Avenue NW). This small, grassy park has the advantage of a central location within walking distance of many hotels, restaurants, and the White House. It also has noontime concerts several days each week in the summer (call Dial-a-Park 426-6975). The many carry-outs along K Street and Connecticut Avenue can supply you with lunch. For a wide variety of frankfurter-type sandwiches try the Best of the Wurst, 1003 Connecticut Avenue NW. Subway construction has been rampant in this area, but should be completed by late 1975.

**Lafayette Park** (between Pennsylvania Avenue and H Street NW, across from the White House). One of the most attractive parks in the city, with plenty of paths, statues, trees, benches, and even a few tables. People watching is a favorite pastime of regulars here, and it gets fairly crowded in the summer. Try Ranchette Carry-Out (826 18th Street NW), about two blocks away, for good sandwiches for your picnic. (See White House walking tour, Chapter 4.)

**The Mall** (stretching between the Capitol and the Washington Monument). This long, green area is a particularly convenient picnic spot if you have been at the National Gallery or the Smithsonian. A good place to pick up your food is at Townhouse Food Store in nearby L'Enfant Plaza. Cheeses, meats, salads, hard rolls, and other good things are at the deli counter.

**Courtyard of the National Collection of Fine Arts and National Portrait Gallery** (between 7th and 9th, F and G Streets NW). The central courtyard is a good spot for a sunny picnic and calm retreat from downtown hustle and bustle. Either bring your own brown bag or buy excellent sandwiches and beer or soft drinks from the food concession in the courtyard.

**Tidal Basin** (between the Washington Monument and Lincoln and Jefferson Memorials). If you are in Washington when the cherry blossoms burst into bloom in April, a picnic alongside the Tidal Basin is a must. Benches and walkways are located under the trees, or you could even picnic on a pedal boat in the Tidal Basin itself. Plan to bring your food with you.

Some food stores that have especially good, prepared, picnic-type edibles are: **The French Market,** 1632 Wisconsin Avenue NW (338-4828); **Magruder's Grocers,** 5626 Connecticut Avenue NW (244-7800); **The International Safeway,** 1110 F Street NW (628-1880); **1789 Market,** 1232 36th Street NW (965-1789); **Waterside Gourmet,** 401 M Street NW (488-8086).

Or, you can buy a picnic box of wine, cheese, fruit, bread, and other delights from the following places. Prices, depending on how elaborate you want the meal, can range from $2.50 to $10 per person. **Capitol Hill Wine and Cheese Shop,** 611 Pennsylvania Avenue SE (543-0880); **Old World Market,** 7426 Wisconsin Avenue, Bethesda, MD (654-4420) and Foxhall Square, 3301 New Mexico Avenue NW (363-3220).

## Flora and Fauna

**Brookside Gardens,** Wheaton Regional Park, Wheaton, MD (949-8230). Georgia Avenue north from Washington about 2½ miles beyond the Beltway (Route 495), right on Randolph Road, right on Glenallan Avenue to entrance. Open Tuesday-Saturday 9 am-5 pm; Sunday 1 pm-6 pm; closed Mondays (except holidays) and Christmas Day. This 25-acre public garden includes a conservatory, formal garden, and several shrub collections. Outdoors, spring bulbs begin to bloom in late March, and assorted colorful flowers continue through the chrysanthemums of October. The conservatory houses lush tropical plants and trees; flowering annuals and perennials; and such unusual features as banana trees, coffee trees, and a small stream. Seasonal displays blossom at Christmas and Easter, and there is a fragrance garden and a rose garden. Group tours may be arranged by phoning in advance.

**Constitution Gardens,** on the Mall, between 21st and 17th Streets NW along Constitution Avenue. Scheduled for completion in 1976, this area just west of the Washington Monument will be full of pathways, plants, benches, and good views of the Monument and the Reflecting Pool.

**Dumbarton Oaks,** 3101 R Street NW (232-3101). Metrobuses 30 or 32 will let you off at Wisconsin Avenue and R Street; walk three blocks east to Dumbarton. Open Labor Day-July 1, except legal holidays, 2 pm-5 pm. Street parking. You don't need to be a greenery buff or landscape lover to appreciate the garden at Dumbarton Oaks for what it is: one of the most exquisite formal gardens in the country. Surrounding a huge Georgetown estate-turned-museum (see Georgetown walking tour, Chapter 3), the garden cascades down 27 acres of terraced hillside and winds around massive fountains and gracefully curving footpaths. Today, the garden is as impressive for its mammoth proportions as it is for perfection of detail and variety of plant life. Holly bushes about 20 feet high guard the entrance to the house, and some of the largest weeping willows and magnolias in the area can be found nearby. Shoulder-high boxwoods line the path to an Oriental area complete with a stand of towering bamboo.

Strict formality is observed, and no picnics, pets, or bicycles are allowed at Dumbarton. It is a peaceful place—a place to rest on a bench or stroll under an arbor, to escape summer heat by a fountain or autumn winds in a wooded alcove. Guidebooks to the garden may be purchased at the 32nd Street entrance to the museum.

**Kenilworth Aquatic Gardens,** Anacostia Avenue and Douglas Street NE (426-6905). Drive north on Kenilworth Avenue to the Quarles Street exit; bear right and turn left at the first intersection; then right on Douglas Street and right on Anacostia Avenue to the entrance. Or, take a U-2 bus up Kenilworth Avenue to Quarles Street. Open daily 7:30 am-6 pm in summer; 7:30 am-4 pm in winter. Parking. Started in 1882 by a government clerk who brought water lilies from Maine to plant on his property on the Anacostia River, the Aquatic Gardens now have 11 acres of ponds planted with thousands of water lilies, lotuses, bamboo, and other exotic plants. There are also abundant stretches of native plants and many birds and small mammals. Summer is the peak season. Plants start to bloom in June and the garden smells and feels like a tropical park all summer long. Try to plan your visit in the morning, since many blooms close against the heat of the day. Picnic tables are located under shady trees, and a park naturalist is available on summer weekends to conduct nature walks.

**National Arboretum,** 24th and R Streets NE (399-5400). From New York Avenue, turn south on Bladensburg Road and left on R Street. Or take bus number 42 from Connecticut or Pennsylvania Avenues NW to 15th and D Streets NW; transfer to bus B-2, "Mount Rainier," to Bladensburg Road and R Street. Open daily except Christmas Day; Monday-Friday 8 am-7 pm; Saturday and Sunday 10 am-5 pm; closes at 5 pm every day November-March. Rest rooms. Parking. You can drive or walk through 415 acres of rolling greenery, alternately wooded and open. The Arboretum is planned, but not "formal." Spring is the peak season here when banks of azaleas spilling down hills and bordering footpaths and roads are ablaze with color. Camellias, boxwoods, magnolias, and cherry and crabapple trees are among the other favorites.

A nature trail, ponds, and a stream complete the Arboretum's natural look, pleasantly incongruous in a thoroughly urban section of Washington. Picnics are not permitted. Flower shows are held from time to time in the auditorium.

**National Zoological Park;** entrances in the 3000 block of Connecticut Avenue NW, Harvard and Adams Mill Roads NW, and Beach Drive in Rock Creek Park (381-7228). From downtown take bus L-2 or L-4 out Connecticut Avenue. Open daily; grounds open at 6 am, buildings at 9 am; closes 4:30 pm in winter, 6 pm in summer. Rest rooms, snack bar, picnic area, cafeteria. Parking $1. Regardless of the excitement generated by its most renowned residents, the National Zoo is a lot more than a repository for the two giant pandas given to the United States by the People's Republic of China. Although you won't want to miss seeing those cuddly creatures, you can also enjoy the more than 2,000 other animals that make the zoo one of the most popular stops for visitors to Washington. Smokey Bear is there, along with hundreds of exotic birds, reptiles, mammals, and scores of animals considered endangered species and now being carefully preserved and bred.

The zoo currently is undergoing a major facelift that will take animals out of cages and put them into natural surroundings. When it's completed in 1976, there will be fewer visible barriers and larger quarters for most animals. In the meantime, many of the animals have been farmed out to other zoos.

The zoo is as educational as it is enjoyable, with exhibits labeled in detail to identify animals and describe their origins. It is thoroughly visitor oriented and even has amenities such as special lighting for viewing nocturnal animals in the Small Mammal House. A favorite of most visitors is the Great Flight Cage—an enormous wire tent that you can stroll through as birds soar overhead and a waterfall splashes below. The Bird House, a habitat for larger species, is another popular place, full of the color and activity of flamingos, turquoise parrots, scarlet ibises, and others.

The pandas, of course, are still the most sought-after zoo residents. Reminiscent of everyone's childhood teddy bears, Ling-Ling and Hsing-Hsing are rolly-polly superstars worth waiting in line for—which you will do in good weather or on weekends. Zoo officials thoughtfully have made the wait easier by setting up exhibits that display panda paraphernalia, including photos, the crates that shipped the pandas from China, and even a recording of one panda greeting another. The pandas sleep nearly all day, so it is best to come at feeding time—9 am or 4 pm.

One caveat: The zoo gets very crowded, especially on weekends during good weather, and the parking lots fill up fast. If at all possible, go during the week and take a taxi or bus.

## Camping and Hiking

The large parks outside of Washington provide a wide variety of settings for camping, hiking, or just strolling. Challenging hiking not far from Washington can be found along the Appalachian Trail, Shenandoah National Park, and in numerous state parks and forests in Virginia and Maryland. Or, for a Sunday stroll, you might want to try the towpath along the Chesapeake and Ohio (C & 0) Canal or paths running through suburban regional parks.

An indispensable guide for hikers, campers, and other outdoor enthusiasts is *Potomac Trail Book* sold at most book stores in the Washington area, or from Potomac Books, Inc., P.O. Box 40604, Palisades Station, Washington, DC 20016. Information on hiking and camping in and around Washington can also be obtained from the following sources:

**American Youth Hostels,** Potomac Area Council, 1520 16th Street NW, Washington, DC 20036 (462-5780).

**Potomac Appalachian Trail Club,** 1718 N Street NW, Washington, DC 20036 (638-5306, weekday nights, 7 pm-10 pm).

**Sierra Club,** Potomac Chapter, 324 C Street SE, Washington, DC 20003 (547-1144).

**The Wilderness Society,** 1901 Pennsylvania Avenue NW, Washington, DC 20006 (293-2732).

In addition, the Tuesday editions of the *Washington Post* and of the *Washington Star* carry information in their sports sections on upcoming hikes sponsored by local hiking clubs. For camping and hiking equipment sales and rentals, look in the Yellow Pages under "Camping."

Here is a listing of areas in nearby Maryland and Virginia where camping and/or hiking are available. There are also good places for other kinds of recreation, for picnicking, and for simply enjoying the outdoors. Camping fees listed are for the site per night, and campsites go on a first-come, first-served basis, unless otherwise noted. Where there is a park headquarters, stop for maps, schedules of special events, and other information.

**MARYLAND**

**Assateague Island National Seashore,** Assateague, MD and Assateague, VA (301-641-1441). About 150 miles. Maryland side: take Route 50 east to Chincoteague Bay and Route 611 south on to the island; Virginia side: Route 50 to Salisbury, Maryland; Route 13 south to Route 175 east, onto the island. Trailer and tent sites. Rest rooms. Although farther from Washington than other places discussed in this chapter, Assateague is unique enough to be worth the trip. One of the few beach areas on the Atlantic Coast to be left untouched by resort development, this 37-mile-long protected island reaches into Maryland and Virginia. It is separated from the mainland by Sinepuxent and Chincoteague Bay and is noted for oysters, crabs, and the wild Chincoteague ponies. The sturdy, shaggy creatures are herded into the channel every year during the last week of July to swim to Chincoteague Island where they are auctioned.

You will find white beaches and banks of sand dunes—a good backdrop for fishing and swimming. The most extensive camping facilities are in the Maryland section, including those in the Maryland State Park.

A hike along the sand dunes will acquaint you with some of the island's wildlife. Besides the ponies, there are falcons and Sika deer (miniature Japanese elk). A 9,000-acre wildlife refuge at the island's southern end provides protection for hundreds of birds, including egrets, herons, geese, and ibises.

At the National Seashore, operated by the National Park Service (Box 294, Berlin, MD 21811), camping is permitted from mid-April to late October. It is a popular spot, so you'll need to arrive no later than Thursday to camp over the weekend. The State Park does take some reservations. Contact the Park Superintendent, Assateague State Park, P.O. Box 293, Berlin, MD 21811 (301-641-2120).

**C & O Canal,** Metropolitan Washington section, from Georgetown to Great Falls (phone Great Falls Tavern: 299-3613). Street parking in Georgetown or in parking turnouts along Canal Road. On July 4, 1828, when President John Quincy Adams turned the first spade of dirt for the C & O Canal, he started not only an era in transportation, but a tradition in Washington outdoor life. The first day of spring brings hundreds of local residents out for a ritual walk along the canal's towpath, a popular pastime every nice weekend on into winter. The canal's history, interesting geology, lush plant and animal life, and well-maintained towpath for hiking and biking make it a deserving favorite.

Canal boats operated from 1850 to 1924 from Washington to Cumberland, Maryland, leaving behind a history that is visible today at old taverns, remains of aqueducts, locks and lockhouses along the route. The towpath along the section from Georgetown to Great Falls runs through the wooded riverside, with paths going down to the river and picnic clearings. In 1971, the entire property along the canal became the Chesapeake and Ohio National Historical Park, after many years of urging by Supreme Court Justice William O. Douglas and other well-known Washingtonians who enjoy hiking along the towpath.

Boat and bicycle rentals are available along the canal and are discussed in the sections on cycling and boating in this chapter. Camping and hiking are most popular beyond Great Falls.

**C & O Canal,** from Great Falls, about 15 miles, to Cumberland, about 184 miles from Washington, (from Chain Bridge to Seneca: 299-3613; from Seneca to Cumberland: 432-5124). Campsites have toilets, grills, and picnic tables. Operated by the National Park Service. Above Great Falls, the canal generally attracts long-distance hikers and campers rather than the Sunday strollers who frequent the Georgetown section. Once a 180-mile artery for transporting coal from Cumberland's mines to Washington's homes and offices, the area is now primarily noted for its scenic woodland surroundings and historic interest. Old ferry landings and lockkeepers' houses still stand, and many areas bear identifying historical markers.

From Seneca to Cumberland there are "hiker-biker" campsites about every five miles. Drive-in campgrounds with space for small trailers, but no hook-ups, are located at McCoy's Ferry (about 110 miles north of Georgetown, near Clear Spring), Fifteen Mile Creek (about 140 miles north, near Little Orleans), and Spring Gap (about 175 miles north, just south of Cumberland). You'll need a map, which you can pick up at the Great Falls Tavern, or by writing: Superintendent, C & O Canal, National Park Service, Box 158, Sharpsburg, MD 21782. There are a number of books about the canal, and a good selection is available at the Great Falls Tavern/museum. Good recreation areas near the canal include: Carderock, Great Falls, Seneca, and Swain's Lock, all discussed elsewhere in this section. Two others, Harpers Ferry and Antietam, are discussed in Chapter 4.

**Carderock Recreation Area,** Carderock (557-8990). About 8 miles. George Washington Memorial Parkway, MD, north about 7 miles beyond the Key Bridge intersection; just past the Naval Ship Research and Development Center a sign directs you to Carderock. Open all year during daylight hours. Parking. Wedged between the Potomac River and C & O Canal, Carderock is alternately grassy, wooded, and rocky. The first two parking turnouts service cleared picnic areas overlooking the river.

Farther upstream is the rocky area for hiking in the woods or climbing on the 40-foot cliffs looming above the river—the latter recommended only for experts with proper climbing equipment. Even the woodland paths here are rather rocky, so wear sturdy shoes to avoid stumbling.

**Catoctin Mountain Park,** Thurmont (301-824-2574). About 65 miles. Take Route 270 (70S) to Frederick, and Route 15 from Frederick to the entrance. Open all year. Campgrounds open mid-April-October only. Trailers over 22 feet long not permitted. Camping fee: $2 per night. Reservations through the Park Reservation System, Box 1976, Cedar Rapids, Iowa 52406 (800-553-8425). Rest rooms. Noted for its mountain vistas and splendid fall foliage, Catoctin is set in Maryland's western arm, wedged between West Virginia and Pennsylvania. Originally inhabited by Indians and later farmed by German, Swiss, and Scotch-Irish immigrants in the 18th and 19th centuries, the area has a rich history. Civil War battlefields are scattered nearby, and in the center of the park is Camp David, the mountain hideaway established by Franklin D. Roosevelt as a presidential retreat. In 1825 the country's first friction matches were made in the adjacent town of Thurmont, and the "Match House," where they were produced, is still standing. (See Frederick-Gettysburg tour, Chapter 4.)

The 5,769-acre park, ranging in elevation from 700 to 1,880 feet, includes well-forested campgrounds, picnic facilities, nature trails, and a scenic, self-guiding, seven-mile auto drive. From March through November, mainly on weekends, local crafts of the 18th and 19th centuries are demonstrated at the park's folk-craft center. Cross-country skiing and snowshoeing trails are open when there is snow, and a mountain stream provides good fishing.

**Cedarville State Park,** Brandywine (301-888-1622). About 25 miles. Route 5 south, about 15 miles from Washington to Route 301; south on 301 to Cedarville Road; left to park entrance. Open all year. Camping fee: $3.50 per day. Rest rooms. No trailer hook-ups. Only a 45-minute drive from Washington, Cedarville feels remote enough to be several more hours into the wilderness. The facilities are adequate, but not so elaborate that you forget you are roughing it. Fourteen miles of marked foot trails wind through the forests; a small pond provides some fishing; and the picnic area has tables and grills. The 90 campsites are well hidden among the trees.

**Cunningham Falls State Park,** Thurmont (301-271-2495). About 65 miles. Follow directions to Catoctin Mountain Park; Cunningham entrance is on Route 15, just before reaching Catoctin. Open all year. Campsites open mid-April-October. Rest rooms. Trailers over 22 feet not permitted. This 4,446-acre park, adjacent to Catoctin Mountain Park, is named for the 40-foot falls on Big Hunting Creek. You can fish for trout, swim, and boat in the 40-acre lake, or you can hike, camp, and picnic in the woodlands—all with a scenic backdrop of rolling green mountains. The lake has two sandy beaches, a bath house, and a concession for boat rentals and bait. It is stocked with fish. Hiking trails are well marked and lead to good mountain views. Campgrounds include rest rooms, tables, and fireplaces.

**Doncaster State Forest,** Charles County. About 35 miles. Take Route 210 south from Washington about 20 miles; turn left on Route 225 about 2 miles to Route 224; right on 224 about 10 miles to Route 344; left on 344; left on Route 6 about a mile to entrance. Open all year. Doncaster is probably one of the most undeveloped state forests in the area, giving it the advantages of peace and the feeling of wilderness, but the disadvantages of unpaved roads and no water or rest rooms. The 1,427-acre forest is used mostly for hunting, is densely wooded, and has a fresh, piney smell. Possum, raccoon, and deer may be spotted from the two-mile circular hiking trail through the woods. There are a few picnic tables in a cleared area, but no camping is permitted. (For further information, write Forest Superintendent, Doncaster, MD 20643.)

**Gambrill State Park,** near Frederick (301-473-8360). About 55 miles. Take Route 270

(70S) north to Frederick; Route 40 northwest to entrance. Open all year. Camping fee: $3.50 per day. A popular mountain park, Gambrill is best known for its scenic overlooks of the surrounding area. Its 1,139 acres are set in an area steeped in Civil War history and dotted with rolling farms and thick forests. Tree-covered Gambrill has 35 camping sites, five miles of hiking trails, a self-guiding nature trail, and complete picnic and playground facilities. A good path leads to 1,660-foot high Knob Summit, where you can enjoy a vast panorama of the surrounding area, including picturesque villages, farms, and Civil War battlefields. (For camping reservations, phone the number above or write: Park Superintendent, Gambrill State Park, Route 8, Frederick, MD 21701.)

**Great Falls Park,** 11710 MacArthur Boulevard, Potomac 20854 (299-3613). At the end of MacArthur Boulevard, about 15 miles northwest of downtown Washington. Open daily 9 am-8 pm summer; 9 am-5 pm winter, except Christmas Day. Snack bar. Rest rooms. Parking. The park maintained on the Maryland side of these impressive falls has woodland paths, picnic clearings (no tables or grills), and a museum that is a restored 19th-century tavern (See Chapter 5 for more details on Great Falls Tavern). The area is most popular on fall weekends, when colorful foliage sparks as much interest as the falls themselves. The C & O Canal has been restored here with signs to explain how the locks work, and museum exhibits to interpret the history of the canal. Great Falls is a good starting point for hiking or bicycling along the canal, and you can rent bicycles and canoes right at the park. (See section on bicycling in this chapter.) Access to the major falls is temporarily closed on the Maryland side.

**Greenbelt Park,** Greenbelt (426-6816). About 12 miles. Capital Beltway (Route 495) Exit 28; south on Kenilworth Avenue; left on Route 193 (Greenbelt Road) to entrance. Open daily. Campsites. Rest rooms. Water. Camping fee: $1 per day; 5-day limit in summer; 14-day limit rest of year. Located only five miles north of the District line, this 1,100-acre park provides an easily accessible retreat from city life. It is well forested, mostly with pines, and has several streams, well-placed hiking trails, picnic groves, and a campground. Trailers up to 30 feet are permitted, but there are no utility hook-ups. The 178 sites are often filled by late afternoon in the summer. Check on guided walks and evening programs.

**Patapsco State Park,** on the Patapsco River between Elkridge and Sykesville (747-6602). About 30 miles. Take Route 29 (Colesville Road) from Washington to Ellicott City. Park extends north and south from there. Water. Latrines. Campsites. Camping fee: $3.50 per night. This 7,600-acre park runs about 20 miles along the Patapsco River, through woods and clearings and past scenic river overlooks and interesting rock formations. Captain John Smith discovered the river in 1608, and it is strategically placed near battle sites of the Revolutionary War, War of 1812, and Civil War. Nearby sites include a huge, old, stone viaduct; the country's first train depot; and the dam that was the world's first underwater power plant. **Patapsco Valley Historical Center** is also located in the park, and on summer weekends a guided historical bus tour leaves from the park twice daily.

There are three camping areas, with a mix of semi-improved and improved campsites, picnic tables and shelters, fireplaces, play fields, and baseball diamonds. There are 15 miles of hiking trails, interpretive nature walks, and fishing areas. (For camping reservations call number above or write: Park Superintendent, Patapsco State Park, 78 Gun Road, Baltimore, MD 21227.)

**Seneca Park,** Seneca. About 20 miles. Take River Road (Route 190) to dead end, about 12 miles beyond the Beltway (Route 495); left on Route 112, about a mile to Seneca Road; left on Seneca Road to the park. Snack bar. Rest rooms. Parking lot. Getting to Seneca is one of the most interesting things about going there. The routes take you through Potomac, a fine Washington suburb full of old and new country estates, scenic farms, and some unfortunate clusters of development houses. Along Seneca Creek you pass through the town of Seneca, a picturesque summer colony, just before you reach the park area. The most notable attraction here is the 114-foot aqueduct that once carried the canal over Seneca Creek. There is also good picnicking along the edge of the Potomac River.

If you hike from Seneca to Swain's Lock (about six miles) you'll walk through some interesting forest, past high cliffs bordering the canal, and alongside a state game refuge.

**Smallwood State Park,** Rison (301-743-

7613). About 30 miles. Route 210 south about 20 miles; left on Route 225 to Sweden Point Road; turn right and continue on into the park. Open 10 am-dusk, March 1-December 10 and December 26-January 5. Museum is open 10 am-6 pm daily, May 30-Labor Day; open weekends from Labor Day-December 1 and March 1-May 30. Museum tours conducted May 30-Labor Day. Rest rooms. William Smallwood distinguished himself as a Revolutionary War general, governor of Maryland, and occasional host to George Washington at **Smallwood Retreat.** Today, the restored Retreat and its surroundings comprise a 333-acre scenic park overlooking a Potomac River tributary. You can walk through the flat, wooded area on two loop roads and picnic in clearings furnished with tables and grills. Children's playground equipment is also provided. The Retreat, an 18th-century brick house, is now a museum furnished with antiques dating from 1600 to 1800.

**Sugarloaf Mountain,** Stronghold. About 35 miles. Route 270 (70S) to Route 109, west on 109 to Comus; right on Route 95 about 3 miles to Sugarloaf. Open daily, except December and January, 9 am-sunset. Snack bar (open weekends). Outhouses. Picnic tables. Parking. No fires permitted. Sugarloaf, rising suddenly from the surrounding farms and woodland, is a good place to enjoy country vistas and natural forests while picnicking. A paved, winding road takes you within one-fourth mile of the 1,282-foot summit and provides three scenic overlook stops along the way. You can climb a trail to the summit and, for longer hikes, follow a logging road on the east side of the mountain. Sugarloaf is part of a 3,000-acre, privately owned area named Stronghold, bequeathed to a nonprofit corporation in 1954 by Gordon Strong of Chicago. His aim, to educate the public in the appreciation of natural beauty, is being well fulfilled in an area where even "unnatural" features like benches and a snack bar are constructed and placed so as not to spoil the surrounding environment.

**Swain's Lock,** C & O Canal (299-3613). About 12 miles. River Road (Route 190) about 5 miles beyond the Beltway (Route 495); left on Swain's Lock Road. Open daily. Snack bar. Rest rooms. Parking limited, and mostly along the road leading to the canal area; it can be very congested on weekends. The towpath gets muddy here in damp weather, but is otherwise firm, well kept, and a good starting point for a short (two-mile) afternoon hike to Great Falls. Swain's Lock is a popular horseback riding spot for nearby residents and, when the canal freezes, a favorite among ice skaters. The canal, the river, and a feeder stream slice through the well-wooded area, which is cleared of underbrush for fine picnicking. Bicycles, boats, and bait are available at the lockkeeper's house.

**VIRGINIA**

**Bull Run Marina,** Lake Occoquan (703-631-0549). About 30 miles. Take Beltway (Route 495) Exit 9, I-66, west to Fairfax Exit; to 123 south; right on Clifton Road; left on Henderson Road to entrance on Old Yates Ford Road. Snack bar. Rest rooms. Open March-November. The marina is set in the 5,000 acres of Lake Occoquan parkland designated for recreation and conservation. It is a convenient spot for fishing, with boat launching ramps, rowboat rentals, and tackle and bait for sale, and the lake is stocked with bluegill, crappie, catfish, and perch. Picnic tables and grills are set under the trees overlooking the water. In the thick woods, there are nature trails and many kinds of birds, wildlife, and wildflowers.

**Burke Lake Park,** Fairfax (273-9400). About 15 miles. Beltway (Route 495) Exit 11 to Route 123 south; about 13 miles to park entrance, just south of the intersection of Routes 123 and 645. Campsites. Rest rooms. Snack bar. Open all year. Camping fee: $3 per night. One of the most interesting lakes in the area, Burke is large and full of tiny coves. You can rent boats, buy bait and tackle, and try your hand at pulling in largemouth bass, black and white crappie, channel cat, bluegill, and other assorted fish. The woods surrounding the lake are good for camping, picnicking, and hiking. There is also playground equipment and a miniature train.

**Great Falls Park,** 9200 Old Dominion Drive, Great Falls (759-2915). About 15 miles. Take Chain Bridge to Virginia Route 123; northwest to Route 193; right on Route 738 into the park. Open daily, except Christmas Day, 8 am-dark. Admission: 50¢ for cars, 10¢ for pedestrians and cyclists. Snack bar. Rest rooms. Parking lot. One of the most impressive sights along the Potomac River is this 50-foot fall of thundering, cascading water. The setting is somewhat more attractive than that of its sister park on the Maryland side of the river because of its close proximity to the water from many areas in the 800-acre park.

A modern visitors center offers natural-history exhibits and short films on the history and conservation of the area. Picnic facilities include tables and fireplaces, and there are more than four miles of trails for hiking through the woods, viewing the river, or exploring the remains of Potowmack Canal, designed in the 18th century by George Washington and used by river boats to skirt the falls.

Fishing for bass, perch, and catfish is popular in this part of the Potomac (see entry on fishing in this chapter), but swimming and boating are prohibited due to the hazardous waters. Schedules for interpretive walks and organized trail hikes are available from the visitors center.

**Lake Fairfax,** Vienna (471-5414). About 20 miles. Capital Beltway (Route 495) Exit 10 to Route 7 west; left on Route 606 to park entrance. Open May-November. Entrance fee: adults $1.25 weekends, $1.10 weekdays; children 50¢. Camping fee: adults $1.25; children 50¢; $3 minimum per family. Trailer hook-ups. Rest rooms. Laundry. Camp store. Water sports and picnicking are big attractions at this large, rolling site. Although a welcome, wooded oasis in Virginia's suburban sprawl, the lake area comes off as less than natural, with its prominent snack bar, swimming pool, and a miniature train circling the lake. Many campsites around the 30-acre lake are snuggled close together rather than secluded, although the forest is fairly dense. Playground and picnicking facilities and fishing supplies are available.

On the way to Lake Fairfax, stop at **Colvin Run Mill** on Route 7, about 5 miles west of the Beltway. (See Historic Sites in Chapter 5.)

**Prince William Forest Park,** Triangle (703-221-7181). About 35 miles. Route I-95 south about 25 miles from the Beltway (Route 495) to Route 619; right to entrance. Open all year. Camping fee: $2 per night. Rest rooms. The largest hiking and camping area within easy reach of Washington, this 12,290-acre park is situated on 18th- and 19th-century farmland that has now reverted back to thick forest. Approximately 35 miles of trails and fire roads provide access to dense areas that include 89 known species of trees and shrubs and numerous resident animals. Exhibits at the park's nature center help interpret the surrounding wildlife and geography. Picnic areas offer tables, fireplaces, water, rest rooms, and a ball field; and self-guiding nature trails begin and end there. Farther into the park is Oak Ridge Campground, with 120 family campsites and more water, rest rooms, fireplaces, and picnic tables. For group tentsites and cabins, you should phone in advance for reservations. Although no trailer facilities are operated on the park itself, Prince William Trailer Village, a private concession, is situated on the park's northern edge (turn right off Route 95 onto Route 234). Fees there are $3.50 per day and up, depending on the type of hook-up required. No reservations are accepted, but for further information, phone 703-221-2474. For additional information on the park, write: Prince William Forest Park, Box 208, Triangle, VA 22172.

**Shenandoah National Park,** Luray (National Park Service 703-999-2242). About 80 miles. West on Route 66 to Route 55; continue west to Front Royal; left at Front Royal to Skyline Drive. Campsites. Fireplaces. Rest rooms. Laundries. Shenandoah, the closest national park to Washington, is included here (even though it is farther away than most other parks mentioned) because it has such a wealth of things to see and do. Its 300 square miles extend along the crest of the Blue Ridge Mountains, offering breathtaking vistas and clear mountain air. Skyline Drive threads through the park, and Washingtonians take to the route in droves during the fall foliage season; so unless you don't mind stop-and-start driving, stay away on weekends in October and early November.

Start your trip to Shenandoah at one of the two visitor centers along Skyline Drive: Dickey Ridge, just five miles south of Front Royal, or Byrd, about 50 miles south of Front Royal and halfway between the intersections of Route 33 and Route 211 with Skyline Drive. There are four campgrounds, with a total of 700 sites, and there are also mountain cottages and lodges. For information about campgrounds, contact Superintendent, Shenandoah National Park, Luray, VA 22835; and for information about lodges, contact Virginia Sky-Line Co., Inc. (P.O. Box 727, Luray, VA 22835). Three lodges, Skyland, Big Meadows, and Lewis Mountain, are open from spring into fall, and it is essential to make reservations well in advance. Big Meadows also has some rooms available in winter and has a year-round visitor center.

Hiking is good in Shenandoah; a 94-mile link of the Appalachian Trail runs the length of the park. Nearly 200 additional miles of trails criss-cross the area, and there are many opportunities to practice mountain climbing. You can enjoy trout fishing in any of 42 streams; rent horses for trail rides; picnic among the pines; or search for a glimpse of a black bear, deer, bobcat, and any of over a hundred bird species. Many side trips also are easily accessible from Skyline Drive, including Luray Caverns, Thunderbird Museum, and Archeological Park. (See Shenandoah Park tour, Chap. 4.)

**Turkey Run Recreation Area,** McLean (557-8991). About 10 miles. Follow signs off George Washington Parkway. Open daily, dawn to dusk. Parking. Located on the Potomac River, Turkey Run provides good water vistas, fine hiking trails down to the river bank, and picnic facilities. It is densely wooded, with fairly rugged terrain and much plant, animal, and bird life. From Turkey Run, you can walk along a good riverside trail for several miles in either direction—northwest to Beltway Bridge or southeast to Chain Bridge.

**Westmoreland State Park,** Box 465, Montrose (804-493-6167). About 60 miles. South on Route 301; left on Route 3 to entrance. Family campsites and camp store. Rest rooms. Restaurant. With over a mile of Potomac River frontage, including a sandy beach and a backdrop of picturesque cliffs, 1,335-acre Westmoreland is a particular favorite among boating, swimming, and fishing enthusiasts. Hiking trails and a nature center are major attractions in the wooded area, where there are campsites (tent and trailer), cabins, and picnic facilities. Cabins are available May through September, at $35 to $65 a week, depending on size. Campsites can be used all year. For reservation information write Virginia Division of Parks, 1201 State Office Building, Richmond, VA 23219, or phone.

Just a few miles from the park are the birthplaces of two of Virginia's most famed native sons—**Wakefield,** the birthplace of George Washington, and **Stratford,** the birthplace of Robert E. Lee. Stratford, just to the south, is now a restored, working plantation. Wakefield, to the north, had to be constructed anew, based on 18th-century plantation designs.

# Sports

## Bicycling

The last decade has seen thousands of Washingtonians take to two wheels for recreation and transportation. To keep abreast, National Capital Parks, a division of the National Park Service, and various suburban agencies have constructed many bike paths in and around Washington, the site of the nation's first commuter bike path. There are also numerous bike rental concessions to meet the growing demand.

National Capital Parks publishes a concise pamphlet, the "Bike Guide," that will direct you to good biking areas in Washington, available from them at 1100 Ohio Drive SW, Washington, DC 20242 (426-6700).

For greater detail, including maps of trails as far away as Baltimore, Pennsylvania, and Delaware, you can get *Greater Washington Area Bicycle Atlas,* published by the Potomac Area Council of American Youth Hostels and the Washington Area Bicyclist Association. The 127-page volume even provides advice about buying and repairing bikes and is available at Washington bookstores for $2 or by contacting the Washington Area Bicyclist Association, Room 323, 1346 Connecticut Avenue NW, Washington, DC 20036 (223-0003).

Bicycle rentals, repairs, and sales are in the Yellow Pages. The following are among the most convenient rental locations; most charge between $1 and $2 an hour:

**Fletcher's Boat House,** 4940 Canal Road NW (244-0461). Open daily March-November and some winter weekends in nice weather.

**Hains Point,** East Potomac Park SW (820-1253). Open April-November on Saturdays, Sundays, and holidays.

**Mall,** 12th and Jefferson Streets NW (no phone). Open daily April-November.

**Rock Creek Park,** 16th and Kennedy Streets NW (820-1253). Open April-November on Saturdays, Sundays, and holidays.

**Swain's Lock,** on the C & O Canal, 4 miles above Great Falls, MD (299-9006). Open daily March-November and later if the weather is good.

**Thompson's Boat House,** Rock Creek Park and Virginia Avenue NW (333-4861). Open daily March-November and later if the weather is good.

Among the many cycling routes in and around Washington, the following paths administered by National Capital Parks are particularly good:

**C & O Canal Towpath.** If you rent a bike at Fletcher's, Thompson's, or Swain's Lock, you'll have easy access to one of the area's most popular cycling routes. From Georgetown to Cumberland, Maryland, the towpath consists of 184 miles of level, packed dirt, and offers picnic areas, recreation sites, campsites, snack concessions, and rest rooms along the way. For more detail, see the entry on the C & O Canal in this chapter.

**Fort Circle.** Located in the Anacostia section of Southeast Washington, this hilly path runs from Deane Avenue and 42nd Street SE (just north of Fort Mahan Park) about six miles south to Good Hope and Naylor Roads SE (near Fort Stanton). It passes through wooded land linking the sites of five old forts built to protect Washington during the Civil War. The fort areas along the packed gravel route are now parks, and there are picnic areas and rest rooms.

**George Washington Parkway.** One of the most scenic cycling routes in the area is this 15-mile path along the Potomac from the foot of the Virginia side of Memorial Bridge south through Alexandria to Mount Vernon. The terrain is fairly level, and the path takes you past park areas and marinas and affords good river views. It passes right through downtown Alexandria, where there is a marked bike lane, and then through parkland to Belle Haven Picnic Area and on to Mount Vernon.

**Mall and Potomac Park.** A good place to start this ride is at the Mall bike rental area, 12th and Jefferson Streets NW. From there, it is fairly level cycling around the Mall, past the Reflecting Pool and memorials, around the Tidal Basin, and onto the three-mile loop around East Potomac Park. The route takes you on bike paths, streets, and sidewalks, and it is a good way to see sights.

**Rock Creek Park.** Starting at Virginia Avenue and Rock Creek Park, you can cycle north on four miles of slightly rolling bike path through wooded parkland to Pierce Mill. The trail, which runs along Rock Creek and passes the National Zoo, can get somewhat crowded on sunny weekends. Beyond Pierce Mill, beginning at Beach Drive and Broad Branch Road NW, four miles of scenic roadway running north are closed to motor vehicles from 9 am to 5 pm on Sundays.

## Boating

Boat lovers in Washington vent their enthusiasm in anything from schooners skimming across the Chesapeake Bay to pedal boats inching around the Potomac Tidal Basin. There is enough water around to make it fairly convenient to rent a boat, take a short guided cruise, or watch a yacht race.

On the Potomac River, canoes and sailboats are especially popular, although you'll also see rowboats and cabin cruisers. If you happen to be on the river at the right time, you may even spot the President's big yacht "Sequoia," or catch a glimpse of the Georgetown University crew practicing in their racing shell. Following are good places to rent boats along the Potomac and the C & O Canal:

**Backyard Boats,** 100 Franklin Street, Alexandria, VA (548-1375). Rents sailboats March-November; canoes all year, depending on the weather.

**Buzzard Point Marina,** First Street and the waterfront SW (488-8400). Rents sailboats most of the year.

**Fletcher's Boat House,** 4940 Canal Road NW (244-0461). Rents canoes and rowboats, March-December, except in bad weather.

**Jack's Boats,** 3500 K Street NW (337-9642). Rents rowboats and canoes, April-November, except in bad weather.

**Swain's Lock,** Swain's Lock Road on the C & O Canal about 4 miles north of Great Falls, MD (299-9006). Rents rowboats and canoes, for use on the Canal only, March-November and later if weather permits.

**Thompson's Boat Center,** Rock Creek Park and Virginia Avenue NW (333-4861). Rents canoes and rowboats, mid-March to mid-November.

Other boat rentals, including houseboats and charter cabin cruisers, are available at Annapolis, Maryland, and other spots on the Chesapeake Bay. See "Boats—Rentals and Charter" in the Yellow Pages for information. A number of parks, some described in this chapter, have boat rental facilities. See in Maryland: Cunningham Falls State Park, Mt. Calvert Regional Park, Rock Creek Regional Park, and Seneca Creek; in Virginia: Bull Run Marina, Burke Lake, Fountainhead Regional Park, Lake Fairfax, and Pohick Bay Regional Park.

For less sporting water activity you might try the pedal boats available at the Tidal Basin, rented April-September by the **Tidal Basin Boat Center** (783-9562), opposite the Jefferson Memorial, which also arranges rides on a swan boat that tours the Tidal Basin. The basin is especially inviting in April when the banks of Japanese cherry trees bordering it burst into cotton candy-like blossoms.

From April until Labor Day, you can tour up and down the Potomac on a **Wilson Line** cruiser, leaving from 6th Street and Maine Avenue SW at 9:30 am and 2 pm. Wilson Line, which operates the large cruise ships, is something of a Washington tradition, having operated continuously since 1876. Excursions to Mt. Vernon last about four-and-a-half hours. There is also a moonlight cruise, from 8 pm to midnight. Phone EX 3-8300 for more information.

One of the most exciting boating experiences in the Washington area is a fast, bounding **raft trip** in Shenandoah River white water. The trips start at Harper's Ferry, West Virginia, at the KOA campground, and, with an experienced guide, take you splashing down the river for four-and-a-half hours. The $12.50 fee includes a picnic lunch. Raft trips are run seven days a week from late May to October, and reservations are required. To reserve a spot or request additional information, phone Blue Ridge Outfitters, 244-9049.

## Fishing

Maryland and Virginia offer good fishing opportunities throughout the year in lakes, rivers, and salt water close to Washington. For information on where to fish and how to obtain a license, contact: Maryland Department of Natural Resources, Tawes Building, Annapolis, MD 21401 (301-267-1230) or Virginia Commission of Game and Inland Fisheries, Box 11104, Richmond, VA 23230 (804-770-4974).

Nonresident anglers can obtain special licenses for limited periods. Trout fishing generally requires an extra fee. At most of the popular fishing spots in the area you can buy bait at concessions on the property or nearby; many also rent tackle. Some good fishing areas are:

**MARYLAND**

**Assateague State Park,** Assateague. Surf and bay fishing; bass, bluefish, flounder, kingfish, sea trout; tackle rental and bait during the summer. (See Assateague in this chapter.)

**Cunningham Falls State Park,** Thurmont. Two stocked trout streams; no boating. (See Cunningham in this chapter.)

**Potomac River,** at Seneca and above. Carp, catfish, crappie, boat rentals and bait at Seneca Park, Seneca, and at White's Ferry, Martinsburg.

**Rocky Gorge Reservoir,** Laurel. Along the Patuxent River; bass, catfish, crappie, sunfish, trout; 800 acres.

**Tridelphia Reservoir,** Unity. Along the Patuxent River; bass, bluegill, crappie, pickerel, pike; 800 acres.

**VIRGINIA**

**Burke Lake,** Fairfax. Bass, crappie, channel catfish, muskellunge, sunfish; 218 acres; boat and tackle rentals; bait. (See Burke Lake in this chapter.)

**Lake Brittle,** New Baltimore. Bass, crappie, bluegill, muskellunge; 77 acres; boat rental and bait.

**Occoquan Reservoir,** Centreville. Bass, bluegill, catfish, crappie, pike; 1,700 acres; boat and tackle rental; bait. (See Bull Run Marina in this chapter.)

**Shenandoah River.** Bass, carp, channel catfish, crappie, sunfish; bait and tackle rental in some areas in Shenandoah National Park. (See Shenandoah National Park in this chapter.)

## Golf

Of the nearly 100 golf courses within driving range of Washington, most are private clubs or military base links. There are, however, nearly 20 public courses where you can take to the fairways for a fee without joining for the season. Most of these are open nearly all year round, weather permitting, and they do get crowded on weekends. It's best to phone mid-week for a weekend starting time. Consult the Yellow Pages for information on practice ranges, equipment, and rentals. Following are some courses you may want to try.

**WASHINGTON**

**East Potomac Park,** Hains Point SW (638-7037). 36 holes; rental clubs; fairly flat course.

**Fort DuPont,** Minnesota and Massachusetts Avenues SE (582-9846). 18 holes; rental clubs.

**Langston Park,** 25th Street and Benning Road NE (399-9682). 18 holes; rental clubs.

**Rock Creek,** in Rock Creek Park at 16th and Rittenhouse Streets NW (723-9832). Two 9-hole courses; rental clubs.

**MARYLAND**

**Falls Road Golf Course,** 10800 Falls Road, Rockville (299-5156). 18 holes; fairly short.

**Greenbrier,** 11607 Rockville Pike, Rockville (881-9893). 9 holes.

**Henson Creek,** Oxon Hill (248-2868). 9 holes; only about 15 minutes from downtown Washington.

**Laurel Pines,** 14601 Laurel-Bowie Road, Laurel (490-4626). 18 holes; well wooded.

**Needwood,** 6924 Needwood Road, Rockville (948-1075). (See Rock Creek Regional Park entry in this chapter.) 18 holes; very popular, so be sure to call first for a starting time.

**Northampton,** 407 Gold Course Drive, Largo (336-7771). 18 holes.

**Northwest Park,** 15711 Layhill Road, Silver Spring (598-6100). 18 holes; 6,660 yards; reputed to be the best public course in the area.

**Oxon Run,** 3000 23rd Parkway, Hillcrest Heights (894-2200). 9 holes; 2,900 yards.

**Sligo Park,** between Forest Glen Road and Arcola Avenue, Silver Spring (585-6006). 9 holes adjacent to creek.

**Valley Springs,** 3601 Brinkley Road, Oxon Hill (894-8488). 9 holes.

**VIRGINIA**

**Burke Lake Park** (see Burke Lake entry in this chapter). (273-9400). 18 holes.

**Jefferson,** 7900 Lee Highway, Falls Church (560-4953). 9 holes; club rentals.

**Loudoun Golf and Country Club,** Route 7, Purcellville. 18 holes; good scenery.

**Pinecrest,** 12001 Lee Highway, Fairfax (278-8555). 9 holes; club rentals.

**Reston,** 11599 North Shore Drive, Reston (620-9333). 18 holes; fairly challenging.

**Twin Lakes,** Centreville (631-9099). 18 holes.

## Hunting

There is everything from duck to deer in the Maryland and Virginia hunting areas near Washington, but you have to be a serious and determined hunter to pay the necessary permit fees and unscramble the myriad rules about seasons, weapons, bag limits, and such. Permit fees for hunting in just one area can run up to about $50 for nonresidents, depending on the kind of game you're after.

Before you even consider hunting around Washington, contact the Virginia Commission of Game and Inland Fisheries and the Maryland Department of Natural Resources (addresses in section on fishing) and ask them for "Virginia Hunters Guide," "Summary of Virginia Game Laws," and "Guide to Hunting and Trapping in Maryland." These free booklets will tell you how to obtain a license; where to hunt; and the regulations pertaining to seasons, limits, and weapons.

After you have your license and a firm grounding in local hunting requirements, if you still are game, here are a few happy hunting grounds you might want to try:

**MARYLAND**

**Cedarville State Park,** Brandywine. Squirrel, deer, quail, rabbit; 2,400 acres; camping available. (See Cedarville in this chapter.)

**Cunningham Falls State Park,** Thurmont. Deer, grouse, squirrel; 4,446 acres; camping available. (See Cunningham Falls in this chapter.)

**Doncaster State Forest,** Charles County. Squirrel, deer, quail, rabbit; 1,485 acres. (See Doncaster in this chapter.)

**McKee-Besher's Wildlife Management Area,** just north of Seneca. Deer, quail, rabbit, waterfowl, squirrel, dove; 1,475 acres.

**Merkle Wildlife Management Area,** near Lyons Creek. Deer, quail, rabbit, waterfowl, squirrel; 910 acres.

**VIRGINIA**

**A. P. Hill Military Reservation,** Caroline County. Deer, squirrel, dove; 77,000 acres.

**Apple Manor Wildlife Management Area,** Fauquier County. Turkey, deer, grouse, squirrel; 4,200 acres.

**Quantico Marine Corps Base;** traverses Fauquier, Prince William, and Stafford Counties. Deer, squirrel, rabbit; 45,198 acres.

## Ice Skating, Indoors and Out

There is hardly a more lively site than the C & O Canal at night after a week or two of sub-freezing weather. Hundreds of skaters slide and swirl merrily along, stopping at campfires dotting the banks to warm stiff fingers and numb toes. During the day, the scene is repeated all along the canal, at the Lincoln Memorial Reflecting Pool, on the Potomac River, and at the ponds at Kenilworth Aquatic Gardens. (See entries in this chapter for details on the C & O Canal and Kenilworth Aquatic Gardens.)

Unfortunately, Washington cannot be classified as a winter wonderland, or anything close to it. Freezes that last long enough to permit skating occur infrequently—generally for a few days in January and February, if at all. To check on whether the ice is solid enough, phone National Capital Parks (426-6700).

A more reliable source of ice can be found at ice skating rinks. The newest and most convenient to downtown is **The Sculpture Rink** on the Mall, designed for ice skating in winter and model boat sailing in summer (7th Street and Constitution Avenue NW; phone National Capital Parks, 426-6700). An oval space measuring 160 by 120 feet, it affords skaters a good view of government buildings along the Mall as they spin and cut figure eights. Skating hours, winter only, are 11:15 am-9:15 pm on weekdays and 9:15 am-10 pm on weekends. Rental skates are available. Another ice rink in the District is at the **Washington Coliseum,** 3rd and M Streets NE (547-5800), open Saturdays and Sundays only, November-March.

Here are a few suburban ice rinks:

**MARYLAND**

**Bowie Ice Rink,** Allen Pond Park, Bowie (262-5688). Open November-April.

**Cabin John Regional Park Ice Rink,** Potomac (365-0585). Another winter sports facility here is the toboggan run. Both are open November-March.

**Wheaton Regional Park Ice Rink** (649-3640). Open November-March.

**VIRGINIA**

**Crystal City Ice Rink,** 23rd Street and Jefferson Davis Highway, Arlington (521-0440). Open October-March.

**Fairfax Ice Arena,** 3779 Pickett Road, Fairfax (323-1131). Open all year.

**Tysons Ice Rink,** 8604 Leesburg Pike, McLean (893-5701). Open all year.

**Village House Ice Rink,** 245 North Washington Street, Falls Church (532-5391). Open September-April.

## Swimming

A sure way to beat the Capital's famed summer heat and humidity is to dip into water, and in the Washington area that can mean anything from a public swimming pool to a lake to the Chesapeake Bay. If you are planning on a daily dip, however, stay at a hotel or motel with a pool. Public swimming facilities can have drawbacks, such as crowds or a distant location.

Most public swimming pools in Washington are large and well staffed with lifeguards. However, don't expect such amenities as snack bars or lounge chairs or an atmosphere even remotely akin to a country club. The phone book lists about 25 public pools under "District of Columbia Department of Recreation." Of these, the **East Potomac Park** pool (Hains Point SW) and the **Georgetown** pool (34th Street and Volta Place NW) have about the best facilities and atmosphere. There are also public pools in the surrounding suburbs, and you can locate them by phoning the county Departments of Recreation listed at the beginning of this chapter.

With Rock Creek and the Potomac River riddled with pollution, the closest large body of water for swimming is Chesapeake Bay. Sandy Point is a large public beach on the bay, located on Route 50-301 about eight miles east of Annapolis. It has picnicking facilities, toilets, and showers. Unfortunately, however, in July and August the Chesapeake Bay is usually bristling with sea nettles—small, stinging jellyfish that make bathing in the bay uncomfortable at most times during those months.

Other possibilities for taking to the water are lakes and pools in nearby public parks and recreation areas described in the hiking and camping section of this chapter. For some of the best, see in Maryland: Assateague National Seashore and Cunningham Falls State Park; in Virginia: Bull Run Regional Park, Lake Fairfax, and Westmoreland State Park.

Among the many hotels and motels you can stay in to enjoy good swimming pools, some of the most convenient are:

**Key Bridge Marriott,** 1401 Lee Highway, Arlington, VA (524-6400).

**Loew's L'Enfant,** 480 L'Enfant Plaza East SW (484-1000).

**Ramada Inn,** Massachusetts Avenue and Thomas Circle NW (783-4600).

**Sheraton-Park,** 2660 Woodley Road NW (265-2000).

**Twin Bridges Marriott,** Route I-95, Arlington, VA (628-4200).

**Washington Hilton,** 1919 Connecticut Avenue NW (483-3000).

**Shoreham Americana,** 2500 Calvert Street NW (234-0700).

## Tennis

There are about 150 public tennis courts in Washington and more in the surrounding suburbs. The problem is finding them and getting to them. Many are tucked away in sleepy neighborhoods you'd never visit otherwise, and there are usually a number of players waiting for turns at the net.

If you seriously want to play tennis, one of the best investments you can make is a handy little directory called *Washington Tennis Guide.* It provides a comprehensive list of public courts, tennis clubs, tournaments, and tennis shops, and it is available at sports shops and tennis clubs or from Rock Creek Publishing Company, P.O. Box 19273, Washington, DC 20036 (462-5602).

Most of Washington's public courts are free and first-come, first-served, but three of the largest require a fee and can be reserved. Fees range from about $1 to $2.50 an hour for outdoor play, depending on the time of day, and reservations must be made in person no more than five days in advance for these courts:

**East Potomac Park,** Hains Point SW (783-5360). 24 courts open 9 am-dark, except in summer when eight courts are lighted until midnight. Five indoor courts are available from mid-October through April, 8 am-midnight, at rates ranging from $7 to $12 an hour. Showers, lockers, snack bar, nearby picnicking, and golf.

**Kennedy Courts,** 16th and Kennedy Streets NW (723-2669). 22 courts open 9 am-dark, April through October and when weather permits during winter. Pro shop and snack bar; picnic area nearby.

**Pierce Mill Courts,** Rock Creek Park at Beach Drive and Park Road NW (no phone). 6 clay courts, open noon-dark on weekdays and 8 am-dark on weekends, May through September.

In general, indoor tennis clubs are available to members only, but there are a few that do offer spot play to the public when time is available. Following are some of these, with fees ranging from about $8 to $14 an hour:

**Cabin John Regional Park Indoor Tennis Courts,** Democracy Boulevard and Seven Locks Road, Cabin John, MD (469-7300). 6 courts; reservations may be made up to 5 days in advance.

**Four Seasons Tennis Club,** Williams Drive, Merrifield, VA (573-5105). 8 courts; reservations made be made up to a week in advance.

**Linden Hill Indoor Tennis Club,** 5500 Pooks Hill Road, Bethesda, MD (530-2224). 6 courts; spot time available only when reserved players cancel.

If you want to stay in a hotel or motel with tennis courts, try the **Washington Hilton,** 1919 Connecticut Avenue NW (483-3000); the **Sheraton Inn-International Center,** 11810 Sunrise Valley Drive, Reston, VA (620-9000); or the **Dulles Marriott,** Box 17235, Herndon, VA (471-9500).

# Chapter Eight

# Fun with Children

ELIZABETH POST MIREL

"In America there are two classes of travel—first class and with children." Humorist Robert Benchley's observation is no joke when you and your bedraggled family encounter closed museum doors, overpriced restaurants, or long lines leading only to boring events.

It doesn't have to be this way. Washington is one of the most exciting places to tour family style.

## Strategy

The difference between a satisfying and a frustrating trip is simply strategy. This means advance planning at home and flexible scheduling on tour.

### Books

While you're busy making reservations and acquiring maps, spend a little extra time and money to send away for some books for the children. These are our favorites:

*Our Nation's Capital Coloring Book,* 75¢ plus 50¢ postage from the United States Capitol Historical Society, 200 Maryland Avenue NE, Room 410, Washington, DC 20515. This 100-page book, also on sale in the Capitol Building Gift Shop, has illustrations of all the main sights plus straightforward explanatory text. It is an excellent source of basic information about Washington.

*Coloring the Smithsonian,* $1.50 plus 45¢ postage from the Smithsonian Bookstore, National Museum of History and Technology, 14th Street and Constitution Avenue NW, Washington, DC 20560. These large line drawings on good quality paper can keep kids busy for hours, and familiarize them with many of the displays at the museums. This, and several other coloring books based on Smithsonian exhibits, is also for sale in museum shops.

**Paper Soldiers of the American Revolution,* $2.50 plus 50¢ postage from Bellerophon Books, 153 Steuart Street, San Francisco, CA 94105. Also on sale at Smithsonian museum shops, this construction and coloring book gives detailed information about military life in Colonial times. The company publishes several other fine activity books with historical themes.

And here are a couple of publications for parents that will give them some additional ideas about what to do with children during their visit:

*Going Places with Children in Washington,* $2.50 postage included, from Green Acres School, 11701 Danville Drive, Rockville, MD 20852. Parents and older children will enjoy perusing this comprehensive, compact guidebook and planning their stay in Washington together. It is also on sale at

Smithsonian and local bookshops.

**Ask Me,* A 1976 Bicentennial Calendar of Events for Kids, $2, highlights activities of particular interest to families. It is available at local book and toy stores and can be ordered through the Children's Museum of Inquiry and Discovery, 3432 Newark Street NW, Washington, DC 20016.

## Food

Food can make or break the budget as well as the mood of a family trip. Eating well at a reasonable cost presents a real challenge. For those who prefer making some of their own meals to eat in their hotel room or for an outdoor picnic, supplies can be purchased at local markets, many of which are open at night and on Sundays, and at carry-outs that dot the city and surrounding areas (see Picnics, Chapter 7). For quick refueling in fair weather you will find fruit stands everywhere and ice cream and hot dog carts around the Mall and heavily trafficked tourist areas.

Fast-food chains probably offer the quickest meals at the lowest possible cost. In our experience, the best of these locally are **Holly Farms** and **Gino's** for fried chicken, and **Roy Rogers** and **Burger Chef** for hamburgers.

When you go the restaurant route, check Chapter 9 for ideas and prices. At the finer restaurants prices are usually lower for lunch, but the standards of preparation remain high, and children are regarded more tolerantly.

However, most restaurants welcome children. Some cater specifically to the family trade. This area has many excellent, inexpensive Chinese, Japanese, French, Greek, and Latin-American restaurants, plus a few good seafood places. We strongly recommend eating early—the closer to 6 pm the better. You are seated faster, served better, and find more attention is paid to youngsters.

## Hobbies

The Washington trip can be especially exciting for children with hobbies or collections. In this chapter and others are many good ideas for satisfying special interests. For instance, the rockhound will be impressed with the mineral collection at the National Museum of Natural History, the model builder with the aircraft at the Arts and Industries and Air and Space buildings, and the doll collector with the first ladies' gowns at the National Museum of History and Technology. The free-flying bird cage at the National Zoo is a must for amateur ornithologists. The U.S. Botanic Garden is the place to talk to plants of all shapes and sizes. Washington is also an ideal place to begin a postcard, stamp, doll, miniature animal, Indian artifact, or other collection. This not only gives a focus to shopping, but also sustains the pleasure of the trip long after the suitcases have been unpacked.

## Hotels

In choosing a hotel, look for the extra facilities that make life for families on the road a little bit easier. If you're traveling with very young children, you may want the convenience of in-house washing machines and clothes dryers. Older children may enjoy watching the movies shown on the TV systems installed in some hotels. The whole family will enjoy a swim in the hotel pool after pounding the pavement on one of those hot, sticky days for which Washington is famous. Also, some hotels offer special family rates or feature family packages during summer months. (See Advice to Travelers, Chapter 2 for hotel information.)

## Babysitting

The best and cheapest way to leave the children at night is to have a friend in Washington make arrangements for you with a local sitter. The going rate is about $1 an hour, and you have the assurance of the friend that the sitter is reliable. Otherwise, you can hire a sitter through your hotel or a private agency. Give them several days' notice, and supply a list of your children's names, ages, and special needs.

Among the larger hotels and motels, Howard Johnson's, the Mayflower, and the Shoreham engage sitters for you. The Sheraton Park and Stouffer's refer you to a service. Some Holiday Inns, Marriotts, Quality Inns, and Ramada Inns make babysitting arrangements for their guests; others refer them to lists or agencies. The following babysitting agencies are used by hotels as well as by individual local residents. Count on a fee averaging $3 an hour plus transportation:

**Assistants, Inc.,** 1022 Wilson Boulevard, Arlington, VA (524-0666).

**Child Care Agency,** Woodward Building,

15th and H Streets NW (783-8573).

**Family and Nursing Care, Inc.,** 1005 Bonifant Street, Silver Spring, MD (588-5848).

Most local colleges and universities prefer to arrange steady employment for their students. However, a few offer possibilities for one-night jobs:

**George Washington University,** 2033 G Street NW (676-6495). Ask for a list of students and get in touch with them yourself.

**Georgetown University School of Nursing,** 3700 Reservoir Road NW (965-3500 5-6 pm weekdays). Write or phone your requirements, and a student will get in touch with you. A $2 fee entitles the family to use the service for the academic year.

**Howard University School of Nursing,** 2400 6th Street NW (636-7456). Your name and requirements are posted, and any interested students contact you themselves.

During the day, it can be fun to split up. One parent may take the children while the other goes to an art museum or some other place not suitable for youngsters. Responsible children can be left at the Hirshhorn Museum or the American Film Institute to see films or cartoons (see Entertainment section in this chapter for details).

# Main Sights

Since you may not be able to see all the important sights in Washington when you tour with children, these tips may help you decide which ones appeal most to your family. (For more information see Chapters 3 and 6.)

**Arlington National Cemetery:** The yearning for the Kennedys lingers on. Most children identify with the era and are impressed with the grave site. The changing of the guard at the Tomb of the Unknown Soldier is a ceremony that holds their interest.

**Bureau of Engraving and Printing:** This tour provides a first-rate answer to the question, "How is it made?" Money interests everyone.

**The Capitol:** Young children, to whom the political process means only incomprehensible dinner conversation, may enjoy seeing the building, but are likely to be bored by the sessions. (Children under six are not even allowed in the galleries.) They prefer the subway ride between the Capitol and the Senate Office Buildings: For older children try the Senate, where the proceedings are less confusing, or a committee hearing (check daily newspapers for listings), where the focus is more defined.

**Federal Bureau of Investigation:** Some children are thrilled by the manhunt, shoot-out focus of this popular tour, but others are frightened by it.

***Jefferson Memorial:** An aesthetically pleasing structure and a great place for little ones to run around.

**John F. Kennedy Center for the Performing Arts:** Kids are awed by the displays of flags in the great halls. The mirrors strike their fancy. The terrace and roof afford a grand and leisurely view of Washington, the Potomac, and Watergate.

**Library of Congress:** Older children may be struck by the architecture of this splendid Italian Renaissance building, but younger children may be more intrigued with the book-processing system in the control room.

**Lincoln Memorial:** The most magnificent of monuments, this building should be visited at night, as well as during the day, for full impact.

***National Archives:** Every member of the family must be impressed with the power of the pen when looking at the Declaration of Independence, the Constitution, and the Bill of Rights resting here in their helium-filled cases. While the yellowing papers themselves are not awesome, the democratic force that emanates from them is. Mechanically minded youngsters will be intrigued with the model of the device that lowers the documents into the bombproof shelter every night and brings them up every morning.

**Supreme Court:** Younger children should not be taken to hear the Court in session, but they may respond well to the short tour of the building and the succinct explanation of the work done here.

*** Washington Monument:** We find the idea of ascending this giant tower more appealing than the actuality. There are long lines, crowded elevators, and tiny windows that are too high for most children. The most fun is counting the 898 steps down. Nevertheless, the thrill of having been "up there" outweighs the hassle, and the experience is memorable for children.

**White House:** The appeal of the White House is the fact that the President lives there. Most children are not interested in interior decor, although the associations generally hold their attention.

# Museums

The **Smithsonian Institution** is a must for a first family visit. The Mall area buildings—the National Museum of History and Technology, the National Museum of Natural History, the Arts and Industries Building, and the Air and Space Building—probably hold more interesting objects per square foot than any other institutional complex. The exhibits—developed, designed, and maintained by a highly professional staff—are as educational as they are entertaining. There's something to tie in with everyone's interests, hobbies, or schoolwork. (For more details see Mall walking tour, Chapter 3; Discovery Room, Museum of Natural History, below; Experimentarium in Animal, Vegetable, Mineral section of this chapter.)

**The Anacostia Neighborhood Museum,** 2405 Martin Luther King Avenue SE (381-6691), with its emphasis on participation, is a place where children can get involved in arts and crafts and in the exhibits relating to black history and heritage and to urban problems (see Chapter 5). Most children do not relate well to the more static atmosphere of art museums. The exceptions are the **Joseph H. Hirshhorn Museum and Sculpture Garden**—children as well as adults are turned on by this collection of massive sculptures and modern art (see Chapter 3)—and the **Explore Gallery,** National Collection of Fine Arts (see below).

In addition to the Mall area buildings, several other downtown and suburban museums provide stimulating—and for younger children less overwhelming—experiences:

**Children's Museum of Inquiry and Discovery** (363-1770). The sponsors of this new children's museum are hoping to have a permanent home by fall, 1975. The exciting idea behind it is to have kids participate in science, arts, and humanities projects and to learn about these activities through their experiences. There will be, for example, chemistry, silk-screening, and dramatic demonstrations by professionals who will then help the children do their own experiments. The museum also hopes to display children's works and provide information.

***Daughters of the American Revolution Headquarters,** 17th and D Streets NW (628-4980). Monday-Friday 9 am-4 pm; closed several days during Christmas vacation. Guided tours 10 am-3 pm. When visiting DAR Headquarters go to the Children's Attic and skip the main gallery, period rooms, and museum of the Children of the American Revolution. Although they contain excellent pieces, they are of little or no interest to youngsters. The Attic displays Colonial dolls, toys, and children's furniture. While the material is high in quality, the exhibit is poorly designed. This makes the experience less rewarding for most children than it could be.

**Discovery Room,** National Museum of Natural History, 10th Street and Constitution Avenue NW (628-4422). Monday-Thursday noon-2:30 pm; Friday-Sunday 11 am-3 pm. Free, but tickets from reception desk at Mall entrance required weekends. Visiting this superbly designed room is a marvelous learning experience. Animal, vegetable, and mineral specimens are yours to see, hear, smell, and touch. Using written materials, film strips, and elementary scientific equipment, you build a body of knowledge about the objects you are studying. You can, for example, examine beetles with a magnifying glass, watch a film on sea urchins, make a variety of sounds by rattling different kinds of seeds, see how logs are cut up into boards, and how rocks become pebbles. The half-hour period allowed in the room on crowded weekends is never enough. You may wish, as we did, that the room had longer hours, larger capacity, and more trained staff members to guide you in making your discoveries.

**Explore Gallery,** National Collection of Fine Arts, 8th and G Streets NW (628-4422). Daily 10 am-5:30 pm. Children can enter this room through a circle cut out of a bright yellow door. They can remove their shoes and socks, run up and down the colorful carpeted ramps, jump on the bronze dog, bang the shining foil mirror, and collapse on mats under the ramp platform where they create their own world. All the while, the audio equipment pipes bird calls, rock music, and a variety of other sounds. The paintings and exhibits are seen on the run or incorporated into the play activities. Even toddlers have a good time here, but the gallery seems to appeal most to three-ten-year-olds. It's the ideal place to leave children while you tour the National Collection of Fine Arts and the National Portrait Gallery, both located in the same building. (See Downtown walking tour, Chapter 3 for details.)

**Explorer's Hall,** National Geographic Society, 17th and M Streets NW (296-7500). Monday-Friday 9 am-6 pm; Saturday and holidays 9 am-5 pm; Sunday noon-5 pm. A children's favorite, this manageable museum provides all ages with varying amounts of stimulation and information. Our three-year-old likes the enormous revolving globe and the set of four simultaneous televisions. Our seven-year-old is intrigued with the gravity and space exhibits, and our nine-year-old concentrates on the Indian displays. While it's fun to pick up the earphones and listen to the taped narrations that accompany each exhibit, most of the information is too weighty for children and less than absorbing even for adults. The museum's displays are based on studies sponsored by the National Geographic Society, and the recordings in some cases seem to be more intent on plugging the organization than on building a body of knowledge. The gift shop features the Society's excellent maps and publications (see Chapter 10).

**National Capital Trolley Museum,** Bonifant Road, Wheaton, MD (384-9797). Saturday and Sunday noon-5 pm; summer also Wednesday-Friday noon-4 pm. Capital Beltway (Route 495) Exit 21, Georgia Avenue north to Layhill Road (Route 182); right on Layhill Road 2 miles to Bonifant Road; right on Bonifant Road; museum on left. Trolley fare: adults 50¢; children 25¢. The best thing about this museum is the one-and-a-half-mile trolley ride through the fields. The staff, all devoted volunteers, are full of facts on the history and mechanics of trolleys, and will eagerly relate them to you. The car barn houses the collection of nonworking trolleys. The museum occasionally shows old films on the theme of transportation. An elaborate model railroad operates Sunday 1 pm-5 pm.

**United States Navy Memorial Museum,** Washington Navy Yard, 9th and M Streets SE (433-2651). Monday-Friday 9 am-4 pm; Saturday, Sunday, and holidays 10 am-5 pm. Closed Thanksgiving, Christmas, and New Year's Day. Parking. Snack bar Monday-Friday 9 am-3:30 pm. As a museum this place gets a low grade, but as an indoor-outdoor playground it ranks among the top. Except for the cases of model ships, the exhibits are poorly designed and are accompanied by little or no explanatory text. A sense of historical continuity is lacking. It's the weaponry displays that draw families here. These use up lots of energy and excite the imagination of active children from toddlers to teenagers. They can climb on cannons, raise and lower the barrels of anti-aircraft weapons, sit inside bomb capsules, ring bells, and man submarine periscopes. The yard outside has tanks, guns, and missiles—most of which beat traditional monkey bars for a good climb. Skip the Navy Combat Art Gallery located next door, Monday-Friday 8 am-4 pm (433-3815), unless you are interested in paintings of ships and portraits of the first female officers.

***The National Historical Wax Museum and Dolphin Theatre,** 4th and E Streets SW (554-2600). Daily 9 am-10 pm April 1-Labor Day; 9 am-8 pm September-March. Dolphin shows at noon, 1:30 pm, 3 pm, 4:30 pm, 6 pm, 7:30 pm April 1-Labor Day; noon-6 pm September-March. Admission to museum: adults $2; children 6-12 $1.25; children under 6 50¢. Admission to dolphin show: adults $1; children 6-12 75¢; children under 6 50¢. Combination ticket: adults $2.75; children 6-12 $1.75; children under 6 $1. Group rates available. Adjoining parking lot 85¢ per hour; $2.75 all day. Cafeteria. The new Wax Museum, scheduled to open in spring of '75 promises to provide even more fun for the family than the old one. It will still show famous scenes from the Bible and from American history, but will have several additional attractions, the most novel of which is a trained dolphin show.

The biblical section of the museum will present tableaux such as Adam and Eve in the Garden of Eden, the Last Supper, and the Crucifixion. The American history section has been expanded and, in addition to such well-known historical events as Columbus sailing to America, Betsy Ross stitching the flag, the battle at the Alamo, and the first man on the moon, it will have ethnic, scientific, and black history exhibits. In the Presidents' Room, visitors will hear a brief history of the United States as they view the chief executives' plastic likenesses. The focus is on personalities. Since the museum was not finished when this guidebook went to press, we are unable to comment on the impact of the displays, the quality of the printed material accompanying the biblical and historical scenes, and the educational value of the audio-visual presentation in the Presidents' Room.

**Washington Dolls' House and Toy Museum,** 5236 44th Street NW (244-0024). Tuesday-Sunday, noon-5 pm. Between Lord and Taylor and Wisconsin Avenue. Admission: adults $2; children under 14 $1. Adults are as intrigued as children with the miniature houses, furniture, figures, and accessories exhibited in this new museum, containing the private collection of Flora Gill Jacobs. The longer you look, the more you see—whether it's at the Victorian parlor complete with photo album, dictionary, globe, chandelier, and vase of flowers; or at the German kitchen equipped with copper pots, pewter plates, and a rosy-cheeked cook; or any of the other buildings and rooms on display. The exhibits, which will change periodically, are set up behind sheets of plexiglass, and many are close to the ground. This makes it easy for visitors of all ages to get a good long look at them. The gift shop features a 12-room doll house filled with examples of items that may be purchased through the museum. Copies of Mrs. Jacobs' books on doll houses are also for sale.

***Woodlawn Plantation,** Touch and Try Room, Route 1, Mount Vernon, VA (780-3118). Daily 9:30 am-4:30 pm. Admission: adults $1.25; children, students, and military 60¢. Group tours of house and garden; advance arrangements preferred. While adults are interested in the tastefully furnished rooms of this early-19th-century plantation, children are especially intrigued with the Touch and Try Room. Here they can beat a drum, rock on an antique horse, draw with quill pen and ink, try needlework, arrange doll-house furniture, walk on stilts, and play games. Doing the things children did 175 years ago gives them a feeling for the late Colonial period. They are also impressed with the furnishings in the children's rooms, and enjoy running through the restored gardens. The gift shop offers an excellent selection of books, crafts, and miniatures. Woodlawn Plantation was given by George Washington to Nelly Custis Lewis, Martha's granddaughter by a previous marriage.

A short walk through the woods leads to the **Pope-Leighey House,** a residence designed by Frank Lloyd Wright and moved to Woodlawn from its original location in Falls Church, Va. (See Mount Vernon driving tour; Seeing the Region, Chapter 4.)

## Animal, Vegetable, and Mineral

Washington charms the resident as well as the tourist with its many, varied, and accessible open spaces. These include downtown and suburban parks, gardens, and zoos.

Visiting the **National Zoo** can be the most pleasurable way to see a great selection of live animals in this area (see Outdoors, Chapter 7). Children are especially taken with the pandas (be sure to go at feeding time or you may not see them do anything but sleep), but wallowing hippos, howling gibbons, free-flying birds, and spectacular strolling peacocks have their undeniable appeal. Right now the zoo is undergoing extensive renovation. Don't be disappointed if some of the children's favorite animals are missing. They'll be back, in nicer quarters, by 1976. The **Aquarium** in the Commerce Department Building is another winner (see Federal Triangle walking tour, Chapter 3).

### Animals

**Al-Marah Arabians,** P.O. Box 410, Barnesville, MD (428-8013). Daily 9 am-4 pm. Closed Christmas, Thanksgiving, and New Year's Day. Capital Beltway (Route 495) Exit 19; Route 270, 5 miles to Route 28; west on Route 28 14 miles to Peach Tree Road; right on Peach Tree Road 2 miles to farm on left. Horse-lovers—and that includes most children—come here to watch the routine tending and special training of these beautiful animals. However, they are not allowed to touch or feed them. The well-maintained farm is home for the largest group of purebred Arabians in the world. Visitors are free to wander through the barns, walk along the fences marking the pastures, and picnic by the pond. Four times a year special "Club Day" exhibitions are held for the public. Inquire at the office.

Two miles farther down Peach Tree Road is the **Arabian Horse Museum,** P.O. Box 307, Barnesville, MD (972-0568). Tuesday-Friday 9 am-5 pm; Saturday and Sunday 1 pm-5 pm. Maintained by the Arabian Horse Owners Foundation, this small building houses objects and artworks relating to the heritage of the species, and a small noncirculating library. It's a place where the devotee, rather than the casual sightseer, would want to spend time.

**The Wildlife Preserve,** 13710 Central Avenue, Largo, MD (249-9200). Capital Beltway (Route 495) Exit 33, east 6 miles on Route 214 to preserve on left. April 19-October, daily 9:30 am-5 pm for tickets; closes at dusk. Admission: adults $4.25; children 3-11 $3; children under 3 free. Student groups of 15 or more April 19-June 15 $2. Snack bar, chicken shack, picnic tables. At the Wildlife Preserve the animals run free and the people are in cages. Large groups of sightseers are driven through the 300-acre area in air-conditioned trams. Through the large windows they get a good view of the North American, South American, African, and Australian animals. Some, like the bison, llama, and zebra, keep their distance. The more curious come up close to the vehicle to get a good look at the humans.

A guide on board each tram supplies information and answers questions about the animals and their lifestyles. After the 45-minute trip through the preserve, you can spend as much time as you wish in the pleasant entertainment area, designed in an African motif. There's an attention-holding, slick film about the animal kingdom, a reptile show in which kids get to hold a snake (and receive a certificate to prove it), a rather bird-brained parrot show, a birds-of-prey demonstration, and a small barn where, after petting goats, deer, and other small animals, children can wash their own hands at sinks operated by foot pedals. There is also an "Artisan's Village" of working craftsmen.

The Wildlife Preserve is a privately owned business, and the excursion, although rewarding, can turn out to be an expensive one for families. The gift shop, however, is unabashedly commercial, and the only educational products that are sold are the glossy preserve brochures.

## Farms

**Beltsville Agricultural Research Center,** Beltsville, MD (344-2483). Monday-Friday 8 am-4:30 pm by appointment only. Capital Beltway (Route 495) Exit 27, Route 1, north 1½ miles to Powder Mill Road, right on Powder Mill Road 7/10 mile to Visitors' Center on the left. Cafeteria 11 am-1 pm Don't come here expecting a folksy farm tour. The purpose of this center is to conduct research on food—how to produce it more efficiently, and how to improve its nutritional qualities. Therefore, in the course of the two-hour visit, you do see many types of animals and plants, but you also gain an understanding of how science has affected and will continue to affect your diet. After an introductory slide show, which is short, interesting, and comprehensible to children, you are driven from barn to barn by a knowledgeable guide. You're likely to see dairy cows being milked (research on longevity), beef cattle munching newspaper (research on feeding animals waste products), sheep and their baby lambs (research on fertility), and flowers and plants (research on the effects of pollution). The interest of younger children is sustained by their involvement with the animals, but they tend to get tired and generally are unable to concentrate by the end of the tour. Older children and adults remain fascinated.

***The National Colonial Farm,** P.O. Box 697, Route 1, Accokeek, MD (283-2113). Daily 10 am-5 pm, but advance arrangements preferred weekdays. South Capitol Street or Capital Beltway (Route 495) Exit 37 south to Indian Head Highway, 10 miles to Bryan Point Road, right on Bryan Point Road 4 miles to farm. Admission: adults $1; children 6-12 25¢; friends, patrons, and military free. Life on a middle-income farm in the late 1700s is accurately reproduced on this beautiful plot of land overlooking the Potomac River across from Mount Vernon. The tools, equipment, crops, herbs, animals, and fowl are those of the Colonial period. With a friendly and well-informed guide we spent a leisurely hour examining corn, handling sickles, petting horned Dorset sheep, walking the acreage, and receiving detailed answers to our questions about Colonial farming practices. Even during winter months there may still be cotton in the fields, rosemary in the herb garden, and a newborn lamb in the barn. The Accokeek Foundation, which runs the farm, also sponsors research on crops of the Colonial period, agricultural practices of the 18th century, and development of practical applications of early farming methods. Because The National Colonial Farm is off the beaten track it is rarely crowded, which makes for a satisfying visit. The intimate atmosphere is likely to be destroyed, however, when the ferry from Mount Vernon to the farm, planned for 1976, is completed.

**Oxon Hill Farm,** 6411 Oxon Hill Road, Oxon Hill, MD (839-1177). Capital Beltway (Route 495) Exit 37 south, right at end of ramp to Oxon Hill Road, immediate right into farm; or South Capitol Street to Indian Head Highway, right on Oxon Hill Road, immediate right into farm. Daily 8 am-5 pm. Tours for individuals, families, and groups; advance telephone arrangements required. Although Oxon Hill is a typical turn-of-the-century working farm, its operations cater to the public's needs and interests. For young children there's always a fuzzy animal to pet, a horse to feed, a goose to gawk at. Older children may be interested in watching the work in the fields, as well as the crafts and the animals. The whole family will enjoy the wagon rides (advance telephone arrangements required) and the explanations of farming procedures by the congenial National Park Service staff. Depending on the season, you may see sheepshearing, gardening, threshing, cider pressing, corn harvesting, molasses making, candle dipping, spinning, or weaving. Groups may arrange to participate in farm activities. New to the farm is the Woodlot Trail, a self-guided nature walk designed to illustrate how farmers used the woods. There are tables and grates provided for picnicking on the grounds.

***Turkey Run Farm,** McLean, VA (557-1378). Capital Beltway (Route 495) Exit 13, Route 193, east 1 mile, left into farm; or George Washington Memorial Parkway to Route 123, right fork onto Route 193, right into farm. Wednesday-Sunday 10 am-4:30 pm. The day-to-day operations of a Colonial homestead are reenacted in this pleasant, wooded setting. Visitors see gardening, animal husbandry, logs splitting, cooking, mending, and other seasonal activities and gain some insight into the quality of the farmers' lives. If you have visited other Colonial farms such as Mount Vernon or Woodlawn Plantation (upper income) and National Colonial Farm (middle income), you'll be able to make some interesting comparisons between them and Turkey Run Farm (lower income). Because the location of this farm is so convenient, it tends to be very crowded on weekends. This makes it almost impossible to view the activities in the tiny cabin or to talk to the small staff working the farm, and without such interaction the visit may not be completely satisfying. Weekday or early morning weekend visits are recommended.

## Nature Centers

**Brookside Nature Center,** Wheaton Regional Park, 1400 Glenallen Avenue, Wheaton, MD (946-9071). Tuesday-Saturday 9 am-5 pm; Sunday 1 pm-5 pm. Capital Beltway (Route 495) Exit 21, Georgia Avenue north to Randolph Road, right on Randolph Road 2 blocks to Glenallen Avenue, right on Glenallen Avenue 7/10 mile into park. Guided walks; advance telephone arrangements required. Films Saturday and Sunday 2 pm and 4 pm. Brookside's strong point is conservation. In addition to its displays of mounted animals, mineral specimens, a beehive, and a push-button nature quiz, the center sponsors work programs in conjunction with local schools for children 12-15, and training programs for college students. (See Playgrounds section below for details on Wheaton Regional Park.)

**Clearwater Nature Center,** Cosca Regional Park, Thrift Road, Clinton, MD (297-4575). Tuesday-Saturday 9 am-4:30 pm; Sunday 11 am-4 pm. Capital Beltway (Route 495) Exit 36, Route 5 south, left on Woodyard

Road (Route 223), left on Brandywine Road (Route 381), right on Thrift Road into park. Guided walks; advance telephone arrangements required. Films Saturday and Sunday 2 pm. The exhibit room of this active, modern nature center has been redesigned as a pioneer cabin. Many of the toys, utensils, accessories, and pieces of furniture are crafted by the staff. Clearwater has crafts classes for children and adults, runs workshops on greenhouse botany, gardening, and preserving, and holds monthly story hours for children ages 4-7.

**Gulf Branch Nature Center,** 3608 North Military Road, Arlington, VA (558-2340). Tuesday-Saturday 10 am-5 pm; Sunday 1 pm-5 pm. MacArthur Boulevard across Chain Bridge, left on Glebe Road, first exit at Military Road, right into center. Guided walks; advance reservations required. Films Saturday and Sunday 2 pm. Working with the handicapped, particularly the blind, is a specialty of this North Arlington center. A nature trail with rope guides and braille notes is readily available (it's not set up permanently because of potential vandalism). Many mounted animals—such as a beaver, wolverine, squirrel, fox, and bat—and a few live animals—such as a guinea pig, snake, and turtle—can be examined by touch. Only the blind are allowed to handle the delicate mounted specimens. The library includes several braille volumes. In addition, the center has two nature trails and presents seasonal exhibits on the flora and fauna of the area.

**Hidden Oaks Nature Center,** 4030 Hummer Road, Annandale, VA (941-5009). Tuesday-Saturday 9 am-5 pm; Sunday 1 pm-5 pm. Capital Beltway (Route 495) Exit 6, Little River Turnpike east, left at first light on Hummer Road, second left on Royce Street into center. Animal pelts, deer antlers, a turtle shell, and a hornet's nest are some of the items set out on the touch table of this small community center. Family nights are scheduled monthly during the winter and every Wednesday during the summer. Other programs include nature walks and park discovery sessions.

**Long Branch Nature Center,** 5500 6th Road South, Arlington, VA (671-7716). Tuesday-Saturday 10 am-5 pm; Sunday 1 pm-5 pm. Route 50 to Carlyn Spring Road exit, under Route 50, south on Carlyn Spring Road, left into center, just past Northern Virginia Doctors' Hospital. Guided walks; advance telephone arrangements required. Films Saturday and Sunday 2 pm. This center, bordered by Glen Carlyn Park, features a large indoor turtle and fish pond, a marsh, and a wildflower garden. Other exhibits change seasonally. A recently opened section of bike trail connects with the county system.

**Meadowside Nature Center,** 5100 Meadowside Lane, Rockville, MD (924-4141). Capital Beltway (Route 495) Exit 21, Georgia Avenue north, past Rossmoor to Norbeck Road, right on Norbeck Road, one block to right on Muncaster Mill Road, left into center. Tuesday-Saturday 9 am-5 pm; Sunday 1 pm-5 pm. Films Saturday and Sunday 11 am, 1 pm, 3 pm. Crafts workshops Sunday 2 pm and 4 pm. Meadowside is the place for peaceful experiences. In addition to the exhibits and activities in the main building, the center maintains two-and-a-half miles of nature trails. The 350 acres of woods, streams, meadows, marshes, and lake are home for most of the animals found in the Maryland area. Migratory birds use the lake as a stopover. The quiet center offers a contrast to the busy Needwood Lake recreation area it adjoins.

**Rock Creek Nature Center,** Rock Creek Park, Military and Glover Roads NW (426-6829). Tuesday-Friday 9:30 am-5 pm; Saturday and Sunday noon-6 pm. Advance arrangements recommended weekdays. This active center presents several weekend programs for children. These include planetarium shows (see Space in this chapter), puppet shows (see Performing Arts in this chapter), guided walks, films, and special nature talks. Exhibits include mounted and live animals, a beehive, push-button nature quiz, and other seasonal displays. The bookshop sells nature books and other children's publications and small gifts.

## Space

**Experimentarium,** Air and Space Building, 10th Street and Independence Avenue SW (628-4422). Tuesday-Friday 1:30 pm, 2:30 pm, 3:30 pm, 4:30 pm; Saturday and Sunday 11 am, noon, 1 pm, 2:30 pm, 3:30 pm, 4:30 pm. This well-done half-hour show examines earth from the perspective of outer space, a feat made possible only by recent manned and unmanned space flights. (See NASA Goddard Space Flight Center; Other Sights, Chapter 5.) It captures the fancy and holds the interest of children of all ages, even though most of the audio information is over their heads. The 59 seats are filled on a first-come first-served basis, so be prepared to spend at least 15 minutes waiting in line.

**Planetarium,** Rock Creek Nature Center, Military and Glover Roads NW (426-6829). Saturday and Sunday 1:15 pm (especially for children 4-7 years old accompanied by an adult) and 4 pm (for ages 7 and above). Free, but tickets must be picked up at information desk 30 minutes before show time. The Rock Creek Nature Center's planetarium program is not as successful as the Smithsonian's Experimentarium program. This is due not only to the less sophisticated equipment, but also to the prevailing didactic atmosphere. Children under four are not admitted to the shows, but even older children soon tire of the novelty of gazing at the projected telescopic views. (See Nature Centers in this chapter for details on Rock Creek Nature Center.)

## Playgrounds

It's difficult—perhaps impossible—to maintain an intensive sightseeing schedule of museums and monuments when touring with children. Planning a trip to the zoo, a visit to a farm, a picnic in the park, or a walk in the garden provides a welcome break and change of scene for the whole family. If a large part of the day cannot be devoted to such an outing, you might work in a quick stop at one of Washington's many unusual playgrounds located close to sightseeing areas or in the nearby suburbs. Some of the equipment is so challenging, you'll find yourself climbing it along with the kids.

**Benning-Stoddert Recreation Center,** East Capitol Street and Stoddert Place SE. Near Robert F. Kennedy Memorial Stadium. Across the East Capitol Street Bridge, first right after Minnesota Avenue on Stoddert Place into the center. This is a large, new, Washington recreational facility. The play equipment—all in good working order—includes wooden jumping boards, see-saws, and slides. Picnic tables and playing fields are scattered around the nicely landscaped area.

**Cabin John Regional Park,** 7400 Lux Court, Rockville, MD (299-4555). Capital Beltway (Route 495) Exit 18, Old Georgetown Road north to Tuckerman lane, left on Tuckerman Lane to park at corner of Westlake Drive. Snack bar. In addition to a large, well-equipped play area—featuring a variety of slides, swings, and climbers for all ages—this 525-acre park has a small farm-animal zoo. A miniature train skirts the playground area weekends in the spring and fall, and daily in the summer (fare: 30¢). Winter specialties are the skating rink (365-0585) and toboggan slide (365-1677). Fair weather finds the picnic areas, tennis courts, handball courts, and ball fields in heavy use. The park is a favorite of area residents.

**Garfield Park,** New Jersey Avenue and E Street SE. Capitol Hill just behind the House Office Buildings. Bordering a pleasant and little-known residential area, this long, narrow park has a grassy play area with metal climbing equipment, swings, slides, picnic tables, and benches. Ball courts and free-form wooden structures are shaded by Interstate Highway 95, which passes overhead. The park is well maintained by the National Park Service.

**Glen Echo Park Carousel,** MacArthur Boulevard and Goldsboro Road, Bethesda, MD (229-3031). Saturday noon-6 pm; Sunday noon-8 pm, April-October. Ride: 20¢. Riding the beautifully restored antique carousel while the calliope thumps out the old standard songs is enough to delight any child and make any adult nostalgic. The park, which functions weekdays as a crafts center, also has a children's theater (see Entertainment in this chapter) and offers free art workshops for children. Unfortunately, the playground is underequipped and suitable only for older children.

**Hains Point,** Ohio Drive SW below the Tidal Basin. A climb on the large, painted, metal equipment on this finger of land between the Washington Channel and the Potomac River is always in order. Hains Point also has biking, golfing, and tennis facilities (see Outdoors, Chapter 7 for details).

**Kalorama Playground,** 19th Street and Columbia Road NW. This playground has standard metal equipment, and its large grassy area is the scene of local community activities and festivals.

**John F. Kennedy Recreation Center,** 7th and O Streets NW (232-3355). This is a central city playground and therefore it comes complete with asphalt surfaces, fences, and a sprinkling of broken glass here and there. While the location is not choice, the equipment is. There's a six-lane, double-bump slide, a real locomotive, fire engine, fishing boat, and truck to play on. A tunnel connects the two play areas. A visit is unusual and instructive.

**Lyon Village Playground,** North Highland and North Edgewood Streets, Arlington, VA. Key Bridge to Lee Highway, left on North Highland just before Spout Run Parkway. Timberform climbing equipment, tire swings, and tot swings, plus tennis courts, basketball courts and a small shelter make this small playground near Georgetown a local favorite.

**Watkins-Buchanan Recreation Center,** 13th and E streets SE (546-1360). Near Pennsylvania Avenue, the main shopping and dining area on Capitol Hill. This city playground, adjoining a local school, has lots of superbly designed equipment, some of which is in need of repair. Our favorite is the brick pyramid with slides running off the top. There's also a cable spider web, rolling log, and wooden see-saw. The playing surface is sand. It's worth a detour from the well-trodden Capitol Hill circuit.

**Woodside Park,** Georgia Avenue and Spring Street, Silver Spring, MD. This small playground, just inside the Capital Beltway (Route 495), is one of the most satisfying in the area. The new equipment consists mainly of a variety of enormous timberform climbing structures. Cargo nets, fireman's poles, and slides are attached in such a way that only those who are skilled enough to use them are able to reach them. Thus, the safety factor is built into the equipment. The play area is spread with small pebbles, making a resilient mud-free surface for romping. There are lots of comfortable places for parents to sit, but many prefer to climb and slide with their children.

**Wheaton Regional Park,** 12012 Kemp Mill Road, Wheaton, MD (622-0056). Capital Beltway (Route 495) Exit 21, Georgia Avenue north to Shorefield Road, right into park. Snack bar. This 500-acre regional recreation area boasts a small farm-animal zoo, extensive playgrounds, picnic areas, hiking trails, bicycle paths, pony ring (ride: 45¢), and a miniature railroad that runs weekends during the spring and fall and daily during the summer (fare: 30¢). Facilities include the Nature Center (see Nature Centers in this chapter), a lake stocked with bass, bluegill, and catfish, a botanical garden, riding stable (622-3311), ice skating rink (649-3640), basketball, handball, and tennis courts, ball fields, and campsites. Wheaton Regional competes with Cabin John for top honors in Washington area parks.

# Entertainment

With frequent performances by resourceful private groups and regularly scheduled institutional programs, Washington has an unusually high number of quality cultural events for children. The only problem is finding out about them and then making arrangements to take advantage of them.

## Information

Check the monthly listings in the "Where and When" section of *The Washingtonian,* the weekly "Calendar" in the Style section of Friday's *Washington Post,* or the weekly "Top Billing" feature in Saturday's *Washington Star.* The best subscription newsletter is "Do You Know," $2 yearly from the D.C. Recreation Department, 3149 16th Street NW, Washington, DC 20010 (696-7226). The National Park Service's "Calendar of Events" (426-6700) and the Smithsonian Institution's "Calendar of the Smithsonian" (381-6264) are also helpful, but their focus is on park and museum events rather than performing arts.

## Dance

**Ballet.** Ballet in Washington means more than the Nutcracker Suite. The **Capitol**

**Ballet** and the **Washington Ballet,** two local companies, give several performances a year for children. In addition, visiting companies, such as the **American Ballet Theatre,** and the **Alvin Ailey City Center Dance Theater** perform frequently.

**Folk.** Folk dancing performances, presented by touring troupes, are exciting for the entire family. Folk dancing classes, great fun for older children and adults, are held Thursday nights, 8 pm at the **Chevy Chase Community Center,** Connecticut Avenue and McKinley Street NW (363-2440), and Tuesday nights, except the first Tuesday of the month, 8 pm at Key Elementary School, Key Boulevard and North Veitch Street, Arlington, VA (527-8998). **The African Heritage Center for African Dance and Music,** 2146 Georgia Avenue NW (462-5305) has weekday evening and weekend daytime classes in African dance, ballet, drumming, and modern dance for adults and children. Many of these may be attended in single sessions for a $3 fee.

## Film

**American Film Institute,** Kennedy Center, 2700 F Street NW (833-9300). AFI shows children's feature-length films and cartoons Saturday 2 pm and Sunday noon. Admission: adults $1.50; children $1. Since performances tend to be sellouts, purchasing tickets in advance is recommended. Series subscriptions are also available.

**Hirshhorn Museum and Sculpture Garden,** 8th Street and Independence Avenue SW (381-6753). Animated films and documentaries for children are shown Saturday 1 pm. Free tickets must be picked up at the information desk, preferably several days in advance, for these popular performances.

**Nature Centers.** Most area nature centers run free films on outdoor themes Saturday and Sunday afternoon. (See Animal, Vegetable, and Mineral section in this chapter.)

## Music

Good bets in performances for families for which there is a charge are concerts at **Wolf Trap Farm Park,** Vienna, VA (938-3800), and **Merriweather Post Pavilion,** Columbia, MD (953-2424). In the spring, summer, and fall both amphitheaters offer musical events in a variety of styles. (See Entertainment, Chapter 6 for details.) You can picnic on the grounds, and if your children become restless during the performance, you can set them free to run on the grass.

Although the **National Symphony** and several local orchestras sponsor occasional performances specifically for children, we have found that often the best concerts for young children are those for people of all ages that are short and free of charge. Fortunately, there are many such concerts in the Washington area. Most are scheduled during school holidays and summer vacations, so checking current listings is essential. These are a few regularly scheduled events to keep in mind:

**Capitol Plaza Concerts.** Pops concerts by the Armed Forces Bands Monday, Tuesday, Wednesday, and Friday evenings, June-August, 8 pm. Call the Capitol (224-3121) for further information.

**Marine Corps Sunset Parade.** Marine Corps Barracks, 8th and I Streets SE (433-4044). Friday 8:15 pm May-September. Free, but make reservations at least a week in advance. The band concert is followed by a drill and marching show.

**National Museum of History and Technology,** Constitution Avenue and 10th Street NW (628-4422). The 18th- and 19th-century classical and American folk instruments from the collection are demonstrated in the Hall of Musical Instruments, third floor, Monday-Friday 11 am.

**Netherlands Carillon Concerts.** On the lawn near the Iwo Jima Memorial, Arlington, VA, on weekends April-September. Popular, classical, and religious songs ring out from the bell tower. Call the National Park Service (426-6700) for further information.

**Watergate Concerts.** Pops concerts by the Armed Forces Bands Sunday, Tuesday, Thursday, and Friday evenings 8:30 pm June-August at the Jefferson Memorial. Bring seat cushions and insect repellent to these convivial sessions. Call the National Park Service (426-6700) for further information.

## Festivals

Concerts, dance, and song in connection with annual festivals include: **Festival of American Folklife,** sponsored by the Smithsonian and the Park Service on the Mall June 25-29, July 2-6 in 1975 (throughout the summer in 1976); **International Children's Festival,** held at Wolf Trap Farm

Park during the month of September, and **The Twelve Days of Christmas,** held in the Kennedy Center during the winter holidays. Check appropriate listings for these and other special musical events.

## Puppet Shows

Children communicate with puppets and vice versa. Two local companies give several excellent performances year round, and visiting companies appear occasionally.

**Bob Brown Marionettes,** Rock Creek Nature Center, Military and Glover Roads NW (426-6829). Saturday and Sunday 2 pm and 3 pm. Free tickets must be picked up at information desk 30 minutes before show time. These highly professional shows deal with nature themes and are as spellbinding as they are informative. The company also performs occasionally at other locations.

**Puppet Theatre.** Smithsonian Institution, Arts and Industries Building, 900 Jefferson Drive SW (381-5395). Theater closed for repairs until 1976.

## Theater

**Adventure Theatre,** Glen Echo Park, MacArthur Boulevard and Goldsboro Road, Bethesda, MD (320-5331). Performances for children are scheduled nearly every Saturday and Sunday 1:30 pm and 3:30 pm. Admission: $1.50. The plays, puppet shows, or concerts capture the children's fancy. After the show, in the spring, summer, and fall, they can ride the carousel. (See Playgrounds in this chapter.)

**Archaesus Productions, Inc.,** Suite 747, 2939 Van Ness Street NW (362-7032). A newcomer to the Washington scene, this company succeeds in its attempt to involve the young audience in its performances. Both kids and adults come away feeling satisfied with the theatrical experience. Archaesus gives free programs at the Kennedy Center and at Glen Echo and other parks at various times throughout the year. Mime, musical, and other performances are presented at several locations, including Baird Auditorium in the National Museum of Natural History, and Cerberus Theatre, 3040 M Street NW. Admission: adults $2; children $1.

**Jelly Bean Theatre,** 5248 MacArthur Boulevard NW (244-1228). Several times a year, Saturday and Sunday mornings 10 am and 11:30 am, Jelly Bean Theatre presents vaudeville shows in the Apex Theatre, 4813 Massachusetts Avenue NW. Admission: $1. Clowns, musicians, and other live, mass-culture performers are the entertaining features.

**Recreation Departments.** Theater for and by children is sponsored by the District of Columbia and surrounding county recreation departments. Periodic performances are cited in magazine and newspaper listings.

## Chapter Nine

# Where to Eat

**ELIZABETH POST MIREL**

**PHYLLIS C. RICHMAN**

**CHARLES F. TURGEON**

Eating out can be one of the principal pleasures of a visit to Washington. In recent years, the restaurant industry here has made substantial strides in the number, quality, and variety of dining opportunities it affords. Only a little while ago, the capital's cuisine consisted mainly of steak and seafood and its culinary approach was both cautious and conventional.

Today, Washington offers foods from many lands, prepared with imagination and served with style. The restaurants are often not all their owners or the public would like them to be, but as a group they are growing in diversity and developing greater skills.

The restaurants selected for this Bicentennial Guide are not a complete catalog of Washington's finest, though many *Washingtonian* magazine award winners are included. Instead, we have chosen those which seem most likely—because of location, reputation, historical association, price or other practical considerations—to be of interest to, or come to the attention of, visitors to the capital.

In clarifying restaurants by cost our approach is to figure the total price of an evening meal for two, including one round of drinks, a moderate bottle of wine, tax, and tip. Obviously, luncheons or meals without alcohol will cost less. In the reviews below the following classifications are used: Very Inexpensive: under $15; Inexpensive: $15-$25; Moderate: $25-$35; Expensive: $35-$45; and Very Expensive: over $45.

To indicate which credit cards are accepted by a restaurant, the following symbols are used: AE-American Express; BA-Bank Americard; CB-Carte Blanche; MC-Master Charge; DC-Diner's Club; CC-Central Charge. C.F.T.

## American

**Arbaugh's,** 2606 Connecticut Avenue NW (234-8980). Daily 5 pm-midnight. AE, CB, DC. Inexpensive. Although Arbaugh's is reputed to be a good barbecue restaurant, dining here is a disappointment. The service is slow and confused. The ribs, although tender, are greasy and painted with an overly peppered barbecue sauce. You can get better fried chicken, crisper coleslaw, and tastier french fries at any fast food outlet. E.P.M

**Duke Zeibert's,** 1722 L Street NW (296-5030). Monday-Saturday 11:45 am-midnight; Sunday 5 pm-10 pm; closed Sunday during July and August. AE, BA, CB, DC. Moderate. This restaurant has been providing Washingtonians with prime examples of no-nonsense American cooking for more years than most of them care to remember. Steaks, chops, roast beef, fried chicken, hearty stews, and first-rate local seafood dominate the bill of fare. Unusually good supporting roles are played by breads and pastries, baked on the premises, and the best garlic pickles this side of New York.

The decor here reflects Zeibert's passion for sports, and the restaurant has long been a haven for Washington's professional football and baseball (remember the Senators?) teams, and for male members of the capital's business community and media. Everyone is more than welcome, however, and they can be assured of a down-to-earth, good meal. C.F.T.

**Golden Temple of Conscious Cookery,** 1521 Connecticut Avenue NW (234-6134). Monday-Thursday 11 am-3 pm, 5:30 pm-9 pm; Friday 11 am-10 pm; Saturday noon-10 pm; closed Sunday. No credit cards. Inexpensive. Don't be put off by the fact that this is a vegetarian restaurant. The food is excellent and reasonably priced. A few of the dishes, such as the garbanzo bean burger, and the mung bean stew, may seem exotic, but the only unusual thing about most of the items on the menu is the quality of the ingredients and the care taken with their preparation. This goes for the Swiss cheese on rye, the eggplant parmesan, the enchiladas, and also the soups, breads, and salads. Kids can always have a nutbutter sandwich (a variation on the peanut-butter-and-jelly theme) and a tasty shake made from goat's milk and honey ice cream. E.P.M.

**Hamburger Hamlet,** 5225 Wisconsin Avenue NW (244-2037). Monday-Friday 11:30 am-10 pm; Saturday until midnight; Sunday noon-9:30 pm. AE, BA. Very Inexpensive. Paying more than twice the price for a ¼-pound hamburger here, compared to a fast food outlet, does not give you double the value. Although the quality of the beef is good, the bun is soggy, the American cheese processed, the blue cheese skimpy, the sauerkraut puny, and the french fries disastrous. E.P.M.

**Harvey's,** 1001 18th Street NW (833-1858). Monday-Friday 11:30 am-11:30 pm; Saturday and Sunday 6 pm-11:30 pm. AE, BA, MC, CB, DC, CC. Expensive. Harvey's calls itself the "Restaurant of the Presidents" and, apparently, several chief executives have dined at the various premises occupied by Harvey's since its founding in 1858. Currently it's located just off K Street in the heart of the business district, whose denizens it serves in great numbers at lunch time. The menu reflects Harvey's origin as an oyster house, but there is plenty of meat as well. The food preparation is strictly American and the kitchen attempts, with mixed success, to represent regional cooking styles from Louisiana to New England. C.F.T.

**Mike Palm's,** 231 Pennsylvania Avenue SE (543-8337). Daily 10:30 am-5 pm, 6 pm-midnight. AE, BA, DC. Inexpensive. This popular Capitol Hill restaurant and rathskeller has a relaxed, comfortable atmosphere. Fresh fish dishes, such as bluefish and rockfish, are well-cooked and lightly sauced. Salads are served crisp and the fresh vegetables are prepared with care. In addition to a variety of meat dishes, the restaurant also serves spaghetti and pizza. E.P.M.

**Mrs. K's Toll House,** 9201 Colesville Road, Silver Spring, MD (JU 9-3500). Tuesday-Saturday noon-2:30 pm, 5 pm-8:30 pm; Sunday noon-8:30 pm. AE, BA. Inexpensive. If as much care were lavished on the food as on the decor, Mrs. K's Toll House would be a fine place to dine. As it is, the meals—consisting of soup, salad, bread, meat or fish entree, hot vegetable, starch, and dessert—can only be characterized as adequate. It is, nevertheless, a pleasant place to take a family. The house is gussied up for seasonal holidays; the gardens are a nice place to stroll in fair weather. Service is responsive, and any item on the menu is served, in a slightly smaller portion, at half-price to children under 10. E.P.M.

## American Continental

**Chez Brown,** 519 13th Street NW (737-2143). Monday-Friday 11:30 am-2:30 pm; Tuesday-Saturday 4:30-10:30 pm. AE, CB, DC. Expensive. Few restaurants remain in the heart of downtown, within walking distance of the National Theatre and the

Smithsonian museums. So we should be grateful that Chez Brown not only persists, but that it also maintains an attractive setting, personalized service, and homey food that is prepared on the premises. It has even resisted the temptation to use frozen vegetables. Although the menu is simple and brief—salmon, sole in wine sauce, omelette, roast lamb, duck with cherries, tournedos, liver, and veal steak—it includes a few unexpected pleasures, such as tongue in Madeira sauce, and seasonal daily specials. Portions are enormous; a serving for one is really enough for two. Prices are commensurate with the amount, and if you can't eat that much, you might think it is a lot to pay for simple, basic food. A spare wine list includes about a dozen reasonably priced choices. Friday and Saturday are operatic evenings, when the entertainment make the prices seem more in line. P.C.R.

**Jockey Club,** 2100 Massachusetts Avenue NW in the Fairfax Hotel (659-8000). Monday-Saturday noon-3 pm, 6 pm-11 pm. AE, BA, CB, DC. Very Expensive. Hunting prints, walnut wainscoting, red-leather banquettes, and elegant table settings are key elements in the sumptous atmosphere that has made this a favored lair for both lions and cubs in Washington's political and social jungle. This clientele expects to be cosseted, and the quality of the service here has always been high. The kitchen's performance has been less dependable as a succession of talented chefs have moved on to other assignments. At present, Jean Claude Galan is in charge and shows competence in providing the Jockey Club's traditional selection of French and American dishes. A meal in this exceptionally comfortable dining room can be a regal experience; occasionally, it isn't. In either case, plan on bringing part of the royal treasury to pay for it. C.F.T.

**Montpelier Room,** Madison Hotel, 15th and M Streets NW (785-1000). Monday-Friday noon-3 pm, 5 pm-11 pm; Saturday 5 pm-11 pm; Sunday 11:30 am-2:30 pm, 5:30 pm-11:30 pm. AE, BA, CB, MC, DC. Very Expensive. Among the area's most elegant formal dining rooms, this restaurant offers exceptional comfort and flawless service. The menu is an amalgam of classic continental dishes and American favorites, whose preparation is nearly always competent, if not inspired. The food is complemented by one of the finest wine lists in Washington. Here one can be assured of successfully celebrating a special occasion or entertaining an important client. The cost, however, can be breathtaking. C.F.T

**Paul Young's,** 1120 Connecticut Avenue NW (331-7000). Monday-Friday 11:30 am-2:30 pm, 5:30 pm-10:45 pm; Saturday 5:30 pm-10:30 pm. AE, BA, DC. Very Expensive. A mecca for Washington's business community and out-of-towners staying at the Mayflower Hotel, this is probably the most "New York" restaurant in Washington. The menu emphasizes American dishes—including local seafood from the Chesapeake Bay—but offers European choices as well. The wine list shares honors with the Montpelier and a few of the top French restaurants. The main dining room is handsome and the service good. C.F.T.

## Beef & Lobster

**Costin's Sirloin Room,** 14th and F Streets NW in the National Press Building (EX 3-3030). Monday-Friday 11:30 am-9 pm; Saturday 5 pm-11 pm. AE, BA, MC, CB, DC. Expensive. The room is spacious and comfortable. It affects a Williamsburg style and almost makes it. The service is cheerful and efficient, and the drinks are a full 4½ ounces. One comes to Costin's for prime beef, and they have it in all the favorite American cuts. The menu also features a surprising choice of continental dishes like crêpes, *quiche Lorraine,* and "Chicken Cordon Bleu." Not so surprisingly, these are rather badly prepared and the side dishes of potatoes, vegetables, and salads are also uninspired. But if your goal is a first-class martini, some very plump oysters, and a whacking good piece of meat, you won't be disappointed. C.F.T.

**Joshua Tree,** 6930 Old Dominion Drive, McLean, VA (821-2894). Monday-Thursday 5 pm-10:30 pm; Friday and Saturday until 11 pm; Sunday noon-9:30 pm. AE, BA, MC, DC. Inexpensive. Joshua Tree is the oldest of the successful Marriott dinner houses, a slick steak place with all the pseudobaronial furnishings you would expect at a steak house plus a surfeit of Southwest and Mexican touches. In addition to grilled chopped sirloin and steaks, Joshua Tree serves lobster tail, roast beef, and lamb chops. While the cooking can't be faulted, the entrees tend to be bland. The salad bar is nice enough, but the complimentary sangria is a dead ringer for cherry pop. No reservations are accepted, and you always seem to have to wait—so Marriott must be doing something right. The snuggly little tables in dark corners are quite romantic if you can ignore the prevailing mass-market aura. P.C.R

**The Market Inn,** 2nd and E Streets SW (347-4455). Open daily noon-2 am; Friday and Saturday until 3 am. AE, MC, CB, DC. Moderate. Steaks "from 5 oz. to 50 oz." and lobsters "purified live from our tank" are the primary attractions here, but it's clear the Market Inn has made it on other assets as well. It's a highly popular meeting place for workers of Capitol Hill and in the many nearby government offices. Patrons have a choice of several dining rooms or a colorful piano bar decorated with what must be the biggest collection of nude paintings in Washington. The martinis are huge, the beer is cold, and in this setting even the world-weary can be persuaded to sing. C.F.T.

**Port O' Georgetown,** 1054 31st Street NW (338-6600). Monday-Thursday 5 pm-11 pm; Friday and Saturday until midnight; Sunday noon-9 pm. AE, BA, CB, MC, DC, CC. Moderate. A simple menu in an elaborate nautical setting is the theme of this Marriott-owned steak and seafood house. Located in the handsomely restored Canal Square complex in Georgetown its dining rooms overlook the old canal. The choice of fare is less interesting than it used to be, having been reduced to five cuts of beef and three kinds of lobster. Their preparation is, at best, straightforward. Still, the food comes hot, the service is good, and the atmosphere relaxing. For plain American food—at a fancy price—this can be a good choice, especially if you stick around for the dancing and floor show. C.F.T.

**Phineas Prime Rib,** 1580 Rockville Pike, Rockville, MD (770-0294). Monday-Thursday 5 pm-10:30 pm; Friday and Saturday until 11 pm; Sunday noon-9:30 pm. AE, BA, MC. Inexpensive. Marriott knows the right buttons to push to activate the salivary glands of the American public. There are no reservations, and it is hard to imagine people willing to spend up to two hours on a Saturday night waiting for a slab of roast beef, but plenty do. What they get is a properly cooked, juicy cut accompanied by a crisp, eggy popover, a carafe of inoffensive red wine, and access to slice-your-own breads and a salad bar that is one of the best in town. The value is undeniable. Lobster tails and a la carte vegetables are also available. And Phineas has , unexpectedly, some of the best desserts around, including a bittersweet chocolate cheesecake and a trifle that is creamy and moist with liqueurs and raspberry jam. Save room. P.C.R.

**Le Steak,** 3060 M Street NW (965-1627). Daily 5:30 pm-11 pm. AE, DC. Moderate. This restaurant capitalizes on an American favorite and gives it a French twist. The only entree on the *prix fixe* menu is sirloin steak. This is preceded by a first-class salad made with Dijon mustard dressing, accompanied by perhaps the best French-fried potatoes made in Washington and followed by a choice of several of the usual French desserts. The wine list is limited, naturally, to a few good reds.

Like most popular restaurants in Georgetown, Le Steak is small and usually plays to a capacity crowd. But the simplicity of the menu, combined with fast and friendly service, means a fast turnover. Bright red walls and Parisian mementos add to the cheerfulness of the atmosphere. C.F.T.

# Eastern

## Chinese

**Golden Palace,** 726 7th Street NW. (783-1225). Monday-Saturday 11 am-3 am; Sunday until 2 am. AE, DC. Inexpensive. Washington's Chinatown is small and not the site of our better Chinese restaurants. The recent opening of the Golden Palace, however, has brought new life and high culinary standards to this intriguing corner of downtown Washington. This restaurant specializes in the light but flavorful foods of southeastern China, usually referred to as Cantonese. Among its most enjoyable creations are the oysters with ginger and spring onions, steamed spareribs with plums, and the squid in crab sauce. Its crowning achievement, however, is *dim sum,* those delectable steamed or fried pastries filled with shrimp, ham, lobster, chicken—whatever strikes the chef's fancy. Regarded as between-meal fare in China, you won't find them on the menu; just tell your waiter you want *his* selection of *dim sum* and stand by for a treat. C.F.T.

**Hu Yuan,** 3211 North Washington Boulevard, Arlington, VA. (527-7208). Sunday-Thursday 11 am-10:30 pm; Friday and Saturday until 11:30 pm. AE, BA, MC, DC. Moderate. This new Chinese restaurant specializes in Peking and Szechuan cuisine and has been very well received by both critics and the general public. Their plaudits are justified because the Hu Yuan offers a highly original menu, employs good quality ingredients, and prepares them with competence and dash. The Peking dishes seem to come off better than the Szechuan, but the kitchen's entire repertoire is well executed. In addition to the standard menu, Hu Yuan has an elaborate, multi-course dinner and some special dishes named after the restaurant's most loyal and/or prominent patrons. One such dish is called "Henry The K." C.F.T.

**Jenny's Pan Asian,** 1745 F Street NW (DI 7-8764). Daily 11 am-3 pm, 5 pm-9:30 pm. No credit cards. Inexpensive. The popularity of this very simple restaurant is owed to at least two factors: rock bottom prices and a capacity to provide a wide variety of Asian dishes. Most of the selections on Jenny's extensive menu are Cantonese, but there are offerings from other parts of China as well as from Korea, Vietnam, Thailand, and Indonesia.

This restaurant is plain in the extreme. Its "upstairs" and "downstairs" dining rooms must be approached through separate but equally dingy doors. The decor is nonexistent, table settings spartan, and the furniture crowded and hard. The downstairs waiters shout their orders through a hole in the ceiling and the food is more often slung than served. But Jenny's army suffers these indignities with good humor because the meals are better prepared than in many Chinese restaurants downtown and the prices are reminiscent of the 1950s. C.F.T.

**The Peking Restaurants,** 711 13th Street NW (ME8-2122). AE, DC, CB; 823 15th Street NW (737-4540). AE, DC, CB; 5522 Connecticut Avenue NW (WO6-8079). AE, BA, MC, DC; 10560 Main Street, Fairfax, VA (273-8812). AE, BA, MC, DC. Daily 11 am-10 pm. Moderate. In recent years, the fastest-growing category among Washington restaurants has been the Chinese. Observing this trend with Confucian serenity—but staying at the head of the pack—has been the capital's long-time favorite, the Peking. It has responded to the current craze for more Chinese dining by maintaining its 13th Street and Connecticut Avenue locations while opening new branches on 15th Street and in Fairfax, Virginia.

The menu at these restaurants offers something from every corner of China's culinary geography. As their name implies, however, the Pekings' strongest suit is northern food, the classic dishes associated with the imperial court. Among the finest, of course, is Peking Duck, but this requires one day's advance notice. Other splendid offerings include the "Chicken velvet," *chiao-tzu* dumplings, and *moo-shu* pork.

Opinions differ about which of the four Pekings is best. Many swear by the cooking at the original 13th Street premises, but for handsome surroundings as well as culinary artistry the newer restaurant at 15th Street is winning increasing favor. At all four locations, one will do best by arranging a large party and calling ahead to discuss your menu. C.F.T.

**Yenching Palace,** 3524 Connecticut Avenue NW (362-8200). Monday-Thursday 11:30 am-midnight; Friday and Saturday until 1 am. AE, BA, CB, MC, DC, CC. Moderate. Among the capital's long-established Chinese restaurants of the first rank, Yenching Palace has been the only serious competition for the Peking. Like the Peking, it offers a broad selection of foods from all over China, but seems most proficient in the mandarin or northern style. Dishes of special excellence include the Yuling chicken, cold five-flavored beef, fried "two kinds" (chicken and pork), dry sautéed beef and chicken with peanuts. The only consistent complaint one can level against Yenching is inconsistency; on one visit the food can be spectacular and on the next quite ordinary. But on one of those nights when the Yenching's chefs are "on," there's nothing to beat it in all of Washington. C.F.T.

## Indian

**Apana,** 3066 M Street NW (965-3040). Tuesday-Sunday 6 pm-midnight, AE, BA, CB, MC, DC. Moderate. In the recent burst of new Indian restaurants in Washington, Apana has emerged as the one with the most sophisticated and extensive menu. Standouts include the marvelously tender and flavorful *tandoori* chicken, the *badami* mutton, and a *mughali korma* that combines cubes of beef in a lightly curried sauce of yogurt, onion, and ground cashews.

In beginning a meal here, you'll find the *samosas*—hot turnover pastries filled with ground lamb, potato and peas—very nice, and the *husaini tikka*—small medallions of lamb grilled over charcoal—good also. Beer seems best as an accompaniment to these north Indian dishes, but Apana also offers an ample wine list. The service is accommodating and the seating unusually comfortable and well-spaced. C.F.T.

**Maharajah,** 1639 Wisconsin Avenue NW (338-4692). Tuesday-Saturday 11:30 am-3 pm; Sunday and Monday 4 pm-10 pm; Tuesday-Thursday until 11 pm; Friday and Saturday until 2 am. AE, BA, MC, DC, CC. Moderate. This is the newest and least pretentious of the Indian restaurants mentioned here. The setting is a small but interesting old row house in Georgetown, its interior furnishings reduced to show the original brick walls. Simple wooden tables accommodate about 40 persons.

The attraction here is the food of northwestern India, simply conceived, freshly made, and cheerfully served. The *samosas* are crisp and well filled, there's a good *biriani* of chicken, rice, and green peas, and a fine selection of lamb dishes. The *puri* bread has an especially rich, whole-wheat flavor. This is one Indian restaurant where dishes come to the table hot, and where patrons are given a choice of just how "hot" they want the spicing. C.F.T.

**Taj Mahal,** 1327 Connecticut Avenue NW (659-1544). Monday-Friday 11:30 am-2:30 pm, 6 pm-10:30 pm; Saturday and Sunday 6 pm-10:30 pm. AE, CB, DC. Expensive. A unique feature here is the comfortable Raja lounge where one can sip a Bombay gin martini amid beaded curtains and handsome brasses. The dining room is equally attractive with lofty ceilings and dramatic red draperies. Taj Mahal does best with one of the classic dishes of the Kashmiri cuisine: *roghan josh.* This involves lamb tenderloin cut in chunks, sautéed in clarified butter, and then combined with an elaborate curry sauce that is authoritative but not overwhelming. Another good bet is the *murg musulam,* tender pieces of chicken cooked in a light curry sauce and topped with ground nuts. Ask for the *piaaz pulao,* a rice pilaf, to accompany your entree. C.F.T.

## Japanese

**Benihana of Tokyo,** 7315 Wisconsin Avenue, Bethesda, MD (652-5391). Monday-Thursday 11:30 am-2 pm; 5 pm-10:30 pm; Friday until 11:30 pm; Saturday 5 pm-11:30 pm; Sunday 4 pm-10 pm. AE, CB, DC. Moderate. This is one of the extraordinarily successful chain of Benihana restaurants that stretches from Boston to Honolulu. It follows their formula of theatrically preparing steak, shrimp, and vegetables on *tepanyaki* grills which are scattered about the dining room and surrounded by seats for the admiring diners. The show is fun, especially for children, but the quality of the food is nothing special. Both the ingredients and the cooking are designed more to avoid offending American palates than to pleasing them. C.F.T.

**Japan Inn,** 1520 Connecticut Avenue NW (332-5528). Monday-Saturday 6 pm-10 pm; 1715 Wisconsin Avenue NW (337-3400). Monday-Friday noon-2:30 pm, 6 pm-10:30 pm; Saturday 6 pm-10:30 pm. AE, DC. Expensive. These two handsome restaurants have capitalized on the mixture of fascination and trepidation most Americans feel about Japanese cooking. They have limited their menu chiefly to beef, shrimp, and chicken, and prepare these familiar foods in ways agreeable to western palates. They have ensured their success by using only the highest-quality ingredients and providing service that is both deferential and efficient. The original Connecticut Avenue Inn offers a choice of western-style tables or floor seating in intimate Japanese dining rooms. At the Wisconsin Avenue location, one can either sit around a *tepanyaki* grill and watch the food being dramatically prepared; perch on a stool by the *tempura* bar to savor delectable morsels straight from the deep-fryer; or opt for the traditional dining room on the second floor. C.F.T.

**Mikado,** 4707 Wisconsin Avenue NW (244-1740). Tuesday-Friday 11:30 am-2:30 pm; 5:30 pm-10 pm; Saturday and Sunday 3 pm-10 pm. No credit cards. Inexpensive.

Although modest in appearance, this establishment has quickly gained a reputation as the best Japanese restaurant in Washington. It is distinguished from its more elaborate competitors by offering a genuine and complete menu—not just grilled steaks and shrimps to please the westerners.

Here you can find *sushi, sashimi,* a full range of *owan* (soups), *menrui* (noodle dishes) and, or course, the more familiar *tempura, teriyaki,* and *yakimono* preparations of shrimp, chicken, and beef. A special treat, served nowhere else in these parts, is the *unagi-no-kabayaki,* or broiled eel.

Ordering these Japanese specialties poses no problem for the newcomer as the menu is translated and the staff helpful. C.F.T.

## Polynesian

**Trader Vic's,** 16th and K Streets NW (393-1000). Monday-Friday 11:30 pm-2:30 pm, 5:30 pm-11 pm; Saturday 5 pm-11 pm; Sunday 4:30 pm-10:45 pm. AE, BA, CB, MC, DC. Very Expensive. Victor Bergeron's "Polynesian" restaurants now dot the globe, and Washington is no exception. They might more aptly be referred to as "polynational" since their vast menus include not only South Pacific favorites, but every thing from sirloin to shish-kabob. What makes this unlikely culinary conglomeration a success is a high standard of food purchasing, competent kitchen work, and glamorous presentations. With each dish wrapped in a South Sea Island atmosphere, preceded by some elaborately executed rum drinks, and followed by fresh pineapple flown in daily from Hawaii, most customers are sure to be satisfied. Trader Vic's local beach house is in the Statler-Hilton and is nearly always filled with a combination of conventioneers, the expense account crowd, and just plain folks out to celebrate a birthday or anniversary. Most need an extra Mai-Tai when they get the bill. C.F.T.

# French

**Le Bagatelle,** 2000 K Street NW (872-8677). Monday-Friday 11:30 am-3 pm, 6 pm-11 pm; Saturday 6 pm-11 pm. AE, BA, CB, DC. Very Expensive. Now in its third year, Le Bagatelle remains as fresh and charming as the rose it has chosen for its symbol. The decor echoes an 18th-century Parisian garden and maître d'hôtel Jacques Scarella succeeds in making each of the restaurant's many patrons feel especially welcome. The kitchen is under the direction of Robert Greault, a chef of rare talent and significant achievements, particularly with seafood dishes. Unhappily, some other portions of Le Bagatelle's menu are not always so perfectly executed. The selection of wines is worthy of the cuisine, and one can usually be certain of superior service. C.F.T.

**Café de Paris,** 3056 M Street NW (965-2920). Daily 10 am-5 am. No credit cards. Inexpensive. Its appearance last year gave Washington its first real French café, the sort that provides coffee, wine, and light dishes to accompany them. The surroundings are quite simple, too, but convey a very Gallic feeling. The menu changes frequently, but whatever soups or pâtés are featured will be among the best in town. Salads, breads, and pastries are remarkable for their true Parisian character. The crowd at midday seems to be mostly Georgetown shoppers; thereafter students and off-duty French restaurant waiters dominate the clientele. Ordinary folk shouldn't feel inhibited, however. As the sign on the door says: "We also speak English." C.F.T.

**Le Canard,** 3288 M Street NW (338-3121). Daily 5:30 pm-11 pm. AE, BA, CB, DC. Moderate. Le Canard represents a hopeful new trend among Washington area restaurants: specialization not only in a national cuisine but in a single type of food within it. The focus at this attractively designed French dining room is on fowl, and the menu offers duck and chicken prepared in 16 different styles. Choices among the accompanying dishes are kept to a minimum. Each guest receives a rather simple pâté, a superior green salad, and a small selection of conventional French desserts. The overall quality is good, and Le Canard's great popularity suggests that specialization is an idea whose time has come. C.F.T.

**Charcuterie Normande,** 3155 Wilson Boulevard, Arlington, VA (528-3323). Monday-Saturday 11:30 am-2:30 pm, 6 pm-9:30 pm; Friday and Saturday until 10 pm. AE, CB, DC. Expensive. Owned and operated by a family from Rouen, it has evolved into one of the most solid performers among the capital area's many French restaurants. The cooking is not elaborate, but it is excellent. True to its name, the Charcuterie offers its own pâtés and galantines for appetizers. The main dishes include some splendid *cervelles* and the seldom seen, but superior, *andouilletes.* There are daily specials—usually veal, chicken or fish—and one is wise to order them. The service is quick, and polite, and hot dishes arrive hot. The wine list is superior for Northern Virginia if somewhat overpriced. C.F.T.

**Chalet de la Paix,** 4506 Lee Highway, Arlington, VA (522-6777). Tuesday-Sunday 11:30 am-2:30 pm, 7 pm-11 pm. AE, BA, MC, DC. Very Expensive. This new and highly ambitious suburban restaurant offers fine French cooking with a Swiss twist. Guests will find themselves comfortably seated in a most attractive dining room whose designers, happily, resisted the impulse to imitate a chalet. The menu reflects the Swiss heritage of owner Lucien Birkler and the considerable culinary talents of Chef Werner Tylla. During the late fall, the menu also includes an extraordinary selection of game. The kitchen's performance while short of perfection, produces an expanding number of beautifully executed dishes. This growing strength is giving Chalet de la Paix an increasing claim to recognition as one of the area's finest French restaurants. C.F.T.

**Chez Andrée,** 10 East Glebe Road, Alexandria, VA (836-1404). Monday-Friday 11 am-2:30 pm, 5 pm-10 pm; Saturday 5 pm-10 pm. AE, BA, MC, DC, CC. Expensive. Off the beaten track, Chez Andrée has been surprising as well as pleasing its patrons for many years. It offers one of the area's most complete French menus and a wine list that boggles the imagination. The selection includes over 200 wines from almost every wine-producing nation and many rare vintages from the finest vineyards of France. Here one is inclined to choose wine before food, but the food is by no means second rate. Mussels in cream sauce, red snapper "Marseillaise," and some superior *cervelles* are among the most appealing dishes. The setting is simple and the service straightforward; it is one's palate that gets the most attention at Chez Andrée. C.F.T.

**Company Inkwell,** 4109 Wilson Boulvard, Arlington, VA (525-4243). Monday-Friday 11:30 am-2:30 pm, 6 pm-10:15 pm; Saturday 6 pm-10:45 pm. AE, BA, CB, MC, DC. Very Expensive. Most people are puzzled when they hear this restaurant's name, then incredulous at the assertion that it rates with the best downtown. But Company Inkwell has overcome its name and enough of the skeptics to regularly play to a packed house. The cuisine is French and is prepared with imagination as well as skill. The service is first-rate and made unusual by the management's practice of introducing guests to their waiters as the meal begins. The decor, for no imaginable reason, is early American barn. One may leave the Inkwell still perplexed, but almost certainly pleased. C.F.T.

**L'Escargot,** 3309 Connecticut Avenue NW (966-7510). Daily 11:30 am-2:30 pm, 5:30 pm-10 pm. AE, BA, MC, CB. Inexpensive. A neighborhood restaurant with a city-wide clientele, L'Escargot succeeds by following the all but forgotten formula of good food at fair prices. The most impressive dishes are French favorites like *cervelles,* but such American entrees as broiled rockfish and crab cakes come off very well also. The owner's objective is to produce simple, mostly French fare at prices low enough to keep patrons returning regularly. This makes L'Escargot more bistro than restaurant, but Washingtonians happily ignore the distinction and keep coming back for more. C.F.T.

**Jean-Pierre,** 1835 K Street NW (466-2022). Monday-Friday noon-2 pm, 6 pm-10 pm; Saturday 6 pm-10 pm; closed Sunday. AE, BA, CB, DC. Very Expensive. Pre-eminence among Washington's French restaurants is hard to come by and harder to keep. In recent years, however, one establishment has not only caught the brass ring and held it but has made the achievement look easy. The restaurant is Jean-Pierre's and—for the moment at least—it has no equal. An important reason for this success is that the key operators also are the owners. Founders Jean Pierre Goyenvalle and Jean Michel Farret preside respectively—and sometimes alternately—over the kitchen and the dining room. Consistency and versatility also figure prominently in making this restaurant a winner. Unlike most of its competitors, Jean-Pierre's manages to produce all its dishes with nearly equal skill nearly all the time. Furthermore, it invites its patrons to go beyond the regular menu and challenge Goyenvalle to prepare, with adequate notice, dishes of rare and complex character. Success can be fleeting, but for now, at least, Washington has a French restaurant worth international comparison. C.F.T.

**Le Provençal,** 1234 20th Street NW (223-2420). Monday-Saturday 11:30 am-3 pm, 5:30 pm-11 pm. AE, BA, CB, DC. Expensive. A bastion of fine French cuisine for many years, Le Provençal has made its reputation by focusing on the brilliantly flavored cuisine of southeastern France. Racks of lamb, sea bass with fennel, an extraordinary *bouillabaisse* and a rich *cassoulet* are among the primary reasons for this success. Confidence in its continuation, however, was shaken this year with the departure of the restaurant's accomplished maître d'hôtel and reports that owner-chef Jacques Blanc was devoting less time to his range. With so many strengths in its unique menu, solid wine list, handsome dining room, and capable staff, Le Provençal is likely to continue as a strong performer. C.F.T.

**Rive Gauche,** Wisconsin Avenue and M Street NW (333-6440). Monday-Saturday noon-2:30 pm, 6 pm-11 pm. AE, BA, CB, DC. Very Expensive. For many years, this was the capital's most prestigous French restaurant. Its superior food and service, its elegant atmosphere, made it the darling of senators and socialites, tycoons and tyros, the movers and shakers of the Washington scene. Sometime in the early '70s, however, this paragon of local eateries seemed to go into a decline. As its quality eroded, prices escalated and Rive Gauche appeared to welcome only patriarchal patrons. Happily, these dark days have passed, and a new spirit of dedication to the highest standards of French restaurant tradition is in evidence. A meal at the Rive Gauche still costs the world, but once again, it's worth it. C.F.T.

**Sans Souci,** 726 17th Street NW (298-7424). Monday-Saturday noon-2:30 pm, 6 pm-11 pm. AE, BA, CB, DC. Very Expensive. Probably no French restaurant in Washington offers a more delightful room in which to dine. Open, airy, gold and green, it defies the stereotyped decor of most of its competitors. Its reputation as a favorite haunt for the powerful has declined somewhat with the departure of the Nixon Administration, but prominent Washingtonians still find it among the most agreeable places for a sophisticated lunch or dinner. Actually, the food is usually only fair to good but for style, comfort, and service Sans Souci is hard to beat. C.F.T.

**The 1789,** 1226 36th Street NW at Prospect (965-1789). Monday-Thursday 6 pm-11 pm; Friday and Saturday until midnight. AE, BA, CB, MC, DC, CC. Expensive. Situated in the Georgetown University area, the 1789 is a college inn with a difference. Its atmosphere is alma mater, but the menu is mostly French. Chef Pierre Dupont presents a menu full of familiar Parisian favorites like *escargots, quiche Lorraine,* frogs legs, and tournedos. But his offerings are rescued from the ordinary by the inclusion of filet of pompano with morels, reindeer with lingonberries and, my particular favorite, "Filet de Veau Charles de Gaulle." This extraordinary dish intersperses medallions of veal tenderloin with pieces of lobster on a bed of white asparagus. C.F.T.

## Inns

**L'Auberge,** Route 50 at the center of Middleburg, VA (703-687-6139). Thursday-Tuesday 11:30 am-3:30 pm, 5:30 pm-9:30 pm. AE, BA accepted but surcharge added for their use. Moderate. The best eating in the Virginia countryside is more Parisian than Old Dominion. The setting, to be sure, is an attractive "hunt country" inn, replete with fireplaces, high ceilings, and antique furnishings. The menu, however, is a happy catalog of French favorites including first course choices of freshly made pâtés and galantines, artichokes with mousseline sauce, *quenelles,* and *escargots.* The entrees feature calf's brains, "Turbot hollandaise," and "Crêpes surprises." These offerings are complemented by a wine list of unusual merit for Northern Virginia. A meal at L'Auberge can make a charming focal point for a weekend outing. The good food and short drive (35 minutes from the Beltway) also make it worth considering as an alternative to more familiar French restaurants in town. C.F.T.

**Blair Mansion Inn,** 7711 Eastern Avenue NW (588-1688). Monday-Friday 11:30 am-2:30 pm, 5 pm-9:30 pm; Saturday 5 pm-10 pm; Sunday noon-9 pm. AE, BA, MC, DC. Moderate. Since this old hostelry almost straddles the District's line at Silver Spring, it may be stretching a point to call it a country inn. Still, if you're hankering for some semblance of what rural dining was like in these parts during the turn of the century, Blair Mansion is the closest spot to downtown.

The mansion itself has considerable charm, it is furnished with antiques, and the service staff wears period dress.

The menu concentrates on local specialties: oysters, rockfish, country ham, roast duck, fried chicken, and a crab imperial that has won great favor here over the years. Recently, however, there have been signs that the kitchen has relaxed its customarily high standards and is making more use of frozen foods. Even the wine list is not as selective as it used to be since its good Maryland-made wines have been displaced by some lesser vintages from New York State. These flaws notwithstanding, Blair Mansion Inn can be an enjoyable place to dine. C.F.T.

**Evans Farm Inn,** 1696 Chain Bridge Road, McLean, VA (356-8000). Daily 11:30 am-2:30 pm, 5 pm-10 pm; Friday and Saturday 5 pm-10 pm. AE, BA. Moderate. Its proximity to Washington and its handsome surroundings have made this the most popular of the area's "country inns." The commodious main building is set on a gentle rise amidst spacious grounds. Dining room window seats offer pleasant views of a restored mill, stables, and barn. For those satisfied with prime rib and a selection of Colonial grogs, a visit will probably prove worthwhile. Those ordering more ambitious items on the menu, however, seem certain to be disappointed. Here the mood matters more than the meal—at least to the proprietors; but all things considered, it's not a bad place for Sunday dinner with the family. C.F.T.

**Mount Vernon Inn,** Mount Vernon Parkway at the entrance to George Washington's home (780-0011). Daily 8:30 am-10:30 am, 11:30 am-5:30 pm. No credit cards. Inexpensive. Its location insures a clientele composed almost entirely of out-of-town visitors; its achievement is that it treats them like hometown folks. Tied to the operating schedule for Mount Vernon, the inn offers only a breakfast and luncheon menu. Its entrees are described in "Founding Father" superlatives, but boil down to simple fare—mainly soups, sandwiches and salads. Never mind; the soups have merit, the dining rooms are clean and comfortable, and the waitresses accord their foot-weary, fellow Americans a surprising degree of civility and charm. Cocktails are not available; but one can order beer, ale, or good carafe wines from California. C.F.T.

**Normandy Farm,** Falls Road (Route 189), 1 mile north of Potomac Village, MD (OL 2-9421). Daily 11:30 am-midnight. AE, BA, CB, DC, CC. Moderate. Set in open country just north of Potomac Village, Washington's most affluent suburban center, this seems the ideal spot for rural dining. The building is attractive and its interior charmingly decorated with handsome woodwork, large fireplaces, and a fine collection of copper cookware. The promise of this setting can go a glimmering, however, with the arrival of one's meal. Normandy Farm's very ordinary dishes seem to be made largely from frozen foods and are clumsily prepared. The only consistently good item is the restaurant's long-time specialty, popovers. If you can make a meal of them, augmented perhaps by some simply broiled meat and a small green salad, a visit may prove worthwhile. C.F.T.

**Red Fox Inn,** on Route 50 at the center of Middleburg, VA (687-2771). Tuesday-Sunday 8 am-11 am, 1 pm-4 pm, 5 pm-8:30 pm. AE, BA. Moderate. Advertised as the second-oldest tavern in America, the Red Fox (not to be confused with the bluegrass club in Bethesda) is rich in historical interest. Its dining rooms are a pleasure to see, and there are comfortable lodgings for guests who would rather spend the night than drive back to the city. The kitchen attempts 19th-century Virginia fare, but with mixed success. The menu's best offering is the country ham with "red eye" gravy; the homemade bread and pecan pie are also worth sampling. Surprisingly, the wine list is better than the food, with some especially attractive bottles among the Spanish and California selections. Red Fox is located just across the street from L'Auberge; one shouldn't ignore the possibility of staying at the former but dining at the latter. C.F.T.

# Italian

**Alfio's La Trattoria,** 5100 Wisconsin Avenue NW (966-0091). Monday-Thursday 11:30 am-midnight; Friday until 2 am; Saturday noon-2 am. AE, BA, DC, CC. Moderate. Like so many Italian restaurants in this country, this one succeeds with a big, predominantly red, dining room, some straw-wrapped chianti bottles, oceans of tomato sauce, and an entertaining corps of waiters. Alfio's follows the formula as well as anyone, but is still guilty of over-boiled pasta, over-aged veal and carelessly prepared side dishes. Nevertheless, the restaurant is very comfortable and nearly always crowded with apparently happy patrons. C.F.T.

**Cantina d'Italia,** 1214-A 18th Street NW (659-1830). Monday-Friday 11:30 am-2:30 pm, 6 pm-11 pm; Saturday 6 pm-11:30 pm. AE, BA, CB. Expensive. Although it's getting some competition now from Georgetown (Nathan's) and the suburbs (Portofino), the Cantina remains Washington's longest-running hit among serious Italian restaurants. Its success is due to its northern Italian menu, superior preparation of veal dishes, exceptionally fine wine list, and the untiring efforts of its owner/maître d'hôtel Joseph Muran de Assereto. Its only drawbacks are the pasta cookery, and a rather confining, underground location. For appetizers, don't miss the finely sliced mushrooms or the artichoke hearts in a seafood sauce. Among the many splendid entrees, try the veal kidneys, the chicken in lemon sauce, and a superior combination of peppers, tomatoes, and onions called "Peperonata Lombarda." C.F.T.

**Firenze,** 5400 Pooks Hill Road (Beltway Exit #19), Bethesda MD (530-2700). Monday-Friday 11:30 am-2:30 pm, 5:30 pm-10 pm; Saturday 5:30 pm-10 pm. AE, BA, CB, DC. Very Expensive. The room is lavishly appointed, the service is excellent, and the menu offers a broad selection of Florentine dishes. There is a superior list of Italian wines, including some rarely seen older vintages. This restaurant used to be associated with the highly regarded Portofino in Arlington. Since their separation, however, the cooking here has slipped somewhat. Still it's good enough to make Firenze one of the better Italian restaurants around. C.F.T.

**La Bella Vista,** 1011 Arlington Boulevard, Arlington, VA (525-9195). Monday-Friday 11 am-11 pm; Friday and Saturday until midnight; Sunday 4 pm-10 pm. AE, BA, CB, DC, CC. Moderate. Its location, atop the Arlington Towers complex in Rosslyn, gives it one of the most spectacular vantage points in Washington. The restaurant's floor is tiered so that many patrons can share the extraordinary view of the Kennedy Center, the Mall, and the monuments along both sides of the Potomac. Unfortunately, the quality of the cooking is less elevated. Most dishes are in the Florentine tradition, but they prove to be more sophisticated in concept than execution. Still, one can eat reasonably well here and an early call for a window seat can make a visit very enjoyable. C.F.T.

**Nathan's,** 3150 M Street at Wisconsin Avenue NW (338-2000). Monday-Friday 11:30 am-4 pm, 6:30 pm-11 pm; Saturday 10 am-4 pm, 6:30 pm-11 pm; Sunday brunch 10 am-4 pm. AE, BA, CB, DC. Moderate. Until Nathan's opened its behind-the-bar Italian restaurant, there was really no place except a home to get genuine, freshly-made pasta. The success that has come with offering this simple but splendid fare not only has made a table at Nathan's hard to get but also has, happily, driven some of its competitors to producing the real article. Besides such smash hits as "Fettucine Alfredo" and "Spaghetti alla carbonara," this restaurant also provides some first-rate entrees of veal like *saltimbocca* and a seldom-seen but superior squid dish. The wine list is good and not too pricey if one has the sense to stick to the Italian selections. C.F.T.

**Portofino,** 526 23rd Street, Arlington, VA (979-8200). Tuesday-Friday 11 am-2 pm, 5 pm-11 pm; Saturday 5 pm-11 pm; Sunday 5 pm-10 pm; Monday 11 am-2 pm. AE, BA, CB, DC. Very Expensive. Certainly this is the best Italian restaurant in suburban Washington and many believe it tops anything in town. Set in a small and rather plain brick house, it offers a sophisticated menu of Bolognese, Milanese, and Florentine favorites, prepared with style and served with grace. Among the entrees, the veal and fish dishes seem to be the best, but all the appetizers are first-rate; only the pasta loses out to Nathan's, in the District. The wine list is exceptionally good because it is unashamedly Italian. It contains some remarkable old red wines from the Piedmont that rival France's finest. Likewise, the Portofino's overall quality challenges the best restaurants in the area. C.F.T.

**Regina d'Italia,** 19 North Moore Street, Arlington, VA (527-0023). Monday-Thursday 11:30 pm-2:30 pm, 6 pm-9 pm; Friday and Saturday until 11 pm. AE, BA, MC. Moderate. Situated on the second level of the RCA building in Rosslyn, this attractively decorated new restaurant offers a fine view of Georgetown and the major monuments along the Potomac. The focus of the cuisine is northern Italy, and the menu offers a good choice of antipasto, noodle dishes, veal, and chicken. Prepared in the Milanese style, most of the dishes are light in character and free of tomato sauce. Generally, the cooking is better here than at the neighboring Bella Vista, but both have a lot to learn from the Portofino. C.F.T.

**Old Spaghetti Mill,** 7201 Little River Turnpike, Annandale, VA (941-6400). Monday-Thursday 5 pm-midnight; Friday and Saturday until 1 am; Sunday 4 pm-10 pm. AE, BA, MC. Very inexpensive. The pitch this place makes to families is a successful one. Its 500 seats are usually jammed, and the food, while not sophisticated, is surprisingly good. The pasta is firm, and the sauces are robust. The chicken livers, so easily overcooked, are particularly well-prepared. The dinner comes with warm Italian bread, tubs of butter and garlic butter, salad, and coffee or tea. There is a limited children's menu. The recordings played in the discothéque are old standards early in the evening, and contemporary songs and requests later. E.P.M.

## Middle Eastern

**Astor,** 1813 M Street NW (331-7994). Daily 11 am-2 am. AE, BA, CD, DC. Very Inexpensive. Restaurant fads come and go as fast as administrations in Washington, but the Astor stays on as one of the town's better bargains. The crowd is young; after all, this is where students and fresh-from-the-Midwest government interns learn about exotic Middle Eastern food and belly dancing. You can still eat for $2, but you can spend a lot more, particularly if you eat in the upstairs rear room where the belly dancers and musicians perform. So if it is just food you are after, avoid the nightclub and stick to the dining rooms, which are "done" in electric-blue vinyl and marbleized formica. As for what to order, the more Greek the better: The hot *poililia,* a delectable hors d'oeuvre platter, is worth sharing between two people. Try *moussaka* or *pastitso,* cinnamony and rich with custard topping; an enormous serving of lamb baked with eggplant; or onion-smothered beef *styfado,* a stew heady with allspice. One of the most endearing traits of the Astor is its inexpensive wine list, with Greek and Mediterranean offerings, many of which are available by the glass. P.C.R.

**The Greek Village,** 1712 Connecticut Avenue NW (232-4768). Daily 11 am-2 am. AE, BA, CB, DC. Inexpensive. This small place is one of the more comfortable of the inexpensive downtown restaurants. The prices climb as you go upstairs where the belly dancers perform in the evening, but even then the cost is low. The Greek Village does a good job with its appetizers, salads, lamb, and macaroni dishes, but its *moussaka* lacks gusto. The *souvlaki* sandwich—chunks of nicely cooked lamb in good quality flat bread—is an excellent choice for a light meal. The house wine is above average, and baklava and rice pudding are made on the premises. E.P.M.

**Traverna Cretekou,** 818 King Street, Alexandria, VA (548-8688). Monday-Saturday 11:30 am-11 pm. AE, BA. Moderate. Washington has been short on good Greek restaurants, and some places you had to go to get a taste of the Aegean weren't much fun. Here's a new one with a full menu of authentic Greek specialties—*taramasalata, spanakopita, sahanaki, moussaka, shish-kabob,* and *baklava*—all served in an attractive Mediterranean setting. Greek wines are offered, both resinated and natural, and the coffee is muddy and marvelous. Taverna's faults are iceberg lettuce and spongy bread, but after years of waiting for good Greek food it is hard to protest. C.F.T.

**Calvert Café,** 1967 Calvert Street NW (232-5431). Daily 11:30 am-midnight. No credit cards (accepts personal checks). Inexpensive. Middle-Eastern food of unusually high quality and low cost have made this a perennial favorite with Washingtonians. The redoubtable Mama Ayesha presides over the kitchen and emerges on occasion to welcome her loyal clientele. Lamb dishes are central to the Calvert cuisine, but chicken, eggplant and yogurt play important roles as well. A new dining room has been opened to accommodate the growing throngs, but regulars still prefer to take their *shish-kabob* and ouzo in the dimly lit bar. C.F.T.

**Rudy's,** 6813 Redmond Drive (in McLean Shopping Center), McLean, VA (893-5023). Monday-Friday 11:30 am-2:30 pm, 5 pm-10 pm; Saturday 5 pm-10 pm. AE, BA. Moderate. Since its opening as a 10-stool lunch counter only three years ago, Rudy's has been a striking success. Now it has bloomed into an elaborately decorated Moorish place that has taken a dominant position among Washington's Middle Eastern restaurants. Rudy's highly unorthodox assortment of dishes features such Levantine appetizers as *homos, baba ghanooj.* For entrees one can order Middle Eastern favorites such as *shish-kabob, donner-kabob* or *chawarma* (marinated roast lamb), or some fine South American sausages, veal sweetbreads in the continental style, or maybe the best hamburger in town topped with kaskaval cheese from Yugoslavia.

Rudy's meteoric rise has been paralleled by an increase in prices, especially drinks. Nevertheless, the prices remain within reason, chiefly because Rudy is providing some of the most uniquely satisfying meals in Washington. C.F.T.

# Middle European

**Csikos,** 3601 Connecticut Avenue NW in the Broadmoor Apartments (362-5624). Thursday-Saturday 6 pm-10:30 pm; Sunday 5 pm-10:30 pm. AE, CB, DC. Expensive. Hungarian food is hard to find in Washington, but connoisseurs of this cuisine, as well as newcomers, are likely to be happily surprised with the fare at Csikos. The standout dishes among the appetizers are salmon with sour cream and horseradish sauce, and some fine meat-filled crêpes. Entrees worth special mention are the "Rabbit, hunter's style with dumplings," and the roast duck with red cabbage. More traditional offerings, like "Veal paprikash" and "Transylvanian goulash" are less interesting. There's a fine selection of Hungarian wines, live zither music, a '30s ambience, and very good service. C.F.T.

**Old Budapest,** 10101 Lee Highway, Fairfax, VA (273-2800). Tuesday-Friday 11:30 am-2:15 pm; Tuesday-Thursday 5 pm-10 pm; Friday and Saturday until 11 pm. AE, BA, MC, CB, DC, CC. Moderate. This large, cheerfully decorated, Hungarian restaurant offers a good menu of Eastern European fare, a solid wine list featuring Hungarian vintages, and *gemütlich* melodies provided by an able violinist and piano player. Unfortunately, the kitchen's performance doesn't always match these assets. Far and away the most successful dish is a hearty fish stew called *szegedi halaszle.* For veal and game, however, devotees of Hungarian cuisine will do better at Csikos. C.F.T.

**Old Europe,** 2434 Wisconsin Avenue NW (333-7600). Monday-Saturday noon-1 am; Sunday 1 pm-midnight. The kitchen closes each day at 11:30 pm. AE, BA, CB, MC, DC. Moderate. The one place in Washington where you can count on first-rate German food is this long-established restaurant and rathskeller. The extensive menu ranges from the simplicity of well-made *wursts* to the sophistication of the house specialty "Schnitzel Old Europe." In the late fall, an impressive selection of game dishes is added.

For those devoted to the pleasures of the German table, there is another formidable attraction: the finest list of Rhine and Moselle wines in the capital area. Rheingaus, Frankens, Nahes, and Pfalzers are all available in rankings from *naturwein* to *trockenbeerenauslese.* Currently, many of the bottles are from the fabulous 1971 vintage. For those who prefer beer, the Old Europe features a number of famous German lagers direct from the keg. C.F.T.

# Seafood

**Chesapeake Bay Seafood House,** The Seasons Apartment Building, 4710 Bethesda Avenue, Bethesda, MD (654-6833); Loehmann's Plaza, 7283 Arlington Boulevard, Falls Church, VA (560-7357); Allentown Mall, 6286 Branch Avenue, Camp Springs, MD (449-6321). Monday-Thursday 11:30 am-2 pm, 5 pm-9 pm; Friday and Saturday until 9:30 pm; Sunday noon-9 pm. No credit cards. Very Inexpensive. These large, plainly furnished restaurants turn out some of the best seafood for what's probably the lowest cost around. Specified items such as fried flounder, clams, and chicken are cheap for adults, even cheaper for children 6-12, and free for children under 6—for all you can eat. The batter is light, the product not at all greasy, and the cooking time just right. Seafood platters, broiled fish, and beef entrees are also available. Spiced shrimp is especially good. Dinners come with excellent coleslaw, crisp hush puppies, but soggy french fries. Beer is sold by the mug or pitcher. There's no dessert. Service is speedy and cheerful. E.P.M.

**Crisfield,** 8012 Georgia Avenue, Silver Spring, MD (589-1306). Tuesday-Thursday 11 am-9:30 pm; Friday and Saturday until 10:30 pm; Sunday noon-9:30 pm. No credit cards. Inexpensive. This is not only the best seafood restaurant in the capital area, it also offers the best value. Located near the railroad underpass in Silver Spring, Crisfield looks more like a second-rate tavern than a first-class source of shell and fin fish in the Chesapeake tradition. Newcomers should ignore appearances and join the line of regulars who willingly queue up for one of the few tables or a berth at the oyster bar.

What draws Washingtonians here in such numbers is the freshness of the seafood and the simple but superior manner in which it is prepared. The oysters have a salty sweetness that marks them as local; most restaurants around town use cultivated "Blue Point" oysters and they're no match for Crisfield's Chincoteagues.

The main courses are equally good. The rockfish, this area's name for a striped bass, is always a good bet, and the baby flounder stuffed with crabmeat may be one of the finest dishes of any type served in Washington. Many of the menu items are prepared "Norfolk style," which means lots of butter and a dash of cayenne. The accompanying French-fried potatoes are unusually delicious and the coleslaw fresh and tangy. No liquor is served, but beer and wine are. C.F.T.

**The Flagship,** 900 Water Street SW (488-8515). Monday-Friday 11:30 am-11 pm; Saturday noon-11 pm; Sunday noon-10 pm. AE, BA, CB, DC. Moderate. Now in its 45th year, the Flagship has sailed with Hogate's to a gargantuan new berth on the Maine Avenue waterfront. In one respect its new quarters are preferable to Hogate's; the cavernous interior has been subdivided into a series of more humanly proportioned dining rooms.

The food here seems on a par with Hogate's. The simpler fried dishes can come off well and the plain boiled lobster is usually a treat. But too great a use of frozen food and too few local items on the menu mark this as a restaurant whose size has forced it to make a mechanistic approach to cooking. Among its saving graces are the rum buns—a Flagship specialty that can make you forget you came for seafood. C.F.T.

**Hogate's Spectacular Seafood Restaurant,** 9th Street and Maine Avenue SW (484-6300). Daily 11-am-11 pm; Sundays until midnight. AE, BA, CB, MC, DC, CC. Moderate. A couple of years ago, this long-time Washington favorite moved into its palatial new quarters along the Maine Avenue waterfront. Qualitatively, things haven't been the same since. Hogate's continues to do a land-office business with tourists, but Washingtonians who prize good seafood have headed for smaller restaurants where the fish are fresher and prepared with more personal attention.

This is not to say one can't get a decent meal at Hogate's. But finding what you want is complicated by a menu devoted largely to prescribed whole dinners. Moreover, there is a curious absence of local shell and fin fish, suggesting that Hogate's has chosen to operate like any inland seafood place and depend largely on frozen fare. Your best chance of getting some of the Chesapeake Bay's bounty in fresh condition is to ask for some grilled rockfish or bluefish. C.F.T.

**O'Donnell's,** 1221 E Street NW (737-2101). Monday-Saturday 11 am-1 am; Sunday and holidays 11 am-midnight. 8301 Wisconsin Avenue, Bethesda, MD (OL 6-6200). Monday-Thursday 11:30 am-10 pm; Friday and Saturday until 10:30 pm; Sunday noon-9:30 pm. AE, BA, CB, MC, DC, CC. Moderate. This old-time seafood house has been satisfying District residents and out-of-towners for decades. Less glamorous but more intimate than the new fish palaces along the Maine Avenue waterfront, it recalls the Washington of 50 years ago. Simple wooden booths provide privacy to diners and veteran waiters serve with courtesy if not speed.

The quality of the seafare here may not be up to Crisfield or the Sea Catch, but the first is far away in Silver Spring and the second very expensive. O'Donnell's is about as good as you're going to do downtown and that's not bad. The oysters here are the local variety and usually quite fresh. Rockfish and flounder can be worthwhile, but crab—particularly Norfolk style—is almost always the best bet. Another specialty of the house worth ordering is the terrapin soup; have it Maryland style, with a dash of sherry. C.F.T.

**Sea Catch,** Fairfax Hotel, 2100 Massachusetts Avenue NW (833-8383). Monday-Saturday noon-3 pm, 6 pm-11 pm. AE, BA, CB, DC. Very expensive. This is the District's most expensive seafood restaurant and, sometimes, it's worth it. Sea Catch has broken with the Chesapeake Bay tradition, and prepares most of its dishes in the French manner. Poaching and sautéeing rather than frying and broiling are the primary cooking methods, and many dishes are topped with delicate, wine-based sauces. Among the best things to order here are the crabmeat crêpes, the *bouillabaisse,* and the crab imperial. These ambitious creations are complemented by the Sea Catch's sumptuous furnishings, its courteous staff, and an exceptional wine list. But prospective patrons should know that the Sea Catch does not always produce a dining experience that merits the prices it asks. C.F.T.

# Spanish and Latin

**El Bodegon,** 1637 R Street NW (667-1710). Monday-Friday noon-2:30 pm, 5 pm-midnight; Saturday 5 pm-midnight. AE, BA, MC. Moderate. A rising star among the city's Spanish restaurants, El Bodegon has come very near to overtaking El Tio Pepe. It offers a fine menu and executes most dishes quite well; the *sopa de ajo,* for example, is probably the best in town. El Bodegon also has a solid wine list featuring some particularly pleasant and reasonably priced Spanish vintages. Flamenco dancing and guitar music enliven the dinner hour, and the service staff is very accommodating. C.F.T.

**El Caribe,** 1828 Columbia Road NW (234-6969). Daily noon-3 pm, 6 pm-11 pm. AE, BA, CB. Moderate. This little Latin restaurant attempts the big job of presenting all the cuisines of South America and, surprisingly, it succeeds. Here one can savor "Cerviche de pescado" from Peru, "Ají de lengua" from Bolivia, and "Lomo saltado" from Argentina. If those names mean nothing to you, order them anyway; you're almost sure to be pleased. The breads are of exceptional quality, and there's a good selection of Spanish wines at fair prices. Guitar playing and singing take over midway through the evening meal, and it's all wildly popular and friendly. Don't forget to finish with El Caribe's special dessert—"Brazo gitano"—a moist, rich cake with chocolate filling and a liqueur-laced frosting. C.F.T.

**El Rio Grande,** 11921 Rockville Pike, Rockville, MD (881-5455). Tuesday-Saturday 5 pm-9:45 pm. No credit cards. Inexpensive. Washington is full of taco houses, but very few places where you can get a taste of authentic Mexican fare. Rio Grande has succeeded by obeying almost none of the conventions of the restaurant trade. It is situated in the owner's home, there is no menu, and diners eat what's put before them. The seasoning is mild, the character of the dish depending almost entirely on the freshness of the ingredients. Those who seek the burning sensations of Tex-Mex cooking may be disappointed. But those who try this special restaurant with an open mind are likely to be back again. An extra attraction is Rio Grande's willingness to prepare special meals if requested a day in advance. C.F.T.

**El Sombrero,** 5401 Lee Highway, Arlington, VA (536-6500). Daily 5 pm-10 pm; Friday and Saturday until 11 pm. AE, BA, CB, MC. Inexpensive. Dressiest among the area's Mexican restaurants, El Sombrero makes an effort to glamorize what is fairly basic South-of-the-Border cooking. Those who prize the fire of traditional Mexican spicing will also find that it has been largely quenched by El Sombrero's kitchen. These anomalies aside, the restaurant offers a relaxing atmosphere, generous drinks, some pleasant appetizers, and one very appealing, if unauthentic, dish: the chicken-filled, sour cream-covered "Enchiladas Acapulco." C.F.T.

**El Tio Pepe,** 2809 M Street NW (337-0730). Monday-Saturday 5:30 pm-11 pm. AE, BA, DC. Moderate. For many years now, this attractive Georgetown restaurant has been the leader among the city's Spanish dining establishments. Today it's getting competition from El Bodegon and some of the Latin-American restaurants that have emerged over the past few years. Still, El Tio Pepe remains the leader, and it is the quality of its cooking that makes the difference. Specialties of the house include "Conchitos Tio Pepe," "Lubina à la vasca," and "Vieiras à la gallega." These seafood favorites are augmented by a good selection of meat and poultry dishes.

El Tio Pepe has an above-average wine list, offering many good selections from Spain's Rioja district. The list includes several older vintages at reasonable prices. Diners here are entertained by unusually talented flamenco dancers and guitar players. C.F.T.

# Lunch

For most tourists lunch is an interlude between sights. They look for a convenient place to get an inexpensive, nourishing, and tasty meal. We have listed a number of restaurants near the main sightseeing areas that seem to meet these requirements. Not included are the cafeterias in the museums and public buildings (see the walking tours in Chapter 3) and the many restaurants that also serve lunch (described elsewhere in this chapter). The cost of lunch can vary widely, but at most of the following restaurants it is possible for two people to get a sandwich or hot entree, a nonalcoholic beverage, and dessert for $10 or less. Only the restaurants indicated accept credit cards. Those marked "Bar" serve liquor; those marked "Limited bar" serve beer and wine.

*This section was prepared by Elizabeth Post Mirel.*

## Capitol Hill

Because Capitol Hill is a mix of offices, retail stores, and homes, the area is a vital one. People walk around here evenings and weekends as well as during the busy weekday lunch hour. Most restaurants are open Sunday.

**A & K,** 307 Pennsylvania Avenue SE (547-8360). Monday-Saturday 11 am-11 pm. Limited bar. AE. Very Inexpensive. Fine salad, lamb, chicken, and other Greek dishes. Also hamburgers. Excellent rice pudding and baklava.

**Duddington's,** 319 Pennsylvania Avenue SE (544-3500). Monday-Friday 11 am-2:30 pm, 5 pm-11 pm; Saturday 5 pm-midnight; Sunday 11:30 am-2 pm. Inexpensive. **Duddington's Underground:** Sunday-Thursday 11:30 am-2 am; Friday and Saturday until 3 am. Bar. AE, BA, MC, DC. Very Inexpensive. Upstairs, there are hot entrees, hamburgers, omelettes, fried potatoes, and a well-stocked salad bar, but frankly the food isn't up to the standards of the extraordinarily pleasant, Scandinavian-style decor. The Underground offers pizza, lasagne, and other Italian platters, and quite good hot subs in a British pub setting.

**Tune Inn,** 331½ Pennsylvania Avenue SW (543-2725). Sunday-Thursday 8 am-2 am; Friday and Saturday until 3 am. Bar. Very Inexpensive. Good sandwiches and French fries and a generous portion of crisp fried chicken cooked to order all served in the back of this friendly, neighborhood bar.

## Georgetown

The Georgetown area is as rich in small restaurants as it is in charming boutiques. As with the shops, quality and value vary. This is the best place to go for good low-cost meals, and other than Capitol Hill, the only spot for Sunday brunch.

**Blimpies,** 1211 Wisconsin Avenue NW (965-4788). Sunday-Thursday 11 am-3 am; Friday and Saturday until 4 am. Also carryout. Very Inexpensive. In the universe of submarines Blimpies' are skimpies.

**Black Olive,** 2934 M Street NW (337-4536). Monday-Thursday 9 am-midnight; Friday and Saturday until 2 am; Sunday noon-9 pm. Also carryout. Very Inexpensive. Good salad, tender if slightly underflavored souvlaki, fried potatoes. Also pizza, omelettes, and dinner platters.

**Booeymonger,** 3265 Prospect Street NW (333-4810). Monday-Friday 7 am-midnight; Saturday and Sunday 10 am-midnight. Mainly carryout. Very Inexpensive. This quality delly offers a variety of good sandwiches, with a choice of breads (seven kinds) and garnishes (mushroom, avocado, sprouts, or cheeses), plus selected cheeses, pastries, and ice cream.

**Clyde's** 3236 M Street NW (333-9180). Daily 11 am-2 am. Bar. AE, BA, MC, DC. Restaurant Very Inexpensive; Omelette Room Inexpensive. Exceptionally good hamburgers and sandwiches in the popular restaurant-bar. All kinds of omelettes cooked in full view in the stylishly furnished Omelette Room.

**Gourmetisserie,** 1624 Wisconsin Avenue NW (338-1531). Tuesday-Friday noon-2 pm; Saturday until 3:30 pm. Inexpensive. It is worth the long walk up the Wisconsin Avenue hill to dine in this tiny caterer's shop on such regional French fare as cheese soufflé, beef stew, and zucchini casserole.

**Hector's,** 3207 M Street NW (333-5073). Monday-Thursday 7:30 am-midnight; Friday and Saturday until 2 am; Sunday 9 am-midnight. Also carryout. Very Inexpensive. Crusty rolls and pepper garnish make these among the best Georgetown subs.

**Ikaros,** 3130 M Street NW (333-5551). Sunday-Thursday 11 am-midnight; Friday and Saturday until 3 am. Also carryout. Very Inexpensive. Nicely seasoned and grilled souvlaki and good spinach pie. Also pizza, spaghetti, and dinner platters.

**The Parlor,** 1531 Wisconsin Avenue NW (337-9796). Monday-Thursday 11 am-11 pm; Friday and Saturday until midnight; Sunday 1 pm 11 pm. Very Inexpensive. Chili and Greek specialties as well as sandwiches and ice cream. Pleasant dining in rear garden in good weather.

**Swenson's,** 1254 Wisconsin Avenue NW (333-3433). Sunday-Thursday noon-midnight; Friday and Saturday until 2 am. Also carryout. Very Inexpensive. Sandwiches made with quality ingredients and put between slices of good bread. The ice cream is worth the calories.

**La Ruche,** 1206 30th Street NW (965-2684). Sunday, Tuesday-Thursday 8:30 am-1:30 am; Friday and Saturday until 3:30 am. Inexpensive. Excellent soups, salads, hot entrees, pâtés, sandwiches, and coffee. Unparalleled pastries. Like the Café de Paris a restaurant in the French café style, but with a less bohemian atmosphere, and lower prices.

**Yes Soup Kitchen,** 1039 31st Street NW (338-7874). Monday and Tuesday 11 am-2 pm; Wednesday-Sunday until 8 pm. Very Inexpensive. Very good vegetarian fare served in the back of a health food store: hot soups, brown rice, coffee and tea in winter; cold soups, salads, and yogurt ices in summer. Excellent cheese cake. Seating expands into garden in good weather.

## Mall

Lunching at the Mall can be as excruciating an experience as parking there. Choices are limited to the cafeterias in the National Gallery of Art and the National Museum of Natural History, and the outdoor hotdog stand. Weekdays you can stretch these possibilities by trying one of the following restaurants, all within a 10-minute walk of the museums, but most are closed weekends.

### EAST MALL

**Barney's,** 621 Pennsylvania Avenue NW (737-2989). Monday-Saturday 6 am-6 pm. Also carryout. Bar. Very Inexpensive. A New York-style delly, but not up to some others in town.

**Kansas City Beef House,** 625 Pennsylvania

Avenue NW (347-6929). Monday-Friday 11 am-8 pm. Bar. AE, DC. Very Inexpensive. Steak sandwiches, hamburgers, and salads—none of which is outstanding.

**MIDDLE MALL**

**Government Services, Inc. Cafeterias.** Federal Office Building 10A, 880 Independence Avenue SW (783-0075). Monday-Friday 7:30 am-8:30 am, 11 am-1:30 pm. Federal Office Building 10B, 600 Independence Avenue SW (783-0082). Monday-Friday 7:15 am-9 am, 11 am-2 pm. Forrestal Building, 1000 Independence Avenue SW (553-4400). Monday-Friday 7 am-8 am, 11 am-2 pm. Very Inexpensive. Cafeterias in these three government buildings are open to the public for breakfast and lunch but cannot accommodate large groups. The selection of soups, salads, hot entrees, and desserts are more or less appetizing depending on the day of the week and the cook in charge. Safe choices are hamburgers, and grilled sandwiches.

**L'ENFANT PLAZA**

To find these restaurants, start at the intersection of L'Enfant Promenade and Independence Avenue (opposite the present National Air and Space Building) and walk one long block south up L'Enfant Promenade. Go past the fountain to Loews Hotel where The Greenhouse restaurant is located, or down the stairs (next to the list of shops) to L'Enfant Plaza Center where the other restaurants are. The parking situation here is even worse than on the Mall.

**The Greenhouse,** Loews L'Enfant Plaza Hotel, L'Enfant Plaza SW (484-1000). Monday-Friday 7 am-3 pm; Saturday until 6 pm; Sunday until 11 pm. Bar. AE, BA, MC, DC. Inexpensive. A good selection of chef's salads, hamburgers, sandwiches, and hot entrees in a pleasant setting.

**Lucky Pierre's** L'Enfant Restaurants, L'Enfant Plaza Center SW (554-1410). Monday-Friday 11 am-2 pm; Saturday noon-3 pm. Bar. AE, CB, DC. Very Inexpensive. Good chef's salad but poor dressings. Fair hamburgers and sandwiches.

**Plaza Café,** L'Enfant Restaurants, L'Enfant Center SW (554-1410). Monday-Friday 7 am-3:30 pm. AE, CB, DC. Very Inexpensive. Cafeteria with outdoor seating in good weather offering a variety of hot entrees, the best of which is freshly carved steamship round of beef.

**The Showcase,** L'Enfant Restaurants, L'Enfant Plaza Center SW (554-1410). Monday-Friday 11 am-2 pm. Bar. AE, CB, DC. Very Inexpensive. Buffet and salad bar with carved meats, such as ham, turkey, and beef, and a variety of salads.

**WEST MALL**

**Bassin's Cafeteria,** 511 14th Street NW (628-1441). Monday-Friday 6:45 am-8 pm. Very Inexpensive. **Bassin's Restaurant,** 14th Street and Pennsylvania Avenue NW (628-1441). Daily 7 am-1 am. Bar. All major credit cards. Very Inexpensive. Well-prepared chicken, beef, pork, and fish entrees, but less successful casseroles. Cafeteria food is similar to restaurant's, except choices are fewer and prices are lower.

**The Fatted Calf,** 415 12th Street NW (638-7003). Monday-Friday 7:30 am-4 pm. 1345 Pennsylvania Avenue NW (638-7698). Monday-Friday 11 am-7 pm; Saturday until 3 pm. Also carryout. Limited bar. Very Inexpensive. Among the best of the downtown hamburger places. The lean, grilled hamburger comes out with a choice of cheese toppings. French fries and onion rings available.

## White House Area

Because of its proximity to downtown offices, this area is dotted with good lunch places that offer a range of prices and styles. The restaurant described here are a sampling of the cafeteria, carryout, club, and delly types. Only a few are open weekends. Crowds reach a peak at 12:30 pm.

**The Best of the Wurst,** 1003 Connecticut Avenue NW (785-1003). Also other locations. Monday-Friday 7-am-5 pm; Saturday 10 am-2 pm. Mainly carryout. Very Inexpensive. The wursts are good, and the subs are among the best in town.

**Chamberlin Cafeteria,** 819 15th Street NW (628-7680). Monday-Friday 7 am-10 am, 11 am-2:30 pm. Limited bar. Very Inexpensive. Good fish entrees. Other hot courses include meats and casseroles. Also salads and sandwiches.

**The Fatted Calf,** 617 15th Street NW (638-8856). Monday-Friday 7:30 am-5 pm; Saturday noon-4 pm. (See Mall area listings.)

**GJS Ranch,** 818 18th Street NW (338-8795). Monday-Friday 11 am-8:30 pm; Saturday until 4 pm. Bar. BA. **GJS Carryout,** 818 18th

Street NW (338-8795). Monday-Friday 7 am-4 pm. Very Inexpensive. One of the nicest chef's salads around plus excellent hamburgers and a variety of sandwiches.

**Hot Shoppes Cafeteria,** 1621 H Street NW (347-9485). Monday-Friday 11 am-2:30 pm. Coffee shop and carryout Monday-Friday 7 am-4 pm. Very Inexpensive. Standard, bland, Marriott food.

**Kay's Sandwich Shop,** 1733 G Street NW (638-6200). Monday-Friday 6:30 am-7 pm. Also carryout. Limited bar. Very Inexpensive. Large variety of sandwiches but best values are plain cold cuts such as corned beef and roast beef. The combinations never seem to taste as good as they sound.

**Loeb's,** 617 15th Street NW (783-9306). Monday-Friday 7:30 am-3:30 pm. Also carryout. Limited bar. Very Inexpensive. First-rate New York-style delly. Good cold cuts, fine bread, efficient service.

**Sholl's Colonial Cafeteria,** 1032 Connecticut Avenue NW (296-3065). Sholl's New Cafeteria 1433 K Street NW (783-4133). Monday-Saturday 7 am-10 am, 11 am-2:30 pm, 4 pm-8 pm. Very Inexpensive. Just plain good food. If served these meals in a country inn, you'd be happy to pay more than double the price. This goes for all the fresh meat, poultry, and fish, French-fried potatoes, cooked vegetables, salads, cheeses, and desserts. The cherry pie has a deserved reputation for its tart, full-bodied taste. Both locations are usually jammed since they are popular with working people for lunch and touring school groups for dinner, but lines move quickly.

Chapter Ten

# Shopping

TINA LAVER

In 1801, the year after Congress moved to Washington, the Center Market opened at 9th Street and Pennsylvania Avenue, midway between the Capitol and "President's House." By that time, the Georgetown Market had already been operating for several years. And business was thriving at Alexandria's Market Square in neighboring Virginia.

The products have changed during the past 175 years, but shopping remains interesting in all these neighborhoods and in many others as well.

Washington's role as a national center has stimulated an intriguing, top-quality shopping mix. Shops run by the federal government, national associations, and museums add a unique flavor. An enormous range of imported goods accommodates the city's embassies and international residents. And a flurry of products commemorating America's past has appeared in time for the Bicentennial celebrations.

Here is a sample of the sweep of shops, arranged by subject.

## Antiques

### Nearby

The best nearby antique shops are clustered in the antique neighborhoods of Georgetown and Alexandria, with a sprinkling in Bethesda, Chevy Chase, Market Square and downtown. Here are some listed by specialty:

**AMERICAN**

**Carousel**, 907 King Street, Alexandria, VA (836-0028). Monday-Saturday 11 am-4 pm. 18th- and 19th-century country American household objects and tools.

**Cynthia Fehr**, 3214 O Street NW (338-5090). Monday-Saturday 11 am-5 pm. Formal 18th- and early-19th-century American and English.

**Early American Shop**, 1319 Wisconsin Avenue NW (333-5843). Monday-Saturday 11 am-5:30 pm. Country and formal 18th- and early-19th-century American, some English, and Canadian.

**F. Rizenberg**, 220 S. Washington Street, Alexandria, VA (836-2087). Saturday 10:30 am-5:30 pm; Sunday 1 pm-5 pm. 18th- and early-19th-century American furniture.

**ECLECTIC**

**Arpad**, 3125 M Street NW (FE7-3424). Monday-Saturday 9 am-5 pm. Formal furnishings and silver.

**Christ Child Opportunity Shop**, 1427 Wisconsin Avenue NW (333-6635). Monday-Saturday 10 am-3:45 pm. Accessories, some furniture, and jewelry on consignment.

**John Wilbraham**, 1073 Wisconsin Avenue NW (333-2571). Monday-Saturday 10 am-5 pm. Small shop with furniture, accessories, nautical fittings.

**Law-Ford**, 1608 Wisconsin Avenue NW (965-4676). Monday-Saturday 10 am-5:30 pm. French, English, and American furniture and accessories.

**Von Barghahn**, 3235 P Street NW (338-7066). Monday-Saturday 11 am-5 pm; Sunday 1 pm-5 pm. Art glass, miniature portraits on ivory, paintings, African objects.

**ENGLISH**

**William Blair**, 4839 Del Ray Avenue, Bethesda, MD (654-6665). Tuesday-Saturday 10 am-5 pm. 18th-century English and Irish furniture, and accessories.

**M. Darling**, 3213 O Street NW (337-0096). Tuesday-Saturday 11 am-6 pm. Formal 18th- and early-19th-century furniture.

**Mendelsohn**, 6826 Wisconsin Avenue, Chevy Chase, MD (656-2766). Monday-Friday 9 am-6 pm; Saturday until 5:30 pm. English and French furniture.

**The Old Antique House**, 817 Pennsylvania Avenue NW (628-5699). Weekdays 9 am-5 pm; Saturday 9:30 am-4 pm. Period and reproduction furniture, china, enamel.

**G. Randall**, 113 N. Fairfax Street, Alexandria, VA (549-4432). Monday-Saturday 11 am-6 pm. Formal 18th- and early-19th-century furniture.

**FRENCH**

**Peter Mack Brown**, 1525 Wisconsin Avenue NW (FE8-8484). Monday-Saturday 11 am-5 pm. 18th-century French furniture and Chinese Export porcelain (Lowestoft).

**ORIENTAL**

**S. Kriger**, 712 12th Street NW (DI7-2607). Monday-Saturday 10 am-4:30 pm. Early jades and bronzes, snuff bottles, and ivories.

### Out-of-Town.

You can spend a day or afternoon antique hunting in historic Harper's Ferry, West Virginia, or in Annapolis or New Market, Maryland (see Chapter 4 for touring suggestions).

***Harper's Ferry,** West VA. About 65 miles. Take 270 (70S) to Frederick, then 340 west to Harper's Ferry. One of the best known shops in this area is **John C. Newcomer**, Washington Street between Union and Polk (304-535-6002). Saturday 11 am-5 pm; Sunday 1 pm-5 pm; weekdays by appointment. Stonewall Jackson's headquarters in Harper's Ferry during the Civil War provide a striking setting for these American antiques. More than a dozen rooms in this restored plantation house are fitted with 18th- and early-19th-century furniture, folk art, textiles, and pottery. While you are there, take the time to wander among the other shops—antiques and junk—spread out along the main street. One train goes from Union Station to Harper's Ferry and back every Saturday and Sunday.

***New Market,** MD. About 50 miles. Follow Route 270 (70S) north toward Frederick. Before entering Frederick, take Route 40 east about 10 miles to New Market. About 30 antique shops line both sides of Main Street in this tiny town dating back almost to the Revolution. The choice ranges from attic leftovers to fine, formal, 18th-century American and English furniture. In between you'll find many country pieces and shops selling Scottish imports, old crystal, recycled clothing, and dried flower arrangements. The hours vary; most are open weekend afternoons or by appointment. New Market once thrived as a bustling thoroughfare between Baltimore and Frederick. The lone hostelry surviving from those days is Mealey's, an inn that still serves good home-cooked food in cozy surroundings. On weekdays, except Monday, it is open for lunch only, 11 am-3 pm; weekends 3 pm-8 pm.

## Art Galleries

**Adams Davidson,** 3233 P Street NW (965-3800). Monday-Friday 10 am-5 pm; Saturday 11 am-5 pm. Paintings, drawings, and water colors of 19th- and 20th-century masters are the specialty, including French Impressionists, Picasso, and the Hudson River School. Contemporary artists were recently added and a third floor Young Collectors Gallery (where prices drop below $1,000).

**Fendrick,** 3059 M Street NW (338-4544). Monday-Saturday 10 am-6 pm. Topnotch contemporary American prints and drawings by artists such as Helen Frankenthaler, Robert Motherwell, and Louise Nevelson are sold here. Look through the bins for prints under $100.

**Franz Bader,** 2124 Pennsylvania Avenue NW (337-5440). Tuesday-Saturday 10 am-6 pm. In the art business since 1939, Bader continues to discover talented local artists before their prices skyrocket. You'll also find striking Eskimo prints and sculpture, and well-priced paintings and graphics. The art is supplemented by art, architecture, and German-language books.

***Henri,** 1500 21st Street NW (659-9313). Tuesday-Saturday 10 am-6 pm; Sunday 2 pm-6 pm. One of the first galleries to open on what has become a flourishing gallery strip, Henri has also set trends in exhibits. Outstanding local artists have debuted here with work varying from massive sculpture and constructions to neo-romantic paintings. Two special shows are planned for the Bicentennial—silk-screened flags and a miniature panorama of the entire United States.

**Jane Haslem,** 2121 P Street NW (338-3014). Tuesday - Saturday 11 pm - 5 pm. Enter through the lobby of the Georgetown House to see this extensive collection of outstanding American prints, focusing on the period from post World War II to the present.

**Lunn Gallery's Graphics International Ltd.,** 3243 P Street NW (338-5792). Monday-Saturday 10 am-6 pm. Georges Rouault, Emil Nolde, Adolph Gottleib, and Joan Miro are among the outstanding 19th- and 20th-century artists whose prints and drawings are sold here. The gallery also represents the estates of Milton Avery and George Grosz, and stocks an outstanding collection of photographs, including those of Walker Evans, Diane Arbus, Man Ray, and others.

**Max Protetch,** 2151 P Street NW (785-0872). Wednesday-Sunday 11 am-6 pm. The latest new-wave art, mainly from New York, is exhibited here: conceptual, minimal, color field, pop, multimedia.

**Mickelson,** 707 G Street NW (NA8-1734). Monday-Friday 9:30 am-6 pm; Saturday until 4 pm. Located behind the National Collection of Fine Arts, Mickelson was the first representative in this country for M. C. Escher, the Dutch printmaker. The gallery, containing an assortment of good contemporary prints and sculpture, adjoins the largest framing shop south of New York, which also stocks some charming reproductions.

**Middendorf,** 2028 P Street NW (785-3750). Tuesday-Saturday 10 am-6 pm; Sunday 1 pm-6 pm. A truly eclectic mix of quality work that ranges in scope from American primitive to conceptual.

***Old Print Gallery,** 1212 31st Street NW (965-3777). Monday-Saturday 10 am-6 pm. Browse through their stock of original 18th- and 19th-century prints, and plates from old publications, matted and arranged by subject—city views, flowers, maps, historical events, cartoons—many for $15.

**Poster Place,** 1666 33rd Street NW (338-9331). Monday-Saturday 11 am-6 pm; Sunday 1 pm-5 pm. Bright colors and bold design are the trademarks in the area's first shop to specialize in original posters by Calder, Dubuffet, Barnett, and other well-known artists. The all-time favorite is Jim Dine's bleeding hearts.

**Pyramid,** 2121 P Street NW (296-1963). Tuesday-Saturday 11 pm-6 pm. Stark, sometimes jarring or surreal images are the specialty of this gallery, which carries the works of artists from the United States, Europe, and South America.

**Washington Gallery of Photography & Your Lab,** 216 7th Street SE (544-1274). Tuesday-Friday 10 am-10 pm; Saturday and Sunday until 6 pm. Signed, original photographs by local photographers, Ansel Adams, Paul Caponigro, and Edward S. Curtis are sold here. Darkroom space, chemicals, and equipment can be rented by appointment at $3 an hour. There is also a photographic book section.

**Wolfe Street,** 420 S. Washington Street, Alexandria, VA (836-1332). Tuesday-Saturday 11 am-5 pm. Most of this two-story town house is stocked with the work of good local artists. Upstairs one room is filled with moderately priced woodcuts, etchings, and engravings from Goya to early-20th-century Americans; another room contains local pottery and handmade jewelry.

# Books

Washington has its share of quality book stores featuring excellent selections of current hardback and paperback books, but here are a few that offer something unusual in the way of price, specialized collections, or old and rare books.

**Audubon Book Shop,** 1621 Wisconsin Avenue NW (337-6062). Monday-Saturday 10 am-5:30 pm. Wildlife, geology, plants, and flowers are among the nature-oriented books and gifts in this shop, run by the Audubon Naturalist Society.

**Booked Up,** 1214 31st Street NW (965-3244). Monday-Saturday 10 am-4:30 pm. The shelves in these two facing storefronts are lined with out-of-print books, primarily fiction, philosophy, and first editions—in excellent condition.

**Discount Books,** 1342 Connecticut Avenue NW (785-1133). Monday-Saturday 10 am-9 pm. Branch in Chevy Chase, MD. Best sellers here are discounted 20 percent, and all other books priced above $2.50 are reduced 15 percent. The store carries paperbacks from over 200 publishers.

***Government Printing Office Book Store,** 710 North Capitol Street NW (783-3238). Monday-Friday 8 am-4 pm; Saturday 9 am-1 pm. Sales outlets in five other government buildings: Department of Commerce, Forrestal, Pentagon, State Department, U.S. Information Agency. The largest publisher in the world, the Government Printing Office (GPO) prints all government materials, totaling some 27,000 publications. Stock at the main store is the most complete and covers everything from camping and growing bonsai to manuals on infant care, African music, and the best-selling *Recorded Presidential Conversations of Richard Nixon.* This is the only GPO store where you can order books, but you can call their information number and request lists of publications by subject. The "Posters and Charts" sheet contains several items of Bicentennial interest, among them an atlas of 18th-century maps and charts.

**Kramer Books,** 1347 Connecticut Avenue NW (293-2072). Monday-Saturday 10 am-9 pm; Sunday noon-5 pm. This Kramer shop handles publisher's overstocks, remainders, and other bargains. Also, foreign language magazines.

**Sidney Kramer Books,** 1722 H Street NW (298-8010). Monday-Friday 9 am-6 pm; Saturday 10 am-4 pm. At the original shop on H Street there is a wide selection of books on economics, political science, foreign affairs, and management. Next door on the second floor an out-of-print shop emphasizes the same specialties.

***McGraw Hill Book Store, Museum of History and Technology,** Constitution Avenue between 12th and 14th Streets NW; Constitution Avenue entrance (381-5248). Daily 10 am-5:30 pm; April 1-Labor Day until 9 pm. Located inside the Museum of History and Technology, this cozy, tiered, and carpeted store is devoted entirely to books concerning American civilization. Drawn from over 200 publishers, the subjects range from folk crafts to applied engineering, from movies to management.

**Modern Language Book and Record Store,** 3160 O Street NW (338-8963). Monday-Saturday 9:30 am-5 pm; Wednesday and Thursday until 7 pm. French, Spanish, and German books in print for children and adults. (For German books, see also Franz Bader, listed under Art Galleries.)

***National Trust for Historic Preservation Book Store,** 784 Jackson Place NW (382-3304). Monday-Friday 10 am-4 pm. Sells handsome Trust publications and other books relating to historic preservation. (See Lafayette Square walking tour in Chapter 3.)

**Organization of American States Book Store,** 19th Street and Constitution Avenue NW (331-1010). Monday-Friday 8:45 am-5:30 pm. Books about Latin America.

***Park-Reifsneider's Antiquarian Book Gallery,** 1310 19th Street NW (833-8082). Monday-Saturday 10 am-4:30 pm. This three-story town house with floor-to-ceiling used books stocks an excellent assortment of Americana, history, biography, and fiction.

# Clothing

## Women

Washington's clothing shops for women cater to diverse incomes and tastes. You can find designer boutiques in the Watergate Mall, high-style-at-a-price on F Street, a potpourri along Connecticut Avenue from the carriage trade's Elizabeth Arden to the working girl's Casual Corner, Saks Fifth Avenue, and other establishment fashion shops in Chevy Chase and Bethesda. But the highest concentration of sartorial splendor per walking step can be found in Georgetown. Here's a sample of the range there plus a few other stores in the metropolitan area you might want to go out of your way to see.

**Ann Taylor,** 1415 Wisconsin Avenue NW (338-5290). Monday-Saturday 10 am-6 pm; Thursday until 9 pm; Sunday 1 pm-5 pm. Ann Taylor carries up-to-the-minute fashions in the moderately expensive price range. Mostly for the younger set, the stock includes interesting accessories and well-styled clothes by Outlander, Bagatelle, Clovis Ruffin, and some designed especially for this popular chain of 25 stores.

**Exit,** 1063 31st Street NW (333-4607). Monday-Saturday 11 am-6 pm. Current fashion arrives here by way of local seamstresses and designers who have produced instant classics such as denim and patchwork skirts, Indian cotton shirts with old appliqués, and hand-painted cocktail dresses. Very *au courant* accessories.

**Frankie Welch of Virginia,** 305 Cameron Street, Alexandria, VA (549-0104). Monday-Saturday 9:30 am-5:30 pm. Best known for her designs of over 600 commemorative and decorative scarfs and an innovative multi-style dress, Frankie Welch is an Alexandria institution. The three-story town house carries country-gentry designer clothing, accessories, and shoes. A revolving sale goes year round on the third floor.

**Jaipur West,** 1618 Wisconsin Avenue NW (333-8877). Monday-Saturday 10 am-6 pm. One of many shops in Georgetown with fabrics fashioned in far-off lands, this one specializes in colorful cotton dresses and blouses from India.

**Junior League Shop of Washington,** 3041 M Street NW (337-6120). Monday-Friday 9:30 am-4 pm; Thursday evening 6 pm-9 pm; Saturday 10 am-3:45 pm. Those with a taste for quality, classic clothes but little to spend come here for the recycled evening dresses, tailored separates, furs, and children's clothing of the society and diplomatic set, sold on consignment. Another excellent consignment shop, if you don't mind the dust, is **Not New**, 125 S. Fairfax Street in Alexandria, VA (549-0649). Monday-Saturday 9 am-4:30 pm.

**Loehmann's,** 7241 Arlington Boulevard, Falls Church, VA (573-1510); 5230 Randolph Road, Rockville, MD (770-0030). Monday-Saturday 9:30 am-5:30 pm; Wednesday until 9:30 pm. The fashionable, budget-conscious women singing Loehmann's praises have included the wives of senators and ambassadors, as well as Betty Ford. The stores, now nationwide, are famous for discounts on high-fashion manufacturers' overstocks. The format is also famous: labels from top national and international designers are removed, the clothing arranged on long racks and tried on in communal dressing rooms lined with mirrors and usually bustling with enthusiastic, uninhibited ladies. The exact percentages of clothing fibers are marked on the price tags, which also advise, "Select carefully. Our garments are not returnable." All purchases must be paid for by check or cash.

**Vogue,** 1657 Wisconsin Avenue NW (338-1914). Monday-Saturday 10 am-7 pm. High-style, European-cut clothes are mainly French mixed with some made across the street at Felix Alonso, the men's branch. There are a number of similar continental-style clothing shops on Wisconsin Avenue between P Street and Reservoir Road.

## For Men and Women

**Saks Fifth Avenue,** 5555 Wisconsin Avenue, Chevy Chase, MD (657-9000). Monday-Saturday 9:30 am-5:30 pm; Monday and Thursday until 9 pm. The

Washington area branch of the New York women's fashion store excels in top-quality sportswear and select designer clothes. It carries more moderate versions of both in its Young Dimensions shop. Among the special sections: Yves St. Laurent and Goldworm boutiques and a Revillon fur salon. The men's departments are also surprisingly good, both the youth-oriented Contemporary Shop and higher-priced suit department, featuring Yves St. Laurent, Brill, and Classico—Saks' own line.

**E. F. Sly & Co.,** 1249 Wisconsin Avenue NW (337-5926). Monday-Saturday 10:30 am-7:30 pm; Monday until 9 pm; Sunday noon-6 pm. This clothing-packed, one-room shop is rumored to make more money per square inch than any other in the area. It is *the* place for theatrical, funky dress for men and women. Where else can you find knee-high sequined boots, jeans jackets inlaid with fake turquoise, or an imitation leopard-skin shirt, whatever the price? Alice Cooper and David Bowie shop here.

**Toast and Strawberries,** 2009 R Street NW (234-2424). Monday-Saturday 10 am-7 pm; Sunday 1 pm-6 pm. The impact of high color and bold prints in blouses, pants, dresses, dashikis, and Yoruba robes crammed into these two small rooms may be overwhelming at first. But the salespeople are only too eager to show you how to tie a waist or a turban, add beads or a batik scarf to complete "the total look." Many of the designs are custom made for the shop and can be duplicated in different fabrics or sizes.

## Men

**Arthur Adler,** 822 15th Street NW (628-0131). Monday-Saturday 9 am-5:45 pm. Branch in Chevy Chase, MD. Specializing in traditional soft-shoulder clothing, this shop carries Southwick of Massachusetts and Norman Hilton. Fabrics are imported directly for its own line of suits and sport coats, including one signature, patchwork, tartan plaid number for $185. Popular with newsmen and congressmen.

**Britches of Georgetowne,** 1247 Wisconsin Avenue NW (338-3330). Monday-Saturday 10 am-6 pm; Monday and Thursday until 9 pm. Branches on Connecticut Avenue and in Montgomery Mall, Rockville, MD. An elegant, neotraditional clothier, Britches has had such success in gauging the tastes of perfectly turned-out young executives that it has opened a handful of offshoots since starting in 1967. The main Georgetown store carries Ralph Lauren's Polo outerwear, Rafael suits and sport coats, Liberty ties, and Cartier watches among its dress wear and gift items. **Britches Western Shop** at 3214 P Street stocks an impressive array of western-style shirts, denims, flannels, suedes, and boots. **Britches Slack Shop** at 1357 Wisconsin Avenue offers a sportier line—the studied casual look for the slighter budget.

**Brooks Brothers,** 1728 L Street NW (659-4650). Monday-Saturday 9:30 am-5:30 pm. Overlooking Connecticut Avenue, this second-floor shop is the smallest of the 14 Brooks Brothers branches. But you can still find the familiar favorites: button-down oxford shirts; straight-cut, pin-striped suits; striped silk ties; and many other quality items—some made for women—in this 150-year-old institution.

**William Fox,** 2136 Pennsylvania Avenue NW (337-7080). Monday-Saturday 9:30 am-6 pm; Thursday until 8 pm. Fine-tailored, updated, traditional clothing. Samuelsohn of Canada is an exclusive, and you'll find an outstanding selection of neckware from $6.50 to $15.

**Georgetown University Shop,** 36th and N Streets NW (337-8100). Monday-Saturday 9:30 am-5:45 pm. Located just off the campus of Georgetown University, this hallowed store stocks favorite collegiate classics. Among the top-quality, full line of clothing for men (and some for women) are Scottish crewnecks in soft colors, Braemar cable-knit sweaters, cashmere tartan scarfs, viyella shirts, plaid pants, blazers.

**Lewis & Thomas Saltz,** 1409 G Street NW (393-4400). Monday-Saturday 9:30 am-5:45 pm. Branches on Connecticut Avenue and in Chevy Chase, MD. This shop has always specialized in traditional clothing of good quality: Oxxford suits, Braemar sweaters, Lacoste sport shirts, Aquascutum rainwear, McAffee shoes, Countess Mara ties.

**Raleigh's,** 1133 Connecticut Avenue NW (785-7028). Monday-Saturday 9:30 am-6 pm; Thursday until 8 pm. Eight suburban branches. A complete men's department store on three floors with Hickey-Freeman and Hart, Schaffner & Marx suits; Eagle and Hathaway shirts; Pierre Cardin and Yves St. Laurent suits and shirts. It also carries clothing for women.

# Crafts

**The American Hand,** 2904 M Street NW (965-3273). Monday-Saturday 11 am-6 pm; Thursday until 9 pm. The American Hand artfully displays the work of a few local, but mainly West Coast potters. Delicate porcelains, luster metallic glazes, decals, silk-screening, and photo resist are some of the sophisticated techniques used in making both sculpture and utilitarian pieces.

**Appalachian Spring,** 1655 Wisconsin Avenue NW (337-5780). Monday-Saturday 10 am-5:30 pm; Thursday until 8 pm. American crafts, traditional and contemporary, brighten this folksy shop full of colorful quilts, patchwork pillows, rag rugs, afghans, and handwoven placemats. There are also handmade folk toys (ask how to use them), silver jewelry, hammered pewter objects, forged iron hooks, flameware pots, and a book of "Old Timey Recipes."

**Artifactory**, 641 Indiana Avenue NW (off Pennsylvania Avenue at 7th Street) (628-3781). Monday-Saturday 10 am-6 pm. A storehouse of traditional African art—textiles, rugs, baskets, musical instruments, clothing, silver and brass jewelry, and a large assortment of trading beads. In her studio here, a local clothing designer produces wearable art.

While you are in this historic Market Square area, you can stop in at the neighboring delicatessen, **Gallery 641** where local artists show their works, and **Litwin's** used furniture store. These stores date from the mid-19th century when the Center Market flourished here.

**Chelsea Court,** 2909 M Street NW; courtyard entrance (338-4588). Tuesday-Saturday 10 am-6 pm. Branch at Watergate Mall. These two workshop/showrooms may be a little hard to find, but are well worth the effort. Pottery, enamelware, jewelry, leather work, stained glass, metal sculpture, and weaving are the contemporary crafts made on the premises by expert artist/craftspeople, who also design to order. You can watch them working upstairs in the Georgetown shop, or around the glass-walled studio on the second level at Watergate Mall. The sign "please touch" sets the tone.

**Cows Outside,** 2412½ 18th Street NW (462-6464). Monday-Saturday 11 am-7 pm. Spiffy hats and caps, skillfully stitched handbags and overnight bags, wallets, and belts are the specialty of this small leather shop, which makes jackets or anything else to order.

**Georgetown Leather Design,** 3265 M Street NW (333-9333). Monday-Saturday 10 am-6 pm. Branches at Tysons Corner, McLean, VA; Springfield Mall, Springfield, VA; and Landover Mall, Landover, MD. The story of a sandal shop that made good. Now 10 years old, the sunny showroom has expansive stock. All the skirts and most of the pants, vests, jumpers, sandals, and hats are made in the basement workroom. (You can peer down a balustraded hole in the floor to the work galley, strewn with chamois leather and cowhide.) They also stock a complete line of shoes for men and women, Frye boots, handbags, belts, and fur-trimmed suede and leather coats. If you don't see your size on the racks, they will reproduce any of their own designs in different colors or sizes.

**Potter's House,** 1658 Columbia Road NW (483-9697). Monday-Friday 10 am-4 pm; Monday, Wednesday, Thursday 8 pm-11:30 pm; Friday-Saturday 8 pm-12 am; Sunday 7:30 pm-11:30 pm. If you'd rather snack than shop, stop by this comfortable, nonprofit coffeehouse and then browse in the adjoining sales area. You'll find small stained-glass, ceramic, and ornamental objects. A rotating art exhibit hangs on the coffeehouse walls.

**Torpedo Factory,** King and Union Streets at the River, Alexandria, VA (836-8564). Daily 10 am-5 pm. Take a World War I munitions-factory-turned-warehouse, clean it up, and divide it into over 100 studios for artists, who pay just $3 per square foot per year in rent, and you have the Torpedo Factory—the latest, greatest break for struggling artists. You can walk through the four galleries and watch the craftspeople working with clay, operating a Shaker loom, painting portraits (even yours), building a harpsichord, silk-screening, and much more. Most of the activity takes place on weekends.

# Department Stores

**Garfinckel's,** 14th and F Streets NW (628-7730). Monday-Saturday 10 am-6 pm; Thursday until 8 pm. Six area branches. With an emphasis on high fashion, the third floor at Garfinckel's showcases designers Ungaro, Givenchy, Missoni, and Gloria Sachs; a Hermes boutique is on the main floor. In men's clothing, Yves St. Laurent, Pierre Cardin, and Jaeger rate separate boutiques. The scarf and handbag departments are topnotch. Gifts on the top floor include Waterford crystal and Boehm porcelain animals and flowers; on the ground floor, Godiva chocolates. The pleasant Greenbrier Restaurant serves tasty a-la-carte platters, sandwiches, and liquor. For a ladies room to end all ladies rooms, don't miss the enchanting lounge on the fifth floor with its caged twin parrots in bright, globe-lighted surroundings.

**Hecht Company,** 7th and F Streets NW (628-5100). Monday-Friday 10 am-6 pm; Monday and Friday until 9:30 pm; Sunday noon-5 pm. Ten suburban branches. Another top department store, Hecht's leads in moderately priced, trendy clothes, gloves, and costume jewelry. There is an extensive selection of contemporary china, home furnishings, an attractive garden accessory shop, Girl and Boy Scout outfitters, and a pet shop with live lovebirds in the children's department. Dining room and snack bar.

**Kann's,** 8th Street and Pennsylvania Avenue NW (347-7200). Monday-Saturday 10 am-6 pm; Thursday until 8 pm. Branch in Arlington, VA. This low-budget department store seems to be lagging behind the times both in its fashions and physical layout—there are elevators and stairs, but no escalators, and a stand-up lunch counter. The linens on the first floor are of top quality and variety; the housewares department is one of the few that still stocks a selection of bread boxes. Plastic shopping bags here are just 10 cents.

***Lord & Taylor,** 5255 Western Avenue NW (362-9600). Monday-Saturday 9:30 am-5:30 pm; Monday, Thursday, Friday until 9:30 pm. Branch in Falls Church, VA. For those familiar with the selection in their New York store, the contents of the two-story Washington version will undoubtedly seem minimal. All men's and women's clothing and accessories are on the street level. Upstairs the children's and home furnishings departments are stronger, with a large selection of Waterford crystal, some handsome antiques and reproductions, including seven pieces from 18th-century collections, selected by the National Trust for Historic Preservation. The Bird Cage restaurant offers a quick, complete, prix fixe lunch.

***Woodward & Lothrop,** 10th and 11th Streets between F and G Streets NW (628-7730). Monday-Saturday 10 am-6 pm; Monday and Thursday until 9 pm. Eleven suburban branches. A strong, general department store, Woodies also has some unusual special sections: a collector's corner for stamps and coins, authentic Williamsburg design reproductions, tuxedo rentals, Boy and Girl Scout outfitters, and Velati's caramels made daily in the North building across G Street, which also houses a large selection of kitchen accessories. A top stock of furnishings—traditional and contemporary—take up the entire sixth floor. Accessories can be purchased out of the chic model rooms. Good eating spots: the seventh floor tea room, salad buffet, and English pub, which serve liquor, or the basement cafeteria.

# Ethnic

**Amerind,** 3116 M Street NW (333-6838). Monday-Saturday 10 am-6 pm. Several cases of authentic Indian jewelry adorn this attractive, wood-columned shop, which also carries books and crafts, including appliquéd shawls and beaded moccasins.

**Batik Walla,** 1251 Wisconsin Avenue NW (965-9564). Monday-Saturday 10 am-6 pm. Branch at Les Champs. Batik wall hangings, antique tapestries, printed cotton bedspreads, blouses, and dresses from India, Ceylon, and Pakistan are the specialties here.

**Iberian Imports,** 225 N. Fairfax Street, Alexandria, VA (549-1050). Monday-Friday 10 am-5:30 pm; Saturday until 6 pm. Stacks of painted tiles in dozens of patterns, Portuguese faïence plates and planters, wrought-iron fixtures, kitchen and bath accessories are highlighted in this shop that focuses on products from the Iberian Peninsula.

**Indian Country,** 3207 O Street NW (333-5009). Monday-Saturday 10 am-6 pm. Now eight years old, this small shop has a fine selection of small, authentic objects, chiefly made by Indians in the Southwest: jewelry and beads, handwoven ties, Zuni fetishes, baskets, Kachina dolls, and drums.

**Indian Craft Shop,** Interior Department, C Street between 18th and 19th Streets NW (343-4056). Monday-Friday 8:30 am-4 pm. This store started in 1938, long before the popularization of American Indian products, as an Eastern outlet for native Indian handcrafts. A wide selection from more than 35 American tribes is sold here, including jewelry, wood carvings, baskets, Kachina dolls, rugs, ivory carvings, block prints, pottery, and records.

**The Irish Walk,** 604 S. Washington Street, Alexandria, VA (548-0118). Monday-Friday 10 am-5 pm; Saturday until 6 pm. You can buy the Irish country dance records played instead of Musak in this store, as well as Sherlock Holmes caps, nubby handknit Irish sweaters, Irish tea, and biscuits.

**Nuevo Mundo,** 313 Cameron Street, Alexandria, VA (549-0040). Monday-Friday 10 am-5:30 pm; Saturday until 6 pm. This handsome shop brings together a fascinating hybrid of handwoven fabrics, handknit sweaters, and decorative objects from Central and South America, mixed with antique jewelry from China, Afghanistan, and Ethiopia; textiles from Egypt; Buddhas from Siam; *santos* from the Philippines; and stylish clothing from all over.

**The Phoenix,** 1514 Wisconsin Avenue NW (338-4404). Tuesday-Saturday 10 am-6 pm. Branch in Alexandria. A good place to find a beautiful selection of quality objects from Mexico: tin boxes, candelabrum, and mirrors; fine silver jewelry; well-made dresses in brilliant cottons; rug fabrics by the yard; accessories; and decorative items.

**Scotland House,** 607 S. Washington Street, Alexandria, VA (836-8855). Monday-Saturday 9:30 am-5:30 pm. The Scots who founded Alexandria would appreciate the selection here; six rooms display everything from authentic tartan wool blankets, scarves, and pants to clan tiles, grouse prints, guide books, crystal, cairngorm jewelry, toys, and complete clothing lines for men and women—nearly all imported from Scotland.

**Zaro's House of Africa,** 315 7th Street SE (546-4734). Monday and Wednesday 12:30 pm-6 pm; Tuesday, Thursday, Saturday 11 am-7 pm. From Tanzania, Zaire, Ethiopia, and Kenya a diverse collection of jewelry, wood sculpture, masks, leather goods, carved animals, clothing, paintings, and ivories. The African recorded music in the background is also for sale.

## Gifts

* **Bicentennial Museum Shop,** 201 S. Washington Street, Alexandria, VA (548-1812). Monday-Saturday 10 am-4 pm; Sunday 1 pm-4:30 pm. A bonanza of Bicentennial-inspired objects to discover, many commissioned especially for Alexandria's celebration. Prints and drawings of Alexandria were winners in a competition for local artists; the pottery was reproduced from originals discovered on an archeological dig in Old Town; the tea-towel design was adapted from early earthenware motifs. Children will covet the hand-painted lead soldiers, Spirit of '76 T-shirts, and delightful paper caps and helmets from the Revolution. Many of the gifts here sell for less than $5.

* **Martin's China, Crystal, and Silver Shop,** 1304 Wisconsin Avenue NW (338-6144).

Monday-Saturday 10 am-6 pm. This is *the* place in Georgetown for quality china, crystal, and silver—contemporary on the first floor, antique on the second. A very special Bicentennial gift would be their handsome creamware federal bowl decorated with Colonial scenes, made for Martin's by Wedgwood, for $150.

**Old Georgetown Coffee House,** 1330 Wisconsin Avenue NW (338-2366). Monday-Saturday 9 am-6 pm; Sunday 10 am-4 pm. The most popular Georgetown emporium per square inch goes way beyond supplying devoted customers with fresh coffee and exotic teas. An enormous selection of delicacies and accouterments for the kitchen are crammed into this one-room bazaar. Unusual spices are packaged expressly for the store. If you don't see something you want, ask. The salespeople are especially cheerful.

**Teri's Parfumerie Française,** 1054 31st Street NW, Canal Square (337-4117). Monday-Saturday 10 am-9 pm. This French parfumerie is a treat of both sights and scents.

**United Nations Association Gift Shop,** 3143 N Street NW (337-5553). Monday-Saturday 11 am-5 pm; Thursday until 7 pm. This small shop is filled with interesting gifts from around the world at small prices: dolls from Guatemala, wall hangings from Ecuador, pottery from Poland, brass candlesticks from Korea, jewelry from everywhere, flags, UNICEF cards, and Uniworld games. Volunteers here speak several languages. Proceeds go to the U.N.

**Wilfred-Rodgers Ltd.,** 132 King Street, Alexandria, VA (548-4543). Monday-Saturday 10 am-5 pm. Elegant shop for china, crystal, and silver.

## For Kids

**Granny's Place,** 303 Cameron Street, Alexandria, VA (549-0119). Monday-Saturday 10 am-5 pm. Classic toys are the specialty here: Raggedy Ann dolls, musical mobiles, Steiff animals, tool chests, Hansel and Gretel records, handcuffs, and harmonicas.

**Lowen's,** 7227 Wisconsin Avenue, Bethesda, MD (652-1289). Monday-Saturday 9:30 am-6:30 pm; Thursday until 9 pm. This is a supermarket of games, books, dolls, art supplies, hobby kits, etc.

**The Red Balloon,** 1208 31st Street NW (965-1200). Monday-Saturday 10 am-6 pm. Branch at Les Champs. Many toys and games are imported from Europe; clothing and wooden toys made by the owners; plus Osh Kosh bib overalls and jackets.

## Government and Museum Shops

The shops included here are those that go beyond the predictable assortment of posters, catalogues, and postcards. None charges tax, and most with membership programs offer discounts to members. Prices mentioned, of course, are subject to change.

***Bureau of Engraving and Printing,** 14th and C Streets SW (964-7244). Monday-Friday 8 am-2:30 pm. The Bureau no longer operates a sales outlet for its handsome engraved and lithographed printings. But you can see the products during a tour and pick up an order form, or buy them at the U.S. Mint Sales Office at the Treasury Department (see below). Small cameo portraits of the presidents and chief justices, as well as finely detailed vignettes of Washington monuments are priced at under $1. Color prints of the U.S. seal and U.S. flag are 50¢ and 75¢.

**Geological Survey,** Public Inquiries Office, F Street between 18th and 19th Streets NW (343-8073). Monday-Friday 7:45 am-4 pm. Topographical and geological maps of the United States and its possessions (on a scale of one inch to 2,000 feet) published by the Geological Survey, cost 75¢ and $1 here. The office stocks 2,000 maps of California alone. A topographical map of the Washington area is available for $2.

***Library of Congress Information Counter,** 1st Street between East Capitol Street and Independence Avenue SE; street-level entrance (426-5000). Monday-Saturday 9 am-5 pm; Sunday 1 pm-5 pm. Marvelous reproductions of old Victorian advertisements and popular artifacts are all based on the Library's collections. The shop also carries stationery, bibliographies, transcripts of symposiums and lectures at the Library, and special Bicentennial items: facsimiles of a 1770 engraving by Paul Revere, rebus picture puzzles circa 1775, and an illustrated catalogue of the Library's Bicentennial exhibit, "To Set a Country Free." The Library's Archives of Folk Song sells recordings of its collections. You can listen to Indian tribal music, sea chanteys, or poetry readings (two in Spanish) in Room G 152 weekdays between 8:30 am and 5 pm before deciding whether to spend $5.

***National Museum of History and Technology,** Constitution Avenue between 12th and 14th Streets NW (381-5113). Daily 10 am-5:30 pm; April 1-Labor Day until 9 pm. The two shops in this building (one aimed at children, the other adults) contain merchandise inspired by the national collections of the museum. Favorite items are Southwest American Indian jewelry and other moderately priced jewelry from around the world, ceramics, carved wood boxes from Poland, hand-painted boxes from Russia, and hand-blown glass paperweights. Traditional toys include corncob and clothespin dolls from Appalachia, doll-house furnishings, and classic-car reproductions. The best-selling records produced by the Smithsonian are the six-record *Smithsonian Collection of Classic Jazz* and nostalgic sounds of the Southern Railway Locomotive 1401. In connection with several manufacturers, the Institution has introduced reproductions (some dating from the Revolutionary era), Stieff silver and pewter copies of porringers, candlesticks, and other household objects; Fieldcrest coverlets, sheets, and towels; Tonka Dioramas (hobby kits recreating settings from the past); and hand-blown replicas of early American glass.

**National Museum of Natural History,** Constitution Avenue at 10th Street NW (381-5186). Daily 10 am-5:30 pm; April 1-Labor Day until 9 pm. A wide range in prices and objects for the naturalist: books, mineral and rock samples, wildflower seeds, prehistoric animal kits, a geology lab, original Eskimo sculpture from Canada, and a portfolio of photographic prints of the North American Indian by Edward S. Curtis.

***The National Archives Sales Desk,** 8th Street and Pennsylvania Avenue NW; Constitution Avenue entrance (962-6121). October-February: Monday-Saturday 9 am-5 pm; Sunday 1 pm-5 pm; March-September: Monday-Saturday 9 am-10 pm; Sunday 1 pm-10 pm. Well-priced facsimiles of documents in the National Archives collection are the big thing here. The most popular, "Charters of Freedom," includes reproductions of The Declaration of Independence, The Constitution, and The Bill of Rights in one booklet for 50¢. A facsimile packet of 38 documents on the formation of the Union is also reasonably priced, and there is a campy collection of color posters from both World Wars ($1 each). Smaller postcard versions recall messages like "Every garden a munition plant" and "Stenographers: Washington needs you!"

**National Gallery of Art,** Constitution Avenue, between 6th and 7th Streets NW (737-4215). Monday-Saturday 10 am-5 pm; Sunday 12 pm-9 pm. Three rooms on the ground floor sell reproductions and pamphlets of the Gallery's collection. Prints start at an irresistibly low 35¢ (or 3 for $1); framed prints range from $6.50 to $30.

***National Geographic Society,** 17th and M Streets NW (296-7500). Monday-Friday 9 am-6 pm; Saturday until 5 pm; Sunday 12 pm-5 pm. This is the only sales outlet for the beautifully produced National Geographic maps, books, records, and filmstrips. Book subjects cover history, geography, nature, and vanishing species—both men and animals. American heritage titles such as "The Revolutionary War" and "Our Country's Presidents" cost under $5.

**Philatelic Sales Windows and Exhibits, Post Office Building,** Room 1315, 12th Street and Pennsylvania Avenue NW; 12th Street entrance (961-7540). Monday-Saturday 9 am-5 pm. All current U.S. stamps are sold at face value; annual U.S. and Canadian souvenir mint sets, stamp-collecting kits, and a "Stamps and Stories" booklet. Order forms are also available at the post office in the Museum of History and Technology.

**Post Office, Museum of History and Tech-**

**nology;** Constitution Avenue entrance. Daily 10 am-5:15 pm. This reconstructed building dating from the early 1860s served as both a post office and general store at its original site in Headsville, West Va. The high-button shoes and now empty tins are still on the shelves, but the structure serves as a branch of the U.S. Postal Service. You can mail letters and packages up to one pound and buy currently available commemorative stamps and stamp albums from the preceding year. A special feature is the unique hand stamp on all letters mailed from here, with the date and "Smithsonian Sta. Washington, D.C." clearly marked.

* **Renwick Gallery of the National Collection of Fine Arts,** 17th Street and Pennsylvania Avenue NW (381-5364). Daily 10 am-5:30 pm; April 1-Labor Day until 9 pm. An impressive collection of handcrafted items and books on American crafts, art, and architecture. Displays here vary with each new show at the museum. Upcoming: handcrafted coffee and tea pots, planters, and alternatives to the paper bag.

**Textile Museum,** 2320 S Street NW (667-0441). Tuesday-Saturday 10 am-5 pm. Central and South American textiles, handmade caps and sweaters on consignment, handpainted needlework canvases from England with floral and Medieval designs ($65 and up), imported yarns, and lace bobbins are among the textile-related items on sale here.

**Treasury Department, Cash Room,** 15th Street and Pennsylvania Avenue NE; Pennsylvania Avenue entrance (964-2746). Monday-Friday 8:30 am-4:30 pm. This ornate, two-story room with its seven varieties of marble has the opulence and tradition one might expect in a room that once stored most of the nation's gold and silver reserves. Completed in 1869 for President Grant's first inaugural ball, it was called the most expensive room in the world at the time. Today, you can buy uncirculated U.S. coins here at face value; cash government checks and bonds; or buy savings bonds. There may be a limit on purchasing certain coins; most recently pennies and half dollars were limited to one roll per customer.

* **U.S. Mint Sales Office, Treasury Department,** 15th Street and Pennsylvania Avenue NW; East Executive Avenue entrance (964-5221). Tuesday-Friday 9:30 am-3:30 pm; Saturday 10 am-2 pm. Official medals (silver-dollar size) of the presidents in bronze and gold plate start at 50¢. You can also pick up order forms here or at banks and post offices for an uncirculated set of 40-percent silver Bicentennial coins.

## Home

**China Closet,** 6807 Wisconsin Avenue, Bethesda, MD (656-5400). Monday-Saturday 9:30 am-6 pm; Thursday until 9 pm. Branch in Falls Church, VA. This enormous shop has outstanding values in contemporary glassware, stainless steel flatware, ceramics, and imported cookware. Everything here is discounted at least 10 percent, a large stock of seconds reduced more.

**The Design Store,** 1258 Wisconsin Avenue NW (337-5800). Monday-Friday 10 am-9 pm; Saturday until 6 pm; Sunday 1 pm-5 pm. Trend-setting imported housewares, furniture by Herman Miller and Knoll International, its own line of contemporary sofas, toys, Marimekko fabrics, women's clothing, and hammocks are among the potpourri of contemporary items.

**Dockside,** Union and King Streets, Alexandria, VA (549-3163). Monday-Friday 9:30 am-9 pm; Saturday until 6 pm; Sunday 11 pm-6 pm. Branches in Rockville, MD, and Reston, VA. Four buildings along the river house inexpensive glassware, china, baskets, rattan and Scandinavian furniture, posters, candles, brass antiques, and much more imported from over 70 countries. Take special note of Building One, where George Washington once worked as a surveyor.

**Kitchen Bazaar,** 4455 Connecticut Avenue NW (363-7760). Monday-Saturday 9:30 am-6 pm; Thursday and Friday until 9 pm. An excellent selection of the latest, imported and domestic cookery items.

**Little Caledonia,** 1419 Wisconsin Avenue NW (333-4700). Monday-Saturday 9:30 am-5:30 pm. This is the place to find a wonderful selection of classic, tasteful objects for the home: traditional patterns in china; a room with copper cookware and countless casseroles; furniture reproductions; hunting prints; silver, pewter, and crystal; more than 80 different designs in tile; a room for children's gifts that includes Beatrix Potter figurines.

**Modern Design,** 5454 Wisconsin Avenue, Chevy Chase, MD (656-2323). Monday-Saturday 10 am-6 pm; Thursday until 9 pm. You will find Forecast, Thayer Coggin, and Directional furniture, and metal sculpture on the first floor; Dansk designs, other accessories, and jewelry on the second level in an environment as contemporary as the contents.

**Scan,** 1054 31st Street NW, Canal Square (333-5015). Monday-Friday 10 am-9 pm; Saturday until 6 pm. Seven area branches. A co-op, Scan imports contemporary furniture, mainly from Scandinavia, keeping its prices below that of most comparable stores. Also some accessories, fabrics, and Rya rugs. Some of the other branches have a larger selection.

**Ursell's,** 3243 Q Street NW (338-9200). Monday-Saturday 9:30 am-6 pm. Ursell's has been carrying well-designed, functional furnishings for almost 30 years, in addition to a wide selection of classic, contemporary, stainless-steel flatware, china, cutlery, wall hangings, and handmade pottery.

## Jewelry

***Charles Schwartz & Son,** 1313 F Street NW (783-1525). Monday-Saturday 9:30 am-5:30 pm. Branches in the Mayflower Hotel and Les Champs at the Watergate. This is an elegant shop for jewelry, china, crystal, and souvenir pieces by Wedgwood, a company that has been producing American commemorative objects since the 18th century. Four creamware, dinner-size plates with scenes of Washington monuments, made for Charles Schwartz, sell for $9 each, or $35 the set. Jasper ashtrays with the U.S. Capitol in relief cost $8.50. Schwartz also carries the gilded American Revolutionary portrait plates of American patriots, bronze double eagles, and George Washington inaugural swords, issued by the privately organized U.S. Bicentennial Society.

***Galt & Brothers,** 607 13th Street NW (347-1034). Monday-Saturday 9:30 am-5:30 pm. America's oldest jewelers, in business since 1802, specialize in gem-quality diamonds and rare stones mounted in traditional or contemporary settings, some designed especially for the shop. Among the outstanding silver pieces is an authentic reproduction of the 1763 Revere "Liberty Bowl," engraved with the names of 15 members of the Massachusetts Bay Colony. It costs $1,200.

**Tiny Jewel Box,** 1143 Connecticut Avenue NW (393-2747). Monday-Saturday 9:30 am-5 pm. It really is tiny, but the stock of treasures from the past is enormous: pocket watches and lockets; sapphire and ruby princess rings; lacy diamond earrings; heavy, gold, bangle bracelets; cameos; garnet-encrusted brooches; and much more.

## Liquor

The spirit of '76 in bottled form is sure to be a favorite Washington souvenir. The District's liberal liquor laws allow stores here to operate long hours, to stock a wide selection, and most important—to offer exceptionally low prices. Then there are special attractions such as Watergate Bourbon, the house brand at **Watergate Liquors** (2544 Virginia Avenue NW, 333-0636), which has become a fast-selling tourist item. Best buys are found in the high-volume liquor stores, on cases, and on house brands, available nearly everywhere. You should also watch newspaper advertisements for sales on national brands. The largest store in the area, reportedly the largest single retail outlet in the country, is **Central Liquor** at 518 9th Street NW. Other biggies are **Calvert Liquor** and **Plain Old Pearson**'s, both on Wisconsin Avenue. Before you get high on the idea, however, you should remember that state laws vary concerning importation. Maryland and Virginia, for example, post tipsters at larger District stores to watch for their state's residents, and other states are often watchful.

# Services

## All-night Drug Stores

**Ethical Prescription Pharmacy Inc.,** 518 Florida Avenue NW (387-6881). 24-hour answering service.

**Peoples Drug Store,** 14th Street and Thomas Circle NW (628-0720) and seven suburban stores.

## Gyms

**Watergate Health Club,** 2650 Virginia Avenue NW (337-7055). Monday-Friday 8 am-9:30 pm; Saturday-Sunday 10 am-5:30 pm. Use of sauna, whirlpool, steam cabinets, exercise and weight rooms, and indoor pool. Costs $4 per person a day; men and women.

**YMCA,** 1736 G Street NW (737-7900). Monday-Friday 6 am-10 pm; Saturday 8 am-8 pm; Sunday 1 pm-6 pm. An all-day pass costs $3. Indoor pool, weights, track, squash, basketball, and handball; men and women.

**YWCA**, 1649 K Street NW (ME8-2100). Slimnastics and indoor swimming at specified times, for a small charge plus membership fee of $5.

## Out-of-town Newspapers

**General Newstand**, 1796 Columbia Road NW (265-1627). Monday-Friday 6 am-7:30 pm; Sunday 6 am-7 pm. Out-of-town and Spanish language newspapers, foreign magazines.

**Universal Newsstand,** 603 15th Street NW (347-6173). Monday-Friday 6 am-7:30 pm; Saturday 6 am-7 pm. 3 other locations, some open 7 days a week until midnight. Top selection of out-of-town and foreign newspapers.

## Shopping Services

**Garfinckel's, Woodward & Lothrop, Lord & Taylor, Hecht Co.,** and **Saks Fifth Avenue** provide consultants to assist with personal shopping or to recommend gift items. Most also furnish wheelchairs and special assistance to handicapped shoppers upon request. The **Hecht Co., Woodward & Lothrop,** and **Kann's** will send packages C.O.D.

# Tobacco

**Betram Briar Pipe Company,** 920 14th Street NW (628-5700). Monday-Saturday 9 am-5:30 pm. Natural wood briar pipes are made on the premises. The store used to make ivory cigarette holders for FDR.

**W. Curtis Draper,** 507 11th Street NW (638-2555). Monday-Saturday 9 am-6 pm. Branch on Connecticut Avenue. Calvin Coolidge used to buy his 60¢ cigars here. Charatan, Savinelli, and Dunhill pipes; tobacco; all accessories.

**A. Garfinkel,** 720 14th Street NW (638-1175). Monday-Friday 9 am-6 pm; Saturday until 5 pm. Once a favorite of Richard Nixon, this shop carries its own line of cigars and nearly 100 blends of tobacco.

**Georgetown Pharmacy,** 1344 Wisconsin Avenue NW (338-3400). Monday-Friday 9 am-8 pm; Saturday until 6 pm; Sunday 9:30 am-3 pm. This pharmacy stocks an unexpected and extraordinary range of handmade cigars from giant Royal Jamaica Goliaths to short, stubby Dannemans from Brazil, and slim miniature Dutch cigars for ladies. Art Buchwald buys his 80¢ Canary Island Flamencos here.

**Georgetown Tobacco and Pipe Store,** 3144 M Street NW (338-1660). Monday-Saturday

10 am-8 pm. Branches at Montgomery Mall, Rockville, MD; and Tysons Corner, McLean, VA. No cigarettes are carried here, but you will find a wide selection of meerschaum and free-hand pipes and accessories.

# One-of-a-Kind

**Fahrney's Pen Shop,** 1418 New York Avenue NW (628-9525). Monday-Friday 8:30 am-5:30 pm; Saturday 9 am-5 pm. Fahrney's has been repairing pens for the presidents since Herbert Hoover. It stocks all the familiar favorites: Sheaffer, Parker, Esterbrook, plus special writing instruments such as the German Montblanc with an 18-karat-gold point.

**G Street Remnant Shop,** 805 G Street NW (393-7895). Monday 9 am-6:30 pm; Tuesday-Saturday until 5:45 pm; Thursday until 8 pm. Two floors are loaded with fabulous fabrics: cottons from Mexico, India, and Brazil; silks from Mainland China; wools from Great Britain; a rack of remnant bargains; and notions from zippers to handmade silk flowers.

**The Map Store,** 1636 I Street NW (628-2608). Monday-Friday 9 am-5:30 pm. The Washington Beltway map outsells all others here, but you can also find a city map of Amarillo, Texas; Hallwag maps from Switzerland; Michelin maps and guidebooks; nautical charts; topographical maps; globes; and much more.

**Needle's Point Studio,** 7013 Duncraig Court, McLean, VA (356-1615). Sunday-Thursday 1 pm-5 pm. You won't find a readymade kit here, but a vibratingly colorful wall of imported textured threads; even-weave fabrics for surface stitchery; a range of tapestry needles and embroidery frames; and lots of encouragement and inspiration for developing your own designs.

**Quality Umbrella and Cane Shop,** 737 11th Street NW (628-0738). Monday-Saturday 9 am-6 pm. "Washington's most complete selection of umbrellas and canes since 1886" reads the sign above the wooden display case, and it's true.

**Sloan's Auctioneers,** 715 13th Street NW (628-1468). **Adam A. Weschler & Son,** 905 E Street NW (628-1281). Both auction houses run special catalogue sales for better furnishings, art, and other quality items. The regular weekly auctions cover miscellaneous objects from homes and commercial establishments. Sloan's catalogue sales come up about every two months, Weschler's about four times a year. Regular weekly auctions take place at Sloan's on Saturdays, starting at 10 am, with inspection the preceding day from 9 am to 5 pm. At Weschler's, regular sales take place on Tuesdays at 9:30 am, with inspection the day before from 9 am to 5 pm.

**Sunspots,** 1054 31st Street NW, Canal Square (338-1500). Monday-Friday 11:30 am-5:30 pm; Saturday 10 am-6 pm. About 400 styles of sunglasses include Christian Dior, Nina Ricci, and lots more.

**Locker Room,** 501 14th Street NW (393-5566). Monday-Saturday 9 am-6 pm. Banners, Redskin jackets, football T-shirts, even helmet-base lamps for the sports fanatic.

**Tandy Leather,** 712 7th Street NW (638-2120). Monday-Friday 9:30 am-5:30 pm; Saturday until 5 pm. This shop carries all the tools of the trade: leather and suede, leather needles, thread, lacings, pattern books, even moccasin kits.

**Treasure of the Pirates,** 4840 Rugby Avenue, Bethesda, MD (656-3500). Monday-Saturday 10 am-5:30 pm; Thursday until 9 pm. The lapidary enthusiast will find a large assortment of mineral specimens and geodes, amethyst rock from South America, polished stones, trays of mountings, ox-teeth and clay beads, and lovely examples of the finished product in an adjoining room.

# Calendar

**MARIAN HOFFMAN**

## May 1975

| | |
|---|---|
| Nordic Day. On the Washington Monument grounds (426-6975). Nordic folk displays, singing, dancing, and ethnic dishes. | May |
| U.S. Customs Department Exhibit. George Washington Bicentennial Center, 201 S. Washington Street, Alexandria, VA (549-0205). Exhibit traces the history of Alexandria's import-export trade after the city was established as one of Virginia's 12 original customs districts. Daily 9 am-5 pm (through July 30, 1975). | All month |
| Beginning of a three-month commemoration in Williamsburg, VA (293-5350). | 15 |
| City of Rockville Crafts Festival. Rockville Mall, Rockville, MD (424-8000). | 16-18 |
| City of Rockville Memorial Day Ceremonies and Parade. Courthouse Square and parade route, Rockville, MD (424-8000). 9:30 am. | 26 |
| Special Memorial Day Services at Arlington National Cemetery. President lays wreath at Tomb of the Unknown Soldier. | 26 |
| The Bolshoi Ballet presents "Spartacus." The J. F. Kennedy Center Opera House, 2700 F Street NW (254-3700). 8 pm. Admission charge. | 27, 28, 29, 31 |
| The Bolshoi Ballet presents "Giselle." The J. F. Kennedy Center Opera House (254-3700). 2 pm. Admission charge. | 28, 31 |
| The Bolshoi Ballet presents "Ivan the Terrible." The | 30 |

| | |
|---|---|
| | J. F. Kennedy Center Opera House (254-3700). 8 pm. Admission charge. |
| 30, 31 | Outdoor Art Show. President's Park, 15th and E Streets NW (629-7344). Art show and sale, music, handicrafts, and dance performances. |
| 30, 31 | The beginning of the U.S. Naval Academy's June Week. Annapolis, MD (301-267-2291). Graduation week celebration, presentation of Color Girl, parades, band concerts. |
| 31 | President's Cup Regatta. Hains Point, East Potomac Park (426-6975). Admission charge. |
| 31 | Montgomery County Historical Society Craft and Antique Show. Montgomery County Historical Society—Beall Dawson House, Rockville, MD (762-1492). |

## 1975 June

| | |
|---|---|
| Summer | Cavalcade of America's musical heritage. The J. F. Kennedy Center, 2700 F Street NW (254-3600). Historical cavalcade in song, dance, and legend will be presented as part of the center's Bicentennial celebration. |
| June | Display of day-blooming lilies at Kenilworth Aquatic Gardens, Kenilworth Avenue and Douglas Street NE (426-6905). |
| 1 | The Bolshoi Ballet presents "Ivan the Terrible." The J. F. Kennedy Center, 2700 F Street NW (254-3600). 2 pm. Admission charge. |
| 1 | President's Cup Regatta. Hains Point, East Potomac Park (426-6975). Admission charge. |
| 1-4 | U.S. Naval Academy June Week. Annapolis, MD (301-267-2291). Graduation Week celebration, presentation of Color Girl, parades, band concerts. |
| 1-8 | Outdoor Art Show. President's Park, 15th and E Streets NW (629-7344). Art show and sale, music, handicrafts, and dance performances. (All month in 1976.) |
| 6-8 | National Professional Craft Fair. Frederick Fairgrounds, Frederick, MD. Features work of 500 professional craftsmen. 10 am-6 pm. Admission charge; children under 12 free. |
| 7 | Spring Fling Art Exhibit. Market Square, Alexandria, VA (256-4683 or 780-7642). Open outdoor art show. 9 am-5 pm. Raindate: June 14. |

City of Rockville Reenactment of the Signing of the Hungerford Resolve. Rockville Bicentennial Square, Rockville, MD (424-8000). 6 pm. — 11

Flag Day Celebration. Fort McHenry, Baltimore, MD (301-837-1793). — 14

East Bank Artists Exhibition. Anacostia Neighborhood Museum, 2405 Martin Luther King, Jr. Avenue SE (381-6991). A display of art work by student, nonprofessional, and professional artists living east of the Anacostia River. (Through August 24, 1975.) — 15

Bicentennial Youth Bike Tour. Begins at Market Square, King and Fairfax Streets, Alexandria, VA (750-6677 for reservations). Guided bike tour of Old Town Alexandria for students, ending with a picnic at Founders Park. 1 pm-3 pm. — 15

Roaring Twenties Day. National Capital Trolley Museum, Bonifant Road, Wheaton, MD (Call Robert Flack 434-2906 after 6 pm). 1:30-4:30 pm. — 15

Exhibit Featuring a Potpourri of Gallery Favorites. Jewish Community Center of Greater Washington, 6125 Montrose Road, Rockville, MD (881-0100). — 19

American Indian Dance Group. Fort Ward Park, 4301 W. Braddock Road, Alexandria, VA (750-6425). 8:30 pm. Admission charge. (Saturday evenings through August 2, 1975.) — 21

American Folklife Festival. On the Mall. A celebration of American civilization, with singing, dancing, crafts, special foods. Crafts: 11 am-5 pm; music: 11 am-8 pm. — 25-29

## July 1975

Bicentex. Department of Health, Education, and Welfare, 330 Independence Avenue SW (245-6975). Special Bicentennial exhibit center, featuring exhibits of each agency. — July

Farm Craft Day. Belle Grove Plantation, Middletown, VA (703-869-2028). Crafts demonstrated include tatting, flaking, braiding, country music. Admission charge. — July

Treasures from the Hermitage and the Russian State Museum. The National Gallery of Art, Constitution Avenue and 6th Street NW (737-4215). Exhibit features pictures by Rembrandt, Picasso, Matisse, and many others. (Through fall of 1975.) — Mid-July

American Folklife Festival. On the Mall. A celebra- — 2-6

| | |
|---|---|
| | tion of American civilization, with singing, dancing, crafts, special foods. Crafts: 11 am-5 pm; music: 11 am-8 pm. |
| 4 | City of Rockville Independence Day Celebration. Richard Montgomery High School, Rockville, MD (424-8000). 7:30 pm. |
| 4 | Independence Day Parade. Wilson Boulevard, between Glebe Road and Bon Air Park, Arlington, VA (525-2400). 10 am. |
| 4 | Fireworks at the Washington Monument (426-6975). Can also be viewed from Iwo Jima Memorial, Arlington, VA (LI5-6700). |
| 4 | Craft Multiples. The Renwick Gallery, 17th Street and Pennsylvania Avenue NW (628-4422). (Through February 16, 1976.) |
| 5-27 | Bicentennial Art Exhibit—Alexandria Seaport City. Atheneum Museum, 201 Prince Street, Alexandria, VA (548-0035). Maritime artifacts and art work on the early history of Alexandria. Monday-Saturday 10 am-4 pm; Sunday 1 pm-4 pm. |
| 12 | Arts and Crafts Show. Market Square and Torpedo Factory, Alexandria, VA (548-1776). 10 am-5 pm. |
| 12, 13, 19, 20 | Steam Train Excursion (548-1776). Southern Railroad's steam train will conduct day trips to Front Royal and back to Alexandria. Admission charge. |
| 12-13 | Gunston Hall Arts and Crafts Show. Gunston Hall Plantation, Lorton, VA (550-9220). Arts and crafts of the 18th, 19th, and 20th centuries will be demonstrated by costumed craftsmen. 1 pm-5 pm. Admission charge. |
| 12-13 | Armed Services Bicentennial Mobile Museums Display. King Street, Alexandria, VA (548-1776). 40-ft. mobile museums representing the Army, Navy, Air Force, and Marine Corps line King Street. |
| 13 | Civil War reenactment. Fort Ward Park, 4301 W. Braddock Road, Alexandria, VA (750-6425). The battle at Fort Donaldson, Tennessee, in February 1862, will be reenacted with costumed Civil War soldiers. 1:30 pm. |
| 19 | "1776." Alexandria Little Theatre, 600 Wolfe Street, Alexandria, VA (683-0496). Admission charge. (Through August 11.) |
| 19 | Virginia Scottish Games and Gathering of the Clans. Episcopal High School Stadium and fields, 1200 Quaker Lane, Alexandria, VA (549-0205). Bagpipe, highland dance, drumming, and Scottish athletic games, collies demonstrating sheep-herding. Food and merchandise sold. 8:30 am-5:30 pm. |

| | |
|---|---|
| Potomac War Gaming (548-1776). A mock battle of the Revolutionary War in miniature. | 20 |
| The Bolshoi Opera presents "Boris Gudunov." The J. F. Kennedy Center, Opera House, 2700 F Street NW (254-3700). 8 pm. Admission charge. | 22, 25, 26, 31 |
| The Bolshoi Opera presents "The Gambler." The J. F. Kennedy Center Opera House, 2700 F Street NW (254-3700). 8 pm. Admission charge. | 23, 26 |
| The Bolshoi Opera presents "Eugene Onegin." The J. F. Kennedy Center Opera House, 2700 F Street NW (254-3700). 8 pm. Admission charge. | 24, 27 |
| The Bolshoi Opera presents "War and Peace." The J. F. Kennedy Center Opera House, 2700 F Street NW (254-3700). 8 pm. Admission charge. | 29, 30 |
| Annual Chincoteague, VA, Pony Swim and Auction. Assateague Island National Seashore, VA (804-336-6161). | 24-26 |
| The Merrie Old England Summer Festival at Boar's Head Inn, Charlottesville, VA (804-296-2181). Old English dances and songs, archery and jousting. | 26-28 |

## August 1975

| | |
|---|---|
| Mini-Folk Festival. Wolf Trap Farm Park, Vienna, VA (426-6975). Displays of ethnic cultures, dancing. Admission charge for events in Filene Center; Wolf Trap Park free. | August |
| Annual Maryland Clam Festival. City Dock, Annapolis, MD (301-268-7676). Steamed and fried clam platters from the Clam Fleet, a Clam Queen contest, and Chesapeake Bay cruises. | 1, 2, 3 |
| The Bolshoi Opera presents "Eugene Onegin." The J. F. Kennedy Center Opera House, 2700 F Street NW (254-3700). 8 pm. Admission charge. | 2 |
| The Bolshoi Opera presents "War and Peace." The J. F. Kennedy Center Opera House, 2700 F Street NW (254-3700). 1 pm. Admission charge. | 4 |
| Civil War Reenactment. Fort Ward Park, 4301 W. Braddock Road, Alexandria, VA (750-6425). 200 "soldiers" in Civil War uniforms reenact the battle of Fort Stevens, 1861. 1:30 pm. | 16 |
| Maryland State Fair. Timonium Fairgrounds, Timonium, MD (301-252-0200). One of the nation's largest state fairs. Admission charge. (Through September 3, 1975.) | 25 |

# 1975 September

| | |
|---|---|
| September | St. Andrew's Annual Antique Show and Sale. St. Andrew's Church, River and Goldsboro Roads, Bethesda, MD (229-3383 or 229-3384). Luncheon, tea, and other goodies. |
| September | President's Cup Canoeing Regatta. On the Potomac River between 14th Street and Memorial Bridges off Ohio Drive SW (426-6975). |
| September | Annual Ramblin' Raft Race. On the Potomac River, from Lincoln Memorial to Hains Point and back (426-6975). |
| September | Annual Croquet Tournament. On the Ellipse at 15th Street NW (426-6975). |
| September | International Children's Day. Wolf Trap Farm Park, Vienna, VA (426-6975). The emphasis is on international culture with craft workshops, puppet shows, and children in native costumes. |
| September | America on Stage. The J. F. Kennedy Center, 2700 F Street NW (254-3600). Largest exhibit ever produced at the center. Traces history of theater, music, dance, and other entertainment from Colonial days to the present. Continues for 18 months. |
| All month | Exhibit devoted to George Washington. Guy Mason Recreation Center, 3600 Calvert Street NW (333-2412). |
| All month | Sorghum Demonstration. Oxon Hill Farm (839-1177). Harvesting of sorghum cane and demonstration of molasses making. Every Sunday in the month. |
| 1 | Annual Labor Day Songfest. The Sylvan Theatre, on the Washington Monument grounds (426-6975). |
| 7 | Montgomery County Birthday Celebration (279-1776). |
| 13 | City of Rockville Septemberfest Block Party. Bicentennial Square, Rockville, MD (424-8000). 4 pm. |
| 14 | Gunston Hall Car Show. Gunston Hall Plantation, Lorton, VA (703-550-9220). Admission charge. |
| 14 | Blacks in the Westward Movement. Anacostia Neighborhood Museum, 2405 Martin Luther King, Jr. Avenue SE (381-6691). The museum's highly acclaimed Bicentennial exhibition. Using photographs, silk screens, text, and artifacts, the exhibit tells the story of the blacks who explored, conquered, |

| | |
|---|---|
| and settled the western portion of America. (Through January 3, 1976.) | |
| The Freedom Train arrives in Washington (820-7300). | 16 |
| Candlelight Walking Tour of Historic Chestertown. Historical Society of Kent County, Lankford Road, Chestertown, MD (301-778-2680). A tour of approximately 10 houses. 6:30 pm-10 pm. Admission charge. | 20 |
| Outdoor Fall Antique Show and Sale. Market Square, King and Fairfax Streets, Alexandria, VA (656-1102). 9 am-6 pm. Rain Date: September 21. | 20 |
| Trolley Car Extravaganza. National Capital Trolley Museum, Bonifant Road, Wheaton, MD (434-2906 after 6 pm). | 21 |
| Annual Tour of Homes. Alexandria, VA (549-1005). Tour of 18th- and 19th-century homes. 11 am-5 pm. Admission charge. | 27 |
| Heritage Week. Historic Annapolis, 18 Pickney Street, Annapolis, Md (301-267-7619). Candlelight, waterfront, and open house tours, Plantation dinner and Hunt breakfast. | 28, 29, 30 |

## October 1975

| | |
|---|---|
| Open House at the Washington Cathedral, Massachusetts and Wisconsin Avenues NW (966-3500). | October |
| Religion and the Artist in America. Westmoreland Church, 1 Westmoreland Circle (229-7766). An art exhibit featuring paintings and sculpture by Washington area artists on spiritual themes. | October |
| Corcoran Gallery of Art Tour. Corcoran Gallery of Art, 17th Street and New York Avenue NW (638-3211). Tours of houses containing excellent private art collections. Admission charge. | October |
| Festival of the Leaves. Front Royal, VA (703-635-7155). Date is determined by when the leaves will be at their peak of fall color. Antique firetruck display, crafts demonstrations, Confederate-house tours. | October |
| International Field Hockey Tournament. West Potomac Park (426-6975). | October |
| National Jousting Tournament. On the Washington Monument grounds (426-6975). | October |
| Annual Fall Foliage Festival, Waynesboro, VA (703-942-8161, ext. 454). Art show, pro-am golf tournament, antique car meet. | October |

| | |
|---|---|
| 5, 6, 7,8 | U.S. Sailboat Show. Annapolis, MD (301-268-8828). Over 400 boats are displayed, over 145 in the water. |
| 9-11 | Alexandria Forum (549-0205). Lectures by national authorities on history, antiques, and historical restoration and preservation. Also banquet and entertainment. |
| 11, 12, 13 | City Celebration. On the Ellipse (393-1976). Arts, crafts, music, and stage shows. |
| 13 | Alexandria Jr. Women's Club—Embassy Tour and Tea (836-3971). Ten embassy tours. Admission charge. |
| 12, 13 | Potomac Country House Tour (365-2055). Five houses, harvest sale, and exhibition of the hounds. Admission charge. |
| 26 | Oktoberfest. Bowie Race Course, Bowie, MD (262-6200). Culture and folklife of Germany. 11 am-5 pm. Admission charge. |
| 27 | Veteran's Day Services at Arlington National Cemetery (697-3509). |

## 1975 November

| | |
|---|---|
| November | Washington, D.C. International Horse Race. Laurel Race Track, Laurel, MD (667-1050). A race for "Horse of the World" honors, with a $150,000 purse. |
| November | YWCA Annual International Fair (638-2100). More than 40 countries participate with embassy booths offering exotic foods and gifts, dancing, fashion show. |
| 1 | Our Changing Land. National Museum of Natural History, Constitution Avenue and 10th Street NW (628-4422). A walk through our changing land; a series of four habitats describing times before man, at colonization, at our independence, and in the present. |
| 6, 7, 8 | Christmas Corner. Christ Church Memorial Parish Hall, 118 N. Washington Street, Alexandria, VA (548-1708). Specialty shops display and sell gift collections. Craft demonstrations, entertainment, special activities. 1 am-4 pm; luncheon 11:30 am-2:30 pm. Admission charge. |
| 7, 8, 9 | DAR Antique Show. Olde Colony Motor Lodge, N. Washington and First Streets, Alexandria, VA (780-7378, 9 am-2 pm). Friday and Saturday noon-10 pm; Sunday until 6 pm. Admission charge. |
| 8 | Washington's Review of the Troops at Gadsby's Tavern. Gadsby's Tavern, 400 Cameron Street, |

| | |
|---|---|
| Alexandria, VA (549-0205). A reenactment of the military review of the troops conducted by George Washington in 1798 in front of the tavern. | |
| The Berlin Opera presents "Lohengrin." The J. F. Kennedy Center Opera House, 2700 F Street NW (254-3700). 8 pm. Admission charge. | 14, 18, 22, 24, 27 |
| Sully Stitchery. Sully Plantation, Chantilly, VA (437-1794). Admission charge. | 15, 16 |
| The Berlin Opera presents "Tosca." The J. F. Kennedy Center Opera House, 2700 F Street NW (254-3700). 8 pm. Admission charge. | 15, 17, 20, 26, 28 |
| The Berlin Opera presents "Cosi Fan Tutte." The J. F. Kennedy Center Opera House, 2700 F Street NW (254-3700). 8 pm. Admission charge. | 16 |

# December 1975

| | |
|---|---|
| Arts of Asia at the Time of American Independence, The Freer Gallery of Art, 12th Street and Jefferson Drive SW (628-4422). Exhibition will provide an insight into the civilizations of the Near and Far East during the period of the American Revolution. | December |
| Christmas caroling. Wolf Trap Farm Park, Vienna, VA (938-3800). | December |
| The Twelve Days of Christmas. The J. F. Kennedy Center, 2700 F Street NW (254-3600 or 426-6975). A series of cultural events. | December |
| Christmas concert at the Renwick Gallery, 17th Street and Pennsylvania Avenue NW (628-4422). | December |
| Christmas Concert. The Folger Gallery, 201 E. Capitol Street SW (546-2461). | December |
| Christmas Festival. Belle Grove Plantation, Middleton, VA (869-2028). Admission charge. | December |
| Christmas Program. Sully Plantation, Chantilly, VA (437-1794). House decorated in natural greens, caroling, refreshments. Admission charge. | December |
| Candlelight Tours of the White House (456-1414). | December |
| Pageant of Peace. On the Washington Monument grounds (426-6975). Opens with the President lighting the National Christmas tree, includes pageant displays, caroling, etc. | December |
| Potomac English Handbell Ringers. 17th and Pennsylvania Avenue NW. Free, but two ticket limit per person. | December |

| | |
|---|---|
| 6 | Scottish Christmas Walk. Parade through Old Town Alexandria (549-0111). Begins at Scotland House, S. Washington Street, ends with Scottish Advent Service at Old Presbyterian Meeting House. Special activities include an international luncheon, food and craft sale, Scottish films, children's plays and toy exhibits. 10 am-4 pm. |
| 6, 7, 12, 13, 14 | Carols by Candlelight. Gunston Hall, Lorton, VA (703-650-9220). Choir and harpsichordist. Friday 8 am-10 pm; Saturday and Sunday 2:30 pm-4:30 pm. Admission charge. |
| 7 | The European Vision of America. The National Gallery of Art, Constitution Avenue and 6th Street NW (737-4215). Illustrates the development of the visual image of the Americas in European minds from the time of Columbus to the late 19th century. (Through March 21, 1976.) |
| 7 | Annual Pearl Harbor Day ceremonies at Iowa Jima Memorial, Arlington, VA (LI5-6700). |
| 31 | Scottish New Year's Eve in Alexandria. Market Square, King and Fairfax Streets, Alexandria, VA (549-0205). Owners of historic houses welcome bagpipers, kilted Scotsmen, and visitors to their homes shortly after midnight. Begins 11:30 pm in Market Square. Advance tickets required. Admission charge. |

## 1976 January

| | |
|---|---|
| January | Presidential Inauguration and Parade. Once every four years you can watch the parade down Pennsylvania Avenue and the swearing-in ceremony on the steps of the Capitol. |
| January | Annual Ice Follies. The Civic Center, Baltimore, MD (301-727-0703). |
| January | Ice Capades. The Capital Centre, Landover, MD (350-3400). |
| January | A Nation of Nations. The National Museum of History and Technology, Constitution Avenue between 12th and 14th Streets NW (628-4422). An exhibit tracing America's evolution from many nations of the world. (Through December 31, 1976.) |
| January | William Wilson Corcoran: Patron of the Arts. The Corcoran Gallery of Art, 17th Street and New York Avenue NW (638-3211). The Corcoran's celebration of the Bicentennial with an exhibition honoring its founder. |

Barbershop Singing in America. The J. F. Kennedy Center, 2700 F Street NW (254-3600). The premiere of a show tracing the history of barbershop singing in this country. 31

The Black Woman. Anacostia Neighborhood Museum, 2405 Martin Luther King, Jr. Avenue SE (381-6991). An in-depth investigation of the black woman's role and contribution to history. (Through April 25, 1976.) 25

## February 1976

Annual Chesapeake Bay Boat Show. Fifth Regiment Armory, Baltimore, MD (301-837-1975). One of the country's oldest indoor boat shows—and the biggest. February

Catoctin Winter Festival. In Catoctin Mountain Park, Thurmont, MD (301-271-7638). Winter sports demonstrations; and if there's snow, dog-sledding and snowmobiling. February

Signs of Life: Symbols in the City. The Renwick Gallery, 17th Street and Pennsylvania Avenue NW (628-4422). Historical and contemporary objects on display in addition to photographs, films, and live video projections of parts of the District. (Through September 26, 1976.) 6

Lincoln Birthday Celebration. The Lincoln Memorial (426-6975). 12

Washington Birthday Celebration. On the Washington Monument grounds (426-6975). 16

The Federal City: Plans and Realities. The Smithsonian Institution Building (The Castle) (628-4422). Exhibit focusing on the architectural and planning history of Washington, DC. 22

## March 1976

Woodlawn Plantation's Annual Needlework Exhibition. On U.S. Route 1 near Mount Vernon (780-3118). March

Kite Day. On the grounds of the Washington Monument (426-6975). Contests and prizes for best-designed kite, best-flying kite, etc. Free kites distributed by the National Park Service. March

St. Patrick's Day Celebration. At the Arlington House (Custis-Lee Mansion), between Lee and Sherman March

| | |
|---|---|
| | Drives, Arlington, VA (557-3153). |
| March | White Water Boat Show. Maryland side of Great Falls, at the Rocky Island Put-in (426-6975). There's a race with no entry fee, but bring your own boat. |
| March | Annual Bouquet of Gems and Minerals. Charles Woodward High School, Rockville, MD (Mrs. Phillip Marcus—942-3044). |
| March | America after the Declaration of Independence. The National Portrait Gallery, F and 8th Streets NW (628-4422). |
| 1-31 | Performance of Original Irish Music. The J. F. Kennedy Center, 2700 F Street NW (254-3600). A commissioned, American, historically-oriented orchestra performs original works composed in honor of the American Irish. |

## 1976 April

| | |
|---|---|
| April | American Music Festival. National Gallery of Art, Constitution Avenue and 6th Street NW (737-4215). Festival will present works of American composers, including world premieres. |
| April | America as Art. National Collection of Fine Arts, G and 8th Streets NW (628-4422). Made up of some 200 paintings, drawings, prints, and sculptures, this exhibition will show how American art has been identified with and related to changing concepts or ideals over the past two hundred years. |
| April | Jefferson Birthday Celebration. At the Jefferson Memorial (426-6975). |
| April | Outdoor Display of Azaleas. National Arboretum, 24th and R Streets NE (399-5400). |
| April | Georgetown House and Garden Tour. St. John's Church, Prospect and O Streets NW (338-1796). Admission charge. |
| 3-9 | Annual Cherry Blossom Time (426-6690). Lasts one week, with a display of cherry blossoms, parade, crowning of Cherry Blossom Queen and princesses. |
| 18 | Easter Sunrise Service at Arlington National Cemetery (LI5-6700). |
| 19 | Egg Roll on the White House Lawn (456-1414). Children eight years and under; must be accompanied by an adult. |
| 23 | Shakespeare in America. Folger Shakespeare Library, 201 E. Capitol Street (546-4800). Largest exhibit of |

Shakespeareana in America, with a series of dramatic presentations.

## May 1976

| | |
|---|---|
| Alexandria Virginia Association's Old Town Tour (549-0205). Includes tours of about 10 18th- and 19th-century homes and gardens. Admission charge. | Early May |
| Annual National Capital Area Scottish Festival and Highland Games. Robert E. Peary High School, Rockville, MD (942-8000). Bagpipe band, traditional Scottish athletic competition. | Early May |
| The Preakness. Pimlico Race Track, Park Heights and Belvedere Avenues, Baltimore, MD (301-542-9400). The middle race of the Triple Crown series. | Mid-May |
| Northern Virginia Folk Festival (combined multi-ethnic folk festival). Thomas Jefferson Community Center, 125 S. Old Glebe Road, Arlington, VA (558-2152). | May |
| The World's Artists and America: Immigrants and Refugees (1876-1976). The Hirshhorn Museum and Sculpture Garden, Independence Avenue and 8th Street SW (628-4422). The exhibit will explore contributions made to the development of art by immigrants and refugee artists. | May |
| Sully Days. Sully Plantation, Chantilly, VA (437-1794). Annual exhibitions of crafts of the 18th and 19th centuries. Admission charge. | May |
| Centennial-1976. The Smithsonian Institution, Arts and Industries Building, 900 Jefferson Drive SW (628-4422). Exhibit will recreate the character of the late 19th century and will present objects that were displayed at the Centennial Exposition in Philadelphia. | May |
| Flower Mart. On the grounds of the Washington Cathedral, Wisconsin and Massachusetts Avenues NW (279-1776). Features flowers, food, and entertainment. | 7 |
| Historical Symposium on the Incomplete or Imperfect Revolution. Library of Congress, 10 First Street SE (426-5000). | All month |
| A Retrospective of John Robinson. Anacostia Neighborhood Museum, 2405 Martin Luther King, Jr. Avenue SE (381-6691). An exhibition devoted to the art of John Robinson, an Anacostia resident and nationally known artist. (Through June 13.) | 9 |

## 1976 June

| | |
|---|---|
| 3 | The Eye of Thomas Jefferson. The National Gallery of Art, Constitution Avenue and 6th Street NW (737-4215). The exhibition will present the esthetic and intellectual world in which Jefferson lived, illustrating with works of art the attitudes and ideas that he encountered, recorded, and assimilated. |
| 4 | Americas: The Decorative Arts in Latin America in the Revolution. The Renwick Gallery, 17th Street and Pennsylvania Avenue NW (628-4422). Concentrates on Latin American countries in the decade of the Revolution, detailing the richness of design, crafts, and the decorative arts. (Through January 2, 1977.) |
| 6 | Service for the Dedication of the Nave. The Washington Cathedral, Massachusetts and Wisconsin Avenues NW (966-3500). |
| 14 or 15 | Silver Spring Chamber of Commerce Bicentennial Flag Day Parade. Georgia Avenue, Silver Spring, MD (585-6300). |
| 29 | Exhibit of Greek Antiquities. Embassy of Greece, 2221 Massachusetts Avenue NW (667-3168). Also performing arts and crafts. (Through December 1976.) |

## 1976 July

| | |
|---|---|
| 4 | First Historic Sound and Light Presentation. The East face of the Capitol (543-2852). |
| 4 | Opening of the Smithsonian Institution's National Air and Space Museum. On the Mall (628-4422). Will have exhibitions on the national development of aviation and space flight. |
| 5 | The Anacostia Story. Anacostia Neighborhood Museum, 2405 Martin Luther King, Jr. Avenue SE (381-6691). A Bicentennial exhibition on the history and development of the Anacostia community. (Through December 27, 1976.) |
| 7 | Dedication of Bonsai Collection. National Arboretum, 24th and R Streets NE (256-3623). |

# Index

# Authors

**Thierry Bright-Sagnier** writes on the entertainment scene for *The Washingtonian* magazine, has published a book on motorcycles, and plays in a bluegrass band.

**J. Timberlake Gibson** has gotten to know Washington working for the federal government, in the executive office of President Harry S Truman, and as a writer for national and local publications.

**Marian Hoffman** is assistant editor of Washingtonian Books

**Katherine Janka,** a freelance writer and a Communications Associate at the National Training and Development Service, spends much of her time enjoying the out-of-doors and writing about it.

**Tina Laver,** a freelance writer, has written regularly on shopping in the Washington area for *The Washingtonian* magazine.

**Elizabeth Post Mirel** is a freelance food, medical, and travel writer and editor of *Going Places with Children,* published by Green Acres School. She is the mother of three children, who accompanied her on her visits to the places she writes about in the chapter on fun with children.

**Phyllis C. Richman** writes about food and restaurants for *The Washingtonian* magazine and other local and national publications.

**Robert Shosteck** is the author of *Potomac Trail and Cycling Guide* and *Weekender's Guide* (Potomac Books, Inc.).

**Phyllie Theroux** is a writer who has contributed frequently to *The Washingtonian* magazine and to national magazines.

**Charles F. Turgeon** is the food critic for *The Washingtonian* magazine.

**Whitney Watriss** works for Fact Research writing and editing a wide range of material, including tourism studies for government and private industry.

**Tony Wrenn,** a historic preservation consultant, has written about the history and architecture of Washington for local and national publications. He is the author of *Walking Tours: Washington, D.C.,* published by the Parks and History Association.